D1572287

A history of the University of Manchester 1973–90

Published in our
centenary year
～ **2004** ～
MANCHESTER
UNIVERSITY
PRESS

A history of the
University of Manchester
1973–90

Brian Pullan with Michele Abendstern

Manchester University Press
Manchester and New York

distributed exclusively in the USA by Palgrave

Published by Manchester University Press
Oxford Road, Manchester M13 9NR, UK
and Room 400, 175 Fifth Avenue, New York, NY 10010, USA
www.manchesteruniversitypress.co.uk

Distributed exclusively in the USA by
Palgrave, 175 Fifth Avenue, New York, NY 10010, USA

Distributed exclusively in Canada by
UBC Press, University of British Columbia, 2029 West Mall,
Vancouver, BC, Canada V6T 1Z2

British Library Cataloguing-in-Publication Data
A catalogue record for this book is available from the British Library

Library of Congress Cataloging-in-Publication Data applied for

ISBN 0 7190 6242 X hardback

First published 2004

11 10 09 08 07 06 05 04   10 9 8 7 6 5 4 3 2 1

Typeset in Sabon with Stone Sans
by Northern Phototypesetting Co Ltd, Bolton
Printed in Great Britain
by Biddles Ltd, Guildford and King's Lynn

Contents

Preface

Work on this history of the University of Manchester in the second half of the twentieth century began in 1998, when the University was preparing to commemorate the 150th anniversary of the foundation of its ancestor, Owens College, in 1851. The committee which planned the celebrations originally had in mind a single, handy volume which would provide a sequel to H.B. Charlton's *Portrait of a University 1851–1951*, written by a distinguished Professor of English Literature to mark the centenary of the institution. But the history began to take on a life of its own, since the rich and varied material which came into our hands demanded more extended treatment, and the committee was kind enough to allow us to make new arrangements and to bring out the work in at least two volumes. The first of these was published at the end of the year 2000, in time to mark the celebrations in 2001. Publication of this second volume will relate to another important anniversary, the centenary of the establishment of an independent University in Manchester in 1903. In that year the Victoria University (the federal university of the north of England) began to be dismantled, the colleges at Leeds and Liverpool were on their way to becoming separate universities, and the title of Victoria University of Manchester was conferred on the former Owens College.

This volume follows the same principles, uses a similar range of sources both written and oral, and takes up the same themes as its predecessor, carrying them beyond the point in 1973 when universities began to face grave financial difficulties and their relationship with the Government became increasingly tense and even sour. The story considers the reigns of two Vice-Chancellors who adopted very different styles, Sir Arthur Armitage (1970–80) and Sir Mark Richmond (1981–90). As before, the aim of the book is to sketch a panorama of the social and political history of the University and to establish a broad framework within which more detailed intellectual histories of parts of the University may be placed. Several interesting studies, monographs exploring in depth the histories of particular faculties and departments, anthologies of personal recollections, accounts of life in smaller communities such as University halls of residence, have already appeared, and we can only hope that others will follow. Once again, we have tried not to write our history only from the point of view of the central establishment or from that of academics only; nor have we relied solely or even primarily on the official records of Senate, Court and Council or on the University's house magazines, ample and informative though these are. Four of the thirteen chapters discuss student affairs and draw heavily on reports and correspondence in student newspapers as well as on the reminiscences of students of the 1970s and 1980s. Like its predecessor, this volume seeks, not just to celebrate the achievements of the University and of individuals and groups within it, but also to deal frankly and honestly with controversial issues which exposed it to criticism.

The main text of the book was written by Brian Pullan, who drew on the many lengthy interviews conducted by Michele Abendstern with academics, administrators, members of the support staff and students who have vivid memories of the period described and analysed in this volume. Michele Abendstern and Steve Chick compiled the statistical appendix.

We owe many thanks to all those who agreed to be interviewed for this book (their names, with a brief account of the positions they held in the 1970s and 1980s, are listed on pp. 306–11); to those who gave us access to personal papers and to collections of material that might otherwise have escaped us (John Griffith, Sir George Kenyon, Tony Trinci, Joan Walsh and George Wilmers); to George Brooke for materials on the Faculty of Theology, to Hilary Kahn for materials on the history of computer science in Manchester, to Richard Davies and Frank O'Gorman for papers about history and historians, and to Gillian White for information about lawyers; to many others, including John Pickstone and Alan Shelston, for enlightening conversations about aspects of the University's history; to Will Eades and the staff of DARO (the Development and Alumni Relations Office) for general support and assistance; to Estates and Services for finding us accommodation and storage space for our materials; to Peter Nockles and his successor as University archivist, James Peters, for expert guidance to materials held in the University Library; to the Vice-Chancellor's office for enabling us to consult Senate and Council minutes not available elsewhere; to Alan Ferns and the staff of the International and Public Relations Office for back numbers of *Staff Comment* and *Communication*;

to Steve Chick, for compiling the graphs in the statistical appendix; to Tracy Carrington and Marian Haberhauer for transcribing the tapes of the interviews; to Peter McNiven of the John Rylands University Library and Andrew Schofield of the North West Sound Archive for arranging to store the tapes and transcripts in their respective institutions; and to members of the staff of Manchester University Press for their expertise in seeing this book through to publication. We are greatly indebted to Bill Beswick, Christine Hallett, Christopher Kenyon, Ken Kitchen and David Richardson for their kindness and patience in reading all or part of the typescript, and for saving us from omissions and errors.

Every effort has been made to obtain permission to reproduce copyright material in this book. If any proper acknowledgement has not been made, copyright-holders are invited to contact the publisher. Acknowledgement is made to the author and Harper Collins for permission to reproduce the poem 'Bill' by Simon Curtis, from *On the Abthorpe Road and Other Poems* (London: Davis-Poynter, 1975).

Abbreviations

ALA	Associate of the Library Association
ASTMS	Association of Scientific, Technical and Managerial Staffs
AUEW	Amalgamated Union of Engineering Workers
AUT	Association of University Teachers
BMFRS	*Biographical Memoirs of Fellows of the Royal Society*
CAFD	Council for Academic Freedom and Democracy
CBE	Commander of the Order of the British Empire
CND	Campaign for Nuclear Disarmament
CURID	Centre for Urban and Regional Industrial Development
CVCP	Committee of Vice-Chancellors and Principals
D.Sc.	Doctor of Science
ESRC	Economic and Social Research Council
FBA	Fellow of the British Academy
FCMA	Fellow of the Institute of Cost and Management Accountants
FDSC	Faculty Development Sub-Committee
FRS	Fellow of the Royal Society
FRSA	Fellow of the Royal Society of Arts
FRSL	Fellow of the Royal Society of Literature
ICI	Imperial Chemical Industries
JCR	Junior Common Room
JCUD	Joint Committee for University Development
Ll.D.	Doctor of Laws
LSE	London School of Economics and Political Science
MANUS	Manchester Area National Union of Students
M.Ed.	Master of Education
M.Sc.	Master of Science
NAG	Nursery Action Group
NALGO	National and Local Government Officers Association
NUM	National Union of Mineworkers
NUPE	National Union of Public Employees

NUS	National Union of Students
OBE	Order of the British Empire
OPSA	Owens Park Students Association
PBA	*Proceedings of the British Academy*
Ph.D.	Doctor of Philosophy
PREST	Policy Research in Engineering, Science and Technology
SALS	South Africa Liberation Society
SDP	Social Democratic Party
SERC	Science and Engineering Research Council
THES	*Times Higher Educational Supplement*
TLS	*Times Literary Supplement*
UCCA	Universities Central Council for Admissions
UFC	Universities Funding Council
UGC	University Grants Committee
UKAEA	United Kingdom Atomic Energy Authority
UMIST	University of Manchester Institute of Science and Technology

Preliminary note

This book is a sequel to the *History of the University of Manchester 1951–73*, published by Manchester University Press in 2000. It takes up the principal themes of the work at the point at which Manchester, like most British universities, was beginning to encounter grave financial problems and to lose confidence in the sympathy and support both of the Government and of public opinion. This second volume is designed to be read on its own, without the need to refer back repeatedly to its predecessor. Some readers, however, may like to be reminded at the outset of a few important facts, that the story may be easier to follow.

The University of Manchester descended from a small local institution, Owens College, founded in 1851 by the will of a Manchester merchant; the name Owens was sometimes used, even in the late twentieth century, to mean all parts of the University other than the Faculty of Technology, which was housed in UMIST, the former Technical College. Between the 1930s and the 1970s the University almost quadrupled the number of its students, which rose from about 2,700 to as many as 10,000 undergraduates and postgraduates. Together with other universities it strove to increase the number of graduates in the country, both for the sake of social justice and to meet the needs of the nation, as politicians defined them, particularly for scientists and engineers. Expansion led to a greater dependence on public money and to more insistent demands that universities should account for the ways in which they spent it.

As the university system grew in the 1960s, Manchester could no longer take its old pre-eminence for granted: it began to encounter many more rivals and to lose a large proportion of its experienced staff to less strongly traditional institutions. It struggled to overhaul its own legislative and administrative structures, which could not immediately respond to the growing numbers of staff and students; a revised version of the University charter and statutes passed into law early in 1973, and, although the new document did not (as many had hoped) undermine the old professorial hierarchy, it did establish ample consultative machinery. The University also strove to contain the unrest of students who no longer regarded access to higher education as a privilege and were inclined to see the University as an instrument of the Government and a servant of a capitalist economy.

From 1970 the Vice-Chancellor was Arthur Armitage, a magisterial and pragmatic lawyer who had been President of Queens' College and taken his turn as Vice-Chancellor of the University of Cambridge. He was appointed as plain Mr Armitage, Cambridge graduate and barrister-at-law, but hastily dignified before his arrival by an honorary Doctorate of Laws bestowed by fiat of Manchester's Chancellor, the Duke of Devonshire. Armitage was knighted in 1975, after his election as Chairman of the Committee of Vice-Chancellors and Principals. He was flanked by several experienced administrators who had made their careers in Manchester, including the Registrar, Vincent Knowles (the constitutional authority and senior civil servant), and the University Librarian, Fred Ratcliffe.

As were many 'civic', 'provincial', 'red brick' or 'modern' universities, the University of Manchester was governed by a Council, which looked after its fabric and finances and employed its staff, and a Senate, which was the supreme academic body. Council consisted of a majority of lay members, most of whom were prominent figures in the city and the region, and were engaged in business or the professions, and of a minority of academics. Between 1972 and 1980 the Chairman of Council was Mr (later Sir) George Kenyon, an engineer and industrialist who manufactured ropes and had many other business interests. Senate was composed of a majority of professors and of a minority of elected members, all of whom were drawn from the teaching staff of the University. The lay Chairman of Council and the Treasurer, together with the Vice-Chancellor, Bursar and Registrar, exercised great influence from on high on the conduct of University affairs ('the Registrar is responsible for committees and students and the Bursar is responsible for buildings and money', explained the notes for new secretaries in the Vice-Chancellor's office). As resources began to shrink and the generosity of governments to diminish, power lay to an increasing extent with the Joint Committee for University Development (JCUD), so-called because it brought together the authority of Senate and that of Council. Ultimate sovereignty within the University lay in theory with the large and usually passive Court of Governors, whose title was shortened to 'Court' in the new charter of 1973. Traditionally, this was a device for interesting prominent local people in the University. Court provided a responsible body to which the University would have on occasion to explain itself, and whose approval it would have to seek when proposing major legislative changes.

I
The 1970s

1

Uncertainty, economy and improvisation

In 1973 the finances of most British universities lay at the mercy of politicians and were subject to capricious cuts in public spending. Their precarious situation was a consequence of the state-financed expansion of the previous decades. What taxpayers gave, their elected representatives could pare and trim when the economy wilted and crisis loomed. In the midst of high inflation both Conservative and Labour governments failed to compensate universities for increases in the cost of living and forced them to scrimp and save whenever opportunities arose.

Until 1977 three quarters of the annual income of the University of Manchester consisted of a block recurrent grant given for general purposes, together with a much smaller sum earmarked for equipment and furniture. These payments came from a sum voted by Parliament, allocated to universities in general by the Department of Education and Science, and distributed to individual universities by the University Grants Committee (UGC). The University was free to use most of the block grant as it chose, assigning various sums at its discretion to central services, faculties, academic departments, and other undertakings. Some of the remaining quarter of the University's revenue sprang from tuition and other fees. Like the block grant, most of these came from the public purse, but arrived by another route, for they were paid on behalf of United Kingdom undergraduates by their local education authorities. They did not depend solely on the rates, for local authorities would eventually recover from central funds most of the money they had paid out. Other sources of income included research contracts (most of them awarded by government departments and a few by industrial concerns), and the proceeds of a large and complex investment portfolio, which served, for example, to fund the pension scheme for non-academic staff.

To finance costly building projects such as libraries, lecture rooms and laboratories which did not directly produce income, the University looked to the UGC for capital grants. Plans to build student flats, however, were financed only in part by the UGC. They now depended in large measure on loans taken out in the open market from banks, building societies and insurance companies, and serviced by the rents which students paid for the privilege of occupying the premises.

Approximately three quarters of the University's expenditure was on salaries and wages. Much of the remainder was devoted to heating, lighting, watering, and generally maintaining premises and equipment. Sharp reductions in the real value of income from public sources, and the Government's reluctance or failure to cover the salary settlements awarded to employees, were certain to have grave consequences for the University. It was in no position to solve its problems by laying off part of its workforce or sacking redundant executives. But the University could not afford to accumulate a deficit which it had no means of clearing away.

At the end of 1973 Edward Heath's administration withdrew guarantees that the Government would protect the finances of universities against the effects of inflation. No more would it proclaim itself ready to look with sympathy upon their plight. Anthony Barber, the Chancellor of the Exchequer, reduced university income from parliamentary grants by about 10 per cent. In February 1974 Arthur Armitage, the Vice-Chancellor of the University of Manchester, described these measures as the severest cuts in living memory. Interpreting the figures for the University Council and Senate, he estimated that the University was about to lose £800,000 from the income which it had anticipated receiving in the current academical year. He appeared to be forecasting a reduction of about 5 per cent in expected cash, for the University's income from all sources was then in the region of £18.5m. and was to rise to almost £22m. in the next session. In the light of later events, the cuts of 1973 may not seem cataclysmic. But they wiped out the reserves set aside for future developments, and were accompanied by other, much harsher reductions in the funding of capital projects. These made it necessary to cancel or postpone, sometimes for many years, important parts of the building programme which the University had planned.

In the wake of the Arab–Israeli war of October 1973, the oil-producing countries of the Middle East had quadrupled the price of oil. The Brown Index, an economist's tool employed to measure the cost of items which figured prominently in university expenditure, pointed to a price rise of about 10 per cent between January 1973 and January 1974. By November 1974 the rate of inflation had doubled, and the University was facing a deficit of about £1m. According to John Carswell, some time secretary to the UGC, 'the shock, not only of a 10 per cent cut but of the breach between the universities and the state – the revelation that the traditional special relationship need not be respected – was shattering'.

In 1973, then, came one of the great turning points in British university history, a transition into a bleaker world governed by the principles of uncertainty, economy and improvisation. The prevailing gloom, however, occasionally gave way to spells of optimism, to a misplaced sense that the worst must be over. Unfulfilled ambitions, hatched in the late 1960s, still dominated the University's plans and maintained their places at the head of lists; until these priorities had been met it would prove difficult to develop new programmes. Planners still expected that the number of students – particularly undergraduates – would go on increasing at least until the early or mid-1980s. Only then would the number of eighteen-year-olds in the British population cease to grow. Greater numbers would bring in more fees, but fees covered only part of the cost of students' courses, which were heavily subsidised; the University could not rely on receiving full compensation for the growth in its numbers.

Research was to suffer more gravely than teaching, and science and medicine would feel most keenly the effects of shrinkage in the equipment grant. Cuts were falling at precisely the time when apparatus installed in the prosperous 1960s was becoming obsolete; the Faculty of Science usually absorbed 60 per cent of this grant, the Faculty of Medicine about 20 per cent. There was reason to remember Rutherford's dictum, 'Gentlemen, we have no money, therefore we shall have to use our brains', though such words were less likely to console scientists who had once enjoyed ample funds and now saw them taken away.

Almost entirely lost was the capacity for mapping the University's future for more than a year or two ahead; indeed, the 'planning horizon', as the UGC liked to call it, was now obscured, and Sir Peter Swinnerton-Dyer, then the Vice-Chancellor of Cambridge, called it 'a mirage across quicksands'. Far from being known at the outset, grants were sometimes dispensed in instalments during the university year. Once they had been predicted with reasonable certainty five years in advance, under the old system of quinquennial planning which still survived in theory in the 1970s and had not been formally abolished. New uncertainties arose when, from 1977, a larger proportion of the University's income began to depend on tuition fees. No-one could be sure how much they would yield until the students had registered in October of each year.

Universities courted public disapproval if they failed to demonstrate their concern with practical activities which would help to revive the country's manufacturing industries, or begin to solve its most urgent social and medical problems. Unless they could justify their existence in these terms, they risked being dismissed as a luxury which the country could ill afford and which governments could trim with impunity, sometimes out of conviction, more often out of drift and infirmity of purpose. Arthur Armitage was a natural optimist, a booster of morale who yearned for development, proclaimed its usefulness to society and the economy, set aside money for it whenever he could, and in certain areas – especially the expansion of the Medical School and its clinical teaching – achieved it. But he had to blow hot and cold breaths upon the University even as the Department of Education and Science and the UGC blew them upon him, even as the petitions of the Committee of Vice-Chancellors and Principals succeeded or failed in their attempts to wring a little more money for universities from the purse of the Secretary of State.

Uncertainty and pessimism prevailed for much of the time between late 1973 and early 1978, though not all the worst fears were realised. Indeed, one of the most drastic cuts – a sudden reduction of 4 per cent in the real value of resources, expected to occur in the session of 1977–78 – did not actually come to pass. The phrase 'cash limits' began to be heard in the mid-1970s. At its most ominous the term suggested that the sums allocated to universities in a given year would be determined before the Government's pay policy was known, and that no-one would subsequently increase them, no matter how steeply prices increased, no matter how large the latest pay settlements turned out to be. In truth the limits did not prove quite so rigid as prophets foretold and politicians threatened; they were sometimes relaxed to allow for unavoidable increases in expenditure.

Optimism flickered in 1978, when *The Times Higher Educational Supplement* (*THES*) could write of 'a remarkable revival in the financial fortunes of universities'; when inflation had fallen to 10 per cent; when the UGC was announcing, albeit with many caveats, the likely level of recurrent block grants for universities for as many as three years in advance; when moves were afoot to remedy injustices concerning academic salaries. Hubristic talk was heard in Manchester of a new building boom, led by the new Library Extension which the University had secured against heavy odds. Student officers extracted from filing cabinets the long-deferred plans for an extension to their overcrowded Union building. But nemesis overtook all universities with the fall of the Callaghan government and the electoral triumph of the Conservatives in May 1979. Amid growing despondency, the University planned and executed another cut in expenditure, this time of 2 per cent, in the hope of breaking even for the time being.

Members of the Economics Faculty debated the causes of inflation and the merits of restricting the money supply and cutting public expenditure, even at the cost of increasing unemployment. Financed for five years by the Social Sciences Research Council, the Manchester Inflation Project followed the lead of two youngish, internationally known professors, David Laidler and Michael Parkin, who had recently migrated from the University of Essex and would leave together for the University of Western Ontario in 1975. Meanwhile, the University's administrators and managers struggled with the consequences of inflation. Economic crisis impinged on the university population at many points, and students became deeply concerned with the cost of living. Close to their hearts were the level of rents in University residences, the cost of refectory meals, the price of wares stocked by the students' Union shop, and the extent of the fee paid by Local Education Authorities to the Union on behalf of each student.

Academics suffered for several years from the so-called 'pay anomaly'. This grievance was the result of a pay pause imposed by the Government at an unfortunate moment in 1975. The effect of the move was to deprive university teachers of salary increases comparable to those awarded just before the pause to their colleagues in other branches of higher and further education, and especially in polytechnics. However, academics' misfortunes, although they seldom admitted it, were mitigated by the protection which most of them enjoyed against loss of employment. Tenure, more sharply defined in Manchester by the new charter and statutes of 1973, counted for something. Early in 1975 the Vice-Chancellor, though warning of difficulties to come in the next two years, gave assurances 'that the University could not resolve its financial problems by declaring staff redundancies, and even if it could, the adoption of such a policy would be completely repugnant'.

Senior members of the University noted the consequences of recession for people less secure than themselves. The North West Industrial Research Unit, run by University geographers, chronicled the heavy losses of jobs during the 1970s in the manufacturing industries of Greater Manchester, in the fields of textiles, engineering, steel, and aerospace. Members of the Extra-Mural Department, headed by Norman Page (the author of *How to Cope with Redundancy*), offered courses to persons newly unemployed or compelled to change careers, coaching them in the art of hunting for posts and presenting themselves at interviews. Students became aware of a neighbouring population jealous of their privileges, as discos at Owens Park were invaded and the dancers barged and jostled by locals who had gathered in Fallowfield pubs, or as the corridors of new residences on the University's main site suffered at the hands of vandals thought to have come from Moss Side. In the words of Lemuel, the Swiftian satirist of the University journal *Staff Comment*, 'our world within the cloisters still reflects the world without, ignore it though we may'.

Since the avoidance of redundancies was the supreme law, it became necessary in spells of gloom to 'freeze' both academic and support posts when they happened to fall vacant through resignation or retirement; kept on ice for a time though seldom abolished entirely, they revived only at those moments when the economic climate softened. The Joint Committee for University Development (JCUD) redeployed some posts, shifting them towards the disciplines in highest student demand, particularly in the Medical School. This policy, practised since about 1970, was a hallmark of the Armitage regime; the process of redistribution went on for about seven years, until it had exhausted most of the possibilities. Despite the difficulties, the total number of full-time teaching posts in the University increased modestly during the 1970s, although it did not match the increase in the number of students and included more temporary staff, the by-product of financial uncertainty. In the session 1973–74 the University (otherwise Owens) employed 1,234 full-time teaching staff; UMIST (otherwise the Tech or the Faculty of Technology), 440; and the Business School, 50. The Calendar for 1978–79 gave the corresponding figures as 1,350 for Owens, 456 for UMIST, and 31 for the Business School. At Owens the overall increase in staff amounted to 9.4 per cent, against an increase in student load of about 12 per cent. Most of the larger schools and faculties grew a little, but none so vigorously as Medicine, whose strength rose from 223 to 264 full-time teachers (teachers of dentistry merely increased from 52 to 56).

Resolute penny-pinching could reduce expenditure on things other than salaries and wages. It was possible to economise on so-called 'minor works' and on the maintenance of buildings, though this was a form of parsimony which might lead to disaster if indefinitely pursued. From 1973–74 all universities were entitled to finance minor works by drawing on general funds, so long as expenditure on buildings, land and professional fees did not exceed 3 per cent of the institution's block grant (a proviso intended to protect teaching and research from their unwelcome competition). Though distinguished from the major building projects for which universities sought special funding from the UGC, minor works might entail costly operations. Many were or should have been undertaken in order to comply with the numerous fire, health and safety regulations introduced during the 1970s, and to meet the demands of insurers. In practice the University postponed maintenance and improvements at intervals throughout the 1970s, thus giving rise to a threat that buildings would soon become seedy and dilapidated if not ramshackle. In 1980 John Crosby, the Director of Building Services, wrote that few universities could now contemplate spending anything like the 3 per cent allowance on alterations to their buildings, even to meet legal requirements. With good reason, then, the Vice-Chancellor warned of 'a drastic and dangerous curtailment of maintenance programmes . . . This kind of policy cannot be sustained for more than one or two years before the fabric of the building begins to suffer long-term permanent damage.' In at least one department, as Harry Cameron remembers, the elderly wiring was a serious hazard, but the Electrical Engineer could get authority to replace it only by threatening to pull the main switch and close Pharmacy down.

Extravagance on heating and lighting became a target for campaigners, and the Communications Officer set out to convince the University communities of the need to economise. His office published alarming figures illustrating the steep increases in expenditure over the past three years and publicly analysed the uneven distribution of costs (it turned out that the recently acquired Medical School and Computer Building accounted for some 60 per cent of consumption, and the Chemistry and Williamson Buildings and the Linear Accelerator for another 15 per cent between them). Homely exhortations followed: to turn off lights, to abstain from backing up central heating radiators with electric fires, to boil no electric kettles between 10.30 am and 3.30 pm.

Some academics, however, would not comply without recrimination, both against the emergency measures adopted by the Government during the second miners' strike of Edward Heath's reign, and against the University's advertising techniques. In February 1974 twenty-seven academics signed a manifesto urging the University not to economise on the use of lighting by changing its office hours, and arguing that the Three Day Week was but a devious attempt by the Government to pillory the miners and strengthen its own bargaining power. In the autumn the Communications Office hit on the acronym SUE, for Save University Energy, and tried to humanise its campaign by designing a pin-up. SUE was a young woman clad in a close-fitting sun-top and superficially resembling Varoomshka ('She Who Asks Why') of *The Guardian*'s strip cartoon. The office was attacked, not for plagiarism, but for blatant sexism: some feminists and their sympathisers were quick to sense an insult to women and to crowd the columns of *Communication*, the University's house magazine, with polemical letters from women lecturers. These were parried by satirical remarks (mostly from men) on the absurdities of political correctness *avant la lettre*, and relieved by ponderous attempts at humour from both sides. Despite hostility to its propaganda, the magazine felt able to report in May 1977 that the consumption of electricity had fallen by about 20 per cent since 1972, although the cost per unit persisted in growing. Another 'intensive energy-saving campaign' followed in 1979.

Austerity claimed several victims. The Vice-Chancellor's At Home came to an end in the autumn of 1975. Founder's Day celebrations, focused on the conferment of honorary degrees, survived the cuts but incurred censure in 1980. Fearing the treacherous weather of an English May, the organisers had erected a covered walk-way to shelter the distinguished guests en route from the Whitworth Hall to their lunch in the refectory; critics thought this an intolerable extravagance.

Improper use of the telephone was suspected. While it lasted, the antiquated system enabled operators to inquire whether callers from inside the University were engaged on University business. Telephonists developed, or so *Communication* warned, an 'intuitive ability' to sniff out long-distance private conversations disguised as business calls. Scurrilous stories circulated of persons using endearments over the telephone and finding themselves immediately disconnected. Were the telephonists eavesdropping, rather than trusting to intuition? Less controversially, bursarial figures earned commendation for their foresight in making bulk purchases of consumables and furniture before these things were urgently needed, thus forestalling the worst effects of the next price rise. They stockpiled punch cards and eight-track paper tape for computer scientists and quantities of modelling wax and platinum foil for dentists. Curtains, carpets and furniture were kept in readiness for new student flats.

From the autumn of 1977 the financial arrangements of universities began to change, in that they came to depend less on the recurrent block grant and more upon tuition fees. These charges rose steeply, and the Government not only set them but also recommended that they be levied at different rates upon different groups of students. Such recommendations were really instructions, since the Government would assume that the universities would be able to raise more income from fees charged at the higher rates which the government favoured. On this premise it would make suitable reductions in their block grant and save some public money. Universities might dislike the differential fees and be urged by staff and students not to charge them, but they could not defy the Government without adding to their already grave financial difficulties. Relatively few British undergraduates suffered from the new policy, because their fees were paid by local education authorities, and neither they nor their parents saw the bills. But the new arrangements weighed heavily on significant minorities within the student population, including many dedicated people who were supporting themselves. In 1977, Trevor Marshall, a Manchester mathematician prominent in the Association of University Teachers, estimated that about 9 per cent of home undergraduates and 23 per cent of home postgraduates were finding their own fees and maintaining themselves; the new fees, now much higher for postgraduates, discouraged mature students and struck yet another blow at university research. However, much of the ensuing debate focused on the hardship inflicted on overseas students, i.e. those who came from outside the European Economic Community, and had acquired no settlement in the United Kingdom.

Fee increases had been on the cards for some time. As long ago as 1963, Lord Robbins and his colleagues had argued in their famous report on higher education that fees ought to be increased in such a way as to meet about 20 per cent of institutional expenditure. One objective of this move was to ensure that universities should not depend too heavily on a single source of finance, the block recurrent grant. Another, perhaps more important aim, was to reduce or even abolish the concealed subsidy offered to all overseas students, even those who came from rich countries or sprang from prosperous parents. Low tuition fees did little to cover the actual cost of courses and earned the country no gratitude, because few students from abroad realised that they were enjoying any favours. Surely it would be better to raise the fees but openly provide scholarships, bursaries or other forms of aid to a limited number of 'better selected students more aware of the help they receive'. Do this, and it would become possible to discriminate between the rich and the poor, the able and the mediocre, the deserving and the undeserving student.

Robbins stopped short of suggesting that overseas students should pay more for the same education than did their colleagues from the United Kingdom. But it could be argued, even if his report did not do so, that the parents and forebears of most overseas students were not and had never been British taxpayers; that the students themselves, returning with British degrees to their own countries, would not directly benefit either the British economy or the British fisc; and that they ought therefore to contribute more generously to the cost of running British universities. The first concession to this principle was made by a Labour Secretary of State for Education, Anthony Crosland, who introduced a higher fee for overseas students with effect from the session of 1967–68. Crosland incurred charges of racism, levelled at him by radical students, the fate of anyone who appeared to be discriminating against foreigners, no matter how strongly he invoked economic arguments in support of his actions. His successors in the late 1970s were likewise charged with trying to reserve British education for the British, and they offended the international sympathies of Manchester and other universities. Only the most vehement critics, however, compared them with the National Front.

Tuition fees remained where Crosland had set them, at £70 per annum for home and £250 for overseas students, until 1975. At that point, fear that the economy was contracting and the number of overseas students expanding began to inspire a series of unpopular measures. Early in 1977 the Council of the University of Manchester noted that despite the differential fees already in force the total number of overseas students in the United Kingdom had risen from 31,000 in 1967–68 to 80,000 in the current year. More than 1,100 such students were in attendance at Owens in the following session, and they represented about 12 per cent of all students in the institution. They accounted for a large proportion of postgraduates; the forecast was that in 1980–81 37 per cent of full-time postgraduate students would come from overseas, compared with 6 per cent of undergraduates. Universities appeared to be contemplating a 'voluntary agreement' to limit the numbers admitted. By the end of 1979 the University of Manchester had resolved to keep the overall proportion, undergraduate and postgraduate, at 10 per cent.

There was reason to fear, however, that the Government might force British universities to do something more drastic than impose quotas. Ill-judged Government policies might lead universities to price themselves out of the international market by charging exorbitant fees and driving potential clients towards the United States or other countries which offered them a cheaper education. From 1975 postgraduates paid about half as much again as undergraduates, presumably because they required more personal attention and used more costly apparatus. By 1980–81, fees for home undergraduates, jacked up by a series of annual increases, had reached £740 a year; home postgraduates now paid £1,105. Overseas undergraduates already launched on their courses would pay £1,165 and postgraduates £1,525. But overseas students entering the University for the first time in the autumn of 1980 would feel the effects of a policy now extended to its logical conclusion by the Thatcher administration. They would pay what were deemed to be 'full-cost fees', for in March 1980 the University Council had adopted the Government's recommendation to charge £2,000 for Arts-based and £3,000 for Science-based courses, while each year of clinical studies spent in the Medical School would cost every overseas student no less than £5,000. Only a fortunate few would receive financial help from within the United Kingdom. Very likely the Government's new fee remission scheme, designed for 'overseas students of outstanding merit', would benefit no more than 500 students in the whole country during its first year of operation, 1980–81, and would never, even when fully expanded, provide for more than 1,500.

As a result of these increases, the proportion of University income derived from fees began to rise until it exceeded the 20 per cent recommended by Robbins years earlier. In 1976–77, fees had accounted for approximately 7.25 per cent of the University's income, but they contributed just over 17 per cent in 1977–78, and the Vice-Chancellor predicted in May 1977 that 22 per cent would come from fees in the following session. Meanwhile the contribution made by the block grant began to shrink, falling from 74.8 per cent of the whole in 1976–77 to 63.6 per cent in 1977–78. But the higher and higher fees demanded of overseas students, quite apart from the moral issues involved, would endanger the University's income if they caused recruitment to flag.

To idealists, any attempt to charge higher fees to overseas students savoured not only of xenophobia but also of hypocrisy. In their view the claim that the country could not afford to subsidise the visitors was false. Surely, in any case, the exploitation of Third World colonies in the past by European powers, including the United Kingdom, had created a huge moral debt, and this the exploiting nations were bound to repay by generosity towards those who came to their countries as students. Other more pragmatic arguments, urged in the Senate, in student newspapers and in some official publications, appealed to national self-interest: students educated in the United Kingdom would become influential figures in their own nations, promoting good will towards Britain, strengthening commercial ties and encouraging their countrymen to buy British products.

Most telling, perhaps, was the contention that without the presence of overseas students the University would be unable to run certain courses vital to British industrial development. The fee increases imposed by the Thatcher administration in particular were putting some 13 per cent of the University's income at hazard. In a letter of December 1979, the Vice-Chancellor argued the case against them to the UGC. Relatively few home students were willing and well qualified to take courses in Computer Science and in Mechanical and Electrical Engineering, and the departments which offered them depended on a high proportion of undergraduates from overseas. When British students obtained good degrees in those subjects they were able at once to command high salaries in commerce or industry and few wished to suffer the straitened circumstances of a research student. Hence overseas postgraduates of high calibre were needed not only to carry forward research projects but also to act as demonstrators for undergraduate courses; indeed, courses designed to make some 850 students from other science departments familiar with computers would be unable to function without their help. Here was an early example of the argument that the educational policies of the Thatcher government, though intended to restore economic well-being, were in fact short-sighted, unintelligent, and prejudicial to progress.

Any whisper that courses might have to close for lack of overseas students sent a frisson of fear through university lecturers in vulnerable subjects, despite past assurances that no compulsory redundancies would be declared. The possible consequences for UMIST, the Faculty of Technology, which contained a far higher proportion of overseas students than did Owens, were spelled out to a parliamentary committee on higher education by Professor Robert Haszeldine, a chemist who had in 1976 succeeded Lord Bowden as Principal. 'If ever there was a mechanism evolved to throw maximum consternation and difficulties in the way of universities like our own at this time, this is one of them,' he observed, invoking the fear that ten or even fifteen courses might have to be closed for lack of takers. The threatened enterprises included one course in power systems engineering which was clearly of national importance. Another committee of MPs, chaired by Christopher Price, professed concern 'about the effects of sudden financial stringency on course availability in the United Kingdom', and concluded that 'the decision of the present government to move to "full cost" fees within a matter of months' was gravely at fault. 'The scale of the increase is unprecedented and the period over which universities, colleges and polytechnics have been asked to adjust to it is too short. It has caused disquiet throughout the academic community as an educational decision taken on mainly financial grounds.'

Universities might protest, but the only answer returned by an implacable Government was that they should become more entrepreneurial and less philanthropic, and beat the recruiter's drum more loudly in countries that could afford to pay the fees. To the disappointment of idealists, several motions urging the University not to impose the recommended increases were lost in Senate in November 1979; the least unsuccessful, in that 30 members voted for it and 70 against, proposed that 'all students be charged a standard fee, namely that applicable to home-based students'. Senate was then prepared to support strong remonstration with the Government, but nothing more. In February 1980, however, spurred on by the Faculty of Arts, it requested the University to consider 'active collaboration with other British universities to discuss approaches that can be made to the Government on these matters'.

Much less money was now available for buildings. In 1976 a UGC report on the future of university libraries reflected that the sum which the Grants Committee had felt able to allocate to capital projects amounted to no more than £11.5m. in the face of a queue of worthy schemes put forward by all universities and costed at £52.8m. It therefore seemed that the Committee had cut its building programme by 78 per cent. The axe had fallen at a moment when Manchester, having met the most pressing needs of faculties and departments for brand new buildings, had begun to give pride of place to central services. One request, for a new General Purposes Building, had reached the head of the line and suffered only a few months delay. Work on this L-shaped construction, expected to cost about £950,000, began in the summer of 1974 and the building came into use in the autumn of 1977. Named after the last Vice-Chancellor, Mansfield Cooper, it set out to accommodate the small faculties of Law and Theology and the large, eclectic Department of Geography, which was part science and part social science, and was located in the Faculty of Arts. On its heels in the queue were requests for extensions to the University Library and to the

Students' Union, both of which had become overcrowded with objects and people. True, the Students' Union building, opened in 1957, was relatively new. But it antedated the great period of university expansion and its architects and planners had anticipated only 4,200 users; in October 1974 Owens was enrolling almost 10,000 full-time students. Then came the Faculty of Economic and Social Studies, which was still cooped up in antiquated quarters in Dover Street, and after that Music and Drama. In December 1973 the UGC appeared to have tampered with the University's own list of priorities by placing the performing arts in front of the social sciences, but correction followed, and Music and Drama were to receive firm promises of new premises only when the year 2000 had passed.

In 1970 the journalist Michael Kennedy had credited the city of Manchester and the University with building a 'space-age campus'. Set up by the Vice-Chancellor, the Space Reallocation Committee appeared to symbolise the new mood of the middle and later 1970s, and with it the University's resolution to adapt to circumstances and even to find relief in the slower pace of development. Some academics and students had long been conscious of the destructive, inhuman and philistine aspects of technological progress, and depressed by the monotony of the brick and concrete blockhouses which now dotted the Education Precinct. According to Christopher Booker (he of *The Telegraph* and *The Spectator*, author of *The Neophiliacs*), 'Around 1967, we suddenly began to hear a new set of words – "conservation", "the environment", "pollution", "ecology" – expressing a growing sense of horror at what our wonderful, runaway technology was doing to our cities, to our countryside and rivers and seas, to other species, to the whole balance of nature on the planet.' Some of these sentiments began, within a few years, to inspire action in the University. A Pollution Research Unit, shared between Owens and UMIST and directed by the Professor of Liberal Studies in Science, flourished during the 1970s and devoted itself both to measuring the effects of noise, dust, oil and chemicals on the atmosphere, on land and on water, and to studying methods of controlling them 'by administration, law and economics'. By 1981 trees, grass and weeds were flourishing in a 'natural' area protected against pruning and landscaping at the back of the Computer Science building, and a colony of goldfinches had moved in. The conservation party, encouraged by the increasing shortages of money for interfering with the environment, was gaining influence in the Education Precinct.

In the summer of 1975 *Communication* carried an article by Dr M.V. Hounsome, Keeper of Zoology at the Manchester Museum, which reflected on the ecological damage, especially to birds and their habitations, inflicted in the recent past by university planning. True, there was now 'much more green in a previously grey environment'. But the planners had perpetrated two serious blunders, in that most of the lawns, shrubs and bushes had gone from the quadrangles of the main building, and the Virginia creeper had been cut down to enable the blackened stone to be cleaned ('We Cleaned the University', boasted Clean Walls Ltd. of Brown Street in the city centre). The plan had created a 'sterile prairie', the nesting places of blackbirds, dunnock and greenfinch had been destroyed, and good mature bushes had given way to puny upstarts which would take years to reach any useful size. 'The old-fashioned 1950s-style "open plan" scheme put into operation all round the campus is not only destructive but hard to understand; it is boring to look at, intimidating to be in and biologically inadequate.'

In justice to university planners, it should be said that they had had to struggle with the shortcomings of an unpromising reservation within the Education Precinct. A main road from north to south bisected the University area and seemed calculated to divide the arts and humanities on the western side from the natural and social sciences which lay to the east. Crossing Oxford Road at right angles were Burlington Street and Brunswick Street, which defied all efforts to close them to traffic; the task could only be accomplished with the city's co-operation, and this, in the light of protests from motorists and others at any attempt to block or divert their accustomed paths, was difficult to obtain. Since it was such a public arena, references to the University as a cloister or an ivory tower were and remained not only clichéd but implausible, although it was not a place where the people of Manchester lingered; they passed through it, in buses or cars or on foot, bound for other destinations. Academic and administrative buildings, set four-square on level ground, gained such authority as they possessed purely by their own height and mass; the landscape gave them no help, and offered no hillocks to stand upon.

A few Victorian and Edwardian buildings shared the space with Elizabeth II biscuit-boxes. The imposing church of the Holy Name, the work of Joseph Aloysius Hansom of the hansom cab and of his son Joseph Stanislaus Hansom, graced with a massive tower topped by an octagon of Adrian Gilbert Scott, survived the depopulation of its parish and defied attempts to annexe it for an extension to the Library. But Simon Curtis, poet and lecturer in Comparative Literary Studies, feared for the pastiche Queen Anne façade of the old Metallurgy

Building, for the red brick terrace of Waterloo Place, for the 'handsome and distinctive cupola, or little dome, of the Manchester Royal Infirmary, that so enhances Manchester's mean sky-line' and for the relief of the Good Samaritan mounted on the face of the same hospital. Two geologists, Dr F.M. Broadhurst and Dr I.M. Simpson, extolled the quality of the Portland stone which adorned Metallurgy on Oxford Road: 'As a result of prolonged exposure to Manchester's acid rainwater the surface of the stone is beautifully etched in places . . . Those who appreciate natural stone would mourn the passing of this building.'

Forming part of the northern boundary of the University's main area on Oxford Road, the Precinct Centre marked the limitations of 1960s planning. The intention of Hugh Wilson and Lewis Womersley had been to bring the University folk and their neighbours together in a shared shopping mall. They had proposed to link the Centre by walkways, 'streets in the sky' well above the level of wheeled traffic, to the nearby housing estates of Hulme and Brunswick. Adjacent multi-storey car-parks, cheap and convenient, should have decanted drivers and passengers into the Centre's square. But none of this, as Lewis Womersley lamented in 1977, had come to pass. The University and the planners themselves had taken office space in the Precinct, and so had other tenants. But shopkeepers were less easily tempted. Ronald Brierley, chairman of the Lettings Policy Committee, explained that the City Council had encouraged competitors to open shops in Hulme and these had drawn away trade, partly because of the difficulty of manoeuvring prams and shopping trolleys through the approaches to the Precinct Centre. Traders had therefore become dependent on student customers, most of whom were present for only two-thirds of the year, and shopkeepers would not take the plunge unless they could count on an especially high turnover during the student season. Of this they were still unsure.

Few academics were prepared to accept 'The Phoenix', the new Bass Charrington pub in the Precinct Centre ('Decor: two floors, pseudo-30s and GO-GO'), as a substitute for the old College Arms, demolished in the name of modernisation and still much lamented. An archetypal grumbler, created by the Gulliver of *Staff Comment*, muttered that 'where once there stood at the college gates a modest hostelry where we might take a *snifta* at our ease, they have made a desert and built far off a gaudy inn where lascivious damsels dance under the eyes of dons who know not what to make of them and students who, alas, know all too well'. *Staff Comment* tried, as though for revenge, to divert drinkers towards 'The Crown' on Epping Walk in Hulme ('Decor: modernised Victorian, but don't go in the vault').

Womersley himself was in trouble, at least with certain vocal students, for his city connections, both with the repulsive Arndale Centre and with the deteriorating Hulme estate. Critics objected in the pages of *Mancunion*, the principal student newspaper, when on the expiration of his consultancy in 1978 the University decided to award him an honorary Master of Arts degree. A photograph of the Vice-Chancellor bore the caption: 'Would You Buy a Used Degree from This Man?' Womersley's fall from grace reflected a certain disillusionment with the god-like role assumed by planners in the destructive 1960s, a loss of confidence in the breed which was echoed in fierce debates about the defects of their own education launched by students in the Department of Town and Country Planning.

Three threatened buildings, monuments to a more gracious age, began to attract the attention of the Students' Union: the old Music College by the University Theatre, close to the Union itself; the terrace houses at Waterloo Place, on Oxford Road between the Manchester Museum and the Precinct Centre; and the former home of the suffragettes Emmeline, Christabel and Sylvia Pankhurst, at 62, Nelson Street. Student activists sympathised with the homeless and felt that students, also short of rooms and roofs, came close to sharing their plight. They feared that the University would demolish handsome and serviceable buildings or leave them empty for years, on the strength of a delusion that the Government and the UGC were about to stump up the money to develop the sites. Suggestions that good buildings be levelled to provide car parks, or to free the environment from clashing architectural styles, appeared outrageous, particularly at a time when the Union itself was sorely in need of living room. 'Such blatant waste of space and extravagance is typical of the capitalist society in which we live', lamented *Mancunion*.

The shell of the Manchester Royal College of Music on Devas Street was left empty when the institution, now merged with the Northern School of Music and renamed the Royal Northern College, moved to new premises north of the Precinct Centre. In October 1973 about fifty squatters, some of whom were students, occupied the disused building for about five weeks. This action produced unusually rapid results, for the University agreed to relieve the College of the building, to make it available both to the Union and to Contact Theatre, and to offer further space to the Union in one of the houses at Waterloo Place. Later the University also adapted the old music practice rooms, now called the Brick House, for use by Contact, the youth theatre company based at the University Theatre. Huffy Drama students, however, resented the favours bestowed on Contact, which they called 'academically superfluous' and artistically ordinary.

No better name than 'The Squat' could be found for the reprieved college building. Unlovely as the name was, it served to remind students that 'elbow action and bum shining at endless committees' was not the sole way to get one's desire, although journalists from *Punch* later remarked that 'since the authorities have virtually legitimised the take-over, the enterprise somehow lacks that authentic aroma-of-barricade'. At times the Union lost interest in The Squat, but defended it as vital territory whenever the University made any move to invade it. This it appeared to be doing in 1977–78, when the stone floor of the Drama Department's studio was becoming a menace to dance and movement classes, and the University proposed that they migrate to The Squat. By 1981, however, The Squat was in decay. When the Union considered commissioning an ambitious decorative scheme on behalf of the Campaign for Nuclear Disarmament (CND), inspired by Bob Dylan's song 'Masters of War', insuperable obstacles were created by graffiti, by embossed wallpaper, and by patches of damp. Dry rot and the deficiencies of Victorian plumbing threatened the building, and repairs were too expensive to contemplate. Hence, in February 1982 The Squat was at last demolished, its downfall coinciding with another student occupation – this time of the University's main building, in protest against Government education cuts. There was serious talk, though it came to nothing, of compensating the Union with a disused Sunday school, once attached to the church of St Ambrose, which lay close to Waterloo Place.

Waterloo Place formed a Grade II listed building of special architectural and historical interest. The houses, numbers 176–188 Oxford Road, were the oldest in the neighbourhood and perhaps the only architectural reminder of the way the world had been before Owens College occupied its Oxford Road site in 1873. They had been built in 1832 by Peter Tuer, whose name survived in a nearby street. There had once been two parades, each of seven houses, but the more northerly terrace had fallen to bulldozers in 1968. The University owned four of the remaining houses and three were in private ownership, but one of these was in the hands of a firm of historic building consultants. Its partners included Donald Buttress of the Department of Architecture, who directed a course on restoration and conservation, and used the premises for teaching. Number 178 Waterloo Place, passed to the

Union and some of the enterprises which it sponsored. The University also agreed to lease Number 184 and the ground floor of Number 182 to J.P. McGill's second-hand book shop. These moves, however, were intended as temporary measures and the fate of Waterloo Place remained uncertain. Not easily convinced by historical and aesthetic arguments alone, the University Council observed in 1976 that Waterloo Place, even when fully owned by the University, could only be 'of marginal value in the provision of accommodation'. Retention of these houses ran contrary to the Precinct Plan, and heavy expenditure alone would bring them up to modern standards; they occupied ground said to be reserved for a new Economic and Social Studies building; and *Communication* spoke of Waterloo Place's 'uneasy role in the "mixed economy" of the Precinct'.

None the less, the planner Lewis Womersley admitted in November 1977 to a change of heart: he now considered that the terrace should be left standing. It was beginning to seem that adaptation, here and elsewhere, could prove less costly than convenient but characterless new buildings. Hence, in a climate of pessimism and parsimony, Waterloo Place survived, maintaining the line of nineteenth- and early twentieth-century buildings that flanked the western side of Oxford Road between Burlington Street and the Precinct Centre. The Metallurgy building, too, was spared and remained on parade as a front for part of the Manchester Museum. Despite the pleas of the Building Design Partnership for a new building of 'calm simplicity' (which critics thought a euphemism for blandness) to displace the fussy old one, the much-needed Museum Extension arose behind Metallurgy's façade, and its colonnaded portico, spared from destruction, became 'a single large illuminated showcase, bringing the Museum right on to the footpath of Oxford Road'.

Number 62 Nelson Street, formerly the Pankhurst residence, faced extinction for the purpose of clearing the way for an extension to Manchester Royal Infirmary. Seemingly condemned, the house stood empty and increasingly dilapidated for two-and-a-half years in the mid-1970s. When plans for the hospital extension were shelved, Community Action, the Union's welfare organisation, approached Manchester Area Health Authority on their own initiative and signed a lease for the house. They proposed to use the building as a 'Community Resources Centre', which would offer (among much else) a 'fully equipped safe play area for students' children', who could no longer disport themselves on Union premises. Some of the money needed for refurbishment might well be forthcoming from Greater

Manchester Council, and Community Action launched an appeal
in the hope of raising the rest. When they approached the Union
controversy followed, for the Union's officers were now scrutinising
their finances, and did not spare Community Action. The predominantly Conservative executive feared that the Union would be
charged with making improper payments, since much of the Nelson
Street enterprise had little to do with the well being of students themselves and the General Secretary of the Union regarded the project as
an unauthorised venture. However, Community Action had helped to
rescue a house of historical interest, and the Pankhurst residence
escaped the fate of Frederick Engels's house in Thorncliffe Grove,
which had fallen without trace to make way for student flats in the
Southern Area Development.

Money earned in the 1960s made some new building possible amid
the penury of the next decade. A new ecumenical chaplaincy building
opened in 1974, on the eastern side of Oxford Road, and was connected
to the Precinct Centre, as one of Gulliver's characters suggested, by a
Bridge of Sighs across Oxford Road. Which was the palace and which
the prison was not stated. Finance came from sums paid to compensate
for the compulsory purchase of two churches demolished in 1967: the
Anglican St Ambrose, built in 1884, and the handsome Oxford Hall, a
Methodist church established in 1825. St Ambrose had yielded to the
Architecture and Planning Building, Oxford Hall to the Computer
Building. The Sharing of Church Buildings Act of 1969 opened the way
to a new arrangement whereby the Anglican, Methodist, Baptist and
United Reformed Churches combined to share the same premises.
These were called St Peter's House, and the Catholics, who might well
have claimed a special interest in St Peter, named their chaplaincy after
his fellow apostle, St Paul, and contemplated sharing common rooms
and other amenities with the occupants of St Peter's. Angular where
other structures were box-like, St Peter's House did not set out to be an
exclusively religious building or hire its rooms solely to religious organisations (freshers being entertained by the History Department one
October were intrigued to find themselves sharing the kitchen with a
Transvestite Society). Indeed, the chaplains acted in the spirit of William
Temple's dictum that the Church exists for those who are not its members, a principle appropriate to an officially secular but not wholly god-
less University.

Since the amalgamation of the great private library in Deansgate
with the University libraries in 1972, the John Rylands University
Library of Manchester had made convincing claims to be the third

great university library in England, ranking with and in some respects surpassing those of Oxford and Cambridge. Known in the trade as Jerusalem, it possessed some of the attributes of a holy enclave in the midst of dark satanic mills. In 1974 the Library as a whole housed more than 2m. volumes, subscribed to more than 8,000 periodicals, and had on its books more than 26,000 registered users (a figure which had reached 32,000 by 1977, and was then equivalent to about double the number of students and academic staff in the University, UMIST and the Business School).

The sparsely populated, lavishly appointed building in Deansgate offered ample room and a quasi-ecclesiastical atmosphere, beneath its stained-glass windows and statues of literary saints, to the few habitués who came to consult its rare books and manuscripts. But the buildings on the main site of the University at Oxford Road were starved of reader and storage space, and one of them was taxed by a UGC working party with 'presenting the worst working conditions for Library staff and readers of any library in their experience'. Books, journals and other holdings kept on the main site were divided between three libraries to the west of Oxford Road, devoted respectively to Arts, to Science and to Medicine. In the labyrinthine Arts Library a placard – one of many inscribed with stern admonitions – proclaimed that 'Studying In This Tunnel Is Prohibited'. In the Christie Science Library, as Diana Leitch recalls, books were double-stacked on window-ledges, and one of the galleries was so narrow that users had to shuffle sideways down its length. Mathematical treatises, precariously balanced on a narrow bar, might at any moment plunge on to the heads of readers consulting the catalogues down below. The building took on a sinister, gothic air when senior staff set out to lock it up at 9.30 on weekday evenings and at 1 p.m. on Saturdays, and were obliged to patrol it to ensure that no undesirables were lurking in any of its niches; one woman brought along her bullterrier for protection. Plans put to the UGC for approval and financial backing proposed to bring the contents of all three buildings together by attaching an extension – a branch larger than the trunk – to the Arts Library.

Already overcrowded, John Rylands seemed, like all university libraries, intent on limitless expansion, and was spurred on with particular urgency by the acquisitive spirit of its librarian, Fred Ratcliffe. It was true that inflation, and particularly the rising cost of periodicals affected by a world shortage of paper, had begun to reduce its rate of growth by 1975. By that time librarians were inviting faculties to cancel subscriptions and greeting suggestions for the purchase of new journals with increasing scepticism. But the UGC took alarm at the number of requests for large capital grants for library buildings with which it was faced. Seeking finance for that purpose, the University faced intense competition from other clamorous institutions. In 1976 the UGC, at the suggestion of a working party headed by Professor Richard Atkinson, adopted the guiding principle of the 'self-renewing library', which really meant the 'self-pruning library'. Rather than amassing new material *ad infinitum* and placing it on immediate access, libraries ought to weed out the less used items and place them in stores close to their main premises, from which their staff would be able to fetch them within twenty-four hours, should they be called for. Should these works, after several years in limbo, fail to attract any reader's attention, they ought then to be removed from the neighbourhood and sent to a national depot, such as the British Library Lending Division. True, this process would increase the administrative costs of libraries, for staff would have to select volumes for relegation, but it might also forestall some of the demands for new buildings.

Responding to the Atkinson report, the University accepted the need for stores on the main site, looked for forgotten cellars and adaptable nooks and crannies, and found them in a disused laboratory, a church hall, and an empty Roman Catholic infants' school in Dover Street. In 1977 the cost of converting the former school, which would require structural book stacks to transfer the load from the first floor to the foundations of the building, appeared to be about £46,000 – a sum which compared very favourably with the £250,000 which a new building of similar capacity would have demanded. The UGC was prepared at the time, so Senate was informed, to allocate £63,000 towards the cost of converting and equipping two buildings in the Precinct. The Library's bindery migrated to the Precinct Centre.

The cost of the new Library Extension stood at approximately £4m. when the UGC at last felt able to include it in the capital building programme for 1978–79. This move was a tribute to the University's powers of persuasion and particularly to the representations it had made to a committee which the Department of Trade had set up under Mr Justice Whitford and briefed to consider possible changes in the law of copyright. Inspired by Fred Ratcliffe, the University had pleaded that its Library should be granted 'legal deposit status' – in other words, that it should join the British Library, the university libraries of Oxford, Cambridge, and Trinity College Dublin, and the national libraries of Wales and Scotland, as one of the institutions entitled to receive from publishers, free of charge, one copy of every copyright work published in the United Kingdom. Justifying the proposal, the University spoke not only of the size and quality of the existing collections but also of the ease with which members of a regional population of some 12.5 million could travel to Manchester rather than London in search of enlightenment. Responding to this plea for devolution, the Whitford Committee concluded that 'The case for establishing a deposit library in Manchester to serve the North of England would seem strong if the geographical dispersal of such libraries could be considered *de novo* . . . ' It was true that publishers, burdened with 'an additional deposit obligation', would almost certainly be unenthusiastic, but they could probably be won over by allowing them to charge the free copies against their tax liabilities. 'We recommend that the proposal of the John Rylands Library be accepted in principle, although recognising that present financial stringencies will necessarily delay its implementation.'

In the event the constraints were never, at least in the late twentieth century, to relax far enough to allow Manchester to establish the deposit library that would so greatly have enhanced the University's reputation. But against heavy odds the Library did get its premises enlarged, thus enabling *Communication* to boast in 1980 that 'In the current atmosphere of stringent economy, it is the only large-scale building project at any UK university.' This undertaking was expected, or so *Mancunion* informed its readers, to treble the amount of usable space in the Library, to increase the book capacity by 1.4 million volumes, and to provide almost 2,000 seats for readers. Doing his bit, the Vice-Chancellor played host at a grand luncheon for the City Council, members of which soon divined that something was expected in return for this hospitality. They agreed that Burlington Street should be closed to city traffic; that the Extension should be built across its western end; and that the buses whose path would be blocked by the expanding Library should be redirected to Booth Street West. Architects tackled the problem of marrying two buildings in which only the ground and the first floors were on the same level. An elegant conference centre arose within a quadrangle formed by the old Arts Library and the new Extension, and took the name of a benefactress who had died in 1975. Muriel Stott was the daughter of an Oldham cotton spinner, noted for her generosity not only to the care of old people but also to the John Rylands Library before its incorporation into the University.

Every year until the end of the 1970s the Government and the UGC expected the University to increase student numbers, especially those of undergraduates, although the Vice-Chancellor gave notice in April

1974 that the rate of growth would have to slow down. Increased dependence on fees reminded everyone how closely the University's income depended on its power to attract students. Admissions tutors, engaged in a complicated gamble and competing with other establishments, were exhorted not to fall short of the targets set up for them lest they lose the University money, and not to overshoot them lest the University be unable to accommodate all the freshers whom they had accepted. In October 1974, 9,977 full-time students were registered at Owens; in October 1980, there were 11,493, marking an increase of about 15 per cent in a period of six years. Only in 1979 did the UGC advise universities to begin reducing the number of students admitted, indeed to hold down the number of home undergraduates entering in October 1980 to 94 per cent of the number admitted the previous autumn. Only in January 1980 did a Council minute comment that 'Essentially the University had now reached its steady state.'

Successful recruitment depended in part on improving the University's reputation for housing its students, particularly newcomers, who had no wish to find themselves roofless in a strange city or live out of suitcases in temporary lodgings for the first few weeks of their careers. In 1976–77 the University succeeded for the first time in guaranteeing all new undergraduates a place in University accommodation, as distinct from privately owned flats or digs – so long as they were not accompanied by spouses (let alone children) and had applied for a place by the due date. To achieve this end it proved necessary to reserve about half the places in University residences for first-year students; few could now hope to spend all their undergraduate years as paying guests of the University, and gregarious stalwarts who lived from start to finish in halls of residence were becoming creatures of the past.

The policy depended on building almost continuously in order to keep pace with expansion. Owens and UMIST collaborated in the enterprise, each institution offering some places to the other's students. In 1974 they were capable of providing between them some 4,700 residential places in accommodation which they either owned or licensed; by 1980 the stock had risen to over 6,000. Generally about 40 per cent of all students lived in University residences, for 13,352 students were registered at the University, UMIST and the Business School in the autumn of 1974, and 17,113 in the autumn of 1980. In December 1976 *Communication* estimated that of 14,000 students in Owens and UMIST, 6,000 lived in University accommodation, 5,500 in private flats and lodgings, and 2,500 at home.

Effort concentrated on building flats for small groups of students of the same sex, who would cater for themselves and not take communal meals in halls or canteens. New buildings rose on the Southern Area Development, on Booth Street East (where UMIST added Bowden Court to Grosvenor Place), and in Fallowfield, where Oak House expanded. Such flats allowed students more independence and more disposable income than did the traditional halls, and they seemed well attuned to the idea that students were legally adults and ought to be treated as such. By the end of 1976 UGC finance had run out entirely and there was no expectation of a renewed trickle of public money before April 1978.

The Southern Area Development, the most memorable architecturally, took the name of Whitworth Park. Shaped like Toblerone bars, the residential blocks provided over 800 places in the first phase of growth between 1974 and 1976, and a second, more modest programme was launched in 1978 and expected to provide another 200-odd places by 1980. The architects, drawn from the Building Design Partnership, attempted to vary the sizes and shapes of the study bedrooms and to eliminate the 'long impersonal corridor with little boxes of rooms leading off it'; the sloping roofs were designed to waste no space; and the blocks, named after the terraced streets flattened to make way for them, were described as 'cosily angular and very much on a human scale' – a well-worked phrase which emphasised the absence of the overweening towers and concrete cliffs of the 1960s. Space, not wasted, was not generous either; invited to grumble, students complained of the difficulty of hanging long dresses in stunted wardrobes, of the lack of space for trunks and cases, and of the awkwardness of working in these surroundings with an architect's drawing board. *Inmate*, the title of the local newsletter, seemed forbidding. But the new settlement was, as one student put it, 'near where it's at'. It spared students the morning trudge from Fallowfield, to which the alternative was a wait in bus queues so long as to suggest that, in the words of a lecturer ensconced on the top deck of a Number 48, 'There must be a lot of students who never get into the University at all.'

Early in 1980 the Vice-Chancellor announced his intention to retire at the end of the session. He had striven to manage the University's finances in such a way as to encourage bold developments in certain intellectual areas, and especially, perhaps, in Medicine; to protect livelihoods against compulsory redundancies; to favour institutions which served the whole University, and particularly the Library; and to enable the University to provide higher education for the still increasing number of young people who were reaching the age of eighteen. In December 1979 he protested against the untold harm inflicted by 'ad hoc reductions in grant and apparently haphazard changes in policy', proclaiming his belief in 'one of the finest and certainly one of the most economic[al] university systems in the world; one which is selective, and caters only for 8–9 per cent of the population, and one which is singularly flexible and adaptive in meeting the country's needs, especially in science, technology and medicine'. Greeted at the time with much grumbling and some polemic, the Armitage years were to take on in retrospect the pure, sweet air of Good King Arthur's golden days. The appreciation delivered to Senate shortly after Armitage's retirement, in the autumn of 1980, spoke of his 'consistent refusal to accept unnecessary restraints'. The obituary placed before Council after his death in 1984, when far worse things had begun to happen to universities, remarked that 'His span of office covered a period that will perhaps come to be regarded as the golden age of the University system, but Sir Arthur was not out of place as one of its princes. Various qualities are brought to mind by his career: energy, probity, compassion, authority, perhaps helped by those distinctive eyebrows, and above all, optimism. Where all around him viewed the future with gloom and depression, Sir Arthur was heard to counsel that this would be to talk oneself into a disaster; the future had to be regarded with optimism. This epitomised his whole outlook to life and work.'

2

The academics:
achievement and self-doubt

'It *is* a great university, even if people never tire of telling you so.'
Academics leaving Manchester for supposedly more benign places were
inclined to pay back-handed compliments to the University. In the
1970s the institution was proud of its achievements and given
to reciting them at length. Needing to assert its distinction and to struggle against its austere appearance, it possessed neither the ancient
universities' sense of natural superiority nor the Londoners' confidence
that ambitious academics would gravitate towards the capital. Senior
Manchester figures, seasoned travellers from Manchester Piccadilly,
Stockport, Wilmslow or Macclesfield to London Euston, strove to
maintain their places on national boards and committees, each trip
diverting them for a day from ordinary duties. One or two became
absentees, devoted to such bodies as the Committee on Safety of Medicines, delegating – or refusing to delegate – their normal responsibilities to Manchester colleagues. Historians yearned for easier access to
the British Library or the Public Record Office, where many of their
sources were to be found. There was a touch of self-doubt, corresponding to the fear of some Mancunians that the heyday of regional
capitals had passed and that their town was condemned to lose its most
eminent citizens to the south. Even *The Manchester Guardian* had
changed its name and moved its head office to Fleet Street. How many
would follow the example of John Barbirolli, the Hallé's conductor,
and insist on remaining in Manchester even when offered plum jobs
elsewhere? According to the journalist David Aaronovitch, who was a
history student in the mid-1970s, Manchester in those days 'hadn't yet
invented the new thing it was to become . . . it was still emerging from
its civic provincialism, and it hadn't quite got around to being exciting.'
   During the 1970s Manchester contributed much to the southward
drift. It lost three distinguished engineers, Alistair Macfarlane, Andrew
Schofield and William Johnson (Professor of Mechanical Engineering
in the Faculty of Technology) to chairs at Cambridge. John Davis, after

twelve years in a Manchester chair, became Cambridge's first Professor of Paediatrics in 1979. Samuel Finer, beringed and dandified, Picasso with a hint of Disraeli, a lecturer who commanded and inspired vast audiences, left to be Gladstone Professor of Government in the University of Oxford. The Reverend James Barr, Manchester's Professor of Semitic Languages and Literature and an eminent figure in the Church of Scotland, became in October 1976 the Oriel Professor of the Interpretation of Holy Scriptures at Oxford, from which position he succeeded two years later to the Regius chair of Hebrew. The Reverend Basil Hall, acclaimed by Manchester as the country's leading Calvinist scholar, resigned the chair of Ecclesiastical History in the hope of finding peace and leisure for writing as Fellow and Dean of St John's College Cambridge. Others headed for London. Geoffrey Allen, Professor of Chemical Physics, departed to become Professor of Polymer Science at Imperial College, *en route* for the chairmanship of the Science Research Council and a knighthood bestowed in the Queen's Birthday Honours List for 1979. After four years as Professor of Physical Geography in Manchester, Tony Chandler accepted the post of Master of Birkbeck. Ian Macdonald, for a short time Manchester's Fielden Professor of Mathematics, became Professor of Pure Mathematics at Queen Mary College. Manchester had maintained its capacity for nurturing and attracting eminent scholars in a variety of subjects, but not all were prepared to regard a Manchester chair as their crowning achievement, and a few succumbed to the blandishments of other institutions.

However, evidence could be found that Manchester was still among the ten leading universities of the country. In 1975 David Walker of *The Times Higher Educational Supplement* attempted to do what the UGC denied doing and establish a ranking order for English (not British) universities. He noted that certain institutions 'come out near the top of every scale that is used'. His criteria included the proportion of students accommodated in University residences; the strength of the A-level results required to qualify for entry; the quality of engineering research and the standard of medical teaching; the number of library books per head of the student and academic population; and the honours secured by leading academics. Entitled 'Old familiars stay at the top', Walker's piece placed seven universities at the top of the pile and numbered Manchester among them, in the company of Leeds, Oxford, Cambridge, Birmingham, Nottingham, and 'London University taken as a whole'. A little below this premier league came a first division composed of Liverpool, Sussex, Sheffield and Bristol, and on their heels trod Reading, Southampton and Essex. Intellectually, Manchester scored highly in disciplines reckoned to be vital to the country's material interests – in medicine, engineering, mathematics, and the physical and biological sciences. Another education correspondent, Ngaio Crequer, formerly President of the Students' Union in Manchester, visited her old haunts in the year of optimism, 1978. 'Superlatives roll off northern tongues at Manchester University', she wrote. 'Wherever you go someone will claim that their building or department is the first, biggest or best . . . There is a kind of Muhammad Ali mentality about the place.' The heavyweight champion to whom she alluded had not suffered from over-modesty ('I am the greatest!!! . . . It ain't bragging if you can back it up . . . I shook the world. Me! Whee!!!').

A heavyweight among universities, Manchester, as Miss Crequer admitted, made few claims to physical beauty, but even its architectural dimness found appreciation in the verses of Simon Curtis, lecturer in Comparative Literature and refugee from the chilly college elegance and remote suburban lodgings of Cambridge:

> The New Arts Block makes Billy grouse.
> Its hutch-like rooms, anonymous,
> Let off bleak corridors of grey.
> The times that we have heard him say
> Of rooms he had, when at the 'Hall',
> With words which seemed to damn us all,
> 'Late Regency, you know – *such* grace!
> 'How spacious rooms breed spacious minds!'
> Grey lino, shelves and desk, white blinds:
> Dull souls will churn out from *this* place.
>
> But spacious rooms are hard to heat,
> Even for those like Bill, aesthete.
> I had Regency lodgings, once,
> Sash-windowed, spacious, fine. The sense
> Of Regency which best pleased me,
> When freezing, unaesthetically,
> Was peopling those high-ceilinged walls
> With bright-eyed and full-bosomed belles
> In Regency décolleté:
> ('Son, we will warm you up, OK')
>
> As I ploughed through, in mittens, coat,
> What some half-witted critic wrote,
> No shillings left with which to boost

A feudal gas-fire's flickering flame,
Because a pint of Marston's best
Had staked its prior financial claim.
Sure, old Bill's imagination,
So suggestible to furnishing,
Has ranged with taste – should get him far,
Further than ever mine, I fear.

I guess it is I suit this place.
But with so much capital in space,
What the hell's old Bill still doing here?'

By British standards Manchester was great at least in the sense that it was large – a complex and populous university, occupying the greater part of the city's huge Education Precinct, its tentacles sprawling outwards to embrace teaching hospitals and establishments at Jodrell Bank or Barton Aerodrome far from its own centre, equipped to teach and conduct research in an enormous range of subjects. It exercised some influence in the region through its supervision of affiliated colleges, particularly those institutions for teacher training which had once formed part of the School of Education founded in 1947, and were now known as the Colleges of Education Division of the Faculty of Education. Eight of these were still under the University's aegis in the mid-1970s, while another four had been transferred, at least for certain purposes, to the new University of Lancaster.

Manchester's was not a federal university in the same sense as the Universities of London and Wales, but had a complicated relationship with its close neighbour, UMIST. Claiming descent from the nineteenth-century Mechanics' Institute and once called the Tech., UMIST had its own Principal, its own Council, its own grant, its own administration and its own Students' Union, but at the same time formed the Faculty of Technology of the University of Manchester. 'Manchester Owens', whose headquarters were on Oxford Road, had about 10,000 full-time students in 1974, UMIST another 3,000; in 1980 the respective figures were approaching 11,500 and 4,400. The two institutions shared a number of facilities, listed in 1982, when UMIST was reaffirming its links with Owens and resisting the charms of Salford, as 'accommodation, computing, health, welfare, sports, careers, appointments, audio-visual and library services . . . ' The magazine *Staff Comment* was supposed to have three editors, one from UMIST and two from Owens. Critics, particularly in hard times, complained that the Science and Technology Faculties, at Owens and

UMIST, tended to overlap, to lay on parallel courses, and thereby expose their necks to administrators bent on rationalisation. But they came together gracefully at one point, in the joint Department of Metallurgy, established during the 1970s by the collaboration of two professors, Ken Entwistle of UMIST and Robin Nicolson of Owens. Constrained by Victorian premises, they had made a joint application to the UGC in 1971, just before money became scarce, and had secured a grant of £1m. for the new building which they eventually occupied in 1975. After Nicolson's departure, Ken Entwistle was to continue the partnership for thirteen years with Ted Smith, sometime Dean of Science at Owens.

Almost as complex, and sometimes less happy, was the University's relationship with the much smaller Business School, otherwise the Faculty of Business Administration, which had just over 100 full-time students in 1974 and 160 in 1980. This was formally part of the University, but enjoyed a high degree of autonomy, for it received its own grant from the UGC, which paid the money through the University, and had a Council of its own. Questions of identity, relationship and control, left unaddressed in the 1970s and 1980s, would return to trouble the University in the following decade.

In the mid-1970s the University (Owens) paid the salaries and wages of approximately 5,400 individuals. About 2,000 of these were academics, administrators and para-academics paid on the 'academic-related' scales, and the remaining 3,400 were ancillary or supporting staff: technicians, electricians, telecommunicators, plumbers, engineers who maintained the heating and ventilation plants, clerical workers and secretaries, porters, cleaners, patrolmen, car park attendants, gardeners, domestics in halls of residence, cooks, chefs, and caterers. The Registrar ruled over a department of forty-four persons important enough to be listed by name in the *Calendar* for the session 1974–75, the Bursar over one of fifty-six (including accountants, planners, building officers, engineers, and the managers of Oak House, Owens Park and the Student Flats), while the University Librarian had a force of forty-one, ranging from Deputy Directors to Assistant Librarians, Grade II. There were other potentates, other less prominent empires. Clifford Haigh, the Manager of Uniformed Services, a former Detective Chief Superintendent of thirty years service, commanded 170 men, of whom 126 were porters, 32 were concerned with security, and 12 looked after car parks. Janet Kelso, the Telephone Supervisor, presided over twenty-three women. Landscape Services employed as gardeners one woman and about sixty men.

Not always heeding the UGC's pleas for economies of scale, the University listed in its *Calendar* some 120 departments, each representing a distinctive discipline which had once clamoured for recognition: the Department of Historical Bibliography consisted only of Fred Ratcliffe, who was really the University Librarian; that of Scandinavian Studies only of G.L. Brook, who was essentially a Professor of English Language; that of Persian Studies only of Professor Boyle; that of Dental Ethics of a single Lecturer in Dental Ethics and Practice Management. The small Faculty of Theology, which contained only sixteen full-time teachers, none the less saw fit to divide itself into six departments.

Centres and units not classified as University departments, but to some extent directed and staffed by their members, included the Hester Adrian Research Centre, whose object was 'to promote, sustain and carry through research into the learning processes in mentally handicapped children and adults'; the Centre for Business Research; the Centre for Urban and Regional Research; and the Pollution Research Unit. Some of these existed to co-ordinate activities which took place in several departments and to counter the kind of blinkered specialisation that could bedevil intellectual inquiry in a strongly departmental university. Certain enterprises offered their technical expertise to colleagues, as the Research Support Unit of the Faculty of Economic and Social Studies offered help in the 'data processing aspects' of research work.

Some senior University figures believed that the University's academic standing had suffered from the swift expansion of the late 1950s and the 1960s, for which it was now paying the price. Addressing the Senate Dining Club in 1979, the retiring Registrar, Vincent Knowles, recalled the promises of Utopia in the famous Robbins report on Higher Education in 1963. 'Universities accepted the challenge and expanded their staff, but I make bold to state that in some cases those staff were not of university standard. I am reminded – as I am sure you all are – of the saying of Fabius Maximus: "to avoid *all* mistakes in the conduct of great enterprises is beyond man's powers" and we did make some mistakes.' Was the University burdened with large numbers of middle-aged lecturers who had too easily obtained tenured jobs and Association of University Teachers were amounting to very little? Professor Henry Lipson, a distinguished crystallographer of the Physics Department at UMIST, was no enemy of progress. He had promoted the cause of women academics and campaigned for the (AUT) in UMIST, but looked askance at the institution's rapid growth under

Vivian Bowden. Dismay struck him on reading the address delivered in 1975 by Brian Manning as President of the University branch of the AUT. Manning's apparent desire to involve everyone in the government of the University, thus entangling all academics in a series of tedious committees which would only agree on trifles, threatened in Lipson's view not only to 'reduce the quality of our output' but also to give rise to a cult of 'uninspired mediocrity' in which 'the days of the Rutherfords, Alexanders and Osborne Reynoldses will never be able to recur' (Lipson had been a protégé of the great Sir Lawrence Bragg, who had succeeded Rutherford at the Cavendish Laboratory in Cambridge shortly before the Second World War). 'My fears are not groundless. This University was once almost the greatest centre of science in this country. As measured by membership of the Royal Society it is so no longer; it has been overtaken by other Universities – Edinburgh, Birmingham, Liverpool, Bristol, for example. I believe that the reason for this is that, as we have become larger, it has become more difficult for the individual to stand out.'

Be this as it might, in 1974 the Royal Society was represented at UMIST by Lipson himself and by Robert Haszeldine, an entrepreneurial chemist; at Jodrell Bank by Sir Bernard Lovell and Francis Graham Smith, a future Astronomer Royal; at Oxford Road by Sir Frederic Williams, the pioneer of the computer, and by Geoffrey Gee, a chemist long engaged in the study of polymers, whose 'ultimate achievement', according to his Royal Society biographer, 'was to secure the place of natural rubber against the growing competition from synthetic rubbers'. Whereas Williams had forsaken computer design and turned to other forms of electrical engineering, his former assistant, Tom Kilburn, had persevered with computer science with such success that, as a colleague declared, 'The mark of Tom Kilburn is on every modern computer in the world today.' He received in 1978 one of the three Royal Medals awarded, on the recommendation of the Council of the Royal Society, 'for his striking innovations in computer hardware over thirty years' and for originating fundamental concepts such as 'paging and virtual memory'. Fritz Ursell, the Professor of Applied Mathematics, was elected to the Royal Society in 1972. Born in Düsseldorf, educated at Clifton and Marlborough, he had worked during and after the war while still classified as an enemy alien with an Admiralty Wave Group whose task was to establish rules for the forecasting of ocean waves, originally to assist with operations in the Pacific. At Manchester since 1961 his work had concentrated 'on the main themes of water waves, ship hydrodynamics and asymptotics', and he was in close touch with ocean engineers, with a mind to solving their theoretical problems.

The British Academy, the Royal Society's counterpart in the humanities and social sciences, had also recognised the distinction of several Manchester academics. Max Gluckman, the social anthropologist, a leading exponent of legal anthropology and comparative jurisprudence, formerly a field-worker in Barotseland and director of the Rhodes-Livingstone Institute, had established a world-famous postgraduate seminar in Manchester and used the Simon Fellowships to bring eminent or promising visiting scholars to the University. Harry Street was an innovative teacher whose range extended from administrative law to torts. He wrote, not only treatises for law students, but works addressed to a much wider public. Between 1963 and 1978 his fundamental study of civil liberties, *Freedom, the Individual and the Law,* published by Pelican, passed through four editions and sold 100,000 copies. 'I have had two objects in view', he once said. 'Telling the citizen what his rights are, and showing what is wrong with the law and how Parliament should set about putting things right.'

John Roskell, the Professor of Medieval History, was a homely, conservative, avuncular man noted for his thorough studies of the English Parliament. Devoted to formality, respectful of the dignity of University officers (but inclined, as were Knowles and Lipson, to think that the University was failing to defend its standards), a guardian of 'due constitutional propriety', he was nevertheless given to a kind of 'resigned derision' marked by a snort, a wink and a grin at the latest fashionable developments. He tried to celebrate his election to the British Academy with a lunch in the almost empty Lancashire Cricket Club restaurant with a scholarly old friend; refused entry for not being members, they celebrated instead with slices of Grosvenor pie and paper cups of coffee from a more plebeian stall on the Old Trafford ground. Reginald Dodwell, the art historian and Director of the Whitworth Art Gallery, was a student of medieval illuminated manuscripts, a 'historian-palaeographer' who, ranging more widely than this description may suggest, had contributed a volume on *Painting in Europe, 800–1200* to the *Pelican History of Art*. Before coming to Manchester he had been Librarian of Lambeth Palace Library, appointed by Archbishop Fisher, and later Librarian of Trinity College Cambridge. After succeeding John White, the founder Professor of the History of Art, in 1966, he had increased the academic staff of the Department from six to fifteen, established an attractive single honours degree and offered an important postgraduate diploma in Art Gallery and Museum Studies. Dodwell was determined to resist the power of London as 'a big vacuum cleaner' which sucked in everything to do with the arts, and found one distinguished ally in Hal Burton, the architect, stage-designer and impresario, who was anxious to leave his collection of modern art to a gallery outside the capital.

James Barr, author of *The Semantics of Biblical Language* and *Comparative Philology and the Text of the Old Testament,* also represented the Academy in the Faculty of Arts. Professor F.F. Bruce, an evangelical Christian and a member of the Brethren, served as Rylands Professor of Biblical Criticism and Exegesis. He was a classical scholar who had turned to the Greek New Testament and particularly to the writings of St Paul. Like Street he was a gifted populariser and his vast corpus of work came to include about fifty books. As retirement approached he himself became the subject of two celebratory volumes. Bruce was sometimes suspected of reading his own books to students in lectures, but his treatment of the subject in print had perhaps become so exhaustive as to leave nothing else to be said, even by himself.

It was a small company which could rapidly become depleted. By the end of the decade two other members of the University, Howard Rosenbrock of Control Engineering, famous for Rosenbrock's Banana Function, and Durward Cruickshank of Chemistry (both at UMIST), had been elected to the Royal Society, and one to the British Academy (Stefan Strelcyn, Reader in Semitic Studies). But of the group mentioned earlier Gluckman and Williams died during the 1970s, Gee and Haszeldine were drawn to the higher levels of administration, Barr left for Oxford, Smith became Director of the Greenwich Observatory at Hurstmonceux, and Roskell, Bruce and Lipson retired. It remained to be seen whether scientists and scholars of equal distinction would come forward to replace them, and whether there would be any equivalent to the quadrumvirate consisting of Flowers, Gee, Williams, and the engineer Jack Diamond, who had shaped the Science Faculty in the 1960s. Perhaps, as Lipson had half-prophesied, the future would lie, neither with brilliant individuals, nor with comet departments characterised by glittering heads and trailing tails, but rather with the solid achievements of soundly managed units and reliable members of teams.

Some members of the University exercised great influence in other spheres, beyond the purview of the Royal Society and the British Academy. Sir Douglas Black, Professor of Medicine, served as Chief Scientist to the Department of Health and was later elected President of the Royal College of Physicians. An appreciation offered to Senate on Black's retirement in 1977 noted that 'Few medical men have his command of English and fewer the capacity to write so lucidly and persuasively. With his pen (which was usually a small stub of pencil) he could render the tortuous jargon of original medical publications (euphemistically known as "the medical literature") into limpid prose that perhaps made clear for the first time the essential message of their authors.' Patrick Byrne had spent much of his working life as a general practitioner at Milnthorpe in Cumbria, from 1932 to 1968; in 1972 he was appointed at Manchester to the first chair in General Practice to be established anywhere in the country. Having written and lectured widely on the subject of vocational training, he became in 1973 President of the Royal College of General Practitioners. A third Manchester man, Professor Eric Easson, an authority on aspects of cancer and Director of Radiotherapy at the Christie Hospital, served from 1975 to 1977 as President of the more specialised Royal College of Radiologists.

It was commonplace that a large number of university librarians in the country had at one time in their careers been under Fred Ratcliffe's wing. It was equally true that many university registrars owed their training and inspiration to Vincent Knowles, maintaining, even as they infiltrated other institutions, a camaraderie so close that they were known as the Manchester Mafia and he (in the wake of Mario Puzo's novels and the resulting films) as the Godfather. Professors of Politics up and down the country were still likely to have had formative experiences in Manchester's large and prestigious Department of Government, which had been one of the great exporters of talent in the 1960s. By 1981, when Professor W.J. Thomas retired, the Department of Agricultural Economics, which did contract work for the Ministry of Agriculture and Fisheries on such matters as farm incomes, costs and management in the region, could boast that six former members held chairs elsewhere within the United Kingdom.

There was a growing expectation that the Vice-Chancellor of the University of Manchester would at some point serve for two years as Chairman of the Committee of Vice-Chancellors and Principals, becoming the principal spokesman for higher education in the United Kingdom, and earning a knighthood in the process. He represented a premier university built on the grand scale. It was less idiosyncratic than the ancient and the federal universities; less brash, young and ultra-fashionable than the 'green fields' or 'Shakespeare' universities of the 1950s and 1960s; wider in range than the former Colleges of Advanced Technology; regarded with confidence and affection by many sixth-form masters and mistresses advising their brighter pupils to make a sound choice of university. In 1975 Manchester won the so-called Unipops contest and brought home the Golden Disc awarded by the Universities' Central Council for Admissions (UCCA) to the institution which had managed to attract the largest number of student applications per available place. An article in *The Economist* in 1978 found in the Department of Liberal Studies in Science proof that the innovative spirit of Manchester, though growing more feeble, could still flourish. It concluded that those who completed the Bachelor's degree course in this subject were 'among the most sought-after graduates from the University'.

In its public statements the University generally celebrated large, expensive, collective enterprises such as the Medical School, the Regional Computer Centre, and the Nuffield Radio Astronomy Laboratories at Jodrell Bank in Cheshire. To explain their pioneering qualities was to justify the sums spent on them and to insist on Manchester's pre-eminence in certain fields of research and teaching. By the mid-1970s the AUT had acknowledged the need to disarm public contempt for universities and distaste for their students. Sir Michael Swann, the former Vice-Chancellor of Edinburgh University, had, it was said, described university teachers as 'pampered, underworked and overpaid', and much university research was being dismissed as irrelevant and trivial. Perhaps the humanities could no longer be relied upon to humanise, and the social sciences were creating rather than solving social problems. Such uncertainties led to a growing preoccupation with university inventions which promised to benefit humankind, and hence with engineering (including medical engineering). Greatly to be welcomed was evidence that university advisers could assist governments to make policy decisions or even, by their scientific and mathematical expertise rather than their Poirot- or Wimsey-like qualities, help the police to solve crimes.

True to the 'Muhammad Ali mentality' noted by Ngaio Crequer, university publicists proclaimed that the Manchester Medical School was the largest in Europe and that its Stopford Building was the largest edifice ever financed by the UGC. Proof of the dynamism of doctors was not far to seek. By agreement with the Regional Health Authority, the Medical School grafted research and teaching on to local hospitals within a few miles of the Education Precinct and accommodated these activities in new or specially adapted buildings. By the mid-1970s there were three teaching hospitals. One was the Manchester Royal Infirmary, as of old; another was Hope Hospital in

Salford, a large district general hospital in which the gastroenterolo-
gist Leslie Turnberg, at first the only professor on the site, undertook
to develop a new academic community; the third was a conglomerate,
the University Hospital of South Manchester. This consisted of a
famous cancer hospital, the Christie; of a children's hospital, the
Duchess of York; and of the forbidding Withington Hospital, a mixture of seasoned Victorian buildings, some of which were handsome,
and functional new ones, most of which were not. Withington had
been the Chorlton Union workhouse, created by the 1834 Poor Law,
and a disused pauper burial ground lay close at hand, the dead now
commemorated on flat stones in the nearby Southern Cemetery which
listed their names under the perfunctory heading 'In Loving Memory
Of'. The Royal Manchester Children's Hospital at Pendlebury officially acquired a University Unit in 1975, although the Professors of
Paediatrics had controlled some beds and even a whole ward in the
hospital for some time before that year.

Equipped with 1,400 beds, Withington was one of the largest hospitals in the country. From 1970 John Evanson held the foundation
chair of Medicine and oversaw the institution's development into a
major teaching hospital; John Brocklehurst developed geriatric medicine from 'a minor and unfashionable speciality into a major presence
in contemporary medicine'; Neil Kessel, joint author of a classic work
on *Alcoholism,* built up the Department of Psychiatry. Research into
the process of ageing was designed, not so much to prolong life, as to
maintain 'vigour to the end of the life span', for example by improving memory in old age. A centre for treating alcoholism arose within
the hospital, where medical, psychological and social help would all
be at hand. Matters such as the development of tolerance to alcohol
were candidates for scientific investigation, as were methods of sober-
ing a patient up, which would no longer be left to the traditional grue-
some remedies.

Some practical people engaged in vital tasks longed for academic
qualifications that would raise their status and carry them more
swiftly to positions of authority. Degree courses generally dealt with
the theories and principles on which everyday practice rested. It
seemed important that nursing should become a graduate profession,
or at least acquire a graduate elite; nurses were not to be regarded as
automatons, who simply carried out the orders of doctors, and exercised no initiative. A Diploma in Community Nursing was first developed under Professor Frazer Brockington in the Department of Social
and Preventative Medicine in 1959, and was designed to bring

together the theory and practice of nursing and to integrate community and hospital nursing. Brockington's successor, Alwyn Smith, set out to establish a nursing degree, from 1969 onwards, and in pursuit of his aim enlisted the aid of Jean McFarlane, a graduate nurse. She had taken a Master's degree in Manpower Studies and had carried out research into nursing education for the Department of Health while serving on the staff of a professional organisation, the Royal College of Nursing. In this capacity she had directed a course capable of training pupils to be nurses, or district nurses, or health visitors. Miss McFarlane came to Manchester as a Senior Lecturer in 1971 and two years later took charge of a separate Department of Nursing. In the summer of 1974 she became the first Professor of Nursing in an English, though not a British, university, for Manchester came in second to Edinburgh.

Under the new professor's guidance the new department, small, intimate and collegiate, the acorn from which the School of Nursing was to grow, tackled the problem of how to advance beyond practical vocational training. It was essential to provide something more than a diluted medical course enlivened only by stiff doses of anatomy and physiology and some attention to sociology. The theory and content of nursing itself, the processes of making decisions in the interests of patients, ought to be explored, the ethics of such controversial matters as abortion and euthanasia to be discussed. 'We always feel very proud that Manchester did this', Lady McFarlane recalls, 'and that Manchester was open to a new discipline and bore with our fumbling attempts to become respectable academics.' In 1975 the department launched a taught Master's degree, designed for people already in the profession, and intended among much else to teach the art of prescribing and evaluating care. Before long, theoretical models conceptualising the relationship between nurse and patient would begin to cross the Atlantic and the words 'nursing process' to be heard in Manchester (as an adage in the profession had it, on the eighth day God created the nursing process, and nobody rested). As medicine became more technical, a high value attached itself to graduate nurses who had a theoretical grasp of developments, and could therefore explain to patients and relatives the more obscure statements uttered by physicians and surgeons on their ward rounds.

Not all was perfect, for the new undergraduate course was sure to be a hybrid, if not a chimera. One student remembers its inner tensions, both intellectual and social. The theoretical and practical aspects of the course did not marry comfortably, two days of lectures contrasting with three days on the wards. Teaching was conducted by contrasting groups of pundits, including stern and sarcastic anatomists and charismatic but remote nurse lecturers. Potential graduate nurses were conscious, perhaps too much so, of being looked down upon by medical students. On the other hand, like high-fliers and fast-streamers in most hierarchical and disciplined organisations, they sensed the jealousy of ordinary trainees and, like officer cadets at Sandhurst, suffered the severest reproofs from instructors. The white dresses of the undergraduate women, contrasting with the green outfits of the rankers in the Manchester Royal Infirmary and the blue and white checks of the Crumpsall Hospital, made them prominent targets, stigmatised by down-to-earth critics as 'all brains and no common sense'.

For all this the Nursing Department secreted the germs of a major enterprise which would become famous both nationally and abroad. When the Australian authorities determined to make nursing a graduate profession, they sent potential heads of departments to Manchester 'to get themselves made respectable academically'. When nurses came to the department, 'it was almost as if they had had an arrested development, and that while they were on the course their whole personality changed' and they acquired the self-confidence to introduce innovations in their own institutions. Jean McFarlane herself became the only nurse to serve on the Royal Commission on the National Health Service which sat from 1976 to 1979. Raised to the peerage in 1980 as Baroness McFarlane of Llandaff, she found herself representing nurses in the House of Lords and took her seat on the crossbenches, the better to follow her own conscience, saying, 'I have never been a Political person with a capital "P", although I have been political with a small "p" – one can't live in an academic world and not be political!'

The reputation of the University as an intellectual metropolis gained much from its prowess in computing. Here its achievements lay in the design of hardware and software and in the application of computers to the solution of intellectual problems and to the processes of storing and retrieving administrative information. As Simon Lavington, a lecturer in the subject, explained, 'The essence of the discipline is evoked by such words as realism, independence, team loyalty and a logical mind. The additional attribute of imaginative innovation can, perhaps inevitably, only truthfully be associated with a small sub-set of the Computer Science community. Perhaps . . . it is on the efforts of these few imaginative innovators that the continued success of the Department of Computer Studies depends.' In

1969 Manchester had been recognised as one of the three main computing centres in the country, entitled to house a Regional Centre, the others (both directed by ex-Manchester men) being in Edinburgh and London. Gordon Black, the Director, had once worked out computer programmes to assist in designing lenses for the British Scientific Instrument Company, and had set up the National Computing Centre, first at Risley, near Warrington, and then in Oxford Road, Manchester. In the mid-1970s he had a staff of forty-four, and another professor, F.H. Sumner, directed an Administrative Computer Unit of ten persons on behalf of the Registrar's and Bursar's Departments.

By 1977 the word 'regional' seemed unduly parochial, since as many as thirty universities were using the Manchester Centre's services (the organisation dropped it only in 1989, when it became the Manchester Computing Centre – a second MCC, as University wits did not fail to point out). It cast its net as far north as Stirling; as far west as Belfast and Coleraine; as far south as Sussex; and as far east as Norwich. Among its clients were the universities of Wales and Ulster. Pure scientists supplied it with small quantities of data which, if left in the hands of human beings unaided by high technology, would have given rise to very complex and time-consuming calculations; social scientists came forward with much larger quantities of information for storing, sorting and analysis. Linguists and literary scholars began to use computers to perform the mechanical tasks that had previously called for a great deal of wearisome human labour – to compile concordances and word counts, to edit variant texts, and to analyse the style of authors.

Although the computer's influence now extended to most parts of the University, including the administration and the Library, the personal computer was still very much a thing of the future, for the system depended on oracular main-frame computers to which users obtained access by means of 'rather dumb terminals', as one academic recalls. Much time was spent on the tedious process of inserting information by means of punched cards and recovering it from lengths of magnetic tape. In March 1974 up to forty minutes could be spent in the Administrative Computer Unit searching for an item on a tape 2,400 feet long, but the organisation was expecting at the end of the year a new model that would make information available within a few seconds upon 'interrogation' by an operator using a visual display unit. About twenty small departmental computers were functioning in 1974, and were engaged mainly on the control of experiments.

Manchester's radio astronomers, their achievements, showmanship and occasional brushes with financial disaster, had attracted public attention since the 1950s. Adept at performing feats of engineering in the service of pure science (for the days of tracking sputniks were long past), they mapped distant quasars and invisible galaxies which could only be plotted by the reception of radio waves. Council received respectfully in 1978 the news that Jodrell Bank was becoming 'the control centre of a massive radio-astronomy complex which would be one of the most powerful in the world'. It was now practising the art of interferometry: rather than build single radio telescopes with bigger and bigger bowls designed to trap more radio waves, astronomers preferred to build a series of smaller telescopes set some distance apart from each other, to focus them on the same radio source, and to blend the signals which they received. To Manchester's astronomers the Science Research Council offered substantial research grants (almost £2m. in 1975, over £3m. in 1978) for the construction of new radio telescopes. These arose at Defford in Worcestershire, at Knockin near Oswestry in Shropshire, and at Wardle in Cheshire. Others were soon to be added at Pickmere and Darnhall, and these, with Jodrell Bank itself, made up a total of six. They were eventually, in the late 1980s, to advance as far as Cambridge and to take the name MERLIN, which stood for the Multi-element Radio-linked Interferometer Network.

Arthurian wizardry and forays into the universe were not enough. Application to earthly problems was also needed in order to secure the University's reputation. Perhaps universities could do something to dispel the blight which had overtaken the country's manufacturing industries. In 1976 A.J. Morton, Professor of Mechanical Engineering, declared that 'when our industries are sick we cannot prosper and the quality of life is lowered for everyone . . . education, the arts and the environment all suffer'. The spiritual, it seemed, depended on the material. It was as though patriotism and self-interest both demanded that attention be paid to engineering, but there was still a fatal reluctance to take up careers in the field on account of its supposed narrowness and indifference towards both people and the environment. A few months later Bernard Holloway, the Secretary to the Appointments Board, argued that the supply of graduate engineers was not in reality falling short of the demand for their services and that the country was, in proportion to the size of its population, educating just as many scientists and engineers as were other western nations. Nevertheless, he felt obliged to warn against a kind of artsy superciliousness lurking in universities, a pernicious form of intellectual snobbery which denigrated practical skills. 'It is of course necessary that universities should continue to provide for and nurture qualities of creative thinking and develop the qualities which make possible a critical appraisal of our society and its institutions; but there must also be the determination to encourage, develop and value those whose talents lie in less academic but more immediately useful directions, and who will produce the economic resources upon which the whole non-economic superstructure of our society depends.' Sometimes, *pace* Holloway, it was the exponents of the arts and social sciences in Manchester who developed a sense of inferiority; a law lecturer has spoken of the guilty feeling, which was to ripen in the subsequent Thatcher years, 'that if you were not inventing a tin-opener that you could sell to the Japanese you were not actually doing anything worthwhile'.

In 1977 Manchester became one of four institutions chosen to put on a new course in Engineering Manufacture and Management, unofficially called the Elite Engineering course (the others so honoured were Imperial College London, the University of Birmingham, and the University of Strathclyde). The object of this enterprise was to equip a new breed of technocrats with abilities in management and a knowledge of languages, together with detailed acquaintance with the processes and organisation of manufacture. These qualities would be imparted, not only by the Engineering Departments, but also by the Faculty of Law, the Departments of Modern Languages, and the Business School. At least in the beginning the UGC would provide earmarked funds to support the course, and by 1981–82 about eighty students would be taking it.

Many talked of developing 'links with industry' and thereby ensuring that the inventions of academics were developed and exploited. Industry would benefit and might well look to universities to solve problems concerning the repair and maintenance of machinery. Much expensive scientific equipment required primarily for teaching purposes remained underused and could profitably be placed, in slack periods, at the disposal of industrial concerns. Firms could reduce their overheads if they ceased to maintain their own research laboratories and commissioned universities to work for them on contract, using the universities' own premises. Between 1969 and 1974 Geoffrey Allen, Professor of Chemical Physics and an expert on polymers, spent half his time working for the ICI Corporate Laboratory at Runcorn in Cheshire, and also arranged that ICI should establish a laboratory within the Chemistry Department at the University and staff it in part with their own employees. He had learnt from Flowers of Physics and Gee of Chemistry that 'academe alone did not produce the right working atmosphere for the scientist. Industry and government had to be involved too.' Dr E.J. Duff, the University's Research Consultancy Officer, strove to interest industrial concerns in the discoveries made by members of the University. He communicated to as many as 4,000 firms, through a publication entitled *Contact* financed by Paterson Zochonis, the news that (for example) 'new fermentation systems' had been contrived in Chemistry and that a 'linear actuator with an integral position detector' had emerged as a result of researches in Electrical Engineering. Duff's service handled and advised on patents and licences to manufacture, and was pleased to report that in 1977 it had helped with the filing of twenty-one patent applications.

Manchester University inventions appeared in exhibitions at Belle Vue in 1976 and at Lewis's department store (under the self-effacing title 'North West Genius') in 1978. The Wolfson Foundation conferred awards for collaboration with industry. Such prizes went to the Department of Medical Biophysics for a computer system called Magiscan, designed to analyse images such as X-ray pictures; to David Auckland of Electrical Engineering, who had worked closely with a Macclesfield firm, for devices known as 'Spin-scan' or 'Ten-scan' which benefited the textile industry by spotting signs of trouble in complex, fast-moving machines before they actually broke down; and to two senior lecturers in Engineering, Tim Henry and Tony Kelly, for schemes for diagnosing the malaise of malfunctioning industrial plant. Some dreamed of overtaking the Suzuki and the Yamaha and reviving the fortunes of the British motor-cycle industry through the efforts of two mechanical engineers, Geoffrey Roe and Terry Thorpe. They applied themselves to the problems of instability ('wobble', 'weave' and 'flutter'); to the design of new front forks; to the improvement of drum brakes; and to the production of silencers which would make speedway and grass track riders less likely to deafen spectators. Well-briefed on this subject, *Communication* was quick to explain that theirs were not just the achievements of superior mechanics and practical tinkerers, but had been accompanied by published papers of 'high technical and mathematical content'. Contributions to the extraction of North Sea oil, the great windfall of the 1970s, promised to come from Peter Montague's work on submarine habitats, otherwise sea-bed houses, for workers in the industry – these being a kind of bathysphere sheltered within an inner and an outer skin, with the intervening space packed with suitable materials.

World food problems, for humans and animals, attracted the attention of university departments, brought large injections of research money, and were often invoked in support of the University's claims to be directly useful to society and the economy. A rich poultry producer, Sir John Eastwood, made a personal gift of £60,000 to the Department of Agricultural Economics. His generosity enabled a senior research fellow, Sue Richardson, to review the broiler industry and establish the efficiency of chickens in converting food into edible products, in providing protein, and in challenging the supremacy of red meat. An idea hatched in the Department of Liberal Studies in Science flowered, like a rose on a dung hill, into a scheme for producing animal food from purified sewage sludge. This, it now seemed, had a protein content of up to 30 per cent and could be put to good use if only it were purged of toxic metals. Like many of the most highly praised enterprises of the 1970s, this project called for the skills of workers in several different disciplines, for it required the help of chemists and engineers to bring it to fruition.

Social problems, including the impact of scientific progress and technical inventions, received due attention from university departments. In 1977 the Department of Liberal Studies in Science acquired an annexe in the form of PREST, a centre for Policy Research in Engineering, Science and Technology, which engaged in independent analysis of the decisions made by Government. Roger Williams became Manchester's first Professor of Government and Science Policy. Close to hand was the problem of the effect on employment in areas such as Tameside of the advent of micro-electronic devices. Would the introduction of word processors cut the number of clerical workers, and would electronic microchips, whose manufacture required relatively little labour, deprive large numbers of people of a living?

Other members of the University staff became involved with problems of crime, punishment, and even detection. Working within close range of the troublesome supporters of Manchester's principal football teams, the Director of the Centre for Youth Studies was well placed to examine disorderly behaviour at sporting events. Ken Pease, a former researcher in the Home Office, now lecturing in Social Administration, analysed the prison population of England and Wales, compared it with that of other European countries, and sought to discover why so large a proportion of the British people had been locked up. A lecturer in Mathematics, Gerry Wickham, helped police accident investigators by analysing skid marks. The career in crime detection of a medical illustrator, Richard Neave, began about 1979 when, after appearing on a television programme and reconstructing the face of a mummy in the Manchester Museum, he received an invitation from Surrey police to perform the same service for a decomposed corpse found in water at Frimley, between Camberley and Farnborough. That particular body was eventually identified by calling upon radiological evidence. But Neave's technique, based on establishing the depth of missing tissue at twenty-three points on the skull, seemed to have great potential and was to prove invaluable on many future occasions.

The activities of the Arts, Music and Theology faculties attracted less attention. It was harder, at least for those in charge of public relations, to identify their contributions to economic well being and social harmony, more difficult to describe, let alone patent, their innovations and inventions. Traditionally, members of the Arts Faculty were anxious to avoid notice, and many believed in keeping their heads well below the parapet, although the dynamic Barri Jones was engaged in popularising archaeology and was known to appear on Saturday morning children's television. Skills in modern languages would clearly be valuable to businessmen and managers, as the plans for the Elite Engineering course had recognised. Recruitment to the departments of modern languages was flagging in the 1970s, but they increased their attractions by making it easier for students to take degrees in two languages, one being the major and the other the minor language, instead of going through the lengthier process of acquiring double honours in two languages of equal status. Through joint degrees in history and one modern language the History Department gained a few students who were competent to read original sources and carry out modest pieces of research on European countries.

French Studies underwent revision and reorganisation, the emphasis now falling, as Professor Rothwell explained, 'on the mastery of contemporary French and the presentation of the latest techniques in the changing world of literary criticism, whilst at the same time opening up for undergraduate study a broad spectrum of French culture'. Instead of slogging through French culture and literature century by century, students would be encouraged to explore these things thematically and pursue the threads of comedy, tragedy, irony, the literature of the town, and other such matters through time without being constrained by chronological barriers. Modern historians experimented with similar approaches, encouraging students to think comparatively and to abandon, not only strict chronological limits, but the practice of studying only one country at a time and concentrating all too heavily on English and European history. This method proved highly controversial, even among the modern historians themselves, some of whom resented the dogmatic streak which they saw in champions of the thematic approach and thought the whole programme not only too ambitious but also too sharply focused on European concepts. But it gave rise to some notable publications, including John Breuilly's volume on nationalism and a series of books on the nobility by Michael Bush.

The enterprising Department of American Studies extended a normal degree course into one which would last four years, students spending one of them in the United States. It earned patronising praise in the University's official journal in the summer of 1981: 'Though perhaps not a world power by the standards of some other university departments, American Studies has carved out for itself a very respectable place among departments of the second rank. There is little doubt, however, that it can claim to be in the first rank in its own field and that it is forging ahead.'

No-one yet knew how far the Government or the general public would be impressed by the evidence of the utility of University researches fed to the media by the Communications Office. Towards 1980 there were complaints that to judge by its public pronouncements the Department of Education and Science seemed unaware that universities did anything other than teach. Many asked whether universities could ever justify their existence by becoming machines producing manpower for those occupations that seemed most to need well qualified graduates. Part of the problem was that even when the University had produced its science graduates they did not flock towards industry and commerce. Indeed, the Secretary of the Careers and Appointments Service tried by citing statistics to explode the left-wing myth that the University had become the servant of capitalism. About 1974 only 21 per cent of male pure and applied scientists were taking up careers in industry, 46 per cent in commerce. Literal-minded critics, seizing upon these data, might well be tempted to argue that the University was not actually very useful to the economy.

However, it seemed unrealistic to expect the University to respond to short-term changes in the job market. By one reckoning educational decisions took as much as ten years to affect the supply of 'trained manpower' to any significant extent: courses had to be planned and advertised and tutors and lecturers recruited to teach them. During the 1970s the market suffered swings in demand which were caused in part by changes in public spending. None the less there was a constant need for certain kinds of ability and this the University could meet: it was well placed to supply both engineers and computer scientists, and was also contributing to a swelling stream of accountants and experts in business finance equipped to meet the needs of commerce. On the other hand during much of the decade spending cuts reduced the demand for social workers, local government officers, librarians, and executive officers in the civil service. Only in certain subjects did the demand for teachers remain buoyant – as in science (especially physics), mathematics, and modern languages. By 1979 the legal profession appeared to be fully stocked if not saturated, and law students were becoming increasingly unsure of their prospects of a good job.

Arts lecturers were quick to complain that the notion of training for employment was beginning to eclipse the ideal of education for its own sake. What universities should do, argued one graduate of the time, is teach their students to question everything (as Miss Sarah Burton, the headmistress in Winifred Holtby's novel *South Riding*, urges her pupils on Armistice Day). Vocational training has a different purpose and says, 'You will learn these things because you need to know them.' While there was no grave risk that Manchester would acquire a reputation for turning out unemployable graduates, the University did not seem outstandingly good at producing graduates who would be instantly snapped up. About 1980 the older civic universities, which maintained large arts and social science faculties, appeared to be playing this game less well than the newer technological universities (these naturally offered a larger proportion of vocational courses). Published figures, based on the proportion of recent graduates still unemployed on 31 December 1978, suggested that Manchester ranked twenty-fifth out of the forty-four British universities, and that with 11.6 per cent unemployed it was faring appreciably worse than the comparable universities of Birmingham, Liverpool and Sheffield, and slightly worse than Leeds. It might be, of course, that Manchester graduates had their values right: that they were inclined to look around for longer before committing themselves to a job, or that they had postponed the search for employment so as not to be distracted from their final year of academic work by a series of interviews held at inconvenient times.

Few commentators in the 1970s would have denied Manchester the status of premier university which it claimed. Drawn, like other universities, into a national network and competing for good students across the whole country and even beyond it, Manchester could claim eminence in a few fields and respectability in most others. If it suffered financial difficulties it shared these with other institutions and had more reserves than many on which to fall back. Self-doubt, such as it was, often sprang from the belief that there were now fewer people of genius at the University, that some quality of greatness had been lost and exchanged for general soundness and competence. Professorial chairs were said to be distinguished if eminent persons had once occupied them, as if they would forever be Tout's chair, Powicke's, Namier's, Vinaver's, Alexander's. Would the University succeed in attracting successors of equal calibre, or would outsiders be moved to say, 'You have the ruins of a great tradition at Manchester'? 'I don't say that we are a race of pygmies, but certainly we are not a race of giants', says one of the actors in a dialogue composed towards 1970 by the economic historian Eric Robinson. 'Perhaps it is more difficult to be a giant among historians today. We seem to other people to be living too much in the shadow of the great men of the past.'

In general, the University succeeded in striking a balance between the traditional and the innovative, the immediately useful and the things that were valuable in a more far-reaching sense. Should philistines triumph, pure science, which did not produce quick results or address the most urgent problems, would be as much at risk as literary or historical scholarship. But the University, partly because it was good at the practical and the 'relevant', was well placed to protect pure science and scholarship. Since much public money had been lavished on universities, it was natural to ask that they contribute to public well being; the greater the financial stringency, the louder the demand for demonstrable practical utility. There was also a natural desire to link them to the trade and industry of the region, in hard times as well as in prosperity: the University had benefited from the philanthropy of manufacturers, and might now be able to revive the manufacturing through scientific expertise.

Little Manchester activity was useless, except to those with a narrow concept of utility. To impart general literacy, to teach students how to think (perhaps even to think about thought), to train them to arrange, analyse and evaluate information in a properly sceptical spirit, to encourage them to respond to literature and to understand how things happened in the world: such things improved the quality of life, and none was without value. The most down-to-earth disciplines, including nursing, strove to understand the abstract principles which lay behind the practicalities. Some pursuits were clearly of more material significance than others, more closely in touch with the needs of commerce, industry, the professions, the world demand for food, the most pressing problems of social policy and public order. But the University was properly concerned with liberal education as well as with vocational training.

Manchester's Muhammad Ali mentality might provoke iconoclasm, its boastfulness barely conceal a fundamental insecurity. But David Aaronovitch, who read history at Manchester in the mid-1970s after spending a year at Oxford, a southerner not easily impressed by the self-congratulation of the north, found that 'an enormous . . . and tolerant, liberal academic institution, full of people of disparate backgrounds and ages, could exist and thrive outside the more favoured universities of Oxford and Cambridge . . . I don't feel at all ashamed of getting a Manchester degree compared to an Oxford degree. I think the course I did was much better. I think they pioneered certain aspects of looking at history in my course. And I bet they did it elsewhere.'

3

The academics:
consultation and conditions

Universities, perhaps, did not achieve distinction *qua* universities, but strove to nurture and attract distinguished scholars and enable them to flourish. It was their task to create a stable framework and a congenial atmosphere within which individuals, groups or teams could make discoveries, communicate them, and pass on their wisdom to students, who would in due course begin to question it.

By the early 1970s most academics had abandoned their dreams of abolishing hierarchy in the academic world and creating a commonwealth of equals. More modestly, they wanted adequate salaries, security of employment, and freedom to conduct research and teaching as they chose without attracting officious inquiries as to how they did these things. Women academics wanted consideration, equitable treatment, and some acknowledgement of the difficulties of pursuing a career while bearing and bringing up children. Most university teachers wanted to be assured of a fair system of promotion which would not depend on the whims of professors alone and would value all-round talents, without throwing all the emphasis on research and publication. Aware of creeping staleness, born of following the same routines in the same institution with the relentless rhythm of a medieval agricultural year, most Manchester academics longed for a regular system of leave of absence. In the opinion of many only an open and accountable system of government would guarantee these benefits. It must not succumb too easily to the iron law of oligarchy, and the price of liberty must always be eternal vigilance.

Ten years of wrangling had produced the amended University Charter which came into force in 1973. Like most compromises it commanded few people's unreserved admiration. Some disappointed critics alleged that it offered neither true democracy nor enlightened absolutism. Others, who claimed to be from the more collegiate parts of the University, said that it merely confirmed existing practices. Some held that academics, who were by nature individualists, would flourish only in a system in which their voices were heard and they could share responsibility for administering their own affairs. Opponents of this liberal view maintained that precisely because of their individualism (their 'analytic' rather than 'synthetic' tendencies, as Mussolini might have put it), academics, once allowed to discuss questions of policy, would waste precious hours far better devoted to pursuing their own subjects. At best their debates would produce a series of muddled compromises, the result of talking till everyone agreed, which allowed no clear and forthright line to be pursued. Better, by far, to have a professor empowered to bang contending heads together, overrule the bloody-minded, shoulder responsibility for boring questions of management, and free colleagues to apply themselves to important academic pursuits. An authoritarian professor who allowed colleagues freedom to follow their own interests might well prove less tyrannical than a democracy which tried to impose an orthodoxy by majority vote. As the women of Canterbury say in *Murder in the Cathedral*:

'We have suffered various oppression,
But mostly we are left to our own devices,
And we are content if we are left alone.'

Whatever the merits of democracy, it was generally agreed to be labour-intensive, and the art of running committees and keeping accurate records of their decisions had now to be learnt by painful experience.

The Charter of 1973 provided for a Senate with a majority (three-quarters) of professors and a minority (one quarter) of elected members; a consultative Assembly consisting of all academics plus an increasing number of para-academics; and a consultative board in every department, although the departmental professor or professors remained responsible to the Senate for departmental affairs. Most budding academic politicians sensed that power was not located in the official organs where the constitution had supposedly lodged it, though they seldom succeeded in identifying where it really lay. A few hardy souls dwelt on the illogicalities of the Charter and called for further revisions. Why, for example, were the powers of boards of examiners and boards of studies so much greater than those of departmental boards, which consisted of much the same people? But such had been the tedium of the constitutional debate that major questions about its product were unlikely to be reopened for several years to come. Reform proposals were more remarkable for their analyses of the existing situation than for any likelihood that the University would act upon them.

Brian Manning, called by an opponent a well-known Leveller (with reference to his interests in the English Civil War), applied himself to the problems of the Senate and called for a smaller and more coherent body enlivened by a much larger proportion of elected members. In 1974–75 Senate had 276 members: 209 professors, who held seats by virtue of their office, and 67 elected members, who, feeling some responsibility to their constituents, were more assiduous attenders. At a recent meeting 64 of the 209 professors had been present, and 53 out of the 67 elected members. But Senate itself was a flaccid body, little given to debating or voting (one historian, not quoted by Manning, was heard to say that it would make a Nuremberg Rally look subversive). Senate was dominated by the Standing (in other words, steering) Committee which predigested most of its important business. Not unnaturally, too, Senate was inclined to rubber-stamp the recommendations of most of the other bodies whose voluminous papers were served up to members of Senate in buff envelopes; only the most dedicated would skim, let alone read them all. But certain matters, such as Bernard Holloway's foreword to the annual report of the Appointments Board, were guaranteed to awaken Senate from its customary torpor, and the publication of Manning's article in *Staff Comment* was preceded and followed by unusually lively debates, one about the inflammatory question of University investment in South Africa and the other concerning membership of the Assembly. However, *Staff Comment*'s reporter conceded that 'the usual role of those attending is to listen, to read and to accept', and agreed that membership of the Senate was useful chiefly for the access to information which it gave. Senate remained a clearing-house for most significant academic business, even if most decisions had effectively been made elsewhere. Bob Burchell of American Studies, who served twice as an elected member of Senate, recalls that 'I was interested, I suppose, in power . . . not in wielding it, but in finding out about it.'

Debates on the subject of the Assembly aroused some passion, though not because the Assembly enjoyed any power or created much sense of community – indeed, it was rarely quorate, and its opinions could safely be ignored. Membership of the Assembly implied that a person was the equivalent at least of a university lecturer, and it could therefore be held to confer tenure: to bestow protection against dismissal for reasons other than misconduct, incapacity or neglect of duty. Statute XV attached to the new Charter conferred membership of the Assembly not only on lecturers and their seniors but also on 'persons holding research, administrative or library appointments of

comparable status' to that of a lecturer. Was this wording to be liber-
ally interpreted, or not? In May 1975 a majority of the Standing Committee of Senate held that membership of the Assembly ought not to
be widened, because such a move would 'extend the job security of
those included and so give the University grave difficulty in dealing
with those on short-term contracts'. But a minority 'saw a significant
gain' in broadening the Assembly out. The statute contained the
germs of an endless, inconclusive debate.

In the absence of diplomacy tension would arise between professors
and their departmental boards, and boards themselves be paralysed by
conflict between rival factions. Much depended on the willingness of
individuals to compromise rather than flounce out of meetings and
cut in the corridors colleagues who would not see the light as they
did; legal prescription was no guarantee of the good relations on
which the effective running of departments depended.

In the new Department of Nursing, as Jean McFarlane remembers,
the Charter merely formalised the practices of the unofficial staff
meetings, which almost always functioned by consensus, for there was
no room for dictatorial management. Much argument went on 'concerning what nursing was about. We used to fight and hammer away
at that. That was part of the exhilaration of developing a subject, I
think. We were all the best of friends really.' Katherine Perera, joining
in 1977 from Padgate, a small teacher training college, found in the
small Department of Linguistics – the creation of the Czech refugee
William Haas – 'a very egalitarian, democratic ethos' (there were only
seven or eight members of staff). The departmental board made the
decisions in practice, and her ideas were listened to attentively almost
from the day of her arrival.

A newly appointed lecturer in Russian History encountered by
virtue of his office the contrasting atmospheres of the Russian Department, where the professor took the chair at meetings and the senior
lecturer kept the minutes, and of the Department of History, where
proceedings were less decorous, debates were conducted with passion,
and votes were often taken. The Department seemed, as a former professor had observed from his position in the chair, to resolve itself into
those who turned red when they lost their tempers and those who went
white when they lost their tempers. The inconsequential tone of some
debates found a satirist in the departmental student newspaper, *The
Clarion*, whose motto was 'Backwards and Forwards with the People'.
The writer conjured up all too vividly an imaginary debate on the compulsory consumption of rhubarb by students, chaired by the jovial

'Dr Rotherham', and conducted by the thinly disguised figures of 'The Emperor', 'The Chancellor', 'The Boxer', 'Napoleon', and 'Brigadier Colditz'. One compromising professor in the mid-1970s became known as the Harold Wilson of the department; no compliment was intended, but perhaps a sly allusion to Wilson's famous remark that 'I'm at my best in a messy, middle-of-the-road muddle'. Reassuringly, however, another historian, Peter Lowe, told the journalist Ngaio Crequer in 1978 that 'In practice, professors have largely accepted what the board says. So we have moved from what is laid down in the constitution. And most professors have seen this as a development worth having.'

In some departments professors became, at least to begin with, chairmen of the board, as in Government, over which Samuel Finer presided before his departure to Oxford. So long as the professorial chairman was a conscientious interpreter of the people's will, conflict between departmental democracy and executive authority could be forestalled. In other parts of the University honour called for a dual monarchy, or at least for a crown prince surrounded by a rival court. Hence the board chairmanship should go to a reader, senior lecturer or lecturer, not a professor. In the early years elections were sometimes vigorously contested and won by close votes. When initial enthusiasm had begun to flag, however, it was sometimes the professors who had to persuade equable members of the department to chair the board or keep its minutes, appealing to their public spirit and perhaps promising to extol their loyal services at the next promotions exercise.

Four years after the introduction of the revised Charter, a meeting of the Staff Forum held an inconclusive discussion on the strengths and weaknesses of the system. Some speakers felt that since most professors were reasonable enough it was not important to raise the legal status of boards. Most professors attended their meetings, if only to listen in silence. Only a few insisted on receiving their boards' recommendations in writing and on sending a formal reply, an 'irksome and cumbersome procedure' calculated to remind junior colleagues of a constitutional position on which more liberal professors did not insist and guaranteed to waste valuable time. Boards, however, could only act through 'professorial tolerance rather than legal power' and some speakers wanted their authority extended in order to curb the few autocrats who refused to observe the spirit of the Charter.

It was to be argued elsewhere that the absence of professorial vetoes of the proposals of a departmental board provided poor evidence that democracy was flourishing – on the contrary, it might well imply that the board had been censoring itself, in order to avoid provoking a constitutional crisis. As a philosopher, Harry Lesser, wrote, 'The timidity even of tenured faculty members is surprising; and the dropping of hints that "the Professor(s)" or "the authorities" are against a proposal can have a remarkable effect . . . '

'Some people felt', wrote the conscientious reporter of the Staff Forum, 'that there must be some individual persons who were in the last resort responsible for what occurred in their departments, and so supported the idea of ultimate professorial responsibility.' In some quarters liberal professors who forgot themselves so far as to cite the opinions of their junior colleagues were reminded by deans that they could not 'hide behind the board's skirts' – the implication being that boards were shrews and scolds who needed to be tamed by a vigorous masculine hand.

Some veterans of the University remember the new regime without affection. David Pailin, recently retired from the chair of the Philosophy of Religion, remarks that the 1973 Charter 'made a right pig's ear of things'. 'I think it's resulted in an awful lot of committees and a lot of talk. Academics are superb at meeting and talking. They're not very efficient at getting things done . . . '. The late Dennis Welland, the University's first and indeed only Professor of American Literature, recalled that 'The departmental board meant an increased involvement by all members of the departmental staff in administrative problems which were only imperfectly understood and, combined with the hostility to any form of professor, dean, vice-chancellor, anything of that sort, meant an enormous waste of time in utterly unprofitable discussion by people who felt that they had now been given a free rein and were insufficiently aware of the kind of factors involved.' A satirical feature in Staff Comment, 'Mother Alma's Advice Column for Lonely Academic Hearts', conjured up the bemused (and fictitious) Professor of Etruscan Studies, who was having trouble with the young man who helped him with the inscriptions: 'every time we have tea together, he says it is a Departmental Board meeting and contrives to upset me. Do you think I should make him a Departmental Board in his own right? At least I could then have my tea in peace.'

Departmental democracy was most inclined to discredit itself when intellectual disagreements developed into personal antagonisms or exacerbated the mutual irritations of colleagues. Forced (as in Browning's 'Soliloquy of the Spanish Cloister') to spend too long listening to each other, they became more openly resentful. Most departments contained at least one cantankerous figure, conscious of not being valued by others as he esteemed himself, quick to give and to sense insult, addicted to sneering at the mediocrity of his colleagues, cherishing grudges and grievances. But such bright apples seldom grew into poisoned trees; academic communities were traditionally tolerant of eccentricity, even prepared to embrace the fallacy that curmudgeonly behaviour was a mark of intellectual distinction, and few departments were deeply divided.

In the larger departments foul humours dispersed more easily. In smaller units, where differences were paraded at board meetings in the presence of students and the professor was drawn into one of the warring factions, the department's reputation was tarnished. The Philosophy Department was torn by disputes as to what was, and what was not, legitimate philosophy, fit to be taught under its aegis. For some it consisted essentially of logic and linguistic analysis, for others of the study of values, social ethics and political thought. Mutual tolerance seemed unattainable. A lecturer complained in *Mancunion*, the principal student newspaper, of 'strange and wondrous occurrences' and 'grotesque goings-on' which had allegedly cost the Department (and the taxpayer) at least a thousand man-hours. It was as if the Department had become a kind of latter-day Borley Rectory, calling for the services of an exorcist to disperse its resident poltergeists. Bizarre incidents included the disappearance of the board's minute book, thought to have been stolen because, unwisely attempting to record debates as well as their conclusions, it had preserved personal denunciations for posterity, and the thief wanted to consign these bitter remarks to oblivion. Despite the chairman's appeal to members to search their homes, their offices and their consciences, the missing records failed to turn up. A member of the Registrar's Department, Mike Buckley, was enlisted to keep the minutes in a more discreet and impartial style. Nobody could know whether the discontent had been brought to the boil by the new constitutional arrangements, which allowed more scope for expressing grievances, or whether the old regime, had it been allowed to continue, could have contained the trouble more effectively.

Manchester's nearest equivalents to F.M. Cornford's masterly *Guide for the Young Academic Politician* were the last 'Letters of Lemuel', which continued to enliven *Staff Comment* in its declining years, and an article by Harry Lesser on how to conduct committees. Lemuel offered an account of academic politics in terms of the Coldfeet faction, the Hothead party, and the Middlemen, providing rich material on each, but particularly on the apoplectic Coldfeet, chronically infuriated by the latest progressive developments. Lesser identified, in the manner of Cornford, several devious tactics for securing victory by unfair means, including the gambit known as 'The Manciple says'. This, he explained, 'is a way of justifying a mode of procedure which is to one's own advantage but obviously somewhat bizarre, by claiming that some university official or body – the Professor, the Dean, the Senate – has ruled that it must be adopted. The subtlety consists in twisting the actual words of the official – only the crudest operators actually invent speeches – so that they are given a meaning that they do not have and were never intended to have, but which it is just possible that you could have supposed that they did have . . . ' More advice followed on methods of provoking colleagues into unreasonable outbursts and thereby discrediting their point of view, or engineering the withdrawal of a proposal by making it impossible for it to be discussed calmly and sensibly.

Some well-intentioned professors found themselves in quandaries. Their initiatives were treated with suspicion as extensions of professorial power, which must at all costs be stopped in its tracks, but failure to innovate resulted in charges of lack of leadership and comparisons with extinct volcanoes. There could be considerable temptation to turn cynic, or take the train for London at every opportunity, or retreat into the congenial pursuit of one's own subject and let departmental administration go hang. But some professors did possess the political skills, patience, and personal qualities which enabled them to maintain a sense of direction.

Official appreciations of departing professors must clearly be treated with scepticism. 'Everything he touches crumbles to dust', said a senior lecturer, ensconced in the Common Room, of one dignitary who had just been fulsomely praised to Senate. But, significantly, farewell eulogies composed in the 1970s tended to build up an image of the ideal professor as a diplomat, a benign adviser who encouraged younger colleagues and gave them their head, and yet, behind the mellow façade, proved to be a man of steel. When the paediatrician John Davis left for Cambridge, his encomiast detected 'more than a hint of lupoid firmness beneath the lambswool exterior; a necessary prerequisite, many would feel, to keep an academic department in some sort of order'. He had been 'able to terminate many a convoluted discussion with an erudite quotation and a puckish turn of phrase which completely pre-empted further comment'. Professor John Cohen, 'an experimental psychologist who writes like a classical scholar', earned praise for his generosity and tolerance of human weakness. His subject, which perhaps contributed to these qualities, was the study of behaviour in uncertainty, including 'questions relating to psychological probability, risk-taking, choice, driver behaviour, gambling, subjective time, information and communication'.

Critics of authority, impervious to the charm of professors and suspicious of their intentions, reflected that two weapons remained in their hands and might still enable affronted elders to revenge themselves on uppity juniors. These were blockage of promotion and denial of leave. It seemed important that procedures for granting or withholding these benefits should be more carefully regulated, particularly because teaching responsibilities were growing: the University ought to recognise prowess in teaching and grant respites from it at regular intervals. Academics often derided the five-yearly visits of the UGC to universities as empty rituals, but it was possible for the locals to exploit them. Non-professors could use audiences with the visitors to ventilate grievances, and if the UGC sympathised the University was unlikely to resist. In 1974 underlings complained that university promotion exercises attached too much weight to research publications, and they also put the case for entitlement, as of right, to sabbatical leave.

By 1977 the Senate had overhauled the criteria for assessing claims to promotion from the rank of lecturer to that of senior lecturer or reader. It had done so by removing the special emphasis on 'a person's academic distinction in his own subject', which had to be established by means of letters obtained from external referees. In theory at least the three crucial items, research or scholarship, teaching, and administration, were now of equal rank. The Standing Committee of Senate, which sat for two or three days every January assessing promotion cases, would award up to three marks for each of these activities, but keep in reserve a couple of bonus points to award at its discretion.

Professors in certain large departments complained of having to invent 'Mickey Mouse jobs', such as minding the departmental coffee machine, in order to enable favoured candidates to secure the necessary credit for administration. Other bodies developed an obsessive concern with awarding a suitable number of points for each of a multitude of departmental chores, in the hope of proving that some promotion candidates had been diligent beyond the call of duty, as their high scores proclaimed. Where the system was also designed to distribute burdens equally, and where it ceased to be a distinction even to be elected chairman of a departmental board, professors could find it hard to demonstrate that aspirants to senior lectureships had done more than an average amount.

The selection of referees was a sensitive issue, since they had not only to be fair and honest but also aware of the constructions which might be put upon all their remarks, including asides: a critical note or unfortunate phrase was liable to be seized upon by some member of the Standing Committee, bored with reading interminable hymns of praise, eager to spot any weakness in a case, and delighted to come across a nuancé letter. Candidates were now permitted to suggest the names of referees, rather than be forced to rely wholly on the professor's choice. The Standing Committee normally required reports from two such authorities, but, as the new regulations stipulated, 'If neither of the referees selected by the Professor[s] has been suggested by the Lecturer a third referee named by the Lecturer shall at his request be consulted by the Professor[s]'.

There was a dearth of practical suggestions as to how teaching should be assessed, and hard evidence of the quality, as distinct from the quantity, of teaching done was generally lacking. Enthusiastic accounts by one professor of the 'electrical effect' of one lecturer on his students, who came out 'bubbling with excitement' at what they had just heard, were dismissed by a colleague as vacuous 'blethering'. Student questionnaires and peer reviews (solemn visits of colleagues to lectures or tutorials) were still for the most part things of the future. Some academics would resist their introduction, saying that students were not to be made judges of their elders and betters, and that the presence of intrusive colleagues was bound to put a lecturer, let alone a tutor, off his stroke.

As did most attempts to ensure equitable treatment, the new procedures consumed much time. An adherent of Lemuel's Coldfeet faction exhorted: 'Consider the regulations now in force for the advancement of the lesser dons and the augmentation of their annual stipend – for that, believe me, sir, is what most nearly concerns and moves these fellows, however much they mumble of equity and the common good. Where once advancement lay wholly in our hands – we who are masters here, rightly masters by every law of reason and good sense, and I could keep a laggard scribbler that would not yield his tome each year a-dangling till he did or, if he crossed me in word or deed, could let him drop into silence for all time – now all is changed. Now, forsooth, I must be forever preferring, praising, writing to this commission or that on behalf of some underling who, the ink scarcely dry on his degree, would yet be rising, rising to thrust me from my chair . . . '

Chairs in Manchester were of three kinds: established chairs, which existed independently of their holders and survived their departure;

personal chairs, given in recognition of the great distinction of a member of the academic staff; and promotional chairs. Advancement to personal chairs remained as unattainable as ever. So high were the standards demanded, so large the number of referees that had to be consulted, so great the risk that at least one of them would appear to be expressing reservations, that even election to the Royal Society or the British Academy would not automatically secure such positions. They were generally confined to highly productive scholars on the verge of retirement. Stefan Strelcyn, Reader in Semitic Languages and an authority on Ethiopia, became a Fellow of the British Academy in 1976. By 1981 the Standing Committee of Senate had decided to recommend him for a personal chair, but news of Dr Strelcyn's sudden death tragically prevented Senate from confirming the recommendation.

However, under Arthur Armitage, the University made more use of a different species of chair, known as the promotional chair and guaranteed to mystify outsiders, who commonly confused it with a personal chair. Should there be some discipline deserving of recognition, and should there be no funds available to create an established chair in the field, it might be possible to seize upon some enterprising person in the department and raise him or her to the purple. For promoting their subjects entrepreneurs could win promotion for themselves. Dick Smith, the Professor of Ancient History, succeeded in getting Barri Jones, a younger colleague of immense energy, active particularly in the field of rescue archaeology, promoted to a chair in Archaeology. It was a skilful move which enhanced Manchester's standing as a centre for research on the later Roman Empire. As did a personal chair, a promotional chair vanished with the resignation, retirement or death of its holder; one could only hope that the time would then be ripe and the money forthcoming to set up an established chair.

On their visit in 1974 the UGC expressed polite surprise on being told that Manchester had no system for regularly granting study leave. True, the concept of such leave existed, and the Council minutes recorded grants of leave made every year for specified purposes. But the rules, if any, which governed such concessions were obscure and practices varied from one department to another. If the University was to maintain its reputation in research it needed to approach the matter in a less haphazard manner. Unfavourable comparisons were drawn with neighbours in Liverpool, believed to enjoy a genuine sabbatical system of entitlement to one term's leave for every six terms served. The University would suffer no financial loss if colleagues undertook to cover for one another and keep the less specialised first-

and second-year courses going in their absence (to replace the final-year options, which depended on the personal research of those who offered them, would generally prove an impossible task). Study leave, argued a textile technologist from UMIST, was the university teacher's equivalent of continuing education. Advocates of regular leave did not tie it solely to the need to pursue scholarly research: let it be granted also for 'research into teaching methods' or 'refreshment of the individual lecturer'.

Anticipating a recommendation from the UGC, the Senate set up a committee on 'Arrangements in Connection with Leave of Absence', under the chairmanship of Harry Street, the distinguished civil rights lawyer. Reporting in May 1975, the committee acknowledged the existing confusion, which 'gave neither incentive nor encouragement to members of staff to apply for paid leave'. Street and his colleagues did not, as the local AUT would have wished, agree that regular study leave should become a contractual right, but did accept the AUT's proposed compromise – a 'discretionary system of entitlement' which also 'incorporated a recognised timetable for the granting of leave, some system of appeal for cases where leave was not granted, and a set of ground rules for deciding such appeals'. The Senate committee declared that 'it benefits the University, as well as members of staff themselves, if its teaching staff are able to develop new lines of thought, reconsider teaching methods, visit new places and examine activities elsewhere, concentrate on important research and generally refresh their minds'. For the first time they specified that 'it is hoped that non-clinical staff will normally be able to take one term of study leave after nine terms of service, if circumstances permit'. This did not reproduce the arrangements in the book of Genesis and was not therefore literally a sabbatical system, but it did represent a considerable improvement on past practice.

The new system ran experimentally for one year, and was then in essence confirmed in 1977. Some cautious souls feared that to grant leave of absence was to imply that the absentees could be spared: would not critics conclude that the University was over-staffed? A voice in Senate suggested overcoming the problem by requiring those who had taken leave to submit reports on their activities, in order to prove that they had not treated the time as extra holidays, tacked on to their already generous vacations. In later years reports would indeed be required. But in the 1970s they were not generally called for, and seemingly unproductive scholars enjoyed leave together with the most prolific of their colleagues.

Despite these improvements in the conditions of service and despite the advance of a patchy and in some places half-hearted form of academic democracy, academics laboured for much of the 1970s under a sense of grievance concerning their salaries. AUT members became more inclined to behave like a trade union and to threaten 'industrial action' (usually inaction), even at the expense of students. They complained that on account of an arbitrary decision by the Secretary of State for Education their pay was no longer comparable with that of other teachers in higher and further education, who had benefited by the Houghton Report of 1974 (Houghton's brief did not extend to universities, but did include public sector higher education, for example in polytechnics). An 'arbitral board' recommended pay increases for university teachers, but Government rules prevented these from coming into immediate effect, and in the summer of 1975 the Government's new anti-inflationary pay policy got in the way. Lecturers' salaries fell short of reasonable expectations by at least £500 a year, those of senior lecturers by not less than £650 a year, and the so-called 'pay anomaly' gnawed at their sense of well being for several subsequent years.

Efforts by the AUT to win public sympathy by demonstrating were not very successful; the sight of a figure in cap and gown, bearing a placard pleading 'Rectify the Anomaly', melted few hearts. Both in 1975 and 1978 the AUT, reflecting that industrial action was never effective unless it threatened to hurt some innocent party whose cries would be heeded, proposed to withhold examination results until a satisfactory settlement was reached. Some members hated the thought of harming students or adding to their anxiety; one high-principled gentleman would rather, he confessed, have joined a conspiracy to assassinate Shirley Williams, the Secretary of State for Education. AUT tactics, had they been carried into effect, would have antagonised the Students' Union, which had become broadly sympathetic to the lecturers' case and approved of their challenge to unpopular Government policies. Fortunately the Government did not call the bluff and agreed, in 1978, to rectify the pay anomaly by stages. For its part the AUT thought it unrealistic to claim full compensation for past inequities by backdating its pay claims to October 1974. The Association's forbearance appeared to have cost most of its members about £2000 per head.

Changes in the position of women academics in the 1970s are difficult to plot, but some improvements were probably made. At the upper end of the hierarchy, the number of women professors increased, though it did so from an almost non-existent base. Violet Cane's appointment as Professor of Mathematical Statistics in 1972 had been headline news, and had come just in time to save Manchester from being blacklisted by the AUT as one of those reactionary institutions that employed no women professors at all. By October 1975 the number had grown to four, through the appointments of Joan Walsh in Numerical Analysis, Jean McFarlane in Nursing, and Gillian White in International Law; Professor White was believed to be the first Englishwoman to be appointed to a chair in Law in the country. By November 1979 Enid Mumford had become Professor of Organisational Behaviour in the Manchester Business School, and Elizabeth Cutter Professor of Botany, thus raising the complement to six.

Some women academics felt uneasy in a man's world, and were conscious of lacking certain dubious qualities which made for success in a gentleman's club – the necessary brashness in company, the necessary loudness and self-confidence in the lecture room, the necessary resistance to taking on unglamorous jobs which carried little credit. They were slower than men to claim that their academic work was so important that it ought to exempt them from mundane tasks; any woman who did so was soon accused of queenly behaviour. In some departments it was second nature for men to steer students with personal problems towards their more sensitive female colleagues. To judge by Harry Lesser's satirical essay on 'How to Handle a Committee', techniques for upsetting a woman were not unknown in the University: 'one merely needs to be patronising and offensive, and then, when she becomes annoyed, to accuse her of becoming hysterical and irrational, at which with any luck she will obligingly fall into the trap and begin to behave hysterically'. It was no longer to be assumed, however, that women academics would resign their posts when they started families: Diana Kloss in Law and Diana Leitch on the Library staff proved the contrary. The Keeper of Geology in the Manchester Museum led the campaign for Diana Leitch's retention and senior members of the University signed a petition declaring: 'We do not wish to lose what Diana has been doing for us'. When Brenda Hoggett, a Lecturer in Law, became pregnant, Professor Wortley lamented: 'What a pity! She's such a clever girl and she'll never make anything now.' His fears were misplaced, for his junior colleague went on to become a Law Commissioner and to join the high court bench (Family Division) as Mrs Justice Hale.

During the 1970s little appeared to have come of the 1960s dream of transforming the University into a workplace democracy, rather than a specialised institution dedicated to extending and communicating knowledge and know-how. However, the institution was well-equipped (some said, sorely encumbered) with committees and consultative bodies, with departmental boards to advise professors and staff-student consultative committees to advise departmental boards on the curriculum and the pastoral care of students. Some saw them as talking-shops, harmful in that they created confusion, wasted time, and worsened resentments by airing them publicly. Others saw in them a device for smoothing the way towards better relations between professors and their colleagues and ensuring that considered decisions were taken. It was almost impossible to avoid making formal arrangements when the staff had grown so numerous that general consultation over coffee or lunch had become impracticable. Staff–student ratios were becoming less favourable, but only in a few areas did they markedly deteriorate. While pay remained a constant grievance throughout the 1970s and AUT officers became increasingly vociferous, some of the conditions of service modestly improved. The University took some steps to standardise the practices of faculties and departments, and to make academics aware, not precisely of their rights (the administration was nervous of the word), but of the privileges which could be available to all.

4

The students:
life and opinions

About 10,000 full-time students registered at Owens for the session of 1974–75, over 11,000 for that of 1979–80. At least 80 per cent were undergraduates. High fees and other obstacles tended to discourage research students, and the proportion of postgraduates sank from about one-fifth to one-sixth of the whole. Part-time degree and diploma students were numbered in hundreds: almost 700 in 1974–75, and over 900 in 1979–80. Most part-timers were now postgraduates; the Robbins Report had concentrated on the need to provide full-time places for a rising generation of young people, although evening degree classes in the Faculty of Economic and Social Studies had survived the Report's publication by several years.

Most undergraduates entered the University at eighteen and left at twenty-one, apart from those in the professional schools, ranging from architecture and planning to medicine and dentistry, whose student life lasted longer. Undergraduates, however, included a significant number of older recruits, known as 'mature students', who had not stepped on to the escalator which normally carried bright, conventional teenagers from the sixth-form to the university floor of the educational edifice. Greeted with enthusiasm by many tutors who found them more articulate and dedicated than run-of-the-mill undergraduates, mature students numbered about 600 in 1978–79. One of the oldest, John Hogan, obtained in 1977 a Combined Studies degree in American Studies, English and History at the age of seventy-one, to the accompaniment of thunderous applause in the Whitworth Hall. He had left school at the age of twelve to work in a mill, and had been by turns a cotton spinner, a joiner, and director of a number of small businesses. At the time of his retirement, at the age of sixty-four, he had been an insurance broker. Rod Cox, when in his early thirties, became General Secretary to the Students' Union for the session 1979-80; he had left school at sixteen, spent a little time at Plymouth Polytechnic, departed to follow the hippie trail to the Middle East, and entered the University of Manchester to read Philosophy when he was twenty-eight. Special arrangements for 'mature matriculation', sometimes by examination and sometimes by interview alone, were made in order to accommodate candidates not equipped with the usual 'A' and 'O' level grades awarded by the usual public examining boards.

In the fields of adult and continuing education, the University provided a great number of short courses, each lasting for a few weeks. Some of these led to certificates, but many were taken for interest and enlightenment alone, and some produced other kinds of result – for example, in successful interviews for jobs. In the year of Sir Arthur Armitage's retirement, 1980, there were 30,000 enrolments in these fields.

Between the 1950s and the 1970s the proportion of women students at Owens rose from 20–25 per cent of all full-time students (undergraduate and postgraduate) at mid-century to 36.75 per cent in 1974–75 and 38.66 per cent in 1979–80. They were less prominent among the part-time degree and diploma students, for they accounted for only about 25 per cent of these in 1974–75, and 29 per cent in 1979–80 (the proportion would rise when undergraduate part-time degrees were reintroduced during the 1980s). Women gained ground in all faculties, but their preferences for certain subjects, whether for social, cultural or genetic reasons, did not greatly change.

Women accounted for more than half of the full-time students in Arts and Education – indeed, for over 60 per cent of those in the Education Faculty in 1979–80. Law and Medicine were at par, for in both those faculties, as in the University as a whole, the female contingent approached 40 per cent. But in Science, the largest faculty, only one student in four was a woman. Schools and universities were often taxed with failing to direct girls towards technology and the physical sciences, and thereby neglecting to provide for the country's needs and to promote social equality.

Closer analysis of the Science Faculty suggested that, in Manchester as elsewhere, the tendency of schoolgirls to choose biology, which did not conjure up the image of a man in a white coat, was being projected into the University. Women inclined towards the descriptive life sciences and the disciplines most closely linked with medicine – to botany, biology, biochemistry, zoology, bacteriology, virology, pharmacy and psychology. A new course on Speech Pathology and Therapy, directed by Betty Byers Brown, created a small women's world of its own. In some years places to read Liberal Studies in Science were evenly divided between women and men. On the other hand, detailed study of the more materialistic and mathematical branches of science attracted fewer women, and they were even less likely to read engineering. In 1979 the five branches of engineering (aeronautical, civil, electronic and electrical, mechanical, and nuclear) attracted 13 women freshers to 222 men, computer science seven women to forty-six men. Neither physics nor chemistry appealed strongly to women students. Mathematics, on the other hand, claimed a substantial female minority, fielding forty-five women to ninety-five men. The new four-year Elite Engineering course, otherwise Engineering Manufacture and Management, enrolled eight men and one woman in its inaugural year.

By the late 1970s just over half the student population of the whole University (including UMIST) were engaged in the scientific, technological and medical disciplines, and just under half in what were broadly categorised as arts subjects (a term which extended beyond the Arts Faculty, and included education, law and the social sciences). Early in the decade the UGC had resigned itself to accommodating student preferences and to allowing arts and social science students to form a majority within universities in general. It was, after all, possible to educate them more cheaply than science students; for that reason they possessed certain attractions at a time of economic crisis, even if they were expected to contribute little to its resolution. Shirley Williams, the Labour Secretary of State for Education and Science, was said to be thinking otherwise in 1977, although a renewed emphasis on science and engineering would, or so some prophets complained, encourage discrimination against women students.

In Manchester, with its burgeoning medical school, it was never likely that scientists would dwindle into a minority, whatever the national trend might be. In February 1978, *Communication* informed its public that 52 per cent of the University's students were enrolled on courses in Science and Technology, and 48 per cent in Arts and Social Sciences. At times some Arts subjects seemed to have lost their powers of attraction – until reformed, modern languages were in the doldrums, and even English was forced on one occasion to keep up its numbers by raiding UCCA's clearing house in search of worthy students who had failed to get into other universities. Only History was praised for its recruiting campaigns, which involved the use of more imaginative publicity (at least one attractive secretary was falsely represented in a photograph as an eager student); much wooing at interview of promising applicants; and the abandonment after agonised debate of the traditional O-level Latin entrance requirement for

History Honours, on the grounds that many schools no longer provided for it. A new scheme for Honours in Combined Studies, intended to raise the status of non-specialists, failed at first to pull in the expected number of takers; it offered more rational combinations of subjects than the old General degree, which had been a free-for-all, but its students still suffered because their courses were juxtaposed rather than integrated with each other, and because they had no home in any particular department.

It was a matter for self-praise on the University's part, and for complaint by some critics, that increasing numbers of students appeared to be flocking into vocational courses that would offer them professional qualifications or exemptions from professional examinations. Accountancy and business finance recruited with marked success during the 1970s. Both pure sciences and liberal arts began to feel threatened as a result; some sociologists viewed with regret the rise of subjects which appeared to encourage early conformity and to deny students a broader education before they settled down to the grind of earning a living.

'You wouldn't believe the kids nowadays . . . They all seem to want to be bloody accountants!' Thus a Professor of Sociology, nostalgic for the 1960s, consuming his ploughman's lunch in the staff bar and chatting to journalists from *Punch* in the autumn of 1976. Like the ageing Oxford Fabians in Angus Wilson's story 'Such Darling Dodos', he was finding himself no longer on the side of youth, for many left-wing academics, uneasy at having their chosen party in power, appeared more radical than most of their pupils. At times, indeed, the students of the 1970s were accused by journalists, observing them from within and without the University, of being dullards and conformists, less politically aware, less idealistic, less susceptible to ideologies than their predecessors. It seemed possible that the student radicalism of the 1960s had been the child of prosperity, the product of some arrogant belief that graduates were so valuable to society that nothing could stop them in their tracks. Perhaps the spectre of unemployed graduates was whipping up, despite the University's assurances that no files would be kept on student political activities, a fear of bad references, jobs denied, and jeopardised careers. Angelos Loizides asked readers of *Manchester Independent*, 'Have you noticed how mellow and calm we have all become? It seems that despite all the fuss about our militancy and revolutionism we are one of the most well adapted and conformist groups in society.' Students, he noted, had offered little support even to the miners in conflict with Edward Heath; they seemed to want only

'better buildings and more money'. A more scathing attack on the
phlegmatic student body came from *New Manchester Review,* a periodical founded by a former Union officer, Andrew Jaspan – 'My, how
things have changed. The class of '78 look, in the words of one tutor,
like corporals out of the Royal Engineers or the WAF . . . '

In reality the 1970s saw plenty of militant activity, and the students
did not entirely consist, as Jaspan's journal complained, of 'predictable computer novices playing sport seriously and getting their
essays in on time'. The campaigns of the South African Liberation
Society were sustained throughout the decade and lost impetus only
when eclipsed by the issue of overseas students' fees. Complaints of
student apathy were not new; even in the 1960s the inertia and indifference of much of the student body had infuriated the politically conscious minority, and the public image of students had always owed
more to the efforts of a small cadre of activists than to majority sentiment. But in the middle and later 1970s the activists seemed more
sharply divorced from the student population at large. It was partly
that higher authority, having learnt political wisdom, rarely antagonised moderate student opinion, and did not repeat the mistakes
which had provoked the mass occupation of the Whitworth Hall in
February and March 1970. There was a core of truth in a fictitious
interview with the Vice-Chancellor on the techniques of repressive
tolerance, as reported in Michael Mauss's satirical column in *Mancunion.* 'It's the same every year, one term recruiting feeble-minded
first-years for their perverse pranks, one term hurling pathetically
ineffective abuse at me and doing precious little else, and then, ker-
pow! We've got 'em by the balls in their third term . . . . Old Charlie
Carter up at Lancaster's got it wrong; booting 'em in the groin when
they're down just makes them martyrs.' Only in the summer of 1976,
in the course of a row about the Union capitation fee, did students
abandon the practice of never resorting to direct action during an
examination term.

Justifiably or not, critics suggested that 1970s students, even the
would-be rebels and nonconformists, lacked originality and strategic
imagination – that they could only mouth outdated slogans, worship
vanished idols, engage in weary rituals such as occupying the telephone
exchange. In search of copy, the *Punch* journalists visited the Grass-
roots 'alternative' bookshop in Waterloo Place (this offered, according
to an advertisement of 1974, items on 'science fiction – claimants –
mysticism – education' and 'politics – underground – tenants – poetry
– women'). Behind the counter they found 'a vague, bearded youth',

'wearing a Che Guevara button on his cardigan; a student image which suddenly looks as quaintly period as the homespun – sandals – parsley-wine of early Letchworth. Rhodes Boyson, thou shouldst be cheering at this hour . . . '. More profoundly, Andy Pearmain, a Philosophy graduate who became Academic Affairs officer in 1977, criticised the Union for 'sectarianism' – the uncoordinated pursuit of particular cherished projects, with no grand design and a hearty contempt for what anyone else was seeking to achieve. Apart from its interest in the South African disinvestment campaign, the Union had ceased to intervene in University affairs and concentrated instead on peripheral 'alternative' projects, which devalued the University and offered a retreat from its way of doing things, rather than seeking either to reform or to disrupt the institution.

It was possible, however, to hear more favourable opinions of the students of the 1970s. Some academics were relieved that students had reverted to realism and praised their sense of proportion. 'This university isn't like Lancaster or Essex,' said Professor Cohen of Psychology, 'little academic hot houses totally cut off from the urban realities of bus queues and slums and housing estates. It's not so easy to fool yourself into thinking that some trivial little campus issue is a world-shaking event.' Advising new arrivals what to expect, a front page article in *Mancunion* for October 1978 observed that 'There has recently been a general rejection of overt politics'. Rather, 'Students have become more involved with their own private lives – in developing more humane and caring attitudes towards each other. They are worried by the rise of fascism [in the form of the National Front], but are generally more contemplative and less active.'

Some students wanted to encourage collaboration rather than competition. Hence, in 1974 those sitting on a Senate Working Party on assessment argued against the traditional system of classifying degrees in steps which descended from first-class honours to the ordinary degree. They pleaded unsuccessfully for some kind of profiling system which would identify strengths and weaknesses without neatly putting every finalist (as the Pete Seager song had it) into boxes made of ticky-tacky. The Union tried to establish an 'essay bank' which would enable students to read each other's work and educate one another, instead of clutching their efforts jealously to their bosoms in the hope of scoring higher marks than their colleagues.

Sarah Kemp, who as Sarah Bentley read History from 1975 to 1978, remembers herself and her contemporaries as 'very middle-class' in the sense that 'I don't think very many of us took a lot of risks; I think most of us came embedded with our parents' or our background morals and values. I don't remember a huge amount of rule breaking . . . '. Many rules, for example in the halls of residence, had been modified and were scarcely worth infringing. But her friends were keen supporters of the right to be gay, and eagerly discussed the right to abortion on demand and the use of illegal drugs. Many others shared a desire to be ordinary, a determination not to be part of a separate, recognisable student estate – a wish to merge with the people of the city, to help or entertain them without being patronising; a fear of seeming precious or arrogant. James Richardson, another student of the 1970s, found it impossible to exist in Manchester without being a football supporter. Pub culture, complete with pool, darts and card games, was a traditional way of making friends. Staying on in the city after leaving the University, he founded one of the first pub chess clubs, at the 'Albert' in Rusholme. A member of the English Department, Ray Barron, writing of the forbidding scene which met the eyes of overseas students, alluded to 'a student life devoted to beer and football in the best democratic tradition'. The cult of real ale created the phenomenon of the beer bore, indulging in the student equivalent of middle class food and wine talk; at least, however, it focused on the quality of the goods offered, rather than the quantity which could be consumed in the smallest possible time.

There were hints, too, of more raffish recreations, of the enjoyment of cannabis, suggestions that drugs other than alcohol and nicotine were becoming accepted features of student culture. By the mid-1970s cannabis was being openly smoked on Union premises, a practice discouraged by the officers, who dreaded the loss of their licence. The police did raid Union premises on the night of 25 November 1976, the first time for eight years, and a dozen offenders, who did not appear to be students, were later convicted. It was prudent to keep the indulgence private, but in some circles students took it for granted that hosts would provide cannabis at parties. Broaching a hitherto forbidden topic, much as student papers had begun to discuss birth control about 1964, *Mancunion* allowed space to a drug dealer named 'Freewheelin' Franklyn' and reported his remarks on readily obtainable hallucinogenic drugs, including magic mushrooms. One student correspondent registered strong objections to this 'irresponsible' publicity, and little was heard of the subject after Franklyn's departure for London.

Most accounts of student culture concentrated on masculine manners and customs, but some relief was afforded by the vignettes of

female student types, from the callow fresher to the formidable finalist, in 'Lines from a Dean's Leaded Window' in 1975:

'Farouche, uncertain, idle Liz,
First year in Arts, in sex, in digs,
Was quick to hear but slow to heed
The call to study and the need to read.'

'Susanna spends nights in libidinal pleasuring,
Mornings in studying History, afternoons
Speaking at women's lib. meetings. Her thesis
On Froude, Freud and freedom is practically done.'

Liz and Susanna were perhaps the same person, *en route* through different phases in the student life-cycle.

All students were members of the Students' Union; nothing came of
politicians' proposals that membership should become voluntary.
From the obligation of all students to belong to it the Union acquired
both authority to represent the student body and the guarantee of a
regular income from public funds. In dry legal terms the Union was
'an unincorporated association' and 'constitutionally separate from
the University'. Individual members of the Union were also members
of the University, but the Union and the University negotiated with
each other as separate entities, and in Union vocabulary the term 'University' tended to mean the University administration rather than the
whole community of scholars. According to the stylised picture presented by *Mancunion* during the 1970s, the University authorities
were generally to be suspected of plotting to undermine the Union by
starving it of funds or encouraging rival organisations and alternative
social centres. The Union was jealous of its autonomy, but none the
less had to depend on the University in at least two respects. It occupied a building which the University owned, and it relied for most of
its revenue on capitation fees, which were in effect subscriptions paid
by or on behalf of each student. After much annual discussion
between the University and the Union, the University would request
the fee, at a rate which it considered justifiable, from the Local Education Authorities, which paid the fee on behalf of most students.

Less formally, the Union was once described as 'a large theatre
workshop for those interested in politics and administration to prac-
tise their talents'. It was the task of the Union to represent students to
the University and to the world; to entertain, inform and advise them;
to see to their welfare; to express their political opinions; and to campaign for the causes they held most dear. Constantly reiterated, in

tones of relief or regret, was the belief that few students were interested in the Union as a political machine or as a debating society. Most
concerned themselves chiefly with the quality of the goods and services which the organisation provided, and asked only that their
elected officers be competent administrators and give proper directions to their permanent staff of managers, secretaries and other supporters. In September 1980 the Union clubhouse offered students a
large coffee-cum-snackbar; three drinking bars, the Cellar, the Ser-
pent and the Solem; television rooms; a games room; reading and
silence rooms; a number of meeting rooms; and a debating hall. Available in the basement were lavatories, baths, showers and washrooms,
two hairdressers, a travel bureau, a newsagent, a bank, and a second-
hand book shop. Membership of the Union gave access to any or all
of at least 150 active societies.

Ngaio Crequer, later a journalist on the staff of the *THES,* proved
to be the last officer to hold the title of President of the Students'
Union. In 1974 a General Meeting of that body, as though suspicious
of supreme beings, abolished the traditional hierarchy of President
and Vice-Presidents and established a cabinet without a prime minister. This gave rise to the boast that Manchester's was the only students' union in the country to have no president. At first the new
collective consisted of four principal officers, each with his or her own
department, working together as equals. They received modest
salaries, equivalent to a full student maintenance grant divided by
twenty-nine and multiplied by fifty-two, so as to stretch it out across
the full calendar year. They were generally called 'sabbatical' officers,
for any student in mid-course elected to one of these posts would usually be given by the University permission to interrupt the course and
resume it when the term of office was over. Some officers, however,
were recent graduates and therefore 'sabbatical' only in name; wisely,
perhaps, the University avoided asking whether they could be called
students when they had ceased to be registered as such.

The General Secretary was the chief administrator of the Union
building. Responsibility for relations with the University passed to the
Education and University Affairs Officer; for external affairs to
the External and National Union of Students Affairs Officer (who did
'all the directly or vaguely political work'); for student welfare to the
Welfare Officer, formerly the Welfare Vice-President. Two other
sabbatical officers joined them in 1975. One took charge of *Mancunion,* which had developed into the principal student newspaper, and
with it of all the Union's publicity; the other, of Events, including the

Introductory Week and most of the light entertainment which the Union subsequently provided. Four lesser officers, who did not enjoy sabbatical status, made up the rest of the Union Executive. They were the Internal Officer, the Postgraduate Officer, the Overseas Officer, and the Ordinary Officer without Portfolio.

Apart from the Executive there was a much larger Union Council which had forty-four members in 1975 and met every three weeks during term; it was composed of a number of junior ministers, most of whom were secretaries for one concern or another, and of representatives of various student constituencies and interests. Election to the Union Council was the first step in the career of many student politicians, enabling them to claim a modicum of experience when they stood for Executive posts. In the 1970s the Union Council was not particularly assertive and did not, as it was to do in the late 1980s, provide a buffer between the Executive and the General Meeting, the two main rivals for power and authority within the Union.

In the absence of a mediator, the Union's constitution threatened to become unworkable. It made for tension between General Meetings, which were entitled to formulate Union policy, and the Executive which was charged with carrying policy out. Their antagonism was sometimes described as a conflict between the principles of 'representative democracy', embodied in the Union's officers, and those of 'direct democracy', personified by the students who assembled once a week to talk and vote like the citizenry assembled in the market place of ancient Athens. One fear was that the Executive, unless constantly called to account, would develop into irresponsible and secretive bureaucrats pursuing schemes of their own; another, that General Meetings were unrepresentative of the student body and clay in the hands of a caucus of dedicated politicos of left-wing persuasion. True, there was an important safeguard, in that General Meetings became quorate and entitled to make valid policy decisions only if 200 students were present. In the view of many critics the quorum (equivalent to a mere 2 per cent of full-time students) was absurdly low, but attempts to raise it were invariably denounced as Tory plots and seemed doomed to failure. Emergency General Meetings, summoned to deal with business that could not wait even a few days, required a quorum of 500, and the same quorum was needed to empower a meeting to pass a binding vote of no confidence upon Union officers and force them to resign.

Summoned on Wednesday afternoons, the traditional time for student sport and academic committees, General Meetings competed with other amusements which many students found more fascinating. Direct democracy was not wholly democratic – it was almost certain to disenfranchise certain groups engaged in academic business which took them away from the site, such as senior medical students and student nurses. Many gatherings proved to be inquorate, for many students were not apathetic so much as antipathetic to badly chaired meetings protracted by complicated procedures which nobody appeared to understand. Nevertheless, debates on one or two weightier issues with economic implications – concerned with proposals that the Union should withdraw from the National Union of Students (NUS) and with negotiations over the capitation fee – attracted audiences of about 1,200. An alternative to the General Meeting was the referendum, conducted through the ballot box; almost 4,000 students voted in 1976 on withdrawal from the NUS, but only 632 on the less interesting question of constitutional reform in 1978.

Relations between the Executive and the General Meeting deteriorated in 1977 and 1978, when a predominantly Conservative Executive held sway and was seeking both to impose tighter financial controls and to ensure that the Union observed charity law. At issue were payments voted by General Meetings which had nothing immediately to do with the well being of Manchester students. Some students objected to the practice of financially supporting, say, the Portuguese Communist Party at a time when the Union building needed refurbishment and the Day Nursery, supported by the Union, was short of funds. The Executive objected in principle to sending contributions to strikers in the long-running Grunwick dispute over union recognition in London (£25) and to the Anti-Nazi League (£99), contending that these payments would be 'ultra vires', beyond their powers as administrators of public funds conferred on a charity designed to promote student welfare. Legal opinions confirmed their misgivings, and emboldened them to argue that General Meetings had no power to order them to break the law. Their opponents urged the Union to provoke and fight a test case, but did not carry the day, despite the passing of votes of 'No Confidence' in members of the Executive at a General Meeting which turned out to have been inquorate at the crucial moment.

Inflation tested the managerial and negotiating skills of Union officers. The bulk of the Union's income came from capitation fees and a smaller but still significant part of it from the profits of trading in the Union's shops and bars and from other sources such as juke-boxes and fruit machines; the higher the capitation fee, the smaller the need for the

Union to charge high prices to break even. In October 1975 *Mancunion* estimated that capitation fees accounted for 85 per cent of income, 'trading surplus and sundry' for 15 per cent. A year later the respective proportions seemed to be closer to 90 per cent and 10 per cent.

On two occasions, in 1975 and 1980, the Union appeared to be floundering in a financial quagmire. Indeed, in 1975 only an advance of £25,000 from the University, to be repaid when the fees came in, maintained the Union's cash flow during the summer. Some difficulties were traceable to mismanagement (usually attributed to one's political opponents), but more were blamed on a capitation fee believed to be among the lowest in the country. The Vice-Chancellor argued that in the teeth of an economic recession the University had a 'moral responsibility' to restrain its demands upon ratepayers, and others in high places spoke of a need to 'endure cuts in services in the same way as the rest of the community'. But these sentiments were attributed to a Machiavellian plan to weaken the Union by starving it of money: perhaps, in its enfeebled state, it would 'more passively accept the new emphasis on Education as a service sector providing for the needs of industry'. On behalf of the University the official journal, *Communication*, maintained that for the sake of fair comparisons with other institutions calculations should take account of the separate fee paid to the Athletic Union, the consortium of sporting clubs: add the two fees together and they amounted to a generous sum. On behalf of the students *Mancunion* retorted that the University was squeezing the Union's fee in order to get a large subsidy for sporting activities and escape the normal obligation to pay for the upkeep of grounds out of the UGC's block grant. Disputes in 1976 and 1977 resulted in direct action by some students, intended to shame the University into increasing its offers, and not always unsuccessful. But relations subsequently improved, with the University offering cash to refurbish the Union building, and even, in May 1980, exceeding the fee increase recommended by the Department of Education and Science.

In general, however, the administration had been right to urge restraint. Should local authorities find universities' demands excessive, their complaints might inspire proposals to finance students' unions by other means – for example, by treating each of them as a department of its university which would have to compete, as every other department did, for a share of the block grant. Such a system would allow the Unions far less independence. Rumour had it in the summer of 1978 that Local Education Authorities were jibbing at the high proportion of fees spent on the salaries of sabbatical officers and permanent staff, to say nothing of the donation of public money to political causes and the subsidising of social activities.

Members of the Union were automatically members of the NUS and of the Manchester Area National Union of Students (MANUS), a 'network' which linked them with local colleges and the neighbouring Polytechnic. At intervals in the past Manchester students had fallen out with the NUS on the grounds that the benefits of membership did not justify the subscription; that the NUS was a tedious talking shop controlled by the London colleges; and that affiliated unions had to waste time and money on sending delegates to attend its chaotic conferences and transact other business. Many students disliked the politics of the NUS Executive, which seemed too moderate in the mid-1960s and both extreme and self-paralysing ten years later. The Men's Union had withdrawn from NUS in 1954 while the Women's Union retained their membership, but in 1959 a General Meeting had voted in favour of returning all components of the federal Union to the NUS. It was, however, tempting to economise amid the stringency of the mid-1970s by cancelling the Union's block subscription to the national organisation.

Proposals to follow the example of Aston University Birmingham, secede from the NUS, and try to go it alone, aroused wider interest among Manchester students than did any other issue of the 1970s. For all its flaws the NUS was the students' national campaigning body, concerned with grants, social security benefits, and resistance to education cuts. Membership offered a number of advantages, especially cheap travel and commercial discounts. But the organisation had failed to maintain the real value of the student maintenance grant; the NUS was hamstrung by a deadlock between three rival political groups, any two of which would combine to defeat proposals made by the third; and it was addicted to discussing international issues, about which it could only gesticulate. Should not students be allowed to join the NUS at their own discretion, rather than be delivered to it en masse by their university union? Defenders of the NUS argued that to undermine it was to weaken still further the position of students in the face of the Government. In any case the University allowed for the block subscription in the capitation fee, and should that subscription be cancelled there was no guarantee that the University would pay an equivalent amount to support services provided by the Union itself. In the view of David Aaronovitch, who was later to become President of NUS, disaffiliation would be 'economic suicide'.

Suicidally or not, early in 1976 a large General Meeting voted by a majority of one (547 votes to 546) to withdraw from the NUS. But the matter was wisely submitted to a referendum, in which 1,694 students voted for disaffiliation and 2,128 against the move, while another 40 abstained. Discuss services and amenities rather than ideologies, said some commentators, impressed by the size of the poll, and student apathy would disappear. Hence the Manchester Union remained with the NUS, though the issue was sometimes reopened at times when other Unions chose to pull out, and Conservatives were to return to the matter at intervals during the 1980s.

In the late 1960s and early 1970s, the University, like most others in the country, had arranged for student participation in many of the bodies concerned with academic affairs and domestic management. These ranged from departmental and faculty boards (which generally made the decisions most affecting student courses) to Senate and Council. A few student representatives attended the University Council by invitation only, but the University was more generous with formal membership of Senate. In 1976–77 it obtained from the Privy Council an amendment to its statutes allowing eighteen representatives of the studentry to become full members of Senate. Twelve students were elected by the faculties, three by Owens Union, and two by UMIST Union. One was to be nominated by the Committee of the Postgraduate Society. The University's departmental structure had the effect of fragmenting the student body, and the constitution ensured that the Union did not provide the only way into the Senate.

Senate and Council membership was for moderates and reformists. Radical students would not have considered sitting even on a departmental board; to do so would have been to capitulate to the establishment, to be deceived by token concessions. James Richardson had already boycotted his school council and declared in favour of a pupils' union which excluded teachers; he was disinclined to change his tactics at the University, believing as he did that governing bodies ought to be overthrown rather than joined or even infiltrated.

While seeking to co-ordinate the efforts of scattered departmental representatives, the Union relied heavily on the power of publicity to improve the lot of students. On occasion it set out to embarrass certain parts of the University, particularly departments said to be teaching badly or making unreasonable demands. At its disposal were its own journal, *Mancunion,* and a new device, the Alternative Prospectus.

Two mainstream student newspapers existed in 1973: *Manchester Independent* and *Mancunion.* The first had grown out of a crisis in

1960 which had led to the establishment of a student paper managed independently of the Union, but under some supervision from senior members of the University. In the 1960s the *Independent* had become a successful journal and won national awards for excellence. By 1974, however, the paper was sinking into debt. It lacked an efficient system of distribution, published irregularly, and complained of hostility on the part of the Union officer concerned with academic affairs. Though still publishing some articles of high quality, *Independent* failed to recover and eventually abandoned the field to *Mancunion,* once only a free news-sheet through which Union officers tried to explain their actions to their constituents. Now, under more enterprising management, it began to acquire many of the better characteristics of *Independent* and by the 1980s both the paper itself and some individual journalists were beginning to win prizes in the annual *Guardian*–NUS competitions for student newspapers.

In 1974 Anne Bourner, a geology student, became editor of *Mancunion* and expanded it into a magazine of up to sixteen pages, including features, reviews and sports reports. She bore with good humour letters addressed to 'Dear Sir', replying 'The Editor is a woman and proud of it', and thereby provoking other correspondence directed to 'Dear Woman'. Sadly, the claims of her degree forced her to resign prematurely, after which a General Meeting in January 1975 voted that *Mancunion*'s editor should become a sabbatical officer, who would look after all the Union's publications. For a time this officer was really a manager, the editorship passing to a collective which accepted or rejected contributions by majority vote, but by the 1980s the paper had an individual editor once more. At first each issue was pasted together and produced on a photocopying machine, incurring the charge that it resembled 'a borrowed set of sociology notes', but from later in the year 1975 *Mancunion* was professionally printed as a tabloid newspaper. By 1978–79 five or six thousand free copies were being distributed by the simple method of leaving piles at prominent points in the Union building. They were paid for partly by an allowance from the Union's budget and partly by advertising revenue. Despite its intermittent fondness for scurrilous gossip columns, the paper escaped the threats of libel actions that had beleaguered *Manchester Independent* in the touchier atmosphere of the late 1960s. Both sides showed restraint, offended senior members of the University preferring to ignore or remonstrate with the paper rather than resort to writs. Charges of sensationalism, inaccuracy and political bias were more likely to come from disapproving students than from academic staff.

At intervals *Mancunion* started debates on the shortcomings of departments, in a measured manner which would have been almost inconceivable in earlier decades. Even in the deferential 1950s attacks had not been unknown, but the rejoinders of the academic staff had been much haughtier. It now seemed, for instance, that the tense personal relationships among academics in Philosophy, a Department said to exist in 'a state of apparent dishonest inefficiency', were communicating themselves to students. Much to its credit, however, the Department found numerous student defenders, who called the paper's account tendentious and objected to its attempts at the public laundering of dirty linen. In November 1977 thirty students signed a letter in which they declared that 'The majority of the business, both academic and social, of the Philosophy Department continues to the satisfaction of all concerned.' Not all departments would have secured so favourable a testimonial. However, a mature student uttered the sinister prophecy that *Mancunion*'s article would stir up trouble rather than promote reform – that it would provoke 'an entrenched reaction detrimental both to harmony and democracy'.

Criticisms of the Department of Town and Country Planning, voiced in *Mancunion* in the autumn of 1976, seemed to echo widespread disillusionment with the schemes of urban planners. A gang of four, who claimed to express views shared by 'most students in our department', complained particularly of the status of so-called 'practical work', because it was not genuinely practical and encouraged fantasies, both architectural and geographical – 'e.g. designing a New Town in four days'. Projects were subject to unexplained academic assessments (as graded course work they formed part of an examination, and the academic judgement of examiners was not open to student challenge). Course reforms, in the view of the plaintiffs, resulted only in a 30 per cent increase in the burden of work, which was neatly complemented by a 30 per cent drop-out rate: most members of the staff insisted that their own courses remain compulsory, and therefore it was always possible to add to the curriculum but never to delete anything by way of compensation. One lecturer, E.J. Reade, was bold enough to back the criticisms, seeking to dispel the illusion that the planner could become a quasi-deity with synoptic vision acting on behalf of society as a whole and rising above the 'sectional interests' of the specialists involved in the enterprise. 'I feel that the University authorities should be profoundly concerned when what is taught in one of its departments is so inhibiting to free intellectual enquiry.' Another lecturer, Chris Wood, adopted a moderate and soothing tone, promising reform and defending the Department against what he saw as a brilliant and unfair piece of journalism.

High failure and drop-out rates in certain quarters attracted *Mancunion*'s attention. Hence the Physics Department, whose methods had seemed especially enlightened in the late 1950s and 1960s, came under fire in 1978 in the wake of numerous failures, followed by re-examinations and some exclusions, of students taking first-year courses in Physics, and in Physics and Electronics. There was a suspicion that the Department had been trying to 'hook' students in order to keep up its quota despite their poor A-level results (there was no surer way of incurring the displeasure of the University authorities than failing to recruit an adequate number of students, at a time when the University's income increasingly depended on student fees). Having secured students' custom the Department had, allegedly, failed to teach them efficiently. Poor lecturing in a fundamental first-year course, 'Vibrations and Waves', attracted much blame. An admissions tutor praised the Department for taking chances on promising students who did not have the best formal qualifications, and pointed out that good textbooks, including some which had been prepared in the Department in Professor Flowers's day, were available to students who disliked the lectures provided. Whatever the rights and wrongs of this particular dispute, it could be said that British universities had always prided themselves on their low casualty rate and invoked it to justify public expenditure upon them. Any departure from this cardinal principle, even in the name of widening access to the University, was cause for concern. Remedial teaching might be needed in universities if schools failed to prepare students for courses that made severe demands upon their mathematical or other skills.

The Alternative Prospectus, addressed to applicants, made more systematic attempts to improve conditions across the University. It sought to offer a candid account of Manchester from the point of view of the 'consumers of education' and to provide a foil to the University's own propaganda, which had become so mendacious, or so philistine, as to enthuse even about the featureless architecture of modern student flats. Potentially, the Prospectus was an effective weapon, since a hostile report could well discourage custom and force a department, fearful of declining numbers, to change its ways. Introducing the work in 1973, the President of the Students' Union, Ngaio Crequer, envisaged that staff-student consultative committees would make or at least approve the entries, and that the Prospectus would tell unvarnished truths about matters of interest to students – including the balance between lectures, seminars and tutorials; the number of contact hours; the standard of lecturing; the adequacy of laboratories; and the effectiveness of consultation. Later the Prospectus claimed to bring student life 'into its environmental context . . . The content of the Physics course at Manchester might be the same as that at Lancaster, East Anglia or Durham, but being a Physics student at Manchester is going to be a hell of a lot different.' Over 4,000 copies were printed and bound and posted to all schools and colleges in the country which taught subjects at Advanced Level.

A problem with the Alternative Prospectus was that, although it was said in 1975 to represent a thousand students' views, it was impossible for outsiders to know how large a sample of opinion in each department it was reporting and how fairly. Exasperated by the questions put to him by newspapers, Professor Dodwell complained of inaccuracies in the Prospectus and asserted that the offending article about the History of Art Department, which no-one would admit to having written, had never been shown to the local consultative committee. By the late 1970s, however, the Alternative Prospectus had mellowed. As John Fryett, then Education Officer of the Union, conceded, it was no longer considered heretical or sycophantic to praise the University or its departments. Dissatisfaction did not have to be total and the redeeming features of departments did not have to be ignored.

Early in 1978 a centre-spread in *Mancunion*, written by Neil Botfish, presented a balanced and reasonably optimistic picture of education in the University: 'most would agree that student life in Manchester is a very good one. The vast majority of staff are friendly and eminently capable in their fields. There is some choice in what we do, especially in the third year, and our views are generally listened to . . . '. He argued, however, that there were 'pockets of discontent all over the University', and that student campaigns would naturally concentrate on eliminating them. The most widespread complaints were of uninspiring lectures, which sometimes became exercises in dictation or efforts to cover blackboards in formulae for students to copy, and of the failure of the University to insist that its teachers be properly trained in their tasks (admittedly it provided courses for newcomers, but attendance at these was not compulsory). John Fryett blamed professors who, themselves unschooled in educational techniques, failed to insist that their staff be better prepared, for fear of exposing their own ineptitude in the classroom. Allegedly, they took refuge in the cosy belief that 'academics should be natural teachers', and entertained the delusion that 'university students are crying out to learn, that their motivation is naturally high, and therefore the university teacher has to do nothing to stimulate interest – pure facts presented traditionally are all that is needed.'

Most students were content if their lectures were lucid and not too long, if their opinions were heard and their questions answered, if their reading lists were not interminable, if their assessment did not depend wholly on conventional three-hour examinations. Most tutors, however, dreaded the occasional group of students, ranging from sullen youths in bother boots to self-conscious, tongue-tied young women, who reacted neither to each other nor to their teacher, sitting in stony silence and avoiding the tutor's eye no matter what pearls were cast before them. Looking upon their unresponsive faces, unable to fathom the thoughts behind them or overcome the instinctual 'when in doubt, say nowt', many were tempted into nervous gabbling and the delivery of impromptu lectures which then precluded any possibility of interventions from the floor. Some students, by nature absorbent, sponges rather than fountains, felt no love of discussion and were exasperated by colleagues who did. A woman appealed to David Aaronovitch, who was responding eagerly to Ian Kershaw's seminars on Nazi Germany, 'Will you stop talking in the seminar? Having discussions! I don't come here to listen to you. I can't take notes when you're there. I've got a degree to get.'

Little, perhaps, could be done for those students who had become more deeply alienated, convinced (at least intermittently) of the dryness of their discipline and the sterility of academic exchange. A literature student wrote:

'Endless corridors I walk down –
Like some nightmarish dream –
A prisoner in your graveyard –
Alice searching for the queen.
. . . .
'I see never-ending textbooks,
Re-occurring black and white,
Eternal lists – type-written
(Christ, can't you even write?)
Yes, you speak of "man's experience",
My friend, you speak in vain,
Your listeners are ignorant
Of hunger, fatigue, pain,
Your words may be impressive,
Your arguments profuse,
A literary critic – you can only reproduce.'

Many students were anxious not to become introverted and self-absorbed, obsessed with their own personal problems or even with those peculiar to student life; they wanted to care for others. The Union ran its own welfare services, supplementing and perhaps surpassing the pastoral care provided by University departments. 'Contact Nightline', available from 8 pm to 8 am, was presented for a time as the Union's equivalent to 'The Samaritans', providing sympathetic listeners to lonely, depressed and worried students; an advertisement exhorted 'Don't Bottle It Up!' Later, in the 1980s, it preferred to call itself a friendly service which could be consulted, even at ungodly hours, on any subject, however mundane. The Legal Advice Centre considered about three hundred cases a year, particularly those involving landlord and tenant relations, consumer complaints, and road traffic offences and accidents. Most of the help was given by Law students, with an academic on hand to deal with the more complex questions. One University and Academic Affairs Officer, Dave Carter, was particularly anxious to provide advice for students seeking to change courses, who often encountered hostility in the departments they were trying to leave. Lisa French, Warden of Ashburne Hall from 1976 to 1989, was impressed by the Union's ability to nag dilatory Local Education Authorities into releasing grant cheques and saving impecunious students from having to live on air until they arrived. The task of welcoming overseas students and helping them to get their bearings was taken seriously; Ashburne Hall supplemented the Union's efforts by presenting an introductory course teaching new arrivals how to flag down buses and how to take their turn in food shop queues. The Union's Welfare Officer was supported by a phalanx of auxiliaries – a full-time Administrative Assistant, and student Secretaries for Accommodation, Grants, Overseas Students, the Nursery, and Health Centre Provision.

Flanking the Union were two semi-autonomous organisations, Rag and Community Action, which turned outwards towards the city and strongly influenced public impressions of students. They represented two different approaches to charity and welfare. Rag, more traditional and more closely connected with halls of residence, involved students, not only from Owens and UMIST, but also from Salford University, from local colleges, and sometimes from the Polytechnic. It was often described as the MASS Rag, referring to Manchester and Salford Students, and was given to stunts, capers and frivolities legitimised by the high-minded purpose of raising money for some sixty local charities. Rated in order of worthiness, these received different proportions of the net takings. Heading the list in 1975 were the Booth Hall Hospital, the Royal Manchester Children's Hospital and the Ancoats Settlement, which each received 6 per cent, and were followed immediately by the Little Sisters of the Poor, entitled to 5 per cent. Rag at its worst conjured up depressing visions of rowdyism, slapstick, minor public school humour, beeriness, brown sauce, and even blatant sexism. Part of its stock-in-trade were attempts to drink pubs dry (sponsored by Watney's, the brewers) and three-legged pub crawls, together with annual entertainments such as the Pyjama Dance (it required nerve or insensitivity or both these qualities to board a bus in a dressing gown and brave the stares of fellow passengers). No Rag procession could be considered complete without a few arrests, charges of public order offences, brief court appearances, and fines. Community Action, by way of contrast, involved its supporters directly in practical welfare work, rather than fundraising, and accused the Raggers on at least one occasion of playing Lady Bountiful and patronising the people who benefited indirectly from their antics.

Emblems of Rag in the 1970s were two whimsical figures, Fred Bogle (who was more leprechaun than evil spirit, and manifested himself to the organisers every year), and Miss Charity Hog, who was a hedgehog and no sow. It was the Bogle Stroll, said to be the largest sponsored charity walk in England, which saved Rag from degenerating into a worn-out festival barely tolerated by the people of Manchester. Started in 1962, the Stroll consisted of an overnight walk, first of forty-seven miles from Blackpool, and then of sixty-four miles from Lancaster, to Manchester. In 1974–75 the route was changed, both to increase the safety of the walkers and to eliminate the rising cost of transporting them in buses to the starting point. Walkers now pounded a triangular course which began and ended at UMIST, and took them – if they had the stamina – to Salford, Worsley, Atherton, Wigan, Chorley, Blackrod, Westhoughton, Walkden, Swinton, and back again to their base. Four formidable hills made the journey more taxing than ever. But in 1975 2,800 walkers and a dog began the walk, and 427 humans finished it; in 1976 2,600 started and 385 completed the course. Most walkers got as far as Wigan. Strolling was not a universal practice, for runners of fierce competitive instincts covered the ground as individuals or as teams, and proved that the fastest could make it home in about seven-and-a-half hours.

Whatever the motives of the participants – and sometimes these had little to do with charity – the Bogle Stroll commonly accounted for almost half Rag's income, while the proceeds of the sale of Rag magazine added another 30 per cent of the whole. Income from the Stroll suffered from difficulties in persuading walkers to exact the promised sums from their sponsors; in 1979, success did not crown the organisers' attempts to programme a computer to send out the necessary reminder letters. A perpetual problem with Rag magazine lay in its penchant for offensive jokes, now deemed to be both sexist and racist, and its stubborn indifference to the dawn of political correctness. Between 1973 and 1975 reports in *Communication* estimated Rag's annual earnings as approximately £30,000. But the takings then began to fall steeply, and the organisation raised no more than £12,000 in 1977 and £16,000 in 1978. In the second of those years it proved necessary to cancel the Rag procession, for the citizens of Manchester were weary of student ritual, and the organisers could not meet the conditions imposed by the police. However, the shock of this break with tradition seemed to concentrate the mind, and Rag showed signs of reviving: the procession took place once more, there was talk of a target of £40,000, and new, public-spirited activities such as organised blood donations began to figure in the programme.

Community Action stood for direct contact between student volunteers and those they were supporting – homeless, elderly, mentally ill, and disadvantaged people in general. Members of the organisation gave advice, encouragement and practical help rather than money. Under its umbrella students undertook many imaginative projects and it set out to support other enterprises which were 'self-help, community-based, run and organised by the local people'. Community Action received an annual allowance from the Union and employed two full-time and one part-time organiser. One of the most enduring activities was the Soup Run, which began when the pubs closed; volunteers asked no questions and exacted no conversation, but handed out bread and soup to anyone who wanted them, providing many clients with their only hot food of the day. Students on the Veg Run begged fruit and vegetables from stallholders in Springfield Market and distributed them to old people, to single-parent families, and to a number of institutions, such as the Ladybarn Community Centre, the Night Shelter for homeless people in Ardwick, and the Battered Wives' shelter in Chorlton.

Early in 1979 Community Action was running about twenty activities, which included clubs and camps for children and young people; schemes for decorating houses; a project for teaching English to Asians; and a Road Show which laid on performances for old people's parties, hospitals, and children's homes. Like Rag, it had ups-and-downs and suffered from organisational weaknesses; like the Union, it frequently failed to attract enough members to the general meetings which were supposed to lay down policy. Determined to impose tighter controls in the hope of keeping the Union financially buoyant and within the law, the mainly Conservative Executives of the later 1970s irritated Community Action by suggesting that it keep its paper-work in better order. One General Secretary, it was said, failed to realise 'that you can't ask someone who is prepared to stand in the street for three hours giving soup to homeless people to fill in forms in triplicate of how much soup they gave out and who to'. Idealism and accountancy did not mix. But Community Action held together somehow throughout the decade.

Preoccupied with the cost of living, oppressed by deficits in personal budgets, lamenting the inadequacy of grants, quailing before bank managers, constrained to earn money rather than pursue academic knowledge throughout vacations, too proud, sensitive or resigned to beg extra subsidies of parents, many students identified themselves with the poor and homeless. Many chose to live in the poorer quarters of the city rather than hold themselves apart in the self-contained world of the halls of residence and the University flats. Between the 1950s and the late 1970s the popularity of various kinds of accommo-dation altered in that many fewer students lived in board lodgings; the 'traditional halls' maintained a steady state but took a smaller share of the expanding market; University self-catering flats began to attract many tenants; and, towards the end of the 1970s, students began to apply for and occupy Council flats rather than rely on private land-lords. Statistics on student residence published by *Mancunion* in February 1980 disclosed the following choices and preferences:

Private accommodation	36.5%
University self-catering	20.5%
University catered halls	19.0%
At home	12.0%
Council property	4.5%
Boarding	3.0%
Direct leasing	2.5%
Hostels	1.0%
No fixed abode	1.0%
	100.0%

The direct leasing scheme was launched experimentally in 1976, the principle being that the University itself should rent accommodation from private landlords and itself let the premises to students. By so doing the University could ensure that properties were not damp, dilapidated or dangerous, and protect students from exploitation by unscrupulous operators. For their part, the landlords, often sorely tried by the provisions of the Rent Act, could be certain of receiving their rent cheques promptly. University student flats could not be shared by men and women, but mixed groups were allowed to rent houses within the direct leasing scheme. *Mancunion*'s figures suggested that in 1980 93 properties, occupied by a total of 347 students, were included in the enterprise. In 1982 the University Council gave authority to expand the scheme to enable 1,000 students to benefit from it in October 1983.

Traditional halls set out to promote community life, local patriotism and a competitive spirit. They provided some pastoral care and strove to counter the impersonality of a large and potentially bleak University. Their critics, as they had always done, associated them with hearty misbehaviour rather than aesthetic sensibility, and with protracted adolescence, pseudo-gentility and petty regulations. Since they were rival claimants on students' loyalty and provided alternative centres of entertainment, some bad blood existed between them and the Students' Union. When the Union officers issued exhortations to hall members and urged them, for example, to vote on rent strikes, certain hall officers took umbrage. Liaison officers were sometimes appointed in the hope of improving relations between the Union and the halls. One thousand-strong, the Owens Park Student Association (OPSA) resembled a parallel Students' Union based in Fallowfield, and was for a time headed by its own sabbatical President.

For some years the high cost of running traditional halls had made it unlikely that new halls would be established. One, however, was reconstructed in the late 1970s, when Ellis Llwyd Jones, a women's hall whose members were known as Elysians, migrated from its original site in Old Trafford and arrived in Victoria Park as a neighbour of Dalton Hall. Intended to provide places for trainee teachers of deaf people, the old premises were sold to Greater Manchester Council when the special schools for deaf children moved out of Old Trafford and the proceeds were used to rebuild the hall. For the time being Ellis and Dalton merely coexisted, but in 1987 they were to come together under the same head of residence and the same committee. From 1990 they would be officially described as a single item, Dalton Ellis Hall.

The status of some residences changed. Since the late nineteenth century, many had been owned by religious denominations and had at some point been licensed by the University to receive some of its students. However, in the 1970s two Catholic-owned halls, St Gabriel's, for women (run by the Sisters of the Cross and Passion), and Allen, for men (built by the diocese of Salford), officially became University halls. The University took leases on both at a nominal rent of £1 per annum plus a sum which would cover the insurance of the buildings. It also undertook to maintain the grounds and gardens and (at St Gabriel's) to pay rates and contribute to security costs. Other religious bodies, in the 1970s and 1980s, began to relinquish their licences and sometimes to dispose of their buildings to purchasers who withdrew them from University use. For these reasons, the Methodist college, Hartley Victoria, was lost to the University in 1974. Summerville, the Unitarian College in Victoria Park which had been accustomed since 1905 to receive some University students, gave up its licence in 1985. In the same year the Northern College (formerly, in successive incarnations, the Congregational College, the Northern Congregational College and the Lancashire Independent College) sold its imposing premises in Whalley Range for use as a training centre by the General, Municipal, Boilermakers and Allied Trade Union, ordinands giving way to officials as secularisation advanced.

Unfriendly commentators on halls of residence veered between predictions that halls would price themselves out of the market by overcharging, and complaints that such was the shortage of accommodation that the wardens could impose whatever absurd rules they liked on students who desperately needed places. Some, it was said, would perform almost any chores at the warden's behest in the hope of a guaranteed place the following year. For a time the Warden of Needham Hall in Didsbury provoked genteel protests against a genteel regime, in which students, greatly daring, contemplated terminating the 'gentleman's agreement' to wear formal dress at Sunday lunch, walking out of dinner before the Warden rang his bell, and perhaps even depriving him of waiters. These mild threats were not, it seems, carried out. Residents of the Moberly Tower, senior students and postgraduates whose average age was twenty-five, complained of regulations more restrictive than any imposed at Owens Park, where 55 per cent of residents were first-year students and the average age was nineteen. Their Warden retorted with complaints of childish misconduct and objections to the vandalising of lifts. Since many of the graffiti which disfigured them referred to the Warden it was hard for the accused to maintain that the crime was an outside job.

In 1975 the Warden of Hulme Hall praised Manchester's halls of residence for their individuality, and rejoiced in their autonomy, the variety of their architecture, and their escape from the dull uniformity and central control which plagued halls in other universities, old and new. A Hulme student murmured, however, that masculine halls did not cater for a variety of types and rested on 'the assumption that every resident is a beer-drinking, rugby-playing heterosexual'. Laddishness, and to some extent lassishness, were perhaps inevitable consequences of segregation, but this ensured (as the separate Women's Union had once done) that women should have the chance to run their own affairs. Dr French of Ashburne was a firm defender of traditional women's halls, which gave female students 'a chance of being properly in parallel and not sat on by a majority of hefty rugger players'.

One hall seemed bent on self-parody to the point of self-destruction. A close neighbour of the Athletic Ground, Woolton was famous for its sporting prowess. Since its foundation in 1959, it had rapidly invented a range of traditions reminiscent of early Betjeman verses on 'The 'Varsity Students' Rag'. Perhaps the proximity of Owens Park and later of Oak House, the immediate targets of many japes and ritual obscenities, spurred Woolton into cultivating an exaggeratedly distinctive identity based on its own version of machismo. In the winter of 1975–76 there was an unpleasant exchange on the premises between the student President of Woolton and a young man wearing the badge of the Gay Society. The Society were accused of exploiting a personal quarrel to draw attention to their cause, but it was certain that a letter, crude in its sentiments if not in its prose and purporting to come from 'Woolton Hall' (though surely not from the whole Junior Common Room), was sent to and published by *Mancunion*. 'I would like to bring to the notice of your readers an alternative society; namely, "Heterosoc," which holds its meetings at present in Woolton Hall. We believe we uphold the morals of the majority, the laws of nature, and the laws of the land, by denying "Gay" people any rights whatsoever.' Copious correspondence followed, on this and other occasions, in which to their credit some Wooltonians wrote anonymously as individuals to express their own regret at the behaviour of dominant members of the hall. The Warden tried to improve the hall's image by drawing attention to its good academic as well as its excellent sporting record, and to his own policy of promoting an atmosphere 'tolerant of individual views and attitudes'. Wooltonians became indignant at their own notoriety, especially when they found that guards accompanied by Alsatian dogs had been deployed at Owens Park on the night of the Seventeenth Annual Woolton Commemoration Dinner, to discourage roisterers from running amok.

Although, at the end of the 1970s, about 40 per cent of the student population were living in residences provided by the University and many wished to spend the maximum permitted time in them (generally two of their three undergraduate years), a large number had neither the desire nor the means to hold themselves apart from the people of Manchester. Cheapness and accessibility made the notorious Hulme estate, which lay to the west of the University, increasingly attractive to students. Conceived by Wilson and Womersley, who were also the University's own planners, and built between 1968 and 1971, Hulme had provided over three thousand deck-access homes and fifteen tower blocks. But it had rapidly decayed into an ultra-modern slum, described by *The Architects' Journal* as 'Europe's worst housing stock', and destined to survive for only twenty years. A survey conducted in 1975 showed that almost all Corporation tenants wanted to leave the huge, crescent-shaped blocks of flats, a quarter of a mile in length and six storeys high, which had been grandiosely named after the Georgian architects of London and Bath. Student comment alternated between condemnation of Hulme's disastrous structures and a desire to defend its inhabitants against sensational charges that the neighbourhood was rife with crime.

By the mid-1970s the University itself was leasing flats containing two or three bedrooms in Bentley House, Hulme, and subletting this Corporation property to students, providing them with 'basic minimum durables'. By 1978 students themselves had begun to apply through the Town Hall to rent flats directly from the Corporation through a scheme for 'Joint Lettings for Single Persons'. Estimates that there were soon as many as a thousand Owens and UMIST students living in Hulme were probably exaggerated, but the figure given in 1980 does suggest a student population of about 700. More resilient, agile, and unencumbered by pushchairs, students were happy to occupy the upper levels of the crescents when families were moved out and rehoused on ground floors, and the flats had the great merit of cheapness: rents were very low, and allowed the students far more disposable income than did the halls. The *THES* reported, on the authority of the Director of Estates and Services, that students had a good effect on the area, and that neighbours had begun to welcome their presence.

Attempts at characterising students have usually depended on dubious stereotypes, on images formed around the most vocal, vehement, idealistic, eccentric, and badly behaved. In the 1970s, however, the press, as though baulked of its prey and frustrated at the dearth of good copy, tended to concentrate on the unspectacular qualities of students and their lack of originality. It was probably true that the ultra-left and the devotees of direct action had become more distant from the ordinary student population and that their methods, if not their ideals, were regarded by the majority with greater impatience and distaste. Rises in the cost of living and the failure of student grants to keep up with them induced a hard-headed concern with the practical–material. Few students were utopian. They were not averse to protesting, but protests usually had specific and limited aims, such as preventing the demolition of a still-useful building or adding a few pounds to the Union capitation fee. Once challenged, authority often made conciliatory moves. As witness the Alternative Prospectus and the attention paid by *Mancunion* to certain academic departments, would-be reformers often resorted to adverse publicity rather than disruptive tactics. The welfare services of the Union and co-operative ventures such as the essay bank encouraged students to help each other and the experience of living and surviving in Manchester could provide an education in itself. As James Richardson remembers, 'I learnt how to live on my own. Learnt about renting flats, learnt about landlords, learnt about money, learnt how to spend it, how to be in debt!' Some hall residents and some Raggers maintained the tradition of indulging in licensed student rowdiness rather than gaining worldly wisdom. Others preferred to merge with the city, even to live in its most run-down places, as if, like medieval Franciscans, they were identifying with the most deprived people in society and were distinguished from them not by their worldly goods but by their hope of a better future, their powers of self-expression and their developing skills.

5

The students:
campaigns and causes

Stern critics accused the radical students of the 1970s of trying to carry on the 1960s by the same means. Raucous pickets, disrupted meetings and occupations of administrators' offices still characterised the ritual of protest; squabbles between left-wing factions threatened to drive disillusioned students to vote for Conservative candidates who would run the Union on a tight rein.

But there were original twists in the story of the 1970s. New methods of protest, including refusals to pay unjust fees or rents, drew attention to grievances though seldom got them rectified. New causes, such as the pacifist campaign to get troops out of Northern Ireland, won support. Both provocation and repression adopted new forms. A student pamphlet of 1970 had thrust into the mouth of authority the words:

> 'We'll call out the cops and arrest all you rabble,
> Revolution's a word that's fit only for Scrabble.'

In reality, however, the practice of summoning the police only took hold a few years later, when militant campaigners adopted the new tactic of imprisoning members of the University Council in a vain effort to cow them into selling unethical investments. The University's largest sit-in, of February and March 1970, had been provoked by a denial of free speech, a resort to injunctions to prevent discussion of a subversive motion which might have resulted in a breach of the law. But before long students themselves were forced to consider the limits of free speech, to question the great Voltairean principle 'I disapprove of what you say, but I will defend to the death your right to say it', and to debate the NUS's policy of 'No Platform for Fascists'. Feminist movements added salt and vinegar to the long-running, hitherto peaceful campaign for a day nursery for the children of students and staff. The half-humorous, half-serious ethos of the 1970s found expression in an attempt, half old-fashioned Rag stunt and half principled statement, to subvert *University Challenge*, the popular television programme, in the winter of 1975–76.

The more idealistic campaigns were directed, not at reforming the structure of the University, but rather at raising its moral stature and freeing it from any taint of racism. This was one of five cankers of the commonwealth: others, providing the boo-words of student politics, were bureaucracy, elitism, fascism and sexism. None of these evils was precisely defined. One correspondent complained to *Mancunion* that 'The word "bureaucratic" seems to have a unique meaning in the Manchester dialect. Broadly translated it amounts to "things we don't like".' She might have said the same of the other favourite targets of radical invective. But fascism did begin to take on an exact meaning in the neo-Nazism of the National Front, which seemed (as will appear later) to be gaining a toehold within the University itself, where followers of the far Right were once thought to be as numerous as those of the extreme Left, and once fought with them on the Union steps. At times some left-wing groups seemed equally violent and intolerant of disagreement; the notion of left-wing fascism appeared to be no contradiction in terms.

Left-wing students divided into pragmatic and disciplined groups, such as the Labour Club and the Communists, who wanted results, and the ultra-Left, for whom the struggle was its own end, the effects and consequences being of secondary importance. James Richardson talks of the 'amorphous and disorganised' participation in activities and events of many students who were disinclined to subscribe to any coherent political programme. Libertarianism was a popular philosophy, for it seemed somehow to promise socialism without an intrusive State, individualism free of unbridled competition and market economics (a Libertarian float graced at least one Rag procession, but what it depicted is not recorded).

In the later 1970s there was a surprising and perhaps unprecedented shift in student politics towards the moderate Right. In 1976, and particularly in the Union elections of 1977 and 1978, Conservatives gained ground and eventually won a majority on the Executive. For the Federation of Conservative Students, then in moderate mood, had begun to assert itself in student politics, and *The Sunday Times* reported a recruiting drive in the universities and colleges throughout the country. Evidently Conservative Party strategists believed that by wooing students they could win or make certain of holding many marginal seats in towns where higher education was strongly represented. Manchester Withington was one such constituency. From

1974 to 1987 it was held by a Conservative, Fred Silvester, but his majority was not so robust that it could be taken for granted, and the so-called 'mortar board vote' had a bearing on his political survival.

In 1977 and 1979, a Lecturer in Government, George Moyser, conducted surveys of student opinion which suggested that 92 per cent of students belonged to no political party, and that of those who did 46 per cent were Conservatives, 31 per cent Labour supporters, and 8 per cent Liberal. Seven per cent were Socialists or Communists, and 8 per cent were of the Far Right. Consulted by *Mancunion* when Moyser's results were published in 1981, Geraint Parry, a Professor of Government, thought that they indicated a tendency to hold right-wing opinions rather than a slide into apathy, and that they suggested a 'conscious, hard-headed decision not to get involved' because the chances of influencing Government were pretty remote.

Journalists wrote of the new short-back-and-sides image of students. However freely the locks of men still flowed, the election manifestos of women candidates for Manchester Union offices often carried photographs depicting short, well-maintained hair, high-necked jumpers, and necklaces which at a distance suggested strings of pearls. Not all candidates supported by the Conservatives were themselves Conservatives; indeed, when the 'blue slate' triumphed in the elections of sabbatical officers in 1977, they included a Communist, Andrew Pearmain, whom the student Right preferred to anyone from the ultra-Left. The following year candidates backed by the Federation of Conservative Students won five out of the six sabbatical posts. But by 1979 student politics had reverted to a more conventional pattern. In the succeeding years most executive offices fell, with rare exceptions, to candidates backed by the Labour Club and to Independents, more often of the Left than of the Right, while the Socialist Workers Party and the Revolutionary Communist Party did their best or their worst at General Meetings and proclaimed the virtues of direct action. The prevailing mood in the Union was against the Government, especially one which stood for education cuts and inadequate grants, and could easily be cast in demonic roles. Only in 1983 did the Labour Club give way to a new combination, the Left Alliance, which included Conservatives, the Social Democratic Party, and a Communist.

Throughout the decade the NUS struggled to defend the economic interests of students. Despite its name it was not a trade union, and the universities neither employed nor paid its members. The NUS could not order or even urge its members to withdraw their labour (save by occasionally 'boycotting' lectures in order to attend rallies or demonstrations, and they seldom did that for more than a day at a time). Students could temporarily scupper administrative machinery by occupying offices, mail rooms and telephone exchanges, and cause considerable annoyance and distress to their staff, but the Socialist Workers Party and local action groups were more inclined than the NUS to favour such tactics. If they combined in sufficient numbers, however, students could interfere with a university's cash flow by withholding rents or accommodation fees which they deemed exorbitant and out of gear with the student maintenance grant.

In their less querulous moments, first-degree students from the United Kingdom recognised their own good fortune in enjoying mandatory awards; they knew that grants to students in other forms of further and higher education were not made automatically, but given at the discretion of local education authorities. However, university students criticised the flaws of the current arrangements. Their complaint was that grants failed to keep pace with inflation and that the golden age of 1962, when for once they had been adequate, showed no signs of returning. Should the grant rise, social security payments – the benefits that students were entitled to claim as unemployed persons during vacations – would often be reduced as though in compensation. Furthermore, the system did not release students, although they now became adults at the age of eighteen, from dependence on their parents. Tuition fees were, or came to be, paid out of public moneys; but parents whose disposable income was above a certain modest level were expected to contribute to their children's maintenance, the extent of their contribution being determined by an annual means-test. Married women's grants, treated as a kind of supplementary wage, were related to their husband's income. Should parents fail to make the expected contributions (and they could not be legally compelled to do so), students would live in penury. Even if parents were scrupulous and paid everything required of them, the standard maintenance grant, determined every year by the Department of Education and Science, was not generous. It was feared that parents and husbands, as paymasters, might exert undue influence over choices of course, and that the less liberal among them might refuse to support studies they did not consider useful or rewarding. From time to time the NUS published alarming estimates, generally around 40–50 per cent, of the proportion of parents who failed to pay the proper contribution towards their children's support at university. Sometimes these shortfalls were due to loss of employment or to family break-ups which occurred after the grant had been assessed for the academical year, rather than to parental indifference or bloody-mindedness; the administrative process of adjusting the grant to changed circumstances could be very slow indeed.

One weapon in student hands was the rent strike, aimed immediately against the University, as the landlord of some 40 per cent of students. The objects of such action were both to force the University to reduce rents and hall fees and to persuade it to urge the Government to restore the real value of the maintenance grant. Manchester University's rents and fees seemed inordinately high: league tables and surveys drew unfavourable comparisons with other institutions which seemed to be managing their affairs better and exploiting students less. These parallels, however, were not always genuine. High rents in the new self-catering residences could be traced to the University's need to borrow in order to build them and to service the loans by raising student rents. It was also Manchester's custom to rent its rooms for thirty-eight weeks in the year, allowing all students the use of their rooms in the Christmas and Easter vacations, instead of the thirty weeks charged for elsewhere. Since the University was itself in the grip of inflation, it could keep the fees down only by further subsidising halls from central funds, by reducing the quality of services, or by increasing conference revenue (none of which measures could be expected to appeal to students).

To organise a widespread rent strike proved at first to be an almost impossible task. In 1974 neither a ballot of residents in University property nor a vote of the Senior Students' Council revealed the required level of support. But a prolonged strike did take place in 1981, when organisers called upon students to hold back all the rent due and to pay it into a fund held by the Union. Sitting on a substantial sum of money and placing it on deposit at a modest rate of interest, the Union would then negotiate with the University and attempt to secure a reduction in the rent. The movements of rents and prices were squeezing the student purse. Although the Thatcher administration set out to conquer inflation, it began by forcing prices up; indeed, the Retail Price Index rose by 20 per cent between May 1979 and May 1980 (indirect taxation was increased and subsidies to nationalised industries had come to an end). In the autumn of 1980, it was clear that the fees of the University's catered halls had risen by 26 per cent on the previous year's and those of self-catering flats by 19 per cent, whereas the standard maintenance grant had increased by only 14.85 per cent. Support for a general rent strike grew apace; it began in January 1981 and lasted for about twenty weeks.

According to reports in *Mancunion,* when the strike was at its height in late February about 1,600 students, representing perhaps two-fifths of the University's lodgers, had paid their rent and fees into the Union's nest egg, which then amounted to some £300,000. Collectors went out into halls of an evening to add to the funds. Students clearly feared retaliation – would strikers be allowed another year in University accommodation, or would they be blacklisted? The University promised no rebates and no victimisation, and assured students that it was doing no more than breaking even; leading figures from the Bursar's and Registrar's Departments, speaking at Ashburne and Needham Halls, kept down the temperature by assuring students that no legal action to recover the rent would be taken until the end of the academical year on 19 June. When letters marked 'Personal from the Bursar' arrived at students' homes during the Easter vacation, he was credited with a cunning move to enlist parents as allies. Be that as it might, relatively few students chose to pay their summer term rent to the Union, and dreams of doubling the fund, and bringing it to a total of £600,000, failed to come true.

Early in June, realising that support was flagging, the Union settled its dispute with the University, in return for a joint press statement about the inadequacy of the grant and a promise of very slight fee increases in the following year. It was claimed that they would be the lowest in the country, and bring Manchester into line with other institutions. At 6.0–6.5 per cent they were slightly lower than the increase in grant for 1981–82, which was to be 7 per cent (the NUS had asked for 21 per cent and had not obtained it). In the next few years, rent strikes, or the threat of them, would tend to be local affairs provoked by local conditions, such as the protest against rodent infestation at Whitworth Park which eventually earned the indignant residents a rebate of £10 in March 1984.

To mature and married students and single parents, improved facilities were just as important as adequate grants. For some of them access to higher education depended absolutely on their ability to make inexpensive arrangements for child care; no longer acceptable was the argument that young families and degree courses did not mix, or that students with children were foolishly improvident and living their lives in the wrong order. Few feminist issues were discussed so concretely as the demand for nursery provision by the University. Feminists claimed that in the absence of adequate nurseries women had no chance of escaping what might well be a 'stifling' home and its surroundings, of finding jobs to make ends meet, or of gathering to discuss their own 'material and ideological oppression'. Nor would they have much chance of pursuing a degree.

Nurseries, or the lack of them, had been a controversial subject since 1965. A small Day Nursery, started by the Students' Union, had existed since that year and moved from one temporary home to another. It was now located at the Oxford Wine Bar, a run-down UMIST property on Oxford Road, scheduled for demolition and licensed by the local authority only on the understanding that specially designed premises would in the near future be built. For all its merits the Nursery was neither spacious nor free of charge nor open at all times. In the autumn of 1979 it was licensed to care for thirty infants aged between six months and four-and-a-half years, and was said to have a waiting list of over fifty more. It gave priority to children from split or single-parent families, and preferred postgraduate to undergraduate parents. All parents were subject to a means-test and the fees ranged from £7.50 to £18.50 a week. Since the nursery was designed to serve, not Owens and UMIST alone, but all institutions in the Education Precinct and possibly Salford University and 'other colleges' as well, it fell far short of meeting the demands made upon it.

There had been some progress, however, at least in principle. Discouraging if not hostile at first, the University had eventually recognised the call for a nursery as legitimate. Hence in 1973 the University and UMIST Councils set up a committee to look into the matter under Thomas Kenneth Ross, a Professor of Chemical and later of Corrosion Engineering and an influential figure in UMIST. He and his colleagues recommended planning a permanent building which would provide fifty or sixty places and be erected in the area bounded by Upper Brook Street, Oxford Road, and Booth Street East. Financial difficulties, however, continued to bar the way, and the project's path was never smooth, since it involved three institutions and six agencies, and all were strapped for cash. Progress depended on substantial contributions from the administrations of the University, UMIST, and the Polytechnic, and on smaller sums from their students' unions. Although Owens Union set aside money for the purpose, the other unions cavilled on the grounds that their administrations had a moral obligation to stump up all the necessary cash, without help from the student body.

By 1978 the cries of an increasingly frustrated Nursery Action Group (NAG), were demanding immediate remedies, presenting petitions, falling out with Union officers, and disrupting a Union debate on the future of universities addressed by the Vice-Chancellor.

Exasperated by the low priority assigned to the Day Nursery, members of NAG accused the Vice-Chancellor of lavish spending on 'prestige projects', such as distributing honorary degrees or tarting up the Refectory, when a mere £12,000 would have set up the less glamorous Nursery. They were misinformed about the likely cost, since an estimate of £120,000 would have been nearer the mark. When the group turned their fury on the Polytechnic in the autumn of 1978 and twice occupied its administrative buildings, the constitutional tension within Owens Union recurred: the predominantly Conservative Executive condemned NAG's behaviour as 'undemocratic', after which the first quorate General Meeting of the Union proceeded to support their demands.

Little had been achieved and no promises exacted, but the issue could scarcely be forgotten. Indeed, it dragged on throughout the 1980s, when the Nursery found another temporary home in two classrooms of the Medlock Infants School in Ardwick; these had been suitably converted by the City Council, whose Education Committee made a grant to set against the rent. The greatest progress was made in 1985 by a mixture of self-help and philanthropy. The Zochonis Charitable Trust made a gift of £5,000 in 1985–86 for the benefit of the Day Nursery and offered a further £50,000 to the University 'for the encouragement of the Students' Union, having regard to the responsibility which it currently bore for the management of a Day Nursery for the children of student parents'. Up to £5,000 of the interest on the capital sum would be paid to the Union every year so long as the University Council remained satisfied with the Union's arrangements. At the same time the Union established a 'child care society', which set up in the old Silence and Reading Rooms on its ground floors a day crèche for children not yet of school age run by a mixture of qualified staff and amateur volunteers. The quest for a permanent home for the Day Nursery continued under the aegis of the Committee on Relations between the University and the Students' Union, and the Committee's chairman, Fred Tye, and secretary, David Richardson, took a strong personal interest in the matter. The search ended at last in 1990, when a Scout Hut became available on Dryden Street, to the east of the University, and the University and the Polytechnic (UMIST then had its eyes on a different site) combined to take it over. Responsibility for the Nursery was now leaving the hands of the students' unions, and in 1992 the University Council recommended that the University and the Polytechnic should set up a limited company to manage the enterprise on which they had agreed.

The grants and nursery campaigns and the rent strikes were skirmishes in wars of attrition and were concerned with practical problems
that seemed almost insoluble in the face of stringency. In contrast, the
University Challenge affair of 1975–76 was an isolated occurrence in
which an original protest failed to make its point. This was directed
against 'elitism', one of the *bêtes noires* of the 1970s, but not an easy
abuse to define. It was generally said to involve the selection by unfair
competition of persons who then flaunted their spurious superiority to
other human beings. In this case the elitism was of two kinds: first, the
elitism of the university system in general, which encouraged students
to give themselves airs when in reality they were no brighter or
worthier than the general run of the population, but just lucky to have
been born at the time when post-Robbins expansion was giving them
unprecedented opportunities; second, the elitism within higher education, which not only regarded universities as superior to polytechnics
and other institutions represented in the NUS, but also offered special
advantages to members of the ancient, well endowed, collegiate
universities of Oxford and Cambridge. The great expansion of the
1960s ought surely to have diluted their privileged position, but
the programme appeared to be reinforcing it.

In 1975 *University Challenge* was already a long-running quiz programme, which had originated when the Robbins Report was in the
offing. Based on an American quiz acclaimed as the best television
game of 1962, it had first been broadcast by Granada Television on 21
September of that year. Arguably the programme did universities a
service by presenting their students as keen, wholesome and knowl-
edgeable, eager to entertain viewers with their intellectual rather than
their athletic skills. But members of the Manchester Students' Union
now determined to enter a team and a studio audience who would
make a mockery of the show. Elected by the Union, the team was not
to be chosen for its brains or powers of recall. One member later told
The Daily Telegraph that 'the idea was to get a team of students whose
intelligence was the same as the man in the street'. In practice, however, the Manchester panel consisted, not of average, self-effacing
students, but of persons who had been prominent in Union affairs,
including David Aaronovitch (a champion of NUS) and Anne Bourner
(formerly editor of *Mancunion*).

The team's manifesto, published in November 1975, announced
that 'we don't believe in supporting any form of sham concerning our
wonderful educational system'. They and their supporters criticised
the programme on the grounds that it excluded the polytechnics; that

the questions had an 'arts and classics' bias redolent of an effete and gentlemanly style of education and unrelated to most university courses; and that Oxford and Cambridge colleges dominated the competition. The Union Press Officer pointed out that forty-two universities were eligible to participate in *University Challenge*, and that thirty-two teams actually entered, but that sixteen of these came from Oxford and Cambridge, the rules equating a college of five hundred members with a civic university of ten thousand.

During the studio recording, at the end of November 1975, the Manchester team managed to reinforce the public's sense of the superiority of ancient universities by losing heavily to Downing College Cambridge, giving fatuous answers to questions but failing to explain their objections to the programme. Broadcast in the new year, the fiasco outraged the Manchester public and irritated many students, who thought the team's pointless tactics an exercise in 'how to use the media to alienate favourable public opinion'. David Aaronovitch, now a distinguished journalist, summarises the views of Manchester citizens as 'Here's this bloody great University, stuck in the middle, has eaten up all these streets bit by bit, and you would have thought the least they could do is give us some reason to feel proud of them. And now look at this.'

The team were goaded into self-justification through a belated press release which maintained that 'the contest is only a memory test, and does not involve any reasoning ability', and that 'the programme is based on competition for competition's sake . . . Our society involves too much competition, instead of co-operation'. Both sentiments had a familiar ring. The first had been applied to university examinations in the 1960s, and the second reflected a widely held belief of the 1970s, also found in the schemes for a Union essay bank and attacks on traditional methods of classifying honours degrees. Bob Burchell, later Professor of American Studies, remembers a student arguing in a departmental board meeting in the mid-1970s that it was wrong to distinguish between students, and that classes should be asked to write their essays collectively and all receive the same mark.

For four years the management of *University Challenge* banned teams from the University of Manchester from the contest. But in the autumn of 1979 a student successfully pleaded for their reinstatement and on that occasion the Union officers agreed that a game could just be a game, to be played according to its rules or not at all. They organised trial contests, using old questions, in which the General Secretary, Rod Cox, assumed the role of the suave quizmaster, Bamber Gascoigne, a product of Eton and Magdalene College Cambridge whom he did not otherwise resemble. Thirty-three candidates vied for places on the team, and the 'fearsome foursome' selected by this process entered the contest and did well enough to reach the semi-final. *The New Manchester Review* might well have repeated its comment, 'My, how times have changed.'

Some students collided with opponents less forgiving than the production team of *University Challenge*. Accusations of police brutality at public protests, arbitrary snatching of demonstrators and harsh treatment of arrested persons in police stations began to circulate. *Mancunion* ran the story of one activist, the Communist Soraya Ali, born in Pakistan, a student of physics at the University from 1973 to 1976, and subsequently enrolled at Didsbury College of Education. She was sentenced to eighteen months imprisonment, partly for inflicting actual bodily harm on a policeman who was allegedly trying to take her fingerprints by force after her arrest for carrying a placard proclaiming 'Down with the Monarchy' during a royal visit to Manchester during the Queen's Jubilee Year, 1977. Other students' experiences proved milder, but were still alarming to them. A few played with fire when they supported the British Withdrawal from Northern Ireland Campaign by distributing leaflets addressed to troops serving with the colours. This activity caused hostile policemen to threaten them with charges of conspiracy and even to use the word 'treason' (Pat Arrowsmith, the peace campaigner, had recently received a prison sentence under the almost unused Incitement to Disaffection Act of 1934). Manchester students gave out some of the offending items in Manchester itself, others at Richmond army camp in North Yorkshire. On 13 November 1975 *Mancunion* published the subversive pamphlet in transparent disguise by heading it 'Information for Discontented Lecturers' and substituting 'Lecturer' for 'Soldier' throughout the text. No action against the paper ensued.

The lengthiest and bitterest campaign of the 1970s attempted to unmask the University and members of its Council and Court as collaborators in the exploitative and racist regimes of southern Africa and demanded that they recover their moral authority by selling their unethical investments. The beginnings of the campaign have been described in the previous volume of this *History*. The force which drove it was the all-party South Africa Liberation Society (SALS) and its attacks concentrated on the small group of business and professional men serving on the University Council who were responsible for managing the University's investments. Before the drama began the Chairman of Council and the Treasurer had sold the few shares in the University's portfolio which were in companies 'whose head office and main activities were unquestionably in South Africa'. 'This', writes Sir George Kenyon in a memoir of the time, 'relieved us of a peripheral irritation which would have undoubtedly weakened our case and the stand we took.' But there remained the more complex problem of investments in international concerns which had affiliated companies in South Africa and drew a fraction of their profits from that country. On this point a substantial majority of the University Council (which had a majority of lay members) took the view that it would be impossible to maintain a balanced portfolio and to fulfil their legal obligations as trustees, especially of the pension funds for the University support staff, if they 'sold shares in companies whose profits came overwhelmingly from other sources' than southern Africa. They hastened, however, to recognise a degree of responsibility for the policies of companies in which the University held shares. On the contrary, the lay officers chose to adopt – and here they were in accord with *The Guardian* newspaper – the policy of 'constructive engagement'. This urged them not to sell shares indiscriminately, for it was all too likely that if they did so these holdings would pass to less principled persons indifferent to anything other than commercial motives. Rather, the University should use its influence as a shareholder to persuade the directors of the companies concerned to pay reasonable wages and have proper regard to workers' welfare.

To the impatience of students, who suspected foot-dragging, Council chose in 1973 to await guidance from the forthcoming report of a select committee of politicians: the Trade and Industry Sub-Committee of the Expenditure Committee of the House of Commons, over which William Rodgers presided. Published early in 1974, the Sub-Committee's report referred to evidence taken from 141 concerns which had interests in over 600 subsidiary and associated companies in South Africa. This document spelt out a code of practice which told British firms how to be good employers. They were urged to pay a minimum wage based, not on the so-called Poverty Datum Line (which represented bare subsistence), but rather on the Minimum Effective Level, which was equivalent to about 150 per cent of the Poverty Datum Line. They were also exhorted to pay fair rates for jobs, regardless of the race of the persons who did them. Following these principles, the University Bursar wrote to over sixty companies in which the University had invested, inquiring into their policies. In the absence of satisfactory answers, the University would sell its shares. A list of eight unsatisfactory companies appeared in *Staff Comment* for June 1975. In December 1978 the Bursar spoke of fourteen companies which had been found wanting and of shares sold to the value of £343,000. He then reported that 'Of the 160 companies in which the University currently holds shares, 60 have some interests in South Africa, but in almost all the South African interest accounts for less than 5 per cent of total sales or profits . . . '.

Neither the principles nor the measures adopted impressed SALS and their supporters. They wanted to see a bolder gesture which would free the University from any suggestion that it was profiting from tainted investments. There was no meeting of minds, for, as one officer of the Students' Union explained in January 1975, 'We are not interested in reforming South African wages. We are interested in supporting those forces fighting for real social change – i.e. for majority rule in that country. The influence of British investment works against this. We are not sufficiently naïve as to believe that we can change the role of British investment. We can, however, dissociate ourselves from it. This is the solidarity the African National Congress and other bodies have asked for – as opposed to a "please patronise us poor blacks better and give us more wages" approach. This is the solidarity we intend to give.' SALS, determined as they were to reject anything that savoured of paternalism or palliation, were sometimes criticised for seeing the problem primarily in political terms and failing to give publicity to starvation and malnutrition in South Africa: it was as though they feared awkward questions about the likely effects of withdrawals of investment upon South African working people and their families.

Throughout most of the 1970s officers of the Students' Union gave general support to the aims of SALS and pleaded at intervals for Council to reconsider its policy and agree in principle on a general disposal of shares. They did not suggest that all of these assets should immediately be 'dumped' on the market, but rather that they should be sold over a reasonable stretch of time. The Students' Union itself discovered in 1973 the embarrassing fact that it had investments in six companies with interests in South Africa and that such investments represented 22.7 per cent of the Union's total holdings. On being instructed to sell them, the Union trustees proceeded at a leisurely pace to avoid 'dumping'.

Meanwhile representatives of the Union did what they could to put their case not only to Council but also to Senate and Court and to propose a 'binding referendum' of all the staff of the University and its students on the simple question 'Do you wish shares in companies

with South African interests to be sold?' The Registrar received a similar proposal signed by 118 members of the academic staff. Like a
Renaissance pope repelling requests that he summon a General Council to reform the Church, the authorities stressed the difficulties which
stood in the way. Constitutionally, no referendum could bind Council
to act in a certain manner; it would be hard to formulate questions so
unambiguous that clear deductions could be drawn from the answers;
it would be essential to consult all members of the University, past and
present – in other words, to go to the great trouble and expense of
consulting the 50,000 members of Convocation, who could perhaps
be relied upon, if they bestirred themselves to reply, to provide a
counterweight to the idealistic views of the University's current students. To call upon Convocation to elect a Chancellor was one thing;
to seek its opinion on the University's investment policy was quite
another matter.

Some students had little faith in the process by which their representatives repeatedly argued the same case in the dignified setting of
the Council Chamber and heard it politely refuted yet again by familiar counter-arguments. At intervals strident pickets lined the stairs
leading to the Chamber, claiming mandates from General Meetings of
the Union and rendering themselves impervious to persuasion. Sometimes Council members had to step over recumbent bodies before
assembling to deliberate. In November 1974 pickets rushed the Chamber and succeeded in detaining members of Council for some time
after the Vice-Chancellor unlocked the doors and emerged to ask them
to disperse. Of this and other incidents Sir George Kenyon writes: 'For
some of us who were used to facing strikes on construction sites it was
bearable, but for the majority, whose contact with reality was often
only theoretical, it was another matter . . . Once the door was barred
by three Brunhilde-like Amazons and with plenty of cameras around
there was the chance of the Vice-Chancellor or the Chairman being
snapped in a posture which could be construed as criminal assault.' It
seemed prudent to instal a telephone, concealed behind a panel close
to the Chairman's seat, to enable the Vice-Chancellor to summon assistance should he and his colleagues again be unlawfully imprisoned. A
door in the corner offered an escape route into the adjacent Museum.
To this day some doors in the area are equipped with spy-holes through
which the manoeuvres of besieging forces may be studied from within,
and which serve as reminders of more troubled times.

Convinced of the justice of their cause, in November 1974 student
supporters of SALS combined intimidation with symbolism. Between

a Union General Meeting and a Council meeting they sold 1,500 white polystyrene crosses, each of which stood for a South African child who would die in the twenty-four hours which separated the two events. Purchasers then planted the crosses on the grass plot outside the Williamson Building, opposite the Main Building, and a vigil was kept despite the heavy rain which descended that night. A number of students, estimated at 450 by *Mancunion,* occupied the foyer of the Computer Building for twenty-four hours, allowing the staff access to any rooms they needed. David Aaronovitch remembers that the anarchists involved in the protest proposed sabotage of the University's main computer system, but the demonstrators realised in time that one of the hospitals was linked to it, and wisely concluded that this fist, altogether too big to be used, would destroy sympathy even for a righteous cause.

Rough tactics did not invariably command the support of student representatives on Council. Direct action by a crowd of students in 1975, on the heels of an inquorate Emergency General Meeting of the Union, could claim no authorisation from the Union itself. On 25 November the Vice-Chancellor, the Honorary Officers, three Pro-Vice-Chancellors, the Registrar and several members of Court and Council were lunching in the club for the University support staff, William Kay House, as guests of its committee before the usual post-prandial meeting of Council. These premises almost directly faced the Union across Oxford Road. According to the official note in the Council minutes, a crowd of between fifty and eighty protesters invaded the club between 1.30 and 2 pm and refused to release either the University dignitaries or their hosts. 'Police assistance was requested by telephone from the main University building soon after 2 pm and, after the arrival of substantial police forces, the intruders withdrew and those guests who had been forcibly detained were able to leave at about 2.40 pm' One story, not in the record, relates that the resourceful University Treasurer, Alan Symons, had feigned heart trouble, secured his own release (did the students perhaps remember the porter who had died of a heart attack during a disturbance at the London School of Economics (LSE)?), and used his liberty to call in the law.

False imprisonment of Council members and a large police presence on or near University premises added a new dimension to the struggle. The Vice-Chancellor later denounced the demonstrators to the Senate, calling the incident 'both violent and dangerous'. 'This grave and serious criminal violence was the work of a small number when one considers the size of the University and it was in no way an action of the Student Union.' Fortunately the police made no arrests and the University took no disciplinary action; some students twitted the demonstrators for not getting themselves run in, while others excused them by imagining the astronomical legal costs of defending a large number of accused persons. The limits of repressive tolerance had been established, but the University was able to maintain for the time being its reputation for making no martyrs.

No similar incidents followed; bad publicity seemed a more piercing weapon. At intervals throughout the 1970s the student press attacked five prominent members of the University Council for their personal connections with firms such as Tootal, Viyella, Hill Samuel, Simon Engineering and Barclays Bank, which were believed to have extensive interests in southern Africa. Such tactics were easy to reconcile with the left-wing belief that the University was in the grip of amoral capitalists who, far from acting as its disinterested advisers, were using their power over the institution to further their own ends. At intervals students picketed the nearest branch of Barclays and succeeded in per-suading some customers to withdraw their accounts. Introductory issues of *Mancunion* pointedly abstained from recommending or even describing the bank to freshers, a form of cold-shouldering accorded to no other high street bank – though high-principled students, it was admitted, could only use the Co-operative Bank, the Trustee Savings Bank and the Post Office with a completely clear conscience. George Kenyon, one of those under fire, pointed out to the Vice-Chancellor in 1976 that he himself was receiving no more than £1.05 per annum from South African sources. Tootals, of which he was a director, had increased the wages of African workers by almost 100 per cent between June 1973 and November 1974. Some years later he reflected in his memoirs that 'Whilst chastising me for my non-existent interests in South Africa . . . the opposition ignored my ownership and close management of a factory in Zambia which was highly successful, entirely for the benefit of Zambia and its people, since we received no dividends whatsoever over twenty years.'

From the winter of 1974–75 another strand of student opinion argued that the tactics of 'occupation and mass protest' would only antagonise those members of Council who had not made up their minds. It would be better to strengthen the economic as well as the moral argument by seeking professional advice and preparing an alternative portfolio of shares. 'Futile gestures of occupation are bor-ing, ineffective and studenty. University Council's business-biased membership must be approached with sound business propositions and not emotive rantings.' The psychology was sound and the aim sensible, but the ambition was not realised and the alternative portfolio was never drawn up. In 1979, International Anti-Apartheid Year, the case was still being argued in much the same terms by both sides, one pleading for disinvestment on moral and political grounds, the other for constructive engagement in the interests of 'human dignity and decent living standards'.

Over the next eight years the attack on the University's indirect investments in southern Africa was to lose much of its impetus. Until about 1987, however, moral disapproval dogged Barclays Bank and continued to take the form of picketing local branches, refusing to recommend the bank in *Mancunion*, urging students to move accounts away from it, and declining to accept Barclays Bank cheques. When the bank eventually withdrew its investments from South Africa, student activists congratulated themselves on the success of an NUS campaign, from 1983 to 1985, which had caused Barclays to lose 12,000 students' accounts and reduced its share of the student market from 27 per cent to 17 per cent. For some time an empty Kit-Kat machine languished in the Union foyer. Since the Union had banned Rowntree-Mackintosh confectionery and would not communicate with the machine's owners, there was no way of getting it removed. But the Union Council voted in favour of removing this particular ban early in 1983.

Towards the end of the 1970s forms of racism found closer to home began to divert some of the attention from South Africa. Among them were immigration controls, schemes for voluntary repatriation, and, above all, the rise of the National Front. Discriminatory fees and limitations on the quota of overseas students not only threatened the University's finances but offended against the international sympathies of many students. Much controversy arose over the issue of free speech and how best to deal with the problem of neo-fascists. Should they be allowed to speak in the Union, reveal the barrenness of their own arguments, and show themselves up? Or was there a serious danger that the Union would confer respectability on these movements by giving them a platform, or even that some students might be seduced by their arguments and black, Asian, Jewish and Muslim students be placed at risk? Should persons known to hold fascist opinions or belong to fascist organisations be barred from the Union, even if while on the premises they kept silent about their views? The Union Executive was once criticised for removing Scientology posters from a Union notice board: members, or so it was said, were surely entitled to 'accept or reject viewpoints' without having the job done for them by presumptuous officers.

Serious doubts arose when the NUS adopted a 'No Platform' policy towards 'openly racist or fascist organisations'. Not only were these to be denied financial or other forms of aid, but their members were to be prevented from speaking at institutions of higher or further education 'by whatever means necessary (including disruption of the meeting)'. This resolution did not define racism or fascism, although it did give examples of racist and fascist organisations, including the Monday Club and the National Front. Objectors called it unduly paternalistic, in that it denied fellow students the right to make their own judgements. One side proclaimed that 'It is the duty of us all to kick these people off the streets as they cannot simply be outvoted', the other that 'to deny freedom of speech is itself the beginning of fascism'.

Faced with the National Front a few years later, the Manchester Union imposed its own bans in 1976 and 1977, not without misgivings on the part of many students. In November 1977 the Union solicitor, Rodger Pannone, opined that members of the Union who had joined fascist organisations could not legally be prevented from speaking in the Union for that reason alone, although the chair of the meeting would be entitled to rule racist remarks out of order. Some students held that James Anderton, the Chief Constable of Greater Manchester, and Sir Keith Joseph, when Secretary of State for Trade and Industry, should both be denied the right to speak in the Union – Anderton on account of his alleged disrespect for 'civil liberties or democracy', Joseph because in an earlier speech he had suggested that the children of unfit mothers might contaminate human stock. In the event Sir Keith earned some credit for his moderate reactions to attempts to disrupt a meeting which he addressed in October 1979 – 'You could humiliate me and show me up if you asked me questions.' 'When will the unorganised Left be prepared to argue, not to shout?' demanded an exasperated member of the Labour Club. It might well be said that universities had a particular responsibility to defeat unpopular opinions by engaging their champions in debate and not by shouting them down. Opponents replied that deafening disapproval would attract public attention and advertise the University's moral stance far more effectively than would civilised discussions, 'the professor's sensible whereto and why'.

Between about 1978 and 1980 opposition to the National Front – to meetings in the town halls of Hyde and Bolton, to a broadcast during the General Election campaigns of 1979 – became a central concern of politically conscious members of the Students' Union. But the Front was not merely a force outside the University, threatening the society around it; allegiance to the Front was believed to be swelling like a malignant tumour within the University itself, which was well worth infiltrating, for about 10 per cent of the University's students came from overseas and formed a prime target for its propaganda. At intervals Front supporters distributed leaflets in the self-catering flats at Grosvenor Place, Cornbrook House, Whitworth Park and Oak House. They also ventured into Owens Park, but steered clear of the more closely supervised traditional halls. The Union Education Office even saw fit to suggest that Cornbrook House had become a 'National Front stronghold', to which the Chairman of the Residents' Council replied that it was no more so than other residences, and urged the Union not to discourage Jews and overseas students from seeking accommodation therein. Neo-fascist literature alleged that overseas students were occupying places that ought to go to British students. Such propaganda was described as not only xenophobic, but also 'anti-semitic, anti-black and sexist'.

Mancunion maintained that 'The Front cell working on our campus is one of the most active in the country', and referred to 'a cell of fascists within the University which calls itself the "Manchester University National Front"'. Few people were publicly named, but a second-year law student did attract opprobrium as an 'outspoken racialist' and was said to be, not only a member of the Front, but also the editor of *Phoenix*, the movement's new student broadsheet. Together with a fellow activist, he was charged under the Race Relations Act of 1976 with distributing at a Stockport school a pamphlet allegedly calculated to arouse racial hatred, but the local magistrates acquitted him and his co-defendant. *Mancunion* published a photograph of the student and his well-groomed fiancée, cherubic and jubilant in their moment of triumph. Both subsequently complained of being bullied by left-wingers in one of the Union bars, not for anything they had said on the premises but for the opinions they were known to hold, and the young man announced with a martyred air his resignation from the National Front. Suggestions that the Anti-Nazi League and the Socialist Workers' Party themselves condoned intolerance and violence were often made, and Conservatives argued that the Left's No Platform policy had misguidedly handed the National Front a genuine grievance – denial of free speech – of which to complain.

Labour and Conservative Governments were both accused of promoting 'British Education for the British' in a manner reminiscent of the National Front slogan of 'Britain for the British'. Campaigns against the increasing fees charged to overseas students were conducted partly by OSAG, the Overseas Students Action Group, whose Co-ordinating Committee, designed to promote action throughout the country, was formed at Sheffield in November 1977; partly by the NUS; and partly by the Manchester Students' Union, which created its own Fees Action Group. Terence Ranger, a courageous History professor who had been deported from Rhodesia for openly sympathising with the movement against white rule in that country, joined the Education Officer of UMIST Union to urge in November 1979 that Senate should not merely deplore the Government's fee policy but actively resist it. A Staff Action Group, SAG, was set up the following month to support student protests against fee increases.

Students launched their most sustained and vigorous agitation in the autumn of 1979, in the face of the fees recommended (in effect imposed) by Mrs Thatcher's Government. Protests took familiar forms, entailing surprise occupations of administrative offices and centres of communication, but police involvement was greater than usual and the defiance more sustained and skilful. Demonstrators succeeded in obstructing the main thoroughfare, Oxford Road, by 'occupying' at least one of its pelican crossings. Sympathisers with arrested persons picketed the magistrates' courts. Protesters occupied the main administrative block from 12 to 20 November 1979, and the majority were evicted by police and bailiffs enforcing a court order in the early hours of 20 November. However, as Dr Beswick, then Bursar-elect, remembers, the students concerned had obtained a master key. They had left certain rooms open but locked others, in which some of them lay concealed like Greek warriors in the Trojan horse. As did the citizens of Troy, the searchers fell for the trick and failed to investigate the locked rooms. Their omission enabled the students to recapture the building for a brief, symbolic period.

Overseas students took up a suggestion that they should withhold the part of their fees which they believed to be unjust. Prepared to help those in genuine difficulties, the University administration issued temporary membership cards, allowing, for example, the use of the Library, to 255 students. When these cards were about to expire, there was much agitation in favour of extending them, and much was made of the possibility that students excluded from the University would lose their entitlement to remain in the United Kingdom and would then suffer deportation. But in mid-December, when thirty-seven students had made no contribution to the University's finances, the Senate rejected by 100 votes to 20 a proposal that the temporary cards remain valid until the end of the academical year in June 1980.

Several hundred students initially supported the campaign by voting for it at Union meetings; a vanguard of 50–100 carried out the
occupations and demonstrations. Early in December 1979 an unfortunate incident inflamed the struggle. Three senior figures, the Vice-
Chancellor himself, the Bursar-elect and the Head of Uniformed
Services, apparently came dangerously close to demonstrators – a situation in which it was easy to be compromised. Reports got about that
the Vice-Chancellor had assaulted a student, who, for good measure,
happened to be Osman Kavala, the Union's Overseas Officer. At an
Emergency General Meeting on 3 December the Union resolved to call
for the Vice-Chancellor's resignation and the Union Executive personally delivered a letter to that effect to the Vice-Chancellor himself. On
13 December the Senate expressed overwhelming sympathy and support for the Vice-Chancellor. But on 3 January 1980 Council received
the news that the Vice-Chancellor wished to retire early from his post,
at the end of the following September. It was only to be expected that
Fight the Fees, a fivepenny campaigners' publication, should ascribe his
decision to 'student pressure'. Since student activists had never acknowledged his good qualities as Vice-Chancellor, jibes at his record
were inevitable. But there was also speculation that he had resigned at
least partly because further expansion had now become impossible and
he was not the man to preside over stagnation and decay. In reality Sir
Arthur Armitage was gravely ill with the cancer that was to end his life
four years later.

Attacks on the Vice-Chancellor had drawn together between 500
and 750 students out of Owens's 11,000, but in the new year, as
though emotionally exhausted and bereft of new ideas, the campaign
lost impetus. The Fees Action Group were criticised for failing to exe-
cute Union policy and for taking decisions at 'unpublicised times, and
at meetings with dwindling numbers'. Candidates at the Union elections took their stand on 'applause for or criticism of last term's political activity, the heaviest for many years'. There were few candidates
for office and a low poll. A series of motions against increased fees for
overseas students, proposed by Union officers at Senate, suffered
defeat on 20 March 1980. Disillusionment with politics appeared to
be gripping most parts of the student body.

Much of the militancy of the 1970s had focused on a University which
professed sympathy with students' aims and was almost equally critical
of Government policy. But students had no power to dissuade the
University from acknowledging financial necessity, no means of spurring

it into actions more forceful than protests delivered through the Committee of Vice-Chancellors and Principals to the University Grants Committee or the Secretary of State for Education and Science. Direct action gave its practitioners the satisfaction of having registered their anger and drawn public attention to the wrongs being done by the Government or by commercial and industrial capitalists. Disruptive tactics had sometimes won small concessions, but the more outrageous they became, the more they stiffened the resistance of authority, which could not appear to surrender to anarchy. Political activists were exasperated by the inertia of most students, their opponents incensed by the publicity they gained and by student journalists' failure to pay attention to normal, worthy student activities.

In January 1980, Neil Botfish, the Union Education Officer, defended the tactics of the Fees Action Group by urging Sir George Kenyon, the Chairman of Council, to recognise that 'although people like him create influence when they so much as open their mouths, students, who have an equal stake in education, cannot. If we have to adopt direct action to make our point firmly heard, that only reflects the oligarchic way the University is run, as well as our concern for the future of education.' That same month, addressing the NUS conference in Coventry, Dr Rhodes Boyson, the Minister responsible for higher education, warned that 'Every unpleasant demo., every sit-in disturbing student studies or administrative action, every objectionable incident, every wild exaggeration of a student leader, will inevitably damage not only the image and interests of the hundreds and thousands of students who work conscientiously day-by-day, but also the standing of the universities themselves.' There was reason to think that the universities had few friends among the general public, and would suffer even more if the impression got about that they could not control their young. Student leaders and Conservative politicians thus proclaimed contrasting views about the likely effects of student campaigns, each side, no doubt, believing what it wanted to believe and inviting the public to do the same.

II
The 1980s

6

New direction

By 1980 the University of Manchester was no stranger to sudden reductions in the purchasing power of expected income. Hitherto it had proved possible to deal with cuts by thrift and 'good housekeeping', as Arthur Armitage called the moratoria and other measures he imposed. British universities in the 1970s had appeared to be companions in equal misfortune, in that the UGC had not – at least, not openly – assessed their supposed strengths and weaknesses when it distributed the shrunken parliamentary grants. In the Thatcher years, however, the cuts proved so severe as to demand that universities should alter their character in order to manage their resources with the utmost efficiency. It was as though the Government had decided that the faults in the economy might be mended by mending the universities, and by causing them to concentrate more heavily on engineering, technology and applied science. Universities should not only develop closer links with business and industry, but also imitate business corporations themselves. A more decisive and hierarchical regime should be introduced, and the quest for consensus be abandoned if, given the loquacity and conservatism of academics, it took too long to achieve. Management, once designed to be the least obtrusive of university activities, now promised to become the queen of sciences. Pilloried as inefficient, regarded as (in the new Vice-Chancellor's words) 'hopelessly starry-eyed and unmaterialistic', universities were mentioned with near contempt in the Government's Green Paper of 1985. They were unfavourably compared with the polytechnics, which provided vocational training and helped the economy to run. Judgements on the excellence or mediocrity of universities, now openly pronounced by the UGC, had grave financial consequences and, by stimulating intense competition, set up a kind of Darwinian struggle for limited resources in which the least fit and adaptable institutions seemed unlikely to survive.

Between 1979 and 1981 all the four principal posts in the University's administration changed hands. It seemed as if a new consortium of managers was assembling and preparing to tackle the problems of a much bleaker era. None, however, was a businessman; all had risen to eminence by climbing academic ladders, albeit in a slightly unorthodox manner, and they did not all share the same values. The University advertised simultaneously the two top jobs of Registrar and Bursar, on the retirement of Vincent Knowles, who had held sway as constitutional authority for a quarter of a century, and on that of Geoffrey McComas, the former colonial officer who had been Bursar of UMIST before coming to Owens. Fred Ratcliffe, the passionate book collector, accepted appointment as Librarian of Cambridge University in the spring of 1980. A joint committee of Council and Senate, appointed to search for a new Vice-Chancellor, met and deliberated at intervals between February and August 1980, whilst its chairman, Sir George Kenyon, consulted advisers in such London venues as the Athenaeum and the Oxford and Cambridge Club, and sounded out potential candidates for the job.

Of the quartet appointed to these positions, one had served the University throughout his career. This was Dr Frederic Bakewell Beswick, known to his friends as Bill, who had, he said, applied for the Bursar's job on the understanding that numeracy was not essential and that literacy, while no hindrance, was not actually required. He believed in management with good humour and an open door ('I never ended up a row without telling the other person a funny story', a technique learned from his former mentor, Professor Walter Schlapp) and appealed to Arthur Armitage, who was not the blandest of Vice-Chancellors, as an eccentric but shrewd character rather than a grey administrator. Dr Beswick had been a medical student in Manchester during and after the war and had served in the Senior Training Corps under a sadistic lieutenant and a respected sergeant. On returning from National Service to be a Demonstrator in Physiology while reading for his Fellowship of the Royal College of Surgeons, he abandoned his ambition to become a plastic surgeon, deterred by the long queue of qualified doctors leaving the armed forces and the prospect of waiting till the age of forty to be made a Senior Registrar. Encouraged by Professor Schlapp, he took to research on 'the transmission of messages across nerve junctions and the organisation of reflex pathways'. Deemed to be even better at dealing with complete individuals, he eventually transferred to the office of Executive Dean of the Medical School, who provided continuity, remaining in post whilst elected Deans came and went after a mere three years in authority. It was he who directed one of the largest operations ever undertaken by the University, the tripling in size of the Medical School and the planning, construction and commissioning of the Stopford Building on Oxford Road to accommodate the expanded School. His methods of persuasion were legendary and stories of them gained in the telling, for he had, it seemed, invited a professor to chair the committee which would allocate space in the palatial new quarters by saying, 'It is the sort of thing that is going to cause whoever it is to lose a lot of friends, and since you haven't got many, I thought I'd ask you!'

Dr Beswick's formal qualifications to be a Bursar might have been challenged on the grounds that he was not a qualified accountant. But the Bursar's duty was to sit atop a pyramid of competent and loyal professionals whose expertise ranged from finance to human relations and tackle 'things that came upwards, that the professionals could not resolve, which really became matters of judgement'. In any case his department was famous for housing men and women of unexpected accomplishments and varied interests – it included, for example, Eric Ogden, an accountant and an ordained minister who was also a well-known specialist in the histories of road passenger transport operators and manufacturers, and who published eleven volumes on the subject between 1974 and 1992. Dr Beswick had a good friend in Neil Smith, the manager of the National Westminster Bank in King Street, whose presence in the background was reassuring, although he was not in practice called upon to produce money. Since the Student Health Centre became a target for economies early in 1981, Dr Beswick's medical experience and knowledge of the National Health Service quickly proved relevant to his duties as a Bursar. He was soon blooded: within his purview lay the security arrangements made when protests were launched against overseas students' fees, the subsequent wrangle with the Union about the bill for damage done during a sit-in, and the protracted rent strike of 1981.

Vincent Knowles was succeeded by Ken Kitchen, who had been a Deputy Registrar for eight years. He was an outstanding Politics graduate of Nottingham University who had embarked on postgraduate work at Oxford, exploring the activities of the Local Authority Association and assessing its performance as a pressure group. Later he had spent three years as an assistant professor at Carleton University in Ottawa. Back in England in 1965, he had, like Beswick, abandoned his first choice of career and taken to academic administration at Manchester, fortified with a useful first-hand understanding of the peculiarities of the academic mind. Over the next six years he had risen swiftly from Administrative Assistant to Deputy Registrar. As secretary to the committee which drafted the revised University charter of 1973, and as a contributor to the JCUD, he was close to the heart of authority and power and able to leave his mark on the constitution. Like Vincent Knowles he was a trainer of administrators and indeed educated them in a more formal manner, for he and a colleague organised courses in a number of relevant disciplines (including law, statistics and finance) which helped to transform members of registrars' departments into a distinctive profession within academia. Until the early 1970s they had been good at writing fluent and accurate minutes, at keeping secrets, and at associating on equal terms with academics, laying before committees the information they needed in order to make decisions. In Manchester they were urged to ask themselves every morning: 'I know I'm an evil, but am I a necessary evil?' Inevitably, given the demands of the 1970s and 1980s, they were becoming technocrats; the days when students would go to the Registrar's room for classes in Greek and Latin would soon fade into memory, if not into myth.

Ken Kitchen was to bring to the Registrar's chair the detached outlook of one who was not a native product. More self-effacing than his predecessor, he was a decorous civil servant, reluctant to become assertive in public, but with a reputation for steadiness, keeping the ship's engines pounding away through typhoon and squall, and dealing imperturbably with the fury of aggrieved parties. With characteristic modesty, he would say of his own achievement in the fifteen years from 1979 to his retirement in 1994, 'I've helped the University's administrative system to evolve without radical change which disrupted the morale of staff . . . I tried to use the talents of staff, by moving them around and promoting them and so on, and getting the best out of them. But it's become much harsher since I left . . . '.

Scholar librarians were part of Manchester tradition, for Fred Ratcliffe, following similar principles to those of Vincent Knowles, had appointed as assistant librarians people who could well have become university lecturers. Michael Pegg, formerly Librarian of Birmingham University, succeeded Ratcliffe and took up office on 1 April 1981. A kindly and not obviously military figure, he had served for five years in the Royal Army Education Corps, spending some time at SHAPE, the European military headquarters in Paris, and had taken a doctorate in French Literature at Southampton. Dr Pegg had published in Geneva a scholarly edition of the works of a sixteenth-century poet, *Les divers rapportz* of Eustorg de Beaulieu. His interests as a bibliographer seemed certain to take him away from Manchester, for they lay in the pamphlet literature of the German Reformation and in tracking down his quarry in the libraries of Switzerland, Sweden and Denmark. Before him was a well-appointed new library extension and approval in principle for the establishment of a deposit library in Manchester. But the chances were that the University, unless nagged or wooed by a Librarian of strong personality, combining charm with persistence, would fail to provide the resources to run the Library adequately at a time of dwindling resources. A new Librarian and a new Vice-Chancellor might rebuild the special relationship between Ratcliffe and Armitage, or they might not. This bond had depended on mutual esteem and informal transactions rather than on institutional structures guaranteed to survive the departure of two such forceful characters. 'There's no point in being a Librarian in a university if you haven't got the ear of the Vice-Chancellor and the respect of the Vice-Chancellor' (thus Fred Ratcliffe in a recent interview).

Pessimism prevailed in several quarters when the quest for a new Vice-Chancellor began. Who could want the job of presiding over an unwieldy, fractious institution whose income was at risk and whose estate was being run down through enforced neglect? The new incumbent would not enjoy the powers of a managing director and would have no authority to reform the University unless Senate and Council chose to give it him. Some members of the search committee, which was well provided with present and future lay officers and with Pro-Vice-Chancellors, talked of the masterful style of Michael Edwardes of British Leyland or Ian McGregor of British Steel; but thoughts of importing such figures to Manchester remained in the realm of fantasy. *Mancunion* quoted 'informed sources in the University administration' as predicting that Armitage's successor would be 'someone who will merely administer cutbacks and try to keep the University going in the face of competition for funds between the departments'. Philip Short of UMIST, editor-designate of *Staff Comment*, wrote of the 'curious miasma of disenchantment which hangs over the whole field of higher education', for universities and their students had the love neither of the Government nor of the general public. Scholars and scientists who fancied the job must be ready to ditch their intellectual lives, to devote themselves to endless committee- and paperwork and prickly industrial relations, for even the AUT had joined the Trades Union Congress. 'We need something of an iconoclast', urged Mr Short, 'someone who will not try to resist the changes that will be forced on this and all other universities, but who will anticipate them and mould them to work in our favour.'

Sir George Kenyon's search committee consulted with Convocation, the Students' Union, the AUT, and other associations which represented the 'ancillary' or 'support' staff of the University. They issued an advertisement, six persons applied for the job, and one of them was interviewed but did not get it. As always with senior posts, the committee reserved the right to take the initiative and approach eminent persons whose names had been suggested by advisers and who would not, perhaps, have risked putting in for the job and being rebuffed. In the past, misunderstandings had arisen from the practice of interviewing distinguished people for chairs for which they had never intended to apply. But such blunders were avoided on this occasion; the chairman took soundings before potential takers encountered his committee in full panoply.

Sir George and his hunting party consulted fourteen eminent figures in the academic world, particularly Vice-Chancellors of other universities and Chairmen and former Chairmen of the UGC. No doubt they were alert to any hint that these dignitaries, if not too long in the tooth, might themselves be prepared to move to Manchester. Some sixty names emerged from the trawl, and perhaps twenty were seriously considered. A few leaked out, or were deduced, rightly or wrongly, by intelligent speculation. Among the more likely, or so it seemed, was Sir Geoffrey Allen, the Chairman of the Science Research Council, who as Professor of Chemical Physics in Manchester had developed a close relationship with ICI; another was Bryan Carsberg, a chartered accountant who was still in post as Professor of Accounting in Manchester, although he had been on leave since 1978, acting as Deputy Director of Research at the Financial Accounting Standards Board in the United States, and was about to take up the Arthur Andersen Chair of Accounting at LSE. Both would go on to great things, Allen to be Head of Research at Unilever and Carsberg to be Director-General of Telecommunications. Less plausible was the notion that the committee might approach Shirley Williams, the former Secretary of State for Education and Science, although the idea was debated at three meetings. Certain promising men, already of great influence, nibbled at the bait but were not hooked, for they withdrew before or after interview; the University failed to attract Sir Peter Swinnerton-Dyer, the Master of St Catharine's College, Cambridge, and future Chairman of the UGC, or Sir Henry Chilver, the civil engineer who was Vice-Chancellor of Cranfield Institute of

Technology in Bedfordshire. As Sir George Kenyon recalled in his unpublished memoirs, 'I think we had a good field, but even then it seemed to me that the good men were a little chary and that there were plenty of also-rans looking for a good job for their final ten years.'

Mark Richmond, a Professor of Bacteriology at Bristol University, received an invitation to meet Sir George at his bank in Lombard Street, where he was escorted towards the top of the building by a pink-coated flunkey and saw the pile on the carpet grow thicker at every level until it reached the density of a near-jungle. Richmond was persuaded to throw his hat into the ring and undergo a process which involved meeting one half of the search committee of sixteen at lunch and the other half at dinner before submitting to a formal interview with them all. As an appreciation of Richmond would reveal in 1990, the committee were 'impressed by the clarity of thought and lucidity of expression which in their meetings with him had been combined with great good humour and a relaxed personal manner . . . '. Referees' reports assured them that 'he was not prepared to court easy popularity but was willing and able to take hard decisions'. His was the name that went forward to Senate, Council and Court for acclamation and appointment to the office of Vice-Chancellor, officially until reaching the retiring age of sixty-seven, although he privately agreed with the chairman to serve for about ten years (his age was fifty-one).

The new Vice-Chancellor was a scientist of high reputation, recently elected to the Royal Society and prominent on national committees related to his discipline. His intellectual achievement lay principally in exploring the process by which living organisms built up resistance against antibiotics and in analysing the molecular and sub-molecular machinery which was responsible for cells winning or losing the fight for survival. Bald facts and colourless statements about his career and qualities were soon published. Members of the search committee assured Council and Court that their favoured candidate 'had a great deal of administrative experience at national, and some at university level' (he had been an acting dean at Bristol); that he 'appeared to be very sensitive to the needs of the University's various groups'; that he possessed 'an energetic and attractive personality'. He had served on the National Committee for Microbiology of the United Kingdom; was on the Board of the Public Health Laboratory Services, which had investigated outbreaks of botulism, smallpox and legionnaire's disease; and formed part of a Board of the Department of Education and Science which oversaw all experiments involving the breeding of new strains of genes. His connection with Porton Down, a Government laboratory concerned with chemical and biological warfare, did not go unnoticed; but he explained to *Mancunion* that his duties there were concerned with the sale of scientific expertise to pharmaceutical companies in order to raise funds for research. Of more weight with most people, however, was Richmond's reputed skill in dealing in a straightforward but conciliatory manner with technicians' unions at Bristol University, where his willingness to grapple with difficult problems and reluctance to suffer fools gladly had won him general acclaim. His experience of university administration was not enormous, but this fact might well be pleaded in his favour. Perhaps he would not be unduly respectful of the ponderous processes of university decision-making, but would at the same time tread cautiously across the treacherous terrain which lay before him.

In the late 1940s Mark Richmond had been head prefect of Epsom College, a public school hard by the Derby racecourse, described in novels by Hugh Walpole and Francis Brett Young, which specialised in educating the sons of doctors. As a rarely-sung verse of the school song proclaimed:

In every branch of learning,
In every art we'll shine,
But chiefly here we cherish
The art of medicine.

Though not a medical man himself, he was determined to enlist the life sciences in the service of medical education. He retained, in middle life, something of the stand-no-nonsense manner of a head of house or a National Service subaltern, and occasionally addressed chair committees and even the Senate in the style of one reminding the fifth form that its attitude left much to be desired. The words 'blunt' and 'sharp' were applied to him in equal measure ('very sharp, and didn't mind showing his sharpness'). Richmond's plain speaking contrasted with the language of the last two Vice-Chancellors, who had both been given to judicious pronouncements and sometimes to obfuscation; his unadorned style was designed to persuade members of the University to face unpalatable facts and give direct answers to awkward questions, of which he had a plentiful supply ('Right. You're under threat. What are you going to do about it?' 'Why should somebody else pick up your tab?' 'Why should we give you a lectureship in Elizabethan literature when we're short of lecturers in Geriatric Medicine?'). 'There is no more money' was to be a constant and inescapable refrain. Compelled by the University's penury to be a beast, he aspired none the less to be a just beast, and neither bore grudges against those who opposed him nor sulked on sustaining the occasional minor defeat in Senate. His humour was of an unsubtle, teasing kind – 'Now we pass from the ridiculous to the sublime', he would say as the Standing Committee of Senate moved on from Science to Arts promotions. Many sensed correctly that rejoinders would not be resented ('Ha! The Dean of Medicine. Have you come to grovel?' 'Grovel, Vice-Chancellor? I doubt I know the meaning of the word. Perhaps you will provide me with a dictionary for my enlightenment . . . ').

An unceremonious man without pomposity, Richmond cared little for the trappings of power, and would drive his official Rover down to Didsbury on Saturday mornings to shop with his wife at the famous cheese emporium. Some thought his informality too studied and took it for condescension rather than affability, especially his practices of receiving visitors with his feet on the desk and of welcoming guests at The Firs in his shirtsleeves. Cynical arts academics observed the attitudes of science professors clustered about him in the Common Room, he reclining in his chair, they perched deferentially on the edges of theirs. He made less pretence of impartiality than his predecessors – getting the sciences right, rejuvenating physics and chemistry, and redeeming biology were his main intellectual concerns. Especially to lawyers, who had enjoyed great kindness at the hands of Arthur Armitage, he was the Pharaoh who knew not Joseph and left them strictly alone. Contrary to appearances, however, he was no philistine, but very well read, and would talk of Galileo's trial for heresy or of Castruccio Castracane, the tyrant of late medieval Lucca, to a Dean of Arts who happened to be an Italian historian. He was a fan of the resident professional musicians, the Lindsay String Quartet, and a collector of early Worcester blue and white porcelain. He proved to be a stout defender of the Manchester Museum and the Whitworth Art Gallery when the finances of both were threatened by the demise of the Greater Manchester Council in 1986.

It may be that the events of the 1980s placed the Vice-Chancellor, more than anyone else, in a false position which he bore with stoicism, in that he was obliged to enforce Government policy even while he denounced it, and therefore stand accused of acting as the Government's agent whilst shedding crocodile tears. 'Part of my personal failure there [in Manchester] was that one didn't communicate the fact that things simply couldn't go on as they'd gone before.' 'One was having to play cards that inside oneself one only partly believed in.'

No Vice-Chancellor could form personal friendships with academics, all of whom had, or must be suspected of having, their own interests to pursue. As did his predecessors, Richmond leaned heavily for advice and support on the honorary officers of the University, business and professional people who helped to manage its finances and advised on its practical problems. Among them, too, offices changed hands about 1980 and began to circulate at a brisker pace. The most experienced, Sir George Kenyon, resigned the chair of Council in 1980, but agreed, in the interests of continuity, to serve as Treasurer for a further two years. The chairmanship then passed to Norman Quick, who had been a member of Council for fifteen years and Treasurer for the last five. He was the chairman and managing director of the Quicks Group of garages, Ford dealers, and had been national president of the Motor Agents Association; a considerable figure locally, he was also the founder chairman of Piccadilly Radio. On his resignation in 1983 a committee of Council acknowledged the passing of the old order in which such people had been willing to follow a lengthy *cursus honorum* before taking on the positions of Chairman, Treasurer and Deputy Treasurer and holding them for spells of seven or eight years. The committee now recommended that four years should be 'the maximum term of office for the holder of any one post', and Quick's successor, Donald Redford, who had risen rapidly since joining Court in 1978, duly served from 1983 to 1987. A law graduate of the University of London, he had practised at the Chancery Bar and was now Chairman of the Manchester Ship Canal Company. Quick and Redford were joined in the inner circle by Ronald Brierley, a retired insurance broker, formerly the deputy chairman of Sedgwick UK Ltd., who became Treasurer in 1983. Quick, Redford and Brierley all had distinguished war records, Brierley having served in Special Operations and been awarded both the Military Medal and the Croix de Guerre. John Zochonis, Chairman of Council from 1987 to 1991, was a generous philanthropist who presided over the family firm of Paterson Zochonis, a trading company first established in Sierra Leone in 1879, and now specialising in soaps, toiletries, detergents, proprietary pharmaceuticals, edible oils, and, indeed, refrigerators. He was awarded, in Nigeria, a title which meant 'Hand that does good for all', and his beneficiaries within the University included the Day Nursery, a number of especially enterprising students, and some others who had unexpectedly incurred financial hardship.

Richmond was unable to take up his duties before August 1981, and an interregnum loomed. A senior Pro-Vice-Chancellor, Dennis

Welland, the Professor of American Literature, author of books on Arthur Miller and Mark Twain, founder and editor of *The Journal of American Studies,* agreed to act in his place and pursue a policy of 'Steady as she goes', although it was hardly possible to issue no orders at all. As a retirement eulogy of Professor Welland later put it, 'To hold the fort whilst awaiting a new commander is a task that has little to recommend it. There is little chance to make a major success: there is much opportunity to promote a disaster. Moreover, the storm clouds which were to lead to the downpour of July 1981 were already gathering – though no-one realised how furious the storm was to be.' The regent did, however, find some advantages in so limited a spell of office – no-one could profit by making an enemy of him, and other Vice-Chancellors, sensing no rivalry, proved very helpful. So did senior colleagues in the University, relieved that he, not they, had been landed with the job.

To some the crisis of 1981 was a tempest, to others a drought, caused by the Government restricting the flow of public funding to universities. 'One of the tasks the Government was elected to undertake', explained Mark Carlisle, the Secretary of State for Education and Science, 'was to reduce, where possible, the level of public expenditure and to reduce the burden on industry and the individual. In that position, education, with the amount that it spends, cannot be exempt, and universities, important as they are, cannot be sacrosanct.' The Government was determined 'to ensure that at the end of this exercise we have perhaps a leaner university system but one better oriented to national needs and operating within the context of what the nation can afford'. As his sterner successor, Sir Keith Joseph, put it, the burgeoning public sector, of which the universities formed part, could not be allowed to crush the trading base. Few politicians praised the universities for their responses to the cuts of the 1970s and some suggested that they had foolishly ignored warnings to retrench. Norman Quick, the Chairman of Council of the University of Manchester, urged stoicism and constructive effort: of course the University must contribute to the general sacrifice and strive to promote economic revival. A *Mancunion* journalist interviewed the great Lord Robbins, who had helped to inspire the expansion of the 1960s. He agreed that 'Whilst we have to spend more on defence and the police – as we do – education should rightly bear its share of the savings necessary to beat inflation.' But he objected to the UGC's decision to impose the cuts selectively, and would have preferred to maintain student numbers and tolerate a poorer staff-student ratio. Few could have expected the universities to escape scot-free, but it was soon to be argued – for example, by a Vice-President of the AUT addressing a packed audience in the Roscoe Theatre at Manchester – that they had been singled out for cuts of unparalleled severity, and that no other part of the public sector had suffered as much.

Universities were believed to think well of themselves, even to be insufferably conceited, but there were several reasons to cut them down to size. These included a simple demographic argument: the number of young people reaching the age of eighteen, which was 907,000 in 1981, would peak at 941,000 in 1983 and thereafter decline, going into a steep drop in the 1990s. Interpreting these figures, some commentators spoke of a 30 per cent fall in numbers, whilst others stressed the fact that the figure for 1988 (854,000) would be no lower than that for 1979. On the simple assumption that the main task of universities was to teach school-leavers, there might be good reason to slim universities down eventually, but it seemed perverse to do so before the peak year was reached. However, in the words of Dr Rhodes Boyson, the Parliamentary Under-Secretary for Higher Education, 'At some stage there would have had to be a degree of rationalisation, but the need for curtailing expenditure has speeded that up.' Mark Richmond described the cuts as part of a 'tunnelling-through' operation, the tunnel, it seemed, being ten years long.

Wallis Taylor, a Manchester demographer, criticised the figures for concealing differences in the birth rates for different social classes, and found evidence of only a slight drop in the births into the social classes (I and II) from which about half the entrants to higher education now came. In any case, as defenders of universities now maintained, a fall in the number of younger students was no argument for dismantling machinery built up over many years, because the spare capacity could be profitably used. Certain age groups and social groups had in the past taken all too small a part in higher education – they included mature students, working-class people, and women (who were fighting shy of certain vital subjects such as engineering, and could perhaps be enticed into them). Universities could save the country and themselves through adult and continuing education, by offering part-time degrees and laying on refresher courses for professional people, for teachers, and for those involved in commerce and industry. Learning was a process which ought to continue throughout a person's active life and perhaps into retirement and old age. 'Leisure', as the dean of a Cambridge college had reminded his students, 'is well spent in reading for a degree', and Norman Quick did not fail to make a similar point in Manchester.

Universities were accused of planning badly in the palmy days when money had flowed freely, in that too many had tried to offer too wide a range of courses. They were not supposed to be isolated homesteads, each trying to provide every conceivable subject for the stay-at-home students of its own region, but to be part of a national system within which students could travel in search of the more rarefied disciplines which interested them. During debates in the House of Commons in July 1981 there was talk of language courses which were only half filled, and Dr Boyson spoke of concentrating in 'economic units' and only in certain selected universities a number of minority subjects such as Italian, Norwegian and Portuguese, and even German and Spanish. Dr Keith Hampson, the Member for Ripon, complained of 'an additive policy' whereby 'a whole range of departments – drama, Russian, Chinese and so on – appeared in all universities, and history and the humanities appeared in the technical universities'. During the 1980s Manchester (which had no Chinese Department but one or two sinologists) was to benefit by the policy of concentration, since Arts departments such as Russian, Middle Eastern Studies and Italian were to grow by attracting established academics from other less favoured universities. But this prospect was far from clear in 1981; Derek Latham, then a Reader at Manchester, reflected gloomily on the vulnerability of his own subject, Arabic and Islamic studies, whose strength lay in postgraduates, at a time when universities were 'mainly viewed as institutions for the instruction of undergraduates'.

Universities, it now seemed, had been churning out in excessive numbers the wrong kinds of graduate – the sort who produced nothing except paper and arguments, who cured no physical or mental diseases, and would be most vulnerable to cuts in public spending because they often sought employment in the overgrown public sector. 'We went overboard on the social sciences in the 1960s', observed Elaine Kellett-Bowman, the Member for Lancaster, who confessed to being a sociologist herself. 'Now, rather late in the day, we are realising that business skills must be learnt.' She might well have added that economics and sociology were (at least in Manchester) taught in Business Schools and that accountancy and business finance were (at least in Manchester) located in Faculties of Economic and Social Studies. Studying the humanities now appeared, in the eyes of critics, to be a kind of self-fashioning, almost of self-indulgence, which benefited the individual and not the community. It was important to them that universities should adopt what the Member for Rugby, Mr J.F. Pawsey, called 'a more vocational structure' 'with fewer academic subjects being taught'. Attacked in the 1960s by radical students for being too eager to meet the needs of 'the military-industrial complex', universities were now being accused by the Government of the 1980s of doing too little for business and industry, and even being blamed for their failure. Graduate unemployment was growing in the early 1980s, and the Education Secretary was said to have expressed on television the view that there was no point in students undertaking higher education when there was no demand for them at the end of their courses. Phrases such as 'short-termism' and 'the new vocationalism' came into academic usage to describe the attitudes of the Government and its supporters. One speaker in the Commons alleged that universities were scraping the barrel and admitting hundreds of students on the strength of minimal qualifications, presumably a mere two Es at A-level (it should perhaps have been said that some universities looked for qualities in students that compensated for unimpressive A-level performances, and that some questioned the value of A-levels as predictors of degree results).

Certain kinds of inefficiency could be laid at the doors of universities. Robert Rhodes James, the Conservative Liaison Officer for Further and Higher Education, spoke of their uneven quality: 'We have institutions of learning that are the envy of other nations, and some that are at least in some sectors an acute embarrassment.' Employers, or so he anticipated, would become hostile to the graduates of less famous universities. Manchester had little reason to fear such contempt, but parts of the University were attacked by students for poor teaching and one or two incurred bad publicity. The Department of Geography figured in *The Daily Express* and *The Manchester Evening News* because it had been conscientious enough to distribute questionnaires seeking student opinion on its courses and a first-year student had made the results public, allowing a biased and inaccurate account of the teaching's weaknesses to get into print. One of *Mancunion*'s correspondents wrote: 'I fail to see how providing ammunition for the national Tory press to attack education can help anyone.' Students, however, remained critical of the lack of training for lecturers on how to teach, and of the University's failure to compel new arrivals to take even the short introductory courses provided for them.

Universities could be proud of their record in preparing students for first degrees, with few failures and little dropping out. But they were less successful in persuading research students to complete their theses promptly or even to produce them at all, despite having received grants from the Research Councils; this was to be a matter of great concern during the 1980s, especially in the social sciences. Post-graduates' dilatory performances did not impress Dr Boyson, who had taken his doctorate in four years at LSE while serving as head-master of a large London comprehensive school.

It was widely asserted that universities had lost public sympathy. Their declining popularity was not entirely due to failure to prevent their more restive students from infuriating readers of the *Mail* and the *Telegraph*. Some institutions, it was said, had lost touch with the local communities which had once fostered and been proud of them; they had joined a national rather than regional network and done lit-tle to justify themselves to their neighbours. Others, creations of the late 1950s and 1960s, had never had local roots and their presence was resented.

In the past the University of Manchester had been accused of destroying the community in the streets near Oxford Road which dis-appeared to make way for its new buildings in the 1950s and 1960s, and also of forcing a brash and noisy student village on the people of Fallowfield. It could, however, plead that its extra-mural and adult education classes did much to involve and interest local people; that the Manchester Museum, the Whitworth Art Galley and the Univer-sity Theatre all gave pleasure to Mancunians; that the Open Days held in the 1970s had pulled in friendly and curious crowds, whilst the out-station at Jodrell Bank never failed to attract a flow of visitors; and that, like most universities, it was a major employer of local people. Norman Quick urged the University to address such locally relevant subjects as vandalism and the collapsing Victorian sewers, both, no doubt, splendid subjects for interdisciplinary research, involving everyone from economic historians to civil engineers. Campus trade unions thought the University humane, if not particularly generous with wages. None of these considerations, however, moved local peo-ple to strong protest at the cuts imposed on the University of Man-chester – partly, perhaps, because far worse penalties were about to descend on the University of Salford, and Manchester appeared to have far less cause for complaint.

Politicians determined the extent of the total grant to all universi-ties; the UGC determined its subsequent distribution. Each could blame the other for unpalatable measures. Professor Welland, the Act-ing Vice-Chancellor of 1981–82, sympathised with the UGC but reproached the politicians. In a powerful speech to graduands and their parents, delivered in July 1983, he expressed his concern that the cuts 'were imposed by a Parliament that probably contained, regardless of party, more graduates, and certainly more graduates of universities other than Oxford and Cambridge, than any previous Parliament'. But they had not been moved to challenge 'the doctrine that higher education is only worth spending public money on when times are affluent'.

Certain former Manchester students were powerfully placed in the education world and must, in Professor Welland's eyes, have been guilty parties. Mark Carlisle, the Member for Runcorn and Education Secretary from 1979–81, had graduated in Law from Manchester in 1952, where he had been Chairman of the Conservative Association and of the Federation of Conservative Students. Speaking at the Manchester Students Union in October 1980, Neil Kinnock, the Opposition spokesman for Education, dismissed him as an 'ostrich between the hawks and the doves', 'a man with libertarian instincts thrust into a Cabinet intent on monetarism' and therefore unable to assert real influence. More was to be hoped, or feared, from Carlisle's subordinate, the jovial, outspoken, bewhiskered ex-headmaster Rhodes Boyson, sometimes alleged to have been put in charge of universities in order to keep him away from schools.

Boyson granted an interview to *Mancunion;* a photograph showed him swathed in a Manchester University scarf and seated beneath a reproduction of Van Gogh's 'Sunflowers'. Unlike Carlisle, he was a former socialist who had lost his faith in human perfectability, and his intellectual interests, cultivated with university help, had led him to a new political position. A native of Rossendale, he had taken a first degree in Politics and Modern History at the University as an ex-service student after the War, and had completed in 1960 an MA thesis on the history of the Poor Law in north-east Lancashire from 1834 to 1871. Boyson's biography of the Quaker cotton manufacturer Henry Ashworth, later submitted for a doctorate at LSE, had drawn him towards the ideology of the Manchester manufacturers, early 'free market radicals', who formed the Anti-Corn Law League. He was once described, he recalled in his autobiography, 'as the last man personally converted to the free market and the free society by Richard Cobden. Theses, like ideas and books, have consequences.' A defender of hard work and discipline in schools, and of rigorous academic standards, he had been a natural ally of the Manchester Professor of English, Brian Cox, and a contributor in the 1970s to Cox's and Dyson's provocative *Black Papers on Education.* Boyson hit it off surprisingly well with another prominent Manchester figure, David Aaronovitch, who was national President of the NUS from 1980 to

1982, and aroused his colleagues' suspicion by his cosy relationship with the Minister. Aaronovitch once described Boyson as 'honest, genial and only a little bit patronising'.

When the expected cuts were finally announced in the summer of 1981, Dr Boyson sympathised with universities for the speed at which they now had to make drastic decisions – constitutionally, he recognised, they resembled the co-operative society of which he had once been a director in the Rossendale valley, and had a similar obligation to consult. But the unseemly haste was, in his view, an inevitable consequence of the threatening economic climate, the catalyst for change, and he would say only: 'The Government are aware of the difficulties they have caused.'

Between the Government and the universities stood the University Grants Committee, traditionally supposed to act as a buffer. Sceptics doubted the Committee's independence of Government, since members were appointed by the Secretary of State, but in 1981 almost all of them owed their positions to the Labour administration which was now out of office. The Committee consisted of a Chairman (a former Vice-Chancellor), of fourteen practising university academics, of two heads of schools, of one director of education, and of two businessmen. Nothing obliged them to account to Parliament for their decisions and many critics disliked the institution in principle for its immunity from proper public control.

It fell to Dr Edward Parkes, Chairman since 1978, to deliver to the Committee of Vice-Chancellors and Principals on 24 October 1980 a warning of things to come which was much mulled over in the following months. Parkes was an engineer educated at Cambridge, the author of a book on *Braced Frameworks* and of papers on elasticity, dynamic plasticity, and thermal effects on structures. He had been Professor of Mechanics at Cambridge and a Fellow of Caius between 1965 and 1974, and had then left to be Vice-Chancellor of the City University for four years. By way of bracing the framework of the universities, or perhaps of softening it up, he told their representatives in effect that the system as a whole could retain its autonomy under the UGC even if individual institutions could not. For fear of provoking direct ministerial interventions, they must discipline themselves and heed the UGC's advice concerning the rationalisation of their structures. It would probably be unnecessary to close whole faculties or entire universities, but individual departments might be in grave danger.

Parkes's committee was no trade union, and did not regard the preservation of academic jobs as its main concern. He coined

the phrase 'pallid growths', subsequently much quoted, which presumably referred to the unsuccessful experiments of the 1960s and
1970s, and perhaps to humanities departments struggling to survive
in technological universities. 'The excision of these feeble limbs is
something where the Committee can help, even if it's only to lend you
a financial pruning knife.' No doubt he was offering money to cover
redundancy payments. 'I think it likely that both you and we may wish
to start new departments and to close existing ones, and the latter may
involve litigation.' On no account should universities foster the
impression that they were unable or unwilling to reform themselves –
'I am opposed to mulish opposition to any form of change, based
upon a sterile concept of academic freedom, which may be the surest
way to its destruction.' Headlines such as 'Senate rejects V.-C.'s plan
for redevelopment scheme' or 'University of X will resist UGC to the
death' would do untold harm. The UGC wanted every university to
be good at certain things, but to concentrate on its strengths and not
to shore up its weakest points.

Professor Welland urged the University not to panic and not to
allow departments and faculties to embark on an undignified scram-
ble for dwindling resources. Dr Parkes's pronouncements indicated
the UGC's intention to apply the Government cuts selectively.
Between January and July 1981 increasingly pessimistic predictions
circulated of the likely extent of the cuts in recurrent grant. March
brought prophecies of an average cut for all universities of 15 per
cent, to be spread over the next three years, and these proved to be
near the mark. There were other imponderables beside the parliamentary grant: the loss of income from overseas students' fees, the
extent of inflation and the magnitude of wage and salary awards, the
performance of investments. In June 1981 the JCUD in Manchester
asked the Faculty Development Sub-Committees to consider ways of
making a 3 per cent cut across the board in the University's expenditure for 1981–82. This estimate proved to be far too moderate.

On 1 July the UGC sent two letters to every university, one describing the adjustments to be made to the system as a whole, and the other
informing the individual university how much public revenue it was
about to lose and giving 'advice' as to which subject areas it should
favour and which not. Reductions in income would be accompanied
by smaller reductions in student numbers, especially in the arts,
humanities and social sciences; the UGC was anxious to protect the
unit of resource (the average amount of money spent on each student)
and to prevent it, though it would be diminished, from going into free

fall. The whole system would sustain a grant reduction of 17 per cent over the next three academical years, but the cuts imposed on individual universities would vary between as little as 6 per cent and as much as 44 per cent, Manchester's neighbour, the University of Salford, suffering worst of all. Student numbers, in the whole system, would drop by 5 per cent; Salford was told to cut them by 30 per cent.

Manchester did not think itself an average university, but it was to suffer an average fate. This prospect was alarming enough. It would be necessary to accommodate cuts of 16 per cent in recurrent funding. Calculations suggested that the University would have to save between £3m. and £4m. in the next session alone, even after swallowing up a reserve fund of £500,000 earmarked for new developments. Savings in the coming year must therefore be of the order of 6 per cent, not 3 per cent. Manchester was apparently asked to reduce the number of full-time home and European Community undergraduates by only about 2 per cent over the three lean years. But the baseline used for the calculation was the number registered in 1979–80, and, since the University had overshot its target in 1980–81, the reduction would be nearer to 5 per cent and would have to be made at a time when the national population of student age was rising. Admissions tutors received instructions to honour the offers they had made to all candidates who had achieved the A-level results asked of them, but they were not to indulge near-misses and not to use the UCCA clearing system to make up numbers. The University drew cold comfort from the fact that the UGC had not invited it to close a single course or tried to inveigle it into unwelcome collaboration with any other institution. Indeed, the Committee's advice to Manchester proved to be very general: to 'protect medicine, look after engineering, maintain economics and area studies, reduce the life sciences, downgrade the arts', as Dennis Austin, a Pro-Vice-Chancellor, summarised it in an account of the affair subsequently published in the journal *Government and Opposition*.

Acrimonious debate in the Commons followed the announcement of the UGC's decisions. Neil Kinnock led the attack, denouncing 'economic theories that will burn the seed corn to gain a minute or two of heat'. Several members impugned the honour and competence of the UGC, accusing its members of favouring the institutions at which they taught or had been educated, of succumbing to class prejudices, of betraying gross ignorance of the technological universities which they had scarcely visited. Dr Parkes was to say later that critics were naïve to suppose that the UGC relied wholly or even principally on visits for its information. Its database was packed with up-to-date returns from all but the slackest of universities, although he did admit that the UGC had itself suffered from a staff cut imposed over the last three years, and was unable to make the best use of the material in its hands. It seemed unlikely that Manchester owed its escape from disaster solely to the presence of one of its most distinguished academics, the family lawyer Peter Bromley, on the UGC.

Much public discussion concentrated on the treatment meted out to three technological universities in particular: Aston University Birmingham, Bradford, and, worst of all, Salford. Such measures appeared to fly in the face of the country's need for engineers and scientists, and threatened to destroy the kind of university best equipped to get immediate employment for its graduates. Seemingly, the policies of the Government and the UGC were at loggerheads. It emerged, however, that although the UGC had created that impression by martyring three down-to-earth institutions, it was none the less recommending, within the system as a whole, a shift in the direction of science, engineering, medicine, technology, and business studies. Parliamentary debates offered little comfort to practitioners of the arts and humanities: in hard times, they did not seem to minister to the country's most urgent needs.

Local indignation focused sharply on the fate of Salford. No doubt aware of this, the Manchester authorities chose to concentrate, not on uttering indignant press statements, but on making representations behind the scenes to Members of Parliament and other influential folk. The new Vice-Chancellor was given neither to hysterics nor to histrionics. This cautious approach disappointed many students and senior members of the University, allowing them to think that the University was too compliant towards the Government and the UGC, and even hastening to do the Government's work for it. There was nothing at Manchester corresponding to CAMPUS, the campaign to promote the University of Salford ('If you think education is expensive, try ignorance'). In a speech of studied moderation, Fred Silvester, the Conservative Member for Manchester Withington, urged the House of Commons to look on the situation in Greater Manchester as a whole and conclude that it was not so bad: Owens, UMIST and the Business School were facing soluble problems, even though Salford was encountering quite unreasonable demands. The University of Manchester, he said, 'is a tightly run ship and has cut its costs by 6 per cent during the last four years. No doubt it will manage well. The size of its science and technology departments is being marginally increased. It is clear that it can meet the Government's criteria and that it will emerge an efficient university. It would be difficult to say that it will be better for the exercise, but it will be as good, or perhaps slimmer . . . '. Events would soon indicate whether the University would now become a fleet-footed greyhound which had shed every ounce of superfluous weight, or whether, under the influence of moratoria which blocked the way of young academics and early retirements which disposed of senior ones, it would be transformed into a stout, middle-aged and lethargic Labrador retriever.

7

Contraction, 1981–84

'As you are aware', wrote the Vice-Chancellor to the Chairman of the UGC on 8 February 1982, 'the University of Manchester, as the largest unitary university in the country, has a scale of problems in absolute terms which is not faced by any other similar university.' The arid prose of official communications did little justice to the upheavals of the previous months. It had seemed that the University would be able to escape bankruptcy only by shedding one-seventh of its academic and supporting staff. Figures presented to Senate in November 1981 showed that the University's annual income was now about £60m., and that expenditure, if allowed to continue unchecked, would amount to £64m. and immediately plunge the University into deep debt.

About £12m. of income and expenditure was attributed to 'self-balancing items', where money was given for a specific purpose and the University enjoyed no discretion in using it; these included research projects, payments of local authority rates, and the purchase and maintenance of equipment for the Regional Computer Centre. Exclude those items from the calculation, and 52 per cent of the remaining expenditure was on the salaries of academic staff and of those para-academics who were paid on 'academic-related' scales and enjoyed similar conditions of service (administrators, librarians, accountants, engineers, building officers and so forth). Another 25 per cent went to pay the support staff of the University, with the result that only 23 per cent of expenditure was on matters other than salaries and wages. In some areas of the University, such as the Faculty of Arts, which spent little on equipment and the fuel needed to operate it, salaries and wages accounted for as much as 95 per cent of expenditure.

During the 1970s it had proved possible to make the necessary economies by leaving posts unfilled or suppressing them altogether when their holders resigned or retired. But in 1981 it seemed clear that the unaided efforts of 'natural wastage' would never solve the problems of the University, which would have to encourage voluntary redundancies and perhaps dismiss academic or other staff against their will. Things unthinkable under Armitage began to seem inevitable under Richmond. Impatient of snivelling, reluctant to give false comfort, largely unknown before his first encounter with a Senate which had spent the summer in a state of paranoid inertia, the new Vice-Chancellor gave a misleading impression of lacking humanity. He was forced to promise sweat and tears without the consoling prospect of ultimate victory and appeared to be ignoring the moral difficulties and legal implications of dismissing staff. For many reasons he chose to press forward as rapidly as possible, rejecting proposals to 'wait and see' or tarry awhile in 'maybe land'. Resistance soon mounted, for, as Dennis Austin observed, 'universities are marvellously arranged to oppose but ill-equipped to govern'. The Senate and the faculties might well have been accused of 'mulish opposition' by Dr Parkes, but to their student critics they were nowhere near obstinate enough.

Natural wastage, early retirements and voluntary severance might conceivably make the required savings, but they would operate in a haphazard manner. Unless the University resorted to planned, compulsory redundancies it would be unable to carry out a balanced and rational reduction of its staff. To some senior academics, who knew whom they wanted to dislodge, the prospect of some dismissals was not unwelcome. A few believed that the University had expanded too fast in the 1960s and that too many lecturers of modest ability had obtained secure jobs too easily. Some of these mediocrities, indifferent to promotion, had lived very comfortable lives, in the manner of eighteenth-century clergymen or the 'monks' of Gibbon's Magdalen ('decent easy men, who supinely enjoyed the gifts of the founder'). A few had published little, left administration to the professors, disappeared at the start of the long vacation and resurfaced only in October. That they engaged in research or scholarship was a charitable assumption rather than a proven fact. 'Dear Mr X, we haven't seen you since the Middle Ages', wrote a group of History students on the door of an eccentric medievalist who could never fathom his own teaching timetable; few academics had Mr X's brilliance to compensate for their failings in routine affairs. Even the stoutest defenders of academic jobs would sometimes mutter behind their hands, 'Lot of idle buggers round here'. There was some duplication of effort, departments in different faculties teaching similar courses to small numbers of students, and certain jealous teachers would have liked to be rid of their rivals. A few subjects were so obscure, or so unappealingly presented, as to attract no takers. Some students appeared to gain little from being taught in small groups, to whose discussions they contributed no more than the occasional monosyllable or request to close the window: could they not be left to attend large lecture or examples classes, and to work on their own, thus reducing the need for tutors? Addressing Conservative students, Dr Boyson had pointed out that prestigious American universities, including Harvard and Yale, were capable of operating with a far less favourable staff–student ratio. Where Britain employed on average one member of staff to 9.3 students, the ratio in France was 1:20 and in Italy 1:23.

A large proportion of the academic and academic-related staff had been granted tenure and appointed to the retiring age of sixty-seven. To this rule the principal exceptions were probationers, part-time and temporary lecturers, and researchers engaged on finite projects and employed on contracts of limited duration. Statute XVII in the University's legislative code was not designed to protect academic jobs in all circumstances, but it allowed dismissal only for proven incompetence or grave misconduct, and not on account of financial stringency. On the face of it the University could declare no academic redundant without committing breach of contract and perhaps being sued for unjust discrimination. There seemed to be only three serious possibilities. One was the principle of 'last in, first out', which would deprive the University of the young blood it badly needed. There might be a case for closing down flagging departments with poor students and few publications, which was the remedy apparently uppermost in the mind of Dr Parkes. Or one might concentrate on inducing the most senior people to take early retirement, shelling out for generous benefits to persuade them to leave, but markedly reducing the annual salary bill. Their disappearance from the payroll would provide the quickest route to the 'savings target', a term which quickly invaded the vocabulary of all responsible academics and dominated their thoughts for years to come.

Manchester shared the plight of most British universities. Their representatives hastened to warn the Government of the folly and financial cost of a policy which might well lead to prolonged litigation. Damages for breach of contract and loss of jobs would be assessed in each individual case by the courts; the sums awarded would depend on the extent to which the plaintiffs would be able to secure alternative employment. Hence the Committee of Vice-Chancellors and Principals foresaw 'bitter and divisive battles, in which the least re-employable get the most compensation, while the best get least'. In the

Commons debates of 1981 Opposition Members made high estimates of the probable costs – up to £100,000 in individual cases, a total bill of £200m. or even £250m., since perhaps 3,000 academics would be dismissed. To sack somebody without knowing the cost of one's action seemed the height of folly. If the cuts were inevitable, they should surely be imposed more gradually, over five or six years rather than three: the additional cost would be very little higher, much rancour would be avoided, and the universities would be better equipped to meet the peak of demand from eighteen-year-old students which they expected in 1983.

When the argument was put to Sir Keith Joseph, however, he refused to offer relief; the Government was interested not only in saving money, but also in forcing universities to take painful decisions worthy of tough managers. Snubbing Laurie Sapper, the General Secretary of the AUT, who had joined the chorus in favour of natural wastage, Sir Keith wrote in February 1982 that Sapper was only offering a choice between 'a random, uncontrolled reduction in university staff over a longer period, from which it would take years to recover, and reorganisation over a shorter period which, although faster and tougher than universities would like, it is still within their power to structure and control'. Sir Keith would pay something towards 'restructuring', but his proposed contribution was no more than £50m.

If the Government refused any stay of execution, the University might perhaps borrow against or sell assets in order to extend the period of readjustment. The dangers of depleting its capital were obvious. In November 1981 Senate heard that income from General Fund investments supported about fifty posts which must be protected. The University owned some property which did not produce a regular income, but it would probably prove difficult to sell: it might, like Waterloo Place, be listed as of historical interest, and it might be tied by legal restrictions imposed by charities and trust funds or by other considerations. In the event the University did call upon its reserves, not to prolong the process of adjusting, but to reach the savings target quickly by financing early retirements. As Mark Richmond recalled years later, if the University could 'throw in a lump of money early on, in cash terms, it would have enormously beneficial consequences downstream, because you weren't, as it were, accumulating interest on the debt'.

In the autumn of 1981, however, compulsory redundancies seemed unavoidable; the Professor of Social and Pastoral Theology could only plead for 'corporate compassion' (hitherto not much in evidence) towards the victims, and ask whether cumbersome bodies such as the Senate could ever do more than react to each stage in the 'fast-moving and technical process' of making the University's savings. At the end of September Senate had indeed reacted volubly to the new Vice-Chancellor's unvarnished account of a grim situation. Some members called for an alternative plan that would not involve dismissals, but their motion was defeated by 49 votes to 28. However, opposition gathered momentum in October and November. The five Professors of History, for example, met and quickly concluded that they could have no obligation to help the University to commit breaches of contract. None of their colleagues was incompetent or less than conscientious; there was no reason, therefore, to respond to any request to nominate any of them for dismissal. Inevitably the History Department was accused of merely protecting its own interests, for, since most of its staff were young or middle-aged, it would suffer little if the University relied on natural wastage and early retirements, and other, more elderly departments would lose a great deal. Were the professors lacking in moral fibre, fearful of unpopularity, yielding to the threats being uttered by active members of the AUT, who were prominent in their department? For all this there was a kind of idealism in History's actions, a desire to see law respected and not overridden by the claims of financial necessity, a conviction that imposing redundancies would destroy forever any fragile sense of community that the University had developed. In History and elsewhere the intention was not to refuse to help the University in any way, for people talked of a 'spirit of common self-sacrifice', and discussed the possibility of accepting a salary cut, or foregoing future pay increases, or covenanting sums of money to enable the University to overcome its financial difficulties.

Martin Southwold, a Senior Lecturer in Social Anthropology, put the case well when he argued that entering into contracts of employment for life encouraged academics to develop a life plan that could not be instantly modified – to specialise in 'work for which there is a narrow market' and not to acquire a wider range of skills and qualifications. Financial ruin would be the consequence of dismissal in breach of contract. 'The University which entered into these contracts with them is us. If we now break these contracts, acting as principals or as accessories, we shall have betrayed not only our colleagues but the University itself: we shall have destroyed the principles of honour and trust without which there cannot be a university.'

The task of identifying methods of cutting expenditure rested with the JCUD and its outposts in the faculties. These subordinate bodies, the Faculty Development Sub-Committees (FDSCs), were small and intimate; their members had been nominated from above, effectively by the deans, and had not been chosen by faculty elections. They were not supposed to represent their own departments and were expected to withdraw when these were discussed; their function was to sit in judgement on the claims of departments to resources. The Sub-Committees' name became an irony when they were called upon to administer cuts; they began to attract from their parishioners the same kind of opprobrium as the UGC when the spirit of Christmas was lost and it mutated into the unredeemed Scrooge. Rumours spread to the effect that some of the FDSCs were concentrating on compulsory redundancies, perhaps even drawing up hit-lists; the fact that they were not accountable to faculties, perhaps even prevented from sharing information with them, made for distrust. The deans of the larger faculties were torn, in that they were usually chairmen both of their faculties and of an FDSC: they were therefore required both to represent the faculty and to pronounce judgement upon it to a central university body, the JCUD, which seemed increasingly remote. Much depended on their personal qualities, their tact and skill, and their understanding of the figures fed to them from above.

The Faculty of Economic and Social Studies owed much to its Dean. Sam Moore, a Senior Lecturer in Statistics, who understood the need for exact measurement and distribution of resources, succeeded in uniting his Faculty and earning its gratitude by promptly resolving to take no action that involved compulsory redundancies and also by arguing with the University about the extent of the cuts so convincingly as to get a couple of percentage points knocked off the Faculty's bill.

Suspicion and ill-feeling ran higher in the Faculty of Arts, which was famous for being the most argumentative in the University. It was now one of the most insecure. The Dean, Professor Brian Rodgers, a geographer, was greeted at one meeting with groans of disbelief by a Faculty which made no show of deference. He bore them patiently. In the interests of goodwill he offered the Faculty a summary of his FDSC's seven-page report to the centre, but the Faculty, which suspected heavy editing, resolved that 'The Faculty Board finds the report of the FDSC, as summarised, unacceptable, and wishes to dissociate itself from it.' Professor Welland, the former Acting Vice-Chancellor, scolded members like a disappointed headmaster for their distrust of higher authority, warning them that such ungracious behaviour could only bring redundancies nearer. Unrepentant, the Faculty breathed new life into its own policy and planning committee, which was chaired by another geographer, Peter Lloyd, and gave advice – which the FDSC was not constitutionally obliged to follow – on ways of achieving the savings. It would be possible, for example, not to fill the expensive chairs of professors who took early retirement: many lecturers and senior lecturers were now well able to administer departments, and the 'iconic figure' of the professor could be shelved for the time being in the interests of economy.

It was not clear how far the FDSCs were expected to make judgements on the ability of individuals and the quality of departments, or whether they were to concern themselves only with such matters as the number of academics approaching retirement age. The officers of the Faculty of Science inquired into the number and quality of applications to departments, the proportion of good degrees awarded, and the career prospects of graduates, thereby applying some of the criteria which the UGC had supposedly used in its assessments of universities. Since the timetable was tight, it was the Dean, the former Dean and the Dean-elect, a body even smaller than the FDSC, who conducted the business. In the words of Jack Zussman, the geologist who had the dubious privilege of being the Dean of Science, 'we took it all into account, and we added it up, and we gave it weightings, and came up with a pecking order in the Faculty, and it was resented terrifically.' 'The atmosphere between departments and people in different disciplines became very difficult, competitive, alarmed, anxious . . . '

In November 1981 the Science Board passed by 93 votes to 17 with 5 abstentions, two resolutions. The first lamented the fact that the Deans had not presented the report for discussion to Faculty members, either in full or in summary form, although the Board also acknowledged 'that constitutional arrangements presently inhibit such discussion', and called for 'urgent changes in these arrangements so as to permit the widest possible debate within the Faculty of all submissions and developments within the FDSC'. The second resolution declared it premature to make detailed proposals for percentage cuts within departments. But the Dean's extraordinary patience came to be appreciated in time; an account of Jack Zussman's work, presented to Senate on his retirement in 1989, was to declare that 'Only a man of Jack's special temperament could have undertaken these onerous duties without ever raising his voice or showing displeasure.' Similar constitutional resolutions were passed by the Arts Faculty and by the Assembly and forwarded to Senate and Council: they called for new arrangements which would oblige the Sub-committees to share information and recommendations in a spirit of total candour, concealing only personal details, and which would make them more broadly representative of Faculty opinion.

Random reductions of staff, dependent on what the Science Faculty called 'Nature's path', would probably preserve the University as a community and save it from litigation. But they would make the institution less effective in teaching and research. Harmful imbalance would develop because vacancies tended to occur most frequently in the areas which the Government and the UGC were most anxious to protect. Turnover was very high in clinical medicine, very low in arts, and academics in such disciplines as computer science, engineering and accountancy might well be able to find more lucrative jobs outside the University. The UGC therefore warned of the undesirable consequences of a general moratorium, for the practice of freezing every post as it fell vacant would damage highly valued sectors of the University such as the Faculty of Medicine, where many jobs were held for short spells by fledgeling doctors completing their training. Even where posts were not to be suppressed, it took time to fill vacancies, and the University benefited at the Faculty's expense from the stretches of time when it was not paying salaries and not functioning at full volume. Professor P.O. Yates complained publicly in March 1982 that 'this University Department of Pathology has already lost, because of the hold-up of reappointments, seven out of its ten qualified staff and 50 per cent of all laboratory workers. So much for the UGC request for the protection of clinical departments from its cuts.'

Vacancies in a Law Faculty caused no distress to patients, whatever they did to legal education; law teachers were often qualified barristers or solicitors, willing to enter or return to practice if their university prospects were not bright enough. Law at Manchester succeeded in shedding the four posts required of it when three lawyers moved into practice and one took early retirement. There was likely to be an awkward period of transition to a professional appointment, involving some retraining. Hence, in December 1981, the Law Faculty asked the Senate to consider a scheme, involving cash settlements and opportunities for part-time teaching, which would tide ex-academic lawyers over the hard times when they had no supporting income.

Early retirements furnished the most civilised alternative to compulsory redundancies, and the terms offered were generous. Pensions, and the lump sums payable on retirement, naturally depended on the number of years served, up to a maximum of forty. By way of 'dangling the gold' (as Dr Beswick has put it), the University offered to purchase extra years of service for those willing to leave. They could also be tempted by opportunities for part-time teaching, a source of extra income over the years before a state retirement pension began to flow in. Furthermore, the University proposed to award them honorary fellowships for periods of up to three years, lest the break with the institution prove too abrupt. Even so, it was hard to believe that many of the early retirements were wholly voluntary: few senior academics were sufficiently stubborn or egotistical to ignore the moral pressure to leave in order to protect the jobs of younger folk. However, as Ken Kitchen remembers, many 'could see how the university world was changing away from what they'd always enjoyed, and they didn't want to be a part of it'. It was also true that pensions were better protected against inflation than were academic salaries, which had fared badly during the 1970s and were under threat again.

Now called upon to act as an academic personnel officer, the Registrar wrote to all academics approaching or passing the age of sixty. By early November 1981 he had interviewed fifty-five interested parties and was extending the operation to everyone over fifty-five; his personal interest was widely appreciated. Some help could be expected from public funds, but the University was improving on the benefits likely to come through the UGC and establishing an Enhanced Premature Retirement Compensation Scheme by calling upon its own resources. It was possible to refuse permission to retire early on these terms by invoking management interest, usually for the protection of small departments which would collapse if key figures left. But in the bleak winter of 1981–82, there was a strong presumption that almost any early retirement would be in the management interest, although it sometimes proved, on this and other occasions in the future, too costly to buy out certain senior people in the field of clinical medicine.

Early in February 1982 the University, as the rules required, notified the UGC of the number of posts at all levels which would be lost by early retirement and other means. The teaching and research staff, estimated at 1,369 in 1981–82, would be reduced by 17 per cent to 1,136 in 1983–84, and the academic-related staff would fall by 15.4 per cent, from 363 to 307. One hundred and twenty-seven posts would be lost by early retirements, which were described to the UGC as redundancies: eighty-seven from the academic staff, and another forty from their academic-related colleagues. The remaining jobs would be lost by 'normal wastage', by resignations and retirements in the fullness of time. As Mike Buckley remembers: 'we were one of the few universities to get through a deal which I used to describe as winning the pools and the lottery all on the same day. The first lot who went, not only got their pensions made up to the full forty years, but they got a year's salary on top, tax free . . . That got knocked on the head, very rapidly, but where you'd already committed yourself to paying [before 5 February 1982] you were allowed to do it. But there were lots of problems, because one of the conditions of it was that you had to get Statutory Redundancy Pay for them, from the Social Fund or whatever it is, so that that reduced the UGC's commitment, and a lot of people strongly objected to letters saying "You've been made redundant", because they thought they were taking voluntary retirement, which they regarded as an entirely different thing. We had a lot of hassle with people objecting very strongly to the wording of the letter. But the wording of the letters had to be that which would enable us to claim the Statutory Redundancy back, because the money we got from the UGC was the compensation, less what you're going to get for Statutory Redundancy.'

The eventual cost of the early retirements was about £3.4m., of which the UGC covered about £2m. and the University about £1.4m. Approximately three-quarters of the scheme's beneficiaries were to leave full-time employment in the University on 30 September 1982, and most of the remainder on 30 September 1983. In November 1982, Senate received twenty-six resolutions of thanks to retiring professors, compared with nine in 1981 and eight in 1980; in November 1983 there were twelve, and the following year eleven. Some of those resolutions betrayed a sense that an era was passing, that there would no longer be room for gentleman scholars such as Donald Cardwell, the Professor of the History of Science, based at UMIST, whose motto had been that 'if a story is worth telling it is worth embroidering', and who had, 'in an age of fierce pressure stemming from financial stress', 'provided a clear reminder of the crucial need for the retention of the more traditional qualities and values of a university'. As David Pailin, the Professor of the Philosophy of Religion, remarked some years later, 'I've felt at times that the colonels have taken early retirement and the corporals have taken over', some academics of no great eminence having been elevated into promotional chairs to take their places. Barbed rumours also suggested that the scholars had moved out and the accountants had moved in. Whatever the justice of this comment, it was true that the random effects of early retirements were potentially disastrous for some areas of the University, including the modern language departments, which found themselves for a time almost wholly deprived of professors. To the Arts Faculty radicals this might be no bad thing, but it had a sorry effect on morale and on the standing of the departments concerned.

The support staff of the University were to fall by just under 15 per cent, from 2,183 in 1981–82 to 1,857 in 1983–84. Overall, the University's staff, both academic and supporting, would shrink from 3,915 to 3,300 (down 15.7 per cent); one hundred and twenty-seven posts would go through early retirement under the terms approved by the UGC, 488 by natural wastage. In July 1981 Council had pronounced it wrong to make disproportionate cuts in non-academic areas where the staff were not protected by tenure; secretaries, technicians and other highly skilled workers were just as essential to the running of departments, and sometimes to their safety, as were many academics. Retirement came to a number of senior cleaners, some of whom, now in their sixties and seventies, were among the most efficient. In October 1981 the Catering Officer bade farewell to fourteen members of his staff, now held to be of retirement age; they had notched up between them 206 years of service to the University, the senior being Mrs L. Nicholson, who had forty-four years behind her. Student journalists, taking up the cause, feared that many jobs would be lost in the catering department of Owens Park. The kitchen equipment in the student village was becoming obsolete and it was believed that rather than replace it the University intended to convert the Park into self-catering flats and pay off its loyal workers. When nothing came of this threat it was soon replaced by another – that the University might turn the catering over to a private company and that this concern would enhance its profits by cutting jobs. In the University Library the turnover among counter assistants was rapid and jobs became easy to suppress; it seemed, in February 1982, that twenty-nine posts were to go, that services to readers would suffer, and that it might now take a week to return books to the shelves.

Tough negotiations proceeded with the most indispensable workers, the technicians. In October 1981 officers of ASTMS were understandably envious of the more generous terms being offered to tenured academic staff, and well aware that their own pensions (dependent on the University of Manchester Superannuation Scheme started in 1925) were less well protected against inflation. However, as Ian Cameron, then Personnel Officer, remembers, there was a difference between the public and private attitudes of the local branch officers, who personally regarded the terms as favourable and signed up for early retirement without withdrawing their public objections. In June 1982 Mr J. Kay, of the Department of Physics, one of only three glassblowers in the University, chided ASTMS for its obduracy, which might well force the University to resort to compulsory redundancies. In reply Mr A. Dawson, of Metallurgy, put the union's case, and wrote of its duty to get the best possible deal for those who remained behind to 'pick up the pieces'. For 'the frozen posts would be lost forever, and a slow assimilation of extra duties without pay will occur'. 'We cannot accept voluntary redundancy unless we are fully involved in monitoring redeployment and retraining. The University uses words like consultation, co-operation, mutual agreement, etc., [only] in so far as it suits them', and Manchester attitudes were said to compare poorly with those of the management at Salford and UMIST. In the words of Harry Kent, who was then Deputy Bursar in charge of Personnel, 'half the technicians in Physics were sixty, and if they were going five years early, how would Physics continue? Because it's not really very conceivable to switch a technician from Engineering to Physics, although that's what the University thought you could do!' Perhaps the early retirements, by clearing paths to promotion, brought some advantages to those who remained to do the extra work. Trouble with the campus unions lay ahead, however, for the financial constraints upon the University were soon to prevent it from continuing to honour national pay agreements, as it had done in the past.

By December 1981, with the early retirement scheme coming to the rescue, most academics felt an ignoble sense of relief. A document known as the Green Book, drafted by the Deputy Registrar Douglas Porter for JCUD, Senate and Council, assured them that 'JCUD believed that a major and radical restructuring of the academic shape of the University was not required', but that 'some limited changes in the academic activities of the University were inevitable'. University teachers might congratulate themselves on staving off compulsory redundancies, but the officers of the Students' Union and some student activists were unimpressed by their performance. During the 1970s home students had scarcely noticed the Government cuts in University funding. They had demonstrated against discriminatory fees, but had deplored the injustice to overseas students rather than the effect on university finance. Now, in 1981, the cuts were impinging on all undergraduates and postgraduates. Students in Economic and Social Studies saw weekly tutorials in econometrics and sociology reduced to fortnightly events (large examples classes, they protested, were no substitute), while the opening hours of the Faculty Library were curtailed. All students' welfare suffered when jobs in the University Health Service were suppressed. Potential students younger than themselves, with equally strong qualifications, would soon be denied university places. As a writer in *Mancunion* put it, students had changed from 'the cream of the system' into its 'rancid milk' and had become 'the discarded milk bottle outside No. 10'. Student leaders now believed that the University authorities were failing to resist educational damage except by mouthing insincere and ineffectual protests. To fight by rustling papers was not enough. By preparing to enforce the cuts, even by discussing them, by doing anything other than denying their existence, universities appeared to be shooting themselves in the feet. Even the AUT, it seemed, thought only of stretching the cuts over five years rather than three. The policy committee in Arts, mocked one of the Faculty's student representatives, 'thought that what Sir Keith was doing was economic and educational nonsense but they also thought that they had better help him to do it'. His headline in *Mancunion* ran: 'AUT 10 – Education 0. Education Relegated'.

Some students sensed that the cuts were not just a temporary measure for managing an economic crisis. They interpreted them as part of a concerted attack on the independence of universities, which the Government believed to be centres of criticism and dissent, and as a fatal blow to the principles of the Robbins Report. But students' solution to the problem – ignore the cuts, reject the UGC's advice, protest and carry on as before – appealed to few academics, for most knew that inaction would bankrupt the University, and that no-one, least of all the next generation of students, would benefit from that catastrophe. A policy of 'waiting for Lefty', of hoping for a change of Government at the next election, carried obvious risks, for the Labour Governments of the 1970s had not been generous to higher education. Students might well have argued that the University should refuse to lower its student intake, thereby allowing the staff–student ratio to deteriorate, but making a little extra money from fees. However, in their reluctance to let conditions get worse, the students did not pursue this idea consistently, and might not have won if they had, for there were threats of financial penalties on universities which stepped out of line.

Diana Mitlin, the Union Education Officer, pleaded at Senate with the candidates for early retirement, begging them not to go. Other students proposed more spirited tactics: let the University demand the resignation of the UGC; let it refuse to carry out research for Government agencies or departments; let it imitate the University of Southampton and, by way of protest, award no honorary degrees. But the Vice-Chancellor told the Students' Union in February 1982 that 'the Government was prepared to go down with flags flying' and 'the more steam you give them the more they stand up for their own actions'. No gestures of defiance, in his opinion, would carry any weight with such a self-confident body.

Rituals, rallies and direct action none the less remained on the cards. In December 1981 students staged a mock funeral, processing round the precinct and bearing shoulder-high the coffin of British Education. A Cuts Collective formed in the Union and resolved to picket Senate, assailing the ears of members with a chant of 'Fight! Fight! Fight!' as they assembled to discuss the 'notorious Green Book' which stood for capitulation to a hated Government. Early in 1982 the Collective forced the University to abandon two meetings of Senate and one of Council. On 15 January students invaded the Senate and forced it to suspend its deliberations, and several days later a picket, said by *Mancunion* to be 300-strong, blocked the entrances to prevent Senate from meeting at all. Students further expressed their feelings by occupying for two days the first floor of the main administrative building and using it for 'holding meetings, producing leaflets and issuing press releases'. However, on Monday 1 February, the Senate succeeded in getting together, the police clearing a passage for members as students tried to block their path and were yanked out of the way by hefty constables. The Vice-Chancellor and some colleagues had taken the precaution of slipping into the Council Chamber an hour before the advertised time of the meeting. One student was charged with assaulting the police, but subsequently escaped with a light fine and costs; two others, according to the student newspaper, received hospital treatment for concussion sustained in the melée, and a third had an epileptic fit after being knocked down by a policeman. Frustrated, the students again occupied part of the main block while Senate was in session; receiving the news in the Council Chamber, the Vice-Chancellor cut the protest down to size, saying 'Now I can't get my raincoat.'

Student occupations annoyed some campus unions, because they created 'hazardous' working conditions and threatened to interfere with the payment of wages (though students disclaimed any intention to do so, and called the suggestion that they might a piece of black propaganda). Neither the AUT nor NALGO (the clerical workers' union) would back the occupation, and they reproved the occupiers for 'disrupting services provided to the whole University community'. Other unions, NUPE, AUEW and especially ASTMS, were said, however, to be more sympathetic. The University obtained a possession order, naming three officers of the Students' Union and banning the students from occupying any building on the campus. Having no stomach for further defiance, the students ended the occupation. Once the University had accepted the cuts, militancy lacked an immediate goal and began to subside, though demonstrations were held in November 1982 when a UGC sub-committee visited the Mathematics Department. Even the Union Education Officer admitted that, with graduate unemployment running at 15 per cent and still rising, the Government was unlikely to agree to more generous funding of higher education.

At least one student journalist believed that the campaign against the cuts was winning less support from students in Manchester than in other universities. Writing in May 1982, Matthew Richardson complained of the extremism which the Cuts Collective had begun to display towards the end of the spring term: 'some of its meetings were more reminiscent of a mobilisation committee for the socialist revolution than a group trying to organise a campaign against *education* cuts', and it seemed like 'an extremist group dedicated to bringing about the downfall of the Conservative Government at any cost', an aim not generally shared. Student activists were disappointed at their failure to attract the attention of the national press; but since they were saying what they might be expected to say, and doing so in a predictable manner, they were not very newsworthy. For all the protests of students anxious to defend the interests of their successors, the total number of full-time students at Owens was to descend from 11,493 in 1980–81 to 11,070 in 1984–85, the proportion of postgraduates rising a little and that of overseas students falling.

As Mark Richmond observed years later, a 'negative resource flow', even a small haemorrhage, causes decision-making to gravitate towards the centre of an organisation, 'and everyone starts to protect their own power . . . the system is going to shrink a bit, and you'll be darned sure, particularly if you're a dean and given the job, you're not going to have your bit shrink'. The centre of power in the University, in so far as one could be identified, was now the supreme resource committee, the JCUD. In times of prosperity the only problem was 'How to queue the things you're going to do'; in times of contraction, the question could only be 'What can we claw out of here?' Since the activities of JCUD's sub-committees had roused suspicion during the first phase of the crisis, Senate in the summer of 1982 approved proposals to make them more democratic. They were to include *ex officio*, nominated and elected elements, the chairman to suggest the balance between them in the light of the local situation, but the JCUD to approve the proposed arrangements. When the Arts group went too far and took advantage of the loose wording to request an elected majority at the Faculty's suggestion, JCUD rejected the proposal, one member saying that he would have no confidence in anything put forward by such a body. Since democracy was often associated with delay if not with obstructionism, money and democracy were expected to mix only up to a point; but the FDSCs were urged to consult with Faculty Boards and endeavour to dispel suspicion.

The JCUD itself was to consist of the Vice-Chancellor as Chairman, the Pro-Vice-Chancellors, three honorary officers (the Chairman of Council and the Treasurer and Deputy Treasurer), and one student on the recommendation of the Council of the Students' Union. The Senate was to elect four members from its own ranks – two from its *ex officio* members, most of whom were professors, and two from its elected members. Deans, though in theory part of the machinery of JCUD, since they chaired its sub-committees, were cast in the role of supplicants. Supposed to know their own bailiwicks and advise on their needs without exaggeration, they had the power to agonise over priorities, but could do little without the centre's permission. An inquisitorial atmosphere prevailed when they attended the JCUD; hanging about in the corridor outside the Senate Committee Room like fags at the door of the prefects' den, they were offered no waiting room in which to cool their heels and read over their papers. The University was not prepared to give faculty groups devolved budgets and tell them to manage them as they chose without committing the crime of asking for more.

The Vice-Chancellor and his advisers, particularly Douglas Porter, strove to formulate comprehensible rules for the administration of resources. The main principle was that JCUD would assign 'savings targets' to faculties, and that only when they had exceeded these by a certain margin would funds become available to them for new appointments. At first the overall target for the whole University was a saving of 16 per cent, to be achieved within three years, but the burden was unevenly distributed and was related to the number of students which faculties were allowed to absorb. Since Arts was called upon to cut its numbers most severely, it was required to save almost 19 per cent; 15.8 per cent was expected of Science, 12 per cent of Clinical Medicine and Dentistry. Lest anyone put it about that the bureaucrats were getting off lightly, the administrative offices were asked to save 18 per cent.

In July 1982 the overall target was reduced to 13 per cent, for the UGC had been more generous than expected, income from overseas students' fees had fallen less steeply than pessimists had predicted, and investments had performed better than many had feared. Generally the policy was to save hard so that the University could pass the targets and start to rebuild, rather than spend profusely and retrench only when insolvency drew nigh. The rules did not allow the University simply to fill posts vacated by persons whose early retirement the UGC had helped to finance: since the UGC was supposed to have raided its purse in order to make possible some kind of beneficial reorganisation, it was necessary to claim that new posts differed from old. When the Bursar, Dr Beswick, and the Director of Building Services, Mr Crosby, took early retirement in 1983–84, a reorganisation of duties followed: the office of Bursar disappeared for the rest of the century, and a Director of Finance and a Director of Estates and Services rose up in the Bursar's place.

Professor Richmond looked with detachment on the University and was not overawed by its reputation. All the signs were that, at least in the sciences, it was losing its former eminence. 'The physics-based subjects were still pretty good, but they really weren't of the same quality and calibre as they had been twenty years before.' Physics and chemistry needed rejuvenation; engineering departments, in his view, did much the same as their counterparts in UMIST; biology, his own subject, was sadly in need of an overhaul. The University had suffered from the migration of many of its brightest academics to older or newer rivals, and now had difficulty in persuading high-fliers to move from south to north. Given the relative costs of housing, a move from London to Manchester would improve one's standard of living, but there would be little prospect of getting back again. As one of Engels's correspondents had written, 'I would rather be hanged in London than die a natural death in Manchester.' One rare triumph, bucking the prevailing trend, was the appointment to a Physics chair in 1984 of Professor Michael Hart, FRS, who had been for eight years the Wheatstone Professor at King's College London. No doubt the nearby Science and Engineering Research Council (SERC) laboratory at Daresbury in Cheshire played some part in his decision to come north.

The Government could not ignore the unintended consequences of its policies: arts folk sitting tight if not pretty; science and engineering losing stars to careers outside universities; a middle-aged spread caused by the retirement of older scholars and a dearth of posts for young entrants, who could only hope for temporary jobs. These evils it now proposed to remedy, positively by financing a small number of posts for youngish lecturers in favoured disciplines, and negatively, by undermining tenure, which had inhibited rational planning.

Between 1982 and 1985 universities were invited to compete for a total of nearly 150 new posts in information technology and almost 800, called New Blood posts, in all other subjects (with a bias towards science, medicine and technology). The Research Councils and the UGC judged the competitions, in which Manchester, framing its bids skilfully and exploiting its good reputation in several fields, did well. The Science Faculty won twenty-two posts (including five in Physics, with one in Radio Astronomy, three in Chemistry, and three in Mathematics); the Faculty of Medicine three; and other faculties six between them. New Blood posts were confined to applicants under the age of thirty-five, were primarily intended to promote research, and did not attract additional students. Those in information technology, of which the University secured eight, had stronger links with teaching as well as research and generally carried an additional load of ten students each. Successful departments such as Physics scarcely felt the cuts. Basking in Government favour, Computer Science was caught up in the ambitious Advanced Information Technology Programme, designed to involve universities and industrial concerns, based at the Department of Trade and Industry, and known as the Alvey Programme. A process of tipping the balance towards science and technology appeared to be taking hold, although it crept rather than galloped, and the University's intention, as stated in November 1981, was only to shift the Arts to Science ratio from about 48:52 in 1980–81 to 47:53 in 1983–84. Alarm and hostility arose, however, in October 1983, when the UGC invited the University to accept a number of extra students in technical and vocational subjects without extra resources; though uneasy about principle and precedent, the University agreed to accept on these terms twenty extra students in engineering, five in social studies, and five in arts.

Conscious of being poorly valued by Government and society, fearful that the University might become an inferior British imitation of the Massachusetts Institute of Technology, the Arts departments began to formulate a reasoned defence of the humanities and to issue warnings against too crude a notion of what was useful to the country. Useful activities, they argued, were not just those that added to the gross national product; culture was not just a luxury to be afforded only in prosperous times. The History Department joined colleagues in thirty other universities in signing a widely circulated letter which proclaimed that 'History is an intellectual training in distinguishing relevant material, in evaluating an argument, and in presenting a logical case. Society cannot live by inventions alone . . . It is a vital part of universities' wider function to help create a society that values reasoned debate, analytical rigour, and intellectual originality . . . History is of *use* as a defence against the misuse of history. The clearest and most critical understanding of the past is crucial, as we confront a complex and difficult present.' Dennis Welland, addressing the Arts graduands of 1983, attacked the 'new philistinism' embodied in a tasteless advertisement issued by the Equal Opportunities Commission. The Commission's object, to attract girls into careers in science, might be laudable, but it was insulting to describe a woman arts graduate as 'Another dead end kid'. ' . . . what kind of insular arrogance or myopia is it that sees no constructive role in a modern European business and exporting society for graduates with the expert knowledge of foreign languages or foreign lands that most of you have acquired during your time here?' The Faculties of Arts, Music and Theology commissioned their most formidable campaigner, Professor Brian Cox of the English Department, to prepare a document on 'Universities and the Arts'. This spirited piece attacked the new vocationalism and emphasised, among much else, the low cost of producing arts graduates.

Perhaps agreeing that pure or fundamental science might soon be attacked for not being immediately useful, the Vice-Chancellor endorsed the case, as did Senate and Council. Richmond assured the Dean of Arts that he did not want Arts to languish, and took a personal interest in the filling of a chair in French, when funds for it became available. He could not, however, fail to remind the University that measures which in effect compelled Science and Medicine to subsidise Arts would be contrary to Government policy.

The notion of tenure and the concept of academic freedom went hand in hand. Tenure, it was often said, enabled academics to speak and write as they found and protected them from dismissal for expressing honest opinions which conflicted with some orthodoxy subscribed to by powerful people. It was also designed to give academics the security and confidence to undertake a major, even a life work, and not simply concentrate on small enterprises which gave immediate results, resulting in a steady flow of forgettable articles but no monumental books. Like most human institutions, both tenure and academic freedom could become corrupt, especially if they were invoked to resist any kind of accountability and used, as a student once complained in print, to defend incompetent lecturing. Arguably, one could distinguish in principle between dismissal for stating heterodox views and dismissal on account of an institution's financial difficulties; Sir Keith Joseph thought it unsporting to invoke academic freedom in defence of individual jobs. Abolition of tenure, however, might well make it easier for the Government or its agents to shut down departments not regarded as useful, and to do so on the grounds that there was no money to support them in hard times.

In 1981 the Committee of Vice-Chancellors and Principals agreed that in future, academics' contracts of employment might have to be drawn up on different lines. Sir Keith Joseph, in 1982, talked of amending university statutes in order to allow institutions to declare academics redundant without incurring the legal complications anticipated the previous summer. Even champions of tenure in Manchester had to concede that the procedures for granting it were not rigorous. They depended upon small sectional committees of professors who gathered in intimate conclave and nodded each other's cases through, for fear of retaliation from colleagues if they made themselves awkward; only those who had candidates for tenure in a particular year bothered to turn up to meetings. Bent on making tenure more defensible, Senate agreed in principle to lengthen the period of probation: it would now be possible to require new lecturers to serve for a fourth probationary year or even longer before the University decided whether to make them permanent or throw them out. Sectional committees were discharged; departments were required to paint more detailed portraits of their candidates; responsibility for granting tenure passed to Faculty Review Committees and ultimately to the Standing Committee of Senate. Lecturers were now supposed to show firm promise, by 'work, commitment and enterprise', of continuing to develop in their professional fields. For new arrivals, the retirement age fell from sixty-seven to sixty-five, but this arrangement did not apply retrospectively to existing contracts.

No such defensive measures prevented the Secretary of State from attacking tenure. He accepted the need for 'reasonable security and continuity of employment', but not the argument that 'academics should be guaranteed continued employment until retiring age, no matter how the circumstances of their university change'. There was no proposal to alter existing contracts, but rather to perform a messy act by creating, as the national President of the AUT complained, a second class of young university teachers who would not enjoy tenure. In the summer of 1984 the new Chairman of the UGC, Sir Peter Swinnerton-Dyer, warned the AUT that its battle to preserve tenure would never end in victory, and that if it fought to the death and lost it would have no say in the arrangements which replaced this important contractual right. Since the universities had themselves taken no drastic action, legislation seemed unavoidable. Senate debated the matter in July 1984 and some speakers pressed the case for a robust defence of tenure and resistance to the Government's mounting intrusions into university affairs. It proved impossible to carry a motion refusing co-operation with the moves initiated by the Secretary of State (this was defeated by 41 votes to 29), but the question of defining and defending academic freedom, which could perhaps be separated from the defence of cast-iron tenure, was referred to the Standing Committee of Senate.

Within the University there were moves to extend rather than diminish security of employment, particularly for the benefit of researchers on short-term contracts in the Faculties of Medicine and Science. Their position was becoming doubly precarious as the supply of lectureships dried up, and they longed for established posts and a recognised career structure. They now had their own professional body, ARMS, the Association of Researchers in Medicine and Science. Their local branch chairman, Dr Allison Keys, in the Department of Surgery, wrote in July 1983 that the previous year the Faculty of Medicine had contained 122 full-time and 12 part-time research staff on short-term appointments, together with 45 technicians who were similarly placed. In their quest for security they sought membership of the Assembly for those who could be regarded as comparable with university lecturers, and this status would have entitled them to the protection of Statute XVII, which governed tenure. By July 1984 the discussions were becoming increasingly complicated, because they raised legal and constitutional questions about the Senate's authority under the Charter to extend membership of the Assembly.

By the summer of 1982 the immediate crisis had passed and many academics were elated by the camaraderie they had discovered through thumbing their noses in unison at higher authority and suspecting it of evil designs. But a long and often dismal process of patching and mending, dependent on makeshift arrangements and large numbers of temporary and part-time appointments, had now to begin.

Applicants for promotion to senior lectureships were among the first to feel the pinch. They found that the path before them, once broad and smooth, had become a defile strewn with sharp rocks and for some almost impassable. Where posts were supported by the UGC (as were almost all posts outside the National Health Service), a distribution of 40 per cent senior to 60 per cent junior staff had to be maintained.

Since 1974 many junior posts had been lost, and the situation worsened when the recent moratorium prevented young people from getting potentially permanent jobs. With fewer juniors around, and the age structure top-heavy, fewer grants of seniority could be made. In 1980 and again in 1981 it had proved possible to make twenty-one promotions in the areas to which the ratio applied, and sixteen followed in 1982. But in each of the next two years the number dropped to eight, and partial recovery came only in 1985, with thirteen promotions: these made only a slight impression, however, on a lengthening backlog of deserving cases. The process became a fierce competition; it was all too possible for a candidate to reach the notional standard for promotion for three years running and still not be preferred to a senior lectureship. Standing Committee of Senate, meeting for two or three days in bleak January weather and sometimes becoming almost comatose, struggled with the task of distinguishing between academics in different walks of life and penetrating the vapours arising from the eulogistic prose of numerous external referees. These pundits, to their exasperation, found themselves being approached year after year and asked to write further letters as their favoured candidates failed to get professional advancement.

Salary problems became increasingly thorny. The University's finances suffered from so-called 'incremental drift', the increasing bill from an ageing workforce which was moving up the salary scales, with few resignations or retirements of senior staff now in prospect. Recurrent grants to universities made very modest allowances for pay and salary increases. In the face of such parsimony, the AUT and other unions had every reason to urge Vice-Chancellors to be more generous. They argued that should the heads of universities fail to improve their annual pay offers they would soon be unable to recruit staff of the right calibre to the few jobs they were able to advertise. But high salary settlements were not covered by the Secretary of State, and it was not clear where or how the money could be found to meet them, as University cupboards grew increasingly bare.

Illusions that financial trials were over soon evaporated; the Universities were not moving into what Churchill had once called 'broad, sunlit uplands'. Axes would not again fall so suddenly and cut so deeply at a single stroke, but a process of attrition was about to begin. By the autumn of 1983 it was clear that the Government intended to require further savings of 1.5 per cent per annum up to the end of the decade and beyond. Recurrent grants, though increased in cash terms, would fall below the estimated level of inflation. Should the inflation curve prove flatter than expected, money would very likely be 'clawed back'.

In 1983–84 the UGC, now under Swinnerton-Dyer's chairmanship, circulated a lengthy questionnaire which could in principle be answered by any individual and any institution in the world of university education. The central question, though not expressly stated, was unmistakable: how would you cope with further cuts? In March 1984 the University's response to Swinnerton-Dyer included the estimate that continued cuts, at the rate of 1–2 per cent per student per annum, would cause a monetary loss of 15.6 per cent by 1995 and a fall in the number of academic posts of 325, or more than 25 per cent of the current establishment. One of the questions raised the possibility of shutting down flagging universities. Fearing that they might be tricked into appearing to approve of closures, the Senate chose not to answer it. By majority vote, however, the Council insisted on doing so, and advised that 'In the unhappy event that closures had to occur, the process should be concluded quickly on advice from a specially constituted body independent of Government and the UGC.'

The University was later to be criticised for its failure to adopt radical solutions. By choosing not to reduce the bill for salaries more drastically, it made it impossible to spend enough money on its fabric and otherwise maintain its property. As Dennis Austin wrote in 1982 in his account of the cuts and their impact, 'All the early talk of redundancies and lean greyhounds was simply moonshine alongside the plain fact that the University was not prepared to have them.' 'It will, I fear, confirm the drift towards mediocrity. By choosing early retirement we have deprived ourselves of the elderly and we have not replaced them with the intelligent young . . . There is no movement now of scholars between universities and a diminishing scholarly interest within each university.' Perhaps the University had taken a soft line to avoid crippling unpleasantness and a breakdown of trust, but it was not alone in doing so; indeed, no tenured university academic suffered compulsory redundancy until 1988, when Edgar Page, a Lecturer in Philosophy at Hull, declined early retirement at the age of fifty-seven and provided a test case.

Events at UMIST demonstrated the strength of the opposition which would face a manager who too ruthlessly pursued a radical academic plan. Here the Principal, Robert Haszeldine, facing deeper cuts than did his colleagues in Oxford Road, produced 'a snapshot of a slimmer UMIST' and tried to introduce policies 'based upon stepwise restructuring for the future, with discriminating assignment of resource to reflect academic quality and national need'. At one point his plan proposed cuts on individual departments which would vary between 3 per cent and 38 per cent and average out at 24 per cent overall. But the political and diplomatic skills which would have made the measures acceptable appeared to be wholly lacking. Professor Cardwell, of the History of Science and Technology, learned of proposals to close his department only by reading about them in a circular addressed to all academic staff. Assurances that the proposals were not 'encased in granite' did little good. Growing opposition to the Principal resulted in votes of no confidence; evidence of loose financial controls, extravagance and other irregularities came to light and eventually made his position untenable. Complaining of 'character assassination', the Principal announced in June 1982 his own decision to take early retirement. He was succeeded, first temporarily and then permanently, by the Deputy Principal, Professor Harold Hankins, whose great gift was not to appear to be leading, but to allow his colleagues to think that the initiative was wholly theirs, whereas in fact they were being imperceptibly nudged in a certain direction for the good of the institution. Though cast at first in the role of Gerald Ford after Watergate, Professor Hankins proved to be far more than a stopgap Principal, and led UMIST for thirteen years with conspicuous success.

Amid the troubles of the 1980s, Manchester had remained a Broad Church, or, as upbeat jargon had it, a 'dynamic, full-service university'. The labour force might be thinner, but the structure was no less sprawling, for few enterprises had closed down. A rare exception was the Centre for Urban and Regional Research in the Faculty of Arts, founded in 1967 but abandoned on the early retirement of its director; it had failed to attract income by means of research grants and its Consultancy Research account was almost £20,000 in the red.

Outside the walls, however, a grimmer fate overtook institutions associated with the University but more cruelly exposed to the cutting winds which blew from the Department of Education and Science. The post-war School of Education, which conferred under the University's aegis the Teacher's Certificate and the Bachelor of Education degree, was virtually dismantled in the early 1980s and the University's regional influence reduced. Demographic arguments, manpower planning, and rationalisation all contributed to the process. Recruitment to secondary schools now appeared to be falling, and a recent increase in the birth rate suggested a shift of emphasis to primary school teaching. The DES was bent on concentrating virtually all teacher training in the area at the Polytechnic, which was overseen not by the University but by the Council for National Academic Awards. These measures weakened the only remaining Catholic college in the strongly Catholic Manchester region, De La Salle College at Hopwood Hall in Middleton, although it continued for the time being to offer other advanced courses. Senate and Council reflected that 'the University would be prevented from performing a service to the region in which it had taken great pride and which the region greatly valued'. Now its relationship with the colleges would shrink to 'a minimal role in respect of the Bolton Institute of Higher Education and to one course at Stockport College of Technology'.

In the near future institutions would still be affiliated to the University, but they were generally in the fields of medical care and nursing rather than teacher training. The Northern College of Chiropody at Salford Technical College and the School of Physiotherapy at the Manchester Royal Infirmary both affiliated in 1985; the Institute of Advanced Nursing Education of the Royal College of Nursing was affiliated, initially for five years, from October 1987, to enable it to offer part-time courses which would lead to the degrees of BA in Nursing Education and BSc. in Nursing Studies. The term 'School of Education', which had once denoted the teachers' training colleges affiliated to the University, was from 1989 officially applied to the Faculty of Education within it. Future influence over the region was to be exercised in a different way, partly through developing connections with industrial firms, particularly in the fields of high technology in which the University excelled.

8

Enterprise and economy

Cuts in public spending forced universities to devise schemes for self-help which would reduce their dependence on public money. Some academics murmured of 'going private', but it was seldom clear what they had in mind; perhaps they dreamed of some English parallel to Ivy League universities, small, select and well groomed, supported by massive fees and the donations of prosperous alumni (a body which the University of Manchester had hitherto failed to cultivate as a source of support).

The University was again forced to adopt a host of economy measures, some of them seemingly trivial, and puritans began to attack minor extravagances as grave lapses of discipline. On the other hand the University had to think of selling its services and of collaborating, not only with public institutions and Government departments, but also with industrial and commercial concerns. Its purpose in doing so was not just to raise money, but to demonstrate its usefulness to society and the economy, to win friends and restore itself to favour; it was important not to get involved in contract or consultancy work which would increase income but have no academic value, or produce results which might be used for intellectually dishonest or nefarious purposes. The University had to consider methods of increasing fee income, for example by pulling in the overseas students who were obliged to pay the full costs of their courses and had therefore become an important financial asset. Modular part-time degrees, enabling mature students to work at any pace they chose and accumulate the necessary credits over several years, would provide alternatives to the intensive courses which traditionally turned out young graduates. The Extra-Mural Department made ready to instruct almost everyone in the mysteries of computing, offering courses on 'The Micro and the GP', 'Packages for Dairy Farmers', 'Small Businesses and Micros' and so forth. More prosaically, it was vital to make University residences earn money all the year round, by accommodating conferences and even families on holiday, lest the property become unused plant, left empty and unprofitable for up to twenty weeks in every year.

Some economy campaigns, particularly the appeal to save electricity, raised echoes of the 1970s. Wiser now, the Communications Office designed no pin-ups, but hammered out the slogan 'Save Energy, Save Money, Save Jobs'; designed a surreal drawing of electric plugs and flexes strangling the campus; reminded everyone that the University spent £2m. a year on energy; and issued admonitory stickers to be stuck on light switches. Helpful suggestions were made, which involved removing covers from fluorescent tubes to make them give more light and taking lifts out of service. Sticking plaster sealing the doors of one of the shafts to the south of the Arts Building served as a symbol of the new austerity.

But there were many reasons why consumption should increase, especially in science departments. New plants for liquid helium and liquid nitrogen had been installed in the Chemistry and Physics Buildings, and the Stopford Building was a constant drain on the University's resources. Not all news was bad; the Computer Board granted £90,000 towards the cost of electricity consumed in the Computer Building in 1982. However, the new Library extension increased the Library's bill by 332 per cent. When the University's engineers, as always, suspected the use of illicit electric fires, they were tartly advised by members of the Bursar's Department that the electric typewriters and word processors spreading through the Main Building were more likely to be the culprits, and these machines could hardly be outlawed. Halls of Residence, which could plead no such excuses, had for a time a bad record, and it was never easy to persuade them to save.

Incentives and methods were much discussed. Make departments and buildings pay their own bills, or let them be credited with a proportion of any savings they made. Convert oil-fired boilers to coal, at high initial cost but with some prospect of long-term economies. There was little evidence that huge savings would be possible, for consumers soon became blasé and careless, and, as Harry Cameron has put it, great 'sourness and worry' sprang from the cuts falling on 'a massive campus'. University engineers could never in conscience abstain from doing things vital to safety, such as maintaining the substations. The Building Committee was empowered to shut down a building if the need arose.

Minutiae bulked large and extravagance on stationery and postage was condemned. Economy envelopes must be used for all internal communications, fine white ones were banned, and all but the most urgent outside letters must go by second-class post. This regime had the disadvantage that when envelopes all became equally unprepossessing they ceased to offer clues as to the importance of their contents. Hence many academics, finding administrative chores doubly distasteful in the threatening climate, were tempted to consign them unopened to the wastepaper bin. An ill-worded directive advised: 'There is little point in sending a thesis by registered mail as this service is designed primarily for objects of some value.' One meeting of the Arts Faculty became obsessed, to its Dean's exasperation, with the royal blue carpet being laid outside the door of the Council Chamber – dispense with carpets, proclaimed one speaker after another, and there would be more jobs for lecturers. Some nostrils flared angrily at the smell of fresh paint in the Stopford Building; its decoration, at a cost of a quarter of a million pounds, did not seem justifiable in the midst of financial crisis. Mr Crosby, the Director of Building Services, assured critics that the painters had switched from a five-year to a seven-year cycle. Years of deepening dinginess, however, could lead to poor morale as well as damaging the fabric. 'It's all so *dirty*!' cried a fastidious young woman up for interview in the Arts Building one Wednesday afternoon. No doubt she took her custom elsewhere.

Social events, any suggestion of pomp or frivolity, became candidates for the guillotine. Their abolition, however, would be bad for public relations. On 5 May 1982 the Queen came to open the new Library Extension (which had been in operation for several months) and, as had her mother in 1951, received a copy of H.B. Charlton's *Portrait of a University,* now a memorial to a vanished world. Hers was the first visit to the University by a reigning sovereign, but not everyone was impressed. A disloyal subject in the Bursar's Department suggested that Ms Diana Dors or Dame Edna Everage, who had at least written books, would have done the job 'just as nicely and at a fraction of the cost'. The officers of the Students' Union became confused. The Executive wanted to invite Her Majesty by letter to cancel her visit and, as the University's Visitor, to inquire 'as to the University's future intentions as regards the Library'; but some dissenters thought that, as professed republicans, they could not do so, because their letter would implicitly recognise the Queen as Head of State. The royal visit went ahead, unchallenged.

Two University journals disappeared from circulation. *Staff Comment* was now twenty years old and had been in the 1960s a lively grumbling magazine, publishing the splendid 'Letters of Lemuel', a Swiftian satire on the University. But it had been flagging for some time and failing to attract the three editors, one from Arts, one from Science and one from UMIST, who were thought desirable. Its humour had become forced, its journalism earnest, its readership increasingly bored. A bacteriologist called it a waste of time and taxpayers' money. A member of the Government Department exhorted: 'Set a good example, end production of your appalling comic. Its continued existence is a monument to ecological savagery and puerile inanity.' Thirty-eight correspondents wrote in the journal's favour, but their support was not enough to save it. It had lost some of its thunder to *Communication*, the features magazine of the Communications Office. This too was to go.

There was, however, more need to justify the University's decisions and report its achievements than ever before. The task fell to *This Week*, the cheaply produced house magazine, which took on some of the duties of the defunct journals. It explained the University's position on most matters and expounded the complexities of its finances with as light a touch as possible. Sometimes, as its mood swung from gloomy to cheery, it was taxed with unseemly jocularity. Correspondents accused it of playing down the parlous state of the Library, of reporting the Vice-Chancellor's remarks at Senate but not those of the opposition, and on one occasion of insensitive gloating over the gains made by a controversial sale of valuable books. But it was prepared to publish correspondence criticising the University's policies and to provide a forum, as *Staff Comment* had done, for complaints about inadequate parking arrangements, the malfunctioning of the telephone system, or the University's failure to cover the cost of running the Senior Common Room and provide it with portering and window cleaning. The convention that creditable news should appear in *This Week* and scandal in *Mancunion* (not always strictly adhered to) served the community reasonably well.

Could the University, in hard times, continue to subsidise institutions such as the Whitworth Art Gallery, the Manchester Museum, the University Theatre and the University Press, or should they be treated as ballast which could be thrown out to increase the buoyancy of the balloon? All of them enhanced the University's reputation, and the Press carried the University's name abroad. Although it had committed the offence of losing money, it could claim to be the third largest university press in the country and one of the oldest. Defenders of the arts argued that the UGC had allowed for all these institutions when calculating the unit costs for Manchester students – as Professor Cox explains it, 'you'd give more for a student at Manchester than you did at Hull, because Manchester has to support an art gallery, it has to support a museum . . . and it's got the University Press, it's also got departments which are far more expensive, like Medicine, it's a very complicated argument. But the point is that we discovered that the University Press's staff were included in the baseline charges.' The argument saved the Press from the threat of immediate closure, but Senate agreed that the Press and other institutions should be 'brought nearer to a self-financing status'.

It was understood that the University would cease to fund the Press's overdraft by the end of the session 1983–84, although it would still act as a guarantor. In 1983 Council delegated the management of the Press to a newly established Press Board, chaired by a lay member of Council. Their minds no doubt concentrated by the threat of being hanged in a year or two, the Press organised two large academic book sales at bargain prices to clear their warehouses, the first in Manchester and the second in Liverpool, to which they transported five tons of books. They strove to increase their share of the market and received small boosts from such events as the award of the Nobel Prize for Literature in 1982 to Gabriel Garcia Marquez – for the Press had sole British rights to the publication of his work in Spanish, and had recently brought out the novella *No-One Writes to the Colonel* in their Spanish texts series for school and university students in Britain. Reports in the financial years 1982–83 and 1983–84 both alluded to a brisk improvement in sales turnover and, by 1984, to net profits of just over £50,000. Books such as *The Industrial Archaeology of the North-West,* by Owen Ashmore, the retiring Professor of Extra-Mural Studies, helped the Press to improve its sales record. Works of local history, treatises on such subjects as the Great Bridgewater Canal, promised to sell, and so did the modestly priced *Family Tree Detective*, a handbook for amateur genealogists. The number of new titles increased from about seventy per annum in the mid-1980s to between ninety and one hundred by 1988, when the Press had a thousand titles in print and was publishing five scholarly journals. In the words of Francis Brooke, who became Publisher in 1988, 'It would be in nobody's interest for the Press to be a private publishing company for members of the academic staff'. The Press was not to be suspected of acting as a kind of school magazine, unduly willing to publish the turgid and unappealing works of Manchester scholars.

Early in 1982, the professional youth theatre company, Contact, which had long been the principal user of the University Theatre, offered to take over both the theatre itself and the Brickhouse, so long

as the company succeeded in negotiating larger grants from the Arts
and Greater Manchester Councils. Although the University agreed to
this proposal in substance, it retained responsibility for the Theatre
building; continued both to subsidise it to the tune of £25,000 per
annum and to perform certain financial services free of charge; and
nominated some members of the Council of Management. It seemed
important to distribute theatre time equitably between the professional company, University departments, and University amateurs. In
May 1982 the Arts Faculty objected to the failure of Council and its
committees to consult academic bodies before making decisions with
academic consequences, for the number of weeks assigned to University use would fall from twelve to six and those allowed to modern
language departments from three to one, so that they could no longer
contemplate putting on plays in French, German or Spanish. By July
the modern language departments had won their case and the real
losers were the amateurs. Rendered homeless, the Stage Society for
members of the University staff turned into a company of strolling
players and took its productions to the Renold Theatre at UMIST, to
the Library Theatre in central Manchester, and to the Grange Arts
Theatre in Oldham. In November 1983 the Society put on *Murder in
the Cathedral* in the church of the Holy Name. When in March 1985
it presented Edna O'Brien's *Virginia* at the Edgar Wood Centre in
Daisy Bank Road, a member consoled himself with the possibility that
its nomadic existence might bring it back to 'something near its original function – the production of plays of highly intellectual and specialised interest which offer a fairly unique experience to University
actors and audience alike'. Hard times, these remarks implied, were
not always harmful to culture.

Reginald Dodwell, the Director of the Whitworth Art Gallery, was
an energetic fund-raiser who sought corporate sponsorship to counter
the effects of the cuts. In the 1980s he raised money to establish the
Bistro (an agreeable eating place which increased the charms of the
Gallery), and to open a Wallpapers Study Room and a Paper Conservation Studio. Neither the Art Gallery nor the Museum could bolster
its fortunes by charging admission fees, but money could be made by
putting temptation in the way of visitors. By the autumn of 1984 souvenir shops selling tasteful artefacts, as in an English country house
open to tourists, had opened in the Museum and the Gallery, whilst a
form of Wendy house stocking similar wares appeared in the concourse below the Senior Common Room in the Refectory building
where students sat on benches to eat their lunchtime sandwiches.

Memorabilia of most kinds – ties, T-shirts, scarves, tobacco-jars, umbrellas, almost any object capable of bearing the emblem of the University – could be purchased here, and much Christmas shopping done on the premises. Its motto, like that of the county of Rutland, might well have been 'multum in parvo'. From these upmarket campus shops, so *This Week* reminded its readers, customers could bear away 'art books, original terracotta sculptures, and handmade glass and porcelain . . . Someone, somewhere, right now, is probably drinking to our health from a set of monogrammed crystal glasses and matching decanter.' The souvenir trade took a new turn with the invention in 1984 of another money-spinner, graduation videos. Purchasers of these items would be able to view at their leisure a display of University pomp and ceremony lasting twenty-five minutes, made personal to them by inserting a close-up, lasting about one minute, showing them receiving their degrees. The University might not be a business, but business could be done on University premises.

Mancunion once quoted a dictum of Carlyle: 'The true university of these days is a collection of books.' In the 1980s, however, the Library did not command universal respect, let alone recognition as the University's core. Most faculties had agreed that, as a service provided to the whole institution, it should enjoy some protection against the full force of the cuts, but this view was not unanimous. It had difficulty in meeting demands, if only because in the recent past emphasis had fallen on the acquisition of stock rather than the recruitment of staff, and the cuts were now diminishing a labour force already too small and strained. Certain things, as Diana Leitch remembers, contributed to a sense that the Library was letting down one of the University's most powerful faculties: the absence, from 1981 to 1986, of a Medical Librarian after the early retirement of David Cook; the disappearance, with the move of the Medical Library into the Main Library, of the comfortable Medical Reading Room; the conviction that the wrong books were being bought – no more were they sent on approval by Haigh and Hochland, the University booksellers, for consultants to inspect before purchase.

To some users and occupants the new building was convenient and spacious – 'there was a lot of water in the walls, and it was cool . . . we spent a lot of money on the air conditioning in the first few years. And we hadn't many computers in, so we didn't have static in the atmosphere', as Pat Cummings remembers. Other aspects of the Library's architecture and decor earned it little affection, particularly the charmless entrance hall which resembled in some users' eyes the

concourse of a London railway station and offered no immediate
encounter with the staff. A graduate student commented on 'the
absurdity of having a luxurious library without the means to run it
properly' – smart surroundings had made the shortcomings of the
overstretched services all the more glaring. Critics disparaged the
Library as 'a drain on resources, the Printed Book Emporium'.

The UGC knew that universities might be tempted to solve financial problems by cutting libraries, and advised against the move, making the University a special grant of £314,000 in 1982 to help with
services and the upkeep of premises. But it soon proved necessary to
suspend a number of periodical subscriptions, since the rising cost of
learned journals threatened to eat up more and more of the acquisitions budget, and it seemed essential to reduce their share from 46 to
40 per cent of the whole. Faculties had to recommend further
economies in 1984–85 and to shave up to 10 per cent off their allo-
cations. How could British libraries and British scholarship continue
to compete with their prosperous American counterparts?

Even in these unpromising circumstances some progress was possible through resort to automation, especially by extending the use of
information technology in order to compile, acquire and search bibli-
ographical databases. Michael Pegg, who had served at an army
organisation attached to NATO, said: 'I want to encourage information work.' Diana Leitch, who held degrees in science from Edinburgh
and had begun her career by compiling *World Textile Abstracts* at the
Shirley Institute in Didsbury, joined with Alan Neville in establishing
a new Science and Medical Information Unit. ' . . . in a little room,
where you couldn't swing a cat round, we had two computers, and we
actually were involved in the first ever scientific information searching, both printed and electronic, in this Library'. 'We were the first
people to go with one of the big international database hosts, STN
International, in 1983 . . . In 1985, we took on board CDRoms . . .
And by 1987, Alan had worked out how to do what's called "A Local
Area Network" . . . ' By October 1984, the Library was announcing,
Soviet-style, a Five Year Plan for making the greatest possible use of
information technology, the Librarian proclaiming at a seminar that
'Any major library which fails to automate is condemned to becoming
a backwater.' It was a far cry from the days when cataloguers had
filled out index cards with steel nibs, and when the introduction of
fountain pens had been regarded as a startling innovation.

No library had enough copies of course books and recommended
articles to satisfy student demand; students had, or claimed to have,

little money to buy books; and the success of many seminars depended on all students having read the same material by the same time. One solution appeared to lie in the zealous use of the photocopying machine, to make vital articles and extracts available in departmental libraries, or even provide handy anthologies of vital texts for students to possess. However, some of these measures led to illicit photocopying so flagrant as to attract the attention of the Publishers' Association, which was probably tipped off from within the University, for many academics were concerned about the effect on their own royalties of unchecked pirating. The law allowed a student or scholar to acquire one copy of an article from a non-profitmaking library for his or her personal use, but it did not permit a course organiser to produce numerous booklets assembling other people's material without seeking permission. Feeling the pinch as much as anyone else, the Association threatened to take legal action against the University for condoningif not encouraging breaches of copyright. In May 1984 the Association agreed not to sue, but insisted that the University enforce strict obser-vance of the Copyright Act. Let warning notices appear on all machines and all illicitly copied material be surrendered to the Association (some departmental libraries were sorely depleted). Let it be understood that 'Multiple copies (e.g. class sets) of copyright material may not be made without prior permission and payment may have to be made.' Eventu-ally, in 1987, it proved possible to agree on an experimental scheme which would license institutions to make multiple as well as single copies for teaching purposes, on designated machines, at a fee of so much per page, without going through the cumbersome process of seeking permission in advance.

Students were quick to complain of deteriorating services, which were not confined to libraries and classrooms. Their welfare, no longer sacrosanct, was falling victim to the overriding claims of economy. The Student Health Service maintained by the University and UMIST cost the institutions £210,000 a year and became a candidate for rationali-sation in 1980–81, even before the heaviest cuts descended. Unlike most such centres, it was not funded by the National Health Service except to give advice on contraception, and it was not recognised as a general practice. The student service operated from nine to five on weekdays, but did not provide emergency cover outside those hours and was not entitled to supply medication for long stretches of time. Its special function was to advise students on problems closely connected with their way of life, of which ordinary GPs sometimes showed little understanding. These included not only the notorious examination stress, the students' occupational disease, but also matters connected with sexual behaviour and experiments with illegal drugs.

Mancunion asserted in February 1981 that over the last seven years the number of consultations each year had increased from 26,000 to 60,000. But were students suffering from ordinary afflictions using the Centre because it was convenient and approachable, when they could easily have applied to a local GP? Was it right that the University, hard pressed to make economies, should pay its specialised health centre to copy the functions of the National Health Service? University strategy was to reduce expenditure by some 25 per cent and to urge students to register with GPs. Students feared they would encounter difficulties as thousands of extra patients began besieging doctors' surgeries in Rusholme, Fallowfield, Chorlton and Withington. The suppression of doctors', nurses' and counsellors' posts in the student service proved to be a lasting grievance, reiterated throughout the decade. Campaigners protested that even before the cuts, when four full-time doctors and three part-timers had been catering for the 16,000 students of Owens and UMIST, provision had fallen far short of a recommendation made in 1979 by the Royal College of Physicians – to the effect that there ought in University practices to be one full-time doctor to every 1,500 students.

Income generation was the only counter to dismal cost-cutting. Home students who cost the country money were regarded with a wary eye, but overseas students, who paid the full cost of their tuition, could be seen as a financial asset. They accounted in November 1981 for £2m. of the £60m. of the University's income. All universities feared that the fees imposed by the Government would drive students away from the United Kingdom in search of better bargains elsewhere. The proportion of overseas full-time students in the University of Manchester did indeed fall from 9.4 per cent in 1980–81 to about 7 per cent in 1982–83, and remained at much the same level in subsequent years; faculties were urged to aim at 10 per cent. By autumn 1981 the Malaysian Government had decided that British fees were too high and Malaysian students almost disappeared from the scene, with recruitment to Mechanical Engineering and to Education declining especially sharply. Universities now had reason to regard overseas students as trophies, and, as Ken Kitchen recalls, they became increasingly reluctant to share recruiting secrets with each other. By February 1983 Manchester was dropping behind in the race, outstripped by universities as varied as Cambridge, Kent and Lancaster. It would be necessary to bombard promising areas with seductive publicity; to offer daily allowances to induce Manchester scholars visiting overseas institutions to stay on long enough to beat a drum for the University; to reward departments which overshot their allotted targets.

It was important that standards should not lapse; student journalists had warned that racial tension might arise in the University if it did favours to rich overseas students in order to boost income, and connived at the practice of treating education as a saleable commodity. The financial gains made from overseas students increased the moral obligation to understand their difficulties and provide for their needs, though the Students' Union at intervals reproved the University for not doing enough to help. Their intellectual and social success depended on a reasonable knowledge of English. Kenneth James was the pioneer of the TEFL [Teaching English as a Foreign Language] unit, and succeeded in devising some instructive entertainments, the Inspector Thackeray plays, whose fame spread beyond Manchester when they were published by Longmans as 'structural readers' and recorded on cassettes. Each piece contained three clues, 'one obvious, one less so and one hidden – in order to test comprehension and maintain interest'.

Development of part-time, continuing, post-experience and adult education was not only a public service but a defence against the argument that, as the numbers of young people fell, universities would become underemployed and could with justice be cut. Arthur Armitage had begun to explore the field in the late 1970s. Recommendations of working parties led to the establishment in 1983–84 of a Board for Part-time Education and the appointment of a Director to supervise from on high the part-time degree courses offered by departments. The first Chairman of the new Board was an enthusiast, Sam Moore, who had started his own career as a part-time degree student before the Robbins expansion and the Open University had pushed part-time undergraduates into the shade. The first Director was Keith Drake, a Senior Lecturer in Education with degrees in History and Economics who had taught in schools in Liverpool and Newcastle-under-Lyne and in the Extra-Mural Department of Liverpool University. Before long his brief was extended to include continuing education and training, a term which referred to the task of bringing professional people and others up to date with new developments in their fields rather than to the mounting of degree courses.

Part-time undergraduate degrees depended on accumulating credits over a number of years by taking, at one's own pace, courses on several different levels, from basic to advanced, which were known as modules and commanded a fee of £100 each. It was a little like the process of earning a Sunday School Bible by the ticket system in *Tom Sawyer*, but more sophisticated and a good deal less haphazard. Students could, if practical, attend the ordinary courses during the day, or go to classes specially provided for them in the evening (evening students, regrettably, had a restricted choice of subjects, since not all lectures and tutorials could be repeated out of normal hours). Ten credits added up to an unclassified ordinary degree, thirteen to a classified honours degree. Some students could content themselves with a few credits and stop short of graduating. All could, as a psychologist commented, avoid the '"sudden death" syndrome encountered by students examined during temporary life crises'.

The new Board approved the first courses in 1984, with a view to admitting the first students in October 1985. Enthusiasm for part-time teaching varied between different parts of the university. Apart from Nursing Education and Nursing Studies, science and technology were not represented in the first batch of part-time degree courses, which were offered by nineteen academic departments spread across five faculties: the others were in Adult and Community Education, American Studies, Economic and Social Studies, Education, History, History of Art, Language Teaching, Literary Studies, and Theology. Scientists and engineers, however, would perhaps be better equipped to provide refresher courses to industrialists and professional or business people eager to be brought up to date.

One of the University's less intellectual tasks was to obtain the greatest possible benefit from its student premises by opening them up to the conference trade. This aim was not new, but the crisis of the 1980s created a pressing need to find new customers. Since the University was not itself a business, it was tempted to hand over some of the work to a firm well versed in catering for profit. At issue was the student village at Owens Park, equipped with three restaurants, rooms for 900 guests and meeting space for 650. This was expected to earn about half the University's annual income from conferences. By the early 1980s it was in need of refurbishment and its residents, conscious of shrinking grants, were pressing for a 'pay-as-you-eat' scheme, so that they would no longer have to contract to buy more meals than they were likely to consume and more than they could afford. Since its foundation in 1964 the running of Owens Park had depended on a division of labour between managers, who were responsible for food and fabric, and tutors, who were in charge of pastoral care. In the late 1970s the system had not worked impeccably, and few managers had lasted long in post: some, bent on ditching unprofitable activities, antagonised the Owens Park Students Association (OPSA). Close a dining-room to students on a term-time Sunday to accommodate a conference of flower-growers, and a manager could expect to make some money but also arouse disproportionate resentment for apparently putting commercial considerations before student needs.

In the summer of 1982 tension mounted when the University Council contemplated farming out catering and cleaning at Owens Park to Grand Metropolitan Hotels Ltd., which already catered at the Business School and at Broomcroft Hall in Didsbury (the residence for Simon Fellows and other academic visitors to the University). Grandmet would use two of the three existing dining-rooms to run a non-profit-making 'pay-as-you-eat' scheme and would see to the cleaning in return for a management fee paid out of Owens Park funds. It would derive its profit from a half-share with the University in the net conference income from Owens Park and from the surplus on the running of the bar, whilst OPSA would receive a half-share of 'the surplus arising from the gaming machines'. Council heard representations to the effect that 'University conference business generally was not realising its full potential', and that the 'marketing strengths and international links' of Grandmet would introduce the University not only to new kinds of conference business but also to 'the "package tour" trade which the North West was so anxious to promote'.

This vision of holidaymakers enjoying Owens Park was seductive to those who had to solve its financial problems. But the students and staff questioned the intentions of a firm which, or so they believed, would cut jobs to increase profits (up to 140 might be at risk). The University officers argued that, since Owens Park was too generously staffed, redundancies were inevitable, and that Grandmet, which had 'numerous operations within a small radius of Fallowfield', was better equipped than the University itself to re-employ staff. Students, however, believed that Grandmet would raise prices, close dining rooms to students, and turn over Owens Park, even during term, to the profitable conference trade. Some members of Council were perturbed at the news that Grandmet had originally been invited to advise on the problems of Owens Park, but had then, by offering to do the job themselves, become interested parties rather than independent consultants. None the less the University officers had chosen to back Grandmet's scheme and put no other proposals forward; by holding no competition they had lost one of the advantages of venturing into the market. Should Grandmet withdraw from the arrangement after the first five years and take its business elsewhere, the University would in the end lose conference trade.

Owens Park staff took umbrage when the proposals appeared in a circular and were not explained to them face to face at a meeting; the Bursar subsequently agreed to talk to them after they had refused to hold any converse with Grandmet. Two campus unions, NUPE and NALGO, called a strike of Owens Park workers on 2 June 1982. One week later, almost a thousand members of NUPE assembled outside the Main Building and, like an outsize chorus, provided a lively setting for a contentious meeting of the University Council. A petition bearing a thousand signatures reached the Chairman of Council at the end of the discussion, which had lasted three and a half hours. With libellous gusto but no evidence, the student press hinted at corruption in high places: had some University officer been offered a directorship of Grandmet, in which the University held shares? Council chose not to refer the proposals back for further consideration, but did decide to approve the principle of 'pay-as-you-eat' and to empower the officers to negotiate further over the summer.

Within the next month, two other companies, Gardner Merchant and Taylorplan Catering, made proposals, but the trade unions representing staff at Owens Park worked out a scheme which would enable the University to retain direct control of the catering with their collaboration. 'Pay-as-you-eat' would come in gradually over the next academical year and the unions accepted the inevitability of some job losses. This being so, the case for privatising the catering, with all the resentment such a move would provoke, became less compelling. It was, in any case, not clear that the conference trade, unaided by private enterprise, was producing disappointing results; on the contrary, *This Week* was beginning to boast about its resilience and reporting that income in 1981–82 had exceeded that of the previous session by 26 per cent. Acting in partnership with Greater Manchester Council, the University was attracting large international conferences to the city and had succeeded in booking seven such events, which were due to take place within the next three years. Thousands of delegates would surely attend gatherings interested in Latin America, science education, the education of the deaf, pure and applied chemistry, and microbiology. If the University itself had no lecture theatre vast enough to accommodate the plenary sessions, then the Palace Theatre up the road, accustomed as it was to Christmas pantomimes and touring musicals, could be pressed into service. So, it later transpired, could the Free Trade Hall, where Princess Anne opened the Fourteenth International Congress of Microbiology in September 1986.

At the end of October 1983, the branch secretary of NUPE, commenting on the University's rising conference income, declared that 'Privatisation can be beaten with common sense and close working between management and the trade unions.' Student interests were more clearly safeguarded by the appointment of a resident Warden for Owens Park, who now replaced the non-resident Chairman of Tutors; the post went in October 1982 to Dr R.R. Frost, a Senior Lecturer in Botany who had considerable experience of Owens Park. By May 1983 it seemed clear that some gains from conference revenue were being used to keep the fees and rents from University accommodation down to levels more closely related to the modest increases of 4 per cent in student grants. About twenty jobs had gone from Owens Park in 1982–83; the Owens Park fee was to rise by only 2.8 per cent in 1983–84.

Other halls of residence succeeded in attracting much conference business. Woolton Hall's rooms were spacious and it raised plenty of revenue during vacations. It was true that self-catering flats now sheltered more students than did Owens Park and the traditional halls, and that, having no dining halls and few public rooms, they were ill-equipped to house conferences. But the glossy bulletin of the University Conference Office, which began to appear in 1984, did not confine its praise to the 'mouth-watering meals' which Woolton and Langdale, Ashburne and Hulme would offer to peckish delegates. It also extolled the virtues of self-catering flats, which would provide a base for families on holiday to visit, for example, the Liverpool International Garden Festival. As the cradle and coffin of the Industrial Revolution, Manchester might not in itself seem an attractive resort. But it was possible to take an 'Industrial Heritage package holiday' at modest cost, and some organisations had historical, if not sentimental, reasons for arranging their gatherings in the city. Indeed, the Boilermakers' Union, founded in Manchester in 1834, deserted the seaside, returned to the city to celebrate their 150th anniversary, and put up at Owens Park in 1984.

Although the University undertook little new building during the 1980s, it did resolve in 1984 to build a new sports and conference complex, which was eventually named the Armitage Centre in honour of the late Vice-Chancellor. This was to rise on the site of some shale tennis courts at the athletic grounds in Fallowfield and cost about £950,000. A grant from the Hulme Trust, University money earmarked for the improvement of student amenities, would provide £400,000, and the rest would proceed from an interest-free loan to be repaid over a period of thirty-five years from the income of the Centre as a venue for conferences and exhibitions. In prospect were, not only a gymnasium, an aerobics room and a climbing wall for aspiring mountaineers, but also a main hall capable of accommodating an audience of 1,000 on 'tiered, upholstered seating'. This could be removed when the auditorium was called upon to house exhibitions or provide courts for badminton players.

Student representatives on Council welcomed the plans but grumbled at the probability that the Centre would be used for conferences during term. They disliked the near-certainty that all customers, including students, would have to pay more to use the Armitage Centre than to use the older McDougall Centre close to the main site of the University on Oxford Road. On the eve of the opening, on 1 December 1986, *Mancunion* conceded that 'All in all, Manchester students have no longer got a reason to gripe about their sporting facilities.' In October 1987, however, they found the Centre closed for sport and monopolised by three major exhibitions; the manager explained that the Centre had been running at a loss, and that the University was pressing him to make it pay.

Exploiting intellectual property was as important as making full use of real estate. During the 1980s the University attempted to go into business on its own account by means of a new holding company, and it also set out to invite certain kinds of enterprise – high-tech firms which would directly benefit from scientific expertise – to become neighbours of the University and settle on land close to the Education Precinct. Sceptics wondered whether, in the early years, the University would earn anything more than pin-money from these ventures, which would require heavy investment and provide no instant solutions to financial problems. But, by demonstrating the practical value of much University research and encouraging the inventors on its payroll, it might be possible to recover some of the approval which universities had once enjoyed in the sight of Government and society; to earn the enthusiastic support and perhaps the patronage of the business community which the Government extolled; and to join with the City in regenerating the area, not so much by reviving the old industries as by developing new forms of technology.

Some professors were lured away from the University, as Christopher Pogson, who had been Professor of Biochemistry since 1979, 'succumbed to the call of industry' and became Head of Biochemistry at the Wellcome Research Laboratories at Beckenham in Kent in 1984. Brian Robert Pullan (not to be confused with the author of this book) had been the first Professor in the newly created Department of Medical Biophysics in 1973 and had, among much else, worked with the radiologist Ian Isherwood on new techniques for diagnostic imaging, 'using the magnetic properties of certain naturally recurring atomic nuclei in the body'. As an appreciation of his work, put before Senate in 1983, explained, 'Brian Pullan has always been fascinated by the transfer of ideas into practice and has often been frustrated by the historical reluctance of British universities and industry to work together to this end. His work has done much to develop collaborative contacts between this University and industry. He has left to explore other ways of achieving the same goals and will still be working actively applying science and technology in medicine.' One might well ask whether the 'historical reluctance', so long deplored, could be overcome from within the University, and whether the crisis of the 1980s would at last provide the incentive to dispel it. Would Vuman, CURID and the Science Park become the signposts pointing to a new era of co-operation between the cloister and the factory?

The name Vuman (derived from 'Victoria University of Manchester') was supplied by the Registrar and the idea behind it came from the Bursar. In the 1950s, when Dr Beswick had been a lecturer in physiology, the departmental staff, led by their professor, had constructed their research apparatus with their own hands. Devices invented and made for particular experiments were discarded, but might well have had commercial potential if only the academic mind had been sufficiently aware of the possibilities. Aware of lost opportunities, Dr Beswick arranged for a search of university departments for ideas and devices which had been developed in the course of research and then laid aside. There was a strong possibility that some of these might be resurrected, that others might be added, and that old and new items might be developed commercially. In future, opportunities should not be missed and inventions should not be sold for less than they were worth.

Vuman was 'a holding company to facilitate the development of income-generating activities' and designed to 'provide the means for University resources and projects to be exploited commercially for the benefit of the University'. A public limited company devoted to the pursuit of commercial profits, it was established in October 1981 as a separate entity from the University (which was an educational charity). Although the Vice-Chancellor and Chairman of Council were appointed directors at the beginning of Vuman's career, they stepped down after a year to eliminate any possible confusion between their duties to Vuman and to the University. However, the holding company was able to make payments to the University by deed of covenant; to pay royalties to inventors or to their departments; to employ two members of the academic staff on secondment; and to retain the services of eleven others as consultants. For guidance it relied heavily on members of the University Council and sometimes on managers who had worked with or for them; Sir George Kenyon became Chairman of Vuman in 1982 on resigning his office as University Treasurer. The National Westminster Bank provided overdraft facilities of up to £500,000 to finance the new company's operations, and the firm of Paterson Zochonis lent it £15,000 per annum, free of interest, for three years. By November 1982 the company had an 'issued share capital' of £200,000 and an 'authorised share capital' of £500,000. By the summer of 1984 it was employing twenty-nine members of staff on its own account and in its subsidiary and related companies.

In its early days the company had four divisions, of which the first three were established during 1982. The computer division concentrated on selling Sirius computers, together with a word-processing programme for scientists, Vuwriter, which ran on these machines and was an invention of the Barclays Unit within the Department of Computer Science. The furniture division dealt in desks and tables designed in the Department of Town and Country Planning, which could be quickly assembled and dismantled on contractors' sites. It was the task of the laser and spectrometer division to manufacture and sell items designed in the Department of Physics. Vuman then proceeded to form a subsidiary company, Medeval, which had nothing to do with the Middle Ages but was devoted to the evaluation of medicines. It was to 'undertake investigations into the temporal course of medicine within the body (viz. its pharmacokinetics) in healthy volunteers', in the hope that the knowledge gained would 'be of benefit to patients by providing a better understanding of the mechanisms and effects of medicines'. Medeval's appeals for volunteers were to become a regular feature of *This Week* during the 1980s and provided opportunities for students to earn money, supplementing their meagre grants without overexerting themselves – in May 1985 *Mancunion* reported that students and other guinea pigs could be paid up to £350, according to the amount of 'inconvenience' they suffered (it was never suggested that they were exposed to risk).

By July 1984 the furniture division was destined for closure, since its commercial prospects did not justify allocating further resources, but others had been established and the variety and complexity of the operations were growing. A Vuman robot had emerged from the combined expertise of three lecturers, in Pharmacy, Mechanical Engineering and Computer Science. There was now a liquid crystals division; an industrial control division which used a computer to watch over industrial processes; and a project which set out to 'analyse the vibration characteristics of machinery as an aid to design and preventive maintenance'. Medeval and Vuman Computer Systems Ltd. now ranked as subsidiary and associated companies, as did another entity, Visual Machines Ltd., which was producing 'image recognition systems based on research carried out in the University's Department of Medical Biophysics'. Yet another company joined Vuman's empire in 1985, a commercial operation for the teaching of English as a foreign language which had grown out of the Faculty of Education; this bore the name of Delta, which stood for 'Direct English Language Teaching Agency'.

In the first full year of trading, 1982–83, Vuman reported a net profit of nearly £67,000 on a turnover of almost £750,000. A turnover of more than £1m. was forecast for 1983–84, but Senate heard warnings that development expenditure would very likely reduce the profits in the current year. The question of how much more capital should be poured into Vuman was to exercise Council at intervals throughout the 1980s. As Sir George Kenyon has commented, 'Vuman is a useful thing, but very long-term . . . it takes ten years to develop a new product, or to develop a new idea, to get it making money commercially.'

Planned in 1982–83 and opened in 1984, the Science Park was a collection of buildings and offices concentrated near the University. As the Bursar later put it, just as chemical reactions are produced by molecules bumping together, scientific progress may be advanced by people bumping together. The project did not involve establishing entrepreneurs in offices on the University site, but the principle was that 'they could use our facilities, and they could talk about this and that to the professors of this and that . . . the idea was to get the board room into the Senate, and we were going to turn the Christie Building into a club, and it was going to cost a million quid, but they jibbed at that'. A promising site lay close to hand, off Lloyd Street and near the back of the University Library. Some City councillors, however, appeared to dislike the University as an 'elite' institution and responded coldly to the idea of opening up the land for development. But Professor Dennis Welland and the Bursar succeeded, by a mixture of charm and persuasive argument, in convincing the one councillor who was beginning to appreciate the power of the Science Park to create jobs for the City: the University, they insisted, would not just be pursuing its own ends, but would make its own resources available to companies which need not have originated in the University. At the next meeting of the City planning committee the University's ally won over a sufficient number of his colleagues and they succeeded in pushing the proposal through the whole Council.

The arrangement eventually made was that the City would lease the site for 125 years to a Science Park Company run by a board of fifteen directors. Although all higher academic institutions in the area would be involved, only the University and UMIST would invest in the Company, together with the City and some established firms. Thirty-five per cent of the shares would go to the University and it would appoint at least three directors (it chose the Bursar; the Treasurer, Ronald Brierley; and a solicitor, Dennis Westbrook, who was a member of the University Council). UMIST would have the chance, should it so desire, to buy 23 per cent of the University's holding, and when it in fact exercised this option F.M. Burdekin, Professor of Civil and Structural Engineering, represented UMIST on the board. The first building on the site was to be a so-called 'incubator unit' intended mainly for small developing companies and confined to those 'operating in genuine high technology fields'. One might well hope that the proximity of such things would 'greatly improve the transfer of University-developed technology into industry', and perhaps members of the University staff would obtain consultancies and earn suitable fees. Perhaps, too, the firms would wish to use the laboratories, equipment, workshops and conference facilities, computers, libraries and information services which lay close to hand, and the University would be able to charge them for the privilege.

First to move into the first building, named Enterprise House and officially opened by the Duchess of Kent in December 1984, were Visual Machines Ltd., an associate of Vuman (which held 25.4 per cent of the shares in it), and Thinking Software. On their heels came the European branch of the Advanced Technology Resources Corporation, and Textile Computer Systems Ltd. The scheme owed much to the vision and influence of a well-known Manchester solicitor, Robin Skelton, who was convinced of the enormous potential of 'high-tech' enterprises. He died in August 1988, and the second building in the Park, opened a year after his death, was named after him. Skelton House originally accommodated Medeval, one of Vuman's companies, together with the National Occupational Hygiene Service, CIM

Microdynamics, and the Colgate-Palmolive Dental Health Unit.

Soon to join them in the Park was a third University enterprise, known as CURID, the Centre for Urban and Regional Industrial Development. Its first director was to be the geographer Peter Lloyd, an expert on industry and employment in the region who was anxious not only to study but also to encourage small businesses. Floated by a grant of £100,000 from one of the clearing banks, by another of £45,000 from the Manpower Services Commission, and by several other grants, CURID's object was to compile and relate to each other two storehouses of information. One database would list the research interests of companies in the North West, and the other the academic and research resources in the area which might prove of interest to those firms. It was hoped that CURID might persuade some firms to take up residence in the Science Park. The process followed the same principles, and pursued much the same aims, as the Research Consultancy Service of the 1970s and its newsletter, *Contact*.

One of the brightest novels of the 1980s, David Lodge's *Nice Work*, was both a campus and an industrial novel, a reincarnation of Mrs Gaskell's *North and South,* a dialogue between the managing director of an engineering firm and a budding lecturer in English literature. 'Is money the only criterion?' 'I don't know a better one.' 'What about happiness?' Some thirty years earlier, Princess Elizabeth had charmed an Oxford audience by calling the universities 'a powerful fortress against the tide of sloth, ignorance and materialism'. It was doubtful whether, in Margaret Thatcher's England, universities could resist materialism, in so far as it meant the call to contribute to the country's economic regeneration; doubtful, too, whether they could avoid being taxed with sloth unless they manifestly resorted to self-help.

Weary of endless talk of income generation and savings targets, many academics inquired plaintively how far and why the University was supposed to have become a business. It was undoubtedly expected to remain solvent and to respect employment law, and it was happy enough to accept endowments from business enterprises; Barclays Bank was reproved by students for its connections with South Africa, but it had financed a chair in Microprocessor Applications in Industry which the University did not hesitate to accept. Partnerships with industry, sociable relations, sharing of resources and discussions of common problems all seemed desirable, though the student press questioned the ability of science parks and high technology enterprises to create employment on a large scale – were they not designing machines to eliminate the need for human labour? It was vital that the University should not, for the sake of making money or demonstrating its usefulness, become the slave of capitalism or the servant of the Ministry of Defence; but something might be gained from dialogue with business enterprises, and from making businesspeople aware of the inventions which stood in need of commercial development. It was clear that the University could not live by economies alone. Nor should it, like the small provincial university in Malcolm Bradbury's novella *Cuts*, devote itself with indecent enthusiasm to cutting, privatising and seeking sponsorship at almost any cost.

9

The Students' Union and
the politicians

Student activists were not the revolutionaries of the 1980s, the bearers or prophets of a new order; instead they seemed fated to be rebels, protesting against changes imposed from on high. The initiative had passed to a neoliberal, sink-or-swim, roll-back-the-State Government which nevertheless contrived to interfere with universities as none of its predecessors had ever done. It appeared to be starving students of public money, ostensibly in an effort to make them more self-reliant (some Labour MPs remarked that the effect of the State's parsimony was to make students stand on their parents' feet rather than their own, and lean on their banks for overdrafts). Students could only react to Government assaults on privileges which they had once regarded as rights, and dream of restoring a vanished golden age. Individually, students suffered from deteriorating services, grants and benefits. Collectively, they – or their elected officers – faced attacks on the autonomy of student unions, measures designed to subject them to tighter control by the administrators of their own universities.

In the early 1970s students had feared with good reason that Edward Heath's Government, suspicious of union officers' liking for left-wing political causes, might introduce such arrangements. Conservative politicians, however, had not had time, and their Labour successors had made no move, to do so. But in February 1980 Mark Carlisle announced the abandonment of the old system of union finance, which had depended on a subscription negotiated by the union with the university and paid, on the university's recommendation, by the local authorities. Henceforth the unions would be financed from the universities' block grants, which would be suitably adjusted. This reform would, or so the Government imagined, persuade university authorities to keep a tighter grip on union expenditure: should this get out of hand, it would begin to vie with the many academic activities making claims on the university purse. Students would now be asking for university money, rather than collaborating with the university to obtain local authority funding; the union would become a university department, rather than a separate entity applying with the university's backing for funds from a different source.

At first the AUT were as apprehensive as the students. Laurie Sapper, their General Secretary, denounced the proposals as 'the height of madness, sowing the seeds of disruption in each and every university'. Indeed, at a meeting in the University of Manchester, he warned his members to look to their claims for promotion and pay, which might well be jeopardised by having another competitor for university funds, a rival which made a 'totally dissimilar call' upon them. Interviewed by a Manchester student journalist, Mark Carlisle explained that the Public Accounts Committee had thought the old system too open-ended. The advantage of the new order was that unions would have to plead for their money 'at local level' and justify their use of this year's grant if they wanted a similar allowance next year. His junior colleague, Rhodes Boyson, argued that to insist on accountability was not to dictate policy; the arrangements were not as illiberal as they seemed.

Although *Mancunion* complained that students' unions in general were being treated like 'church hall youth clubs', the University showed no signs of reverting to the paternalism of the 1960s and again concerning itself with such matters as the libellous contents of the Union newspaper or the immoral presence of contraceptive dispensers in the Union building. Union finance did not in practice present the serious problems which pessimists had foreseen, and, despite the cuts, the Union did not approach insolvency, as it had done in the 1970s. Much was due to the wise counsel of the Union manager, Vic Silcock, who was appointed in the early 1980s: as David Richardson remembers, he 'combined infinite patience, strong left-wing conviction and sound business sense, and became a much respected and valued confidant to successive Union executives'.

Two issues, however, did prove both delicate and controversial. The new arrangements imposed on the University itself a duty to ensure that the Union observed charity law and did not use public money for purposes not relevant to the well being of students, including political campaigns and demonstrations. 'I do not see it as the role of university students', said Mark Carlisle, 'to get involved in matters outside the university.' Furthermore, as a result of events during the 1980s, in Manchester and elsewhere, universities incurred a legal obligation to guarantee free speech within the law: they would have to ensure that controversial speakers at union meetings obtained a hearing and were not shouted down for expressing views which conflicted with union policy. As controllers of the purse, universities would have power to fine or withhold funds from unions deemed guilty of misconduct or of damaging university premises, and Whitehall might well press them to discipline students who had assaulted or silenced unpopular politicians. The University never attempted to fine the Union collectively, but did take disciplinary proceedings against four of its members in 1986 amid much turbulence and some angry complaints that the University was violating the independence of the Union.

Between 1982 and 1985 the University made over to the Union a sum of between £520,000 and £570,000 annually, allowing between £45 and £52 per student. Since the Government permitted students' unions level funding in 1981–82, the University eventually subjected the Union to the average cut of 13 per cent suffered by faculties and departments, but did so in two stages rather than three, reducing their funds by 8 per cent in 1982–83 and 5 per cent the following year. Responsibility for paying its own electricity bill passed gradually to the Union. In January 1983 the General Secretary, Andy Whyte, vowed that the Union would declare none of its staff redundant and that, unlike the University, it would honour nationally agreed wage settlements. Allowances to societies and funding for campaigns would increase, but less would be spent on social get-togethers and other events, on exchange visits with students' unions in Poland, and on repairs and maintenance. Student spending power would very likely fall in the immediate future and take the Union's trading income with it; the outlook appeared to be bleak.

However, at least one student urged the Union to stop complaining about cuts and realise its own economic power: it had substantial assets and a large capacity for borrowing. The Union did not follow the suggestion that it should acquire its own houses and flats or even purchase a block in Hulme, but, with Mr Silcock's help, it did manage its affairs well and did not allow its premises to decay. The place received a thorough facelift in the summer of 1983, when attempts were made to banish the 'school dining room look' of the Coffee Bar and to tart up the discotheque in the Cellar Bar. Jo White, the new General Secretary, called it 'the largest, most hectic and most successful refurbishment programme the Union has ever seen'. Since it promised to boost the Union's trading income by making the building less depressing, the redecoration was probably a sound investment.

Cramped conditions had been a grievance for twenty years, and after the demolition of The Squat in 1982 plans to find the Union extra room in far-flung places came to nothing. But early in 1985 the Union realised that it might soon have the means to build on the adjacent plot which had long been reserved for its eventual use. For the officers had, *Mancunion* reported, 'uncovered' a large sum in a Capital Reserve Fund, dedicated to the sole purpose of building an extension. The joint signatures of the Union Manager and the University's Director of Finance would be able to authorise the use of the money. It would not cover the entire cost of a high-tech building, which was estimated at '£379,000 net of furniture and fittings'. But the University was always on the look-out for more space in which to hold examinations and if the Union built a large auditorium it could be used occasionally for that purpose. Hence the University agreed to give some help, and Council to approve the arrangements, on the understanding that the Union would commit the entire Reserve Fund, expected to amount to about £230,000 by the summer, to the enterprise.

Optimists dreamed of completing a new building within two years. However, excavations began only in the autumn of 1989. By that time the estimated cost had risen to a little over £1m., but the project went ahead and the Union acquired a profitable night club. In a statement, '12 Things You Never Knew About Your Union', made at the time of the elections of 1990, the Union claimed that although the real value of their share in the block grant had fallen since 1981 by 40 per cent, they were making a surplus every year and adding it to their 'reserves for long-term planning. It is only thanks to these reserves that we can afford the new building. THE UNIVERSITY IS NOT PAYING FOR THIS NEW BUILDING. THE UNION IS.' Council minutes of 1988 and 1989 congratulated the Union on good financial management – in the year ending on 3 July 1988 the operating surplus had reached about £102,000, leaving a net surplus of £7,000 after transfer to reserves. The Union's policy was to offer good service and expect customers to pay for it: 'We can't be as cheap as some places because we don't cut corners and we pay decent wages.'

Much had been made for many years of the contest for money and attention within the Union between campaigns and services: left-wing students emphasised the first, Conservatives the second. In certain periods, especially in 1982–83, *Mancunion* published more stories about national or regional demonstrations, marches and rallies involving a few Manchester students, than about the internal affairs of the University. This did not mean, however, that the Union was spending vast sums on such activities. When Conservative ministers eventually commissioned a survey of seventy-one students' unions in

1989, they found that none spent more than 2 per cent of its income on supporting political groups and that about two-thirds spent less than 0.5 per cent. Arguably, though, proof of any such expenditure would lay a union open to charges of improper conduct and invite the University to move in and curb it.

In the autumn of 1983 Sir Michael Havers, the Attorney-General, sent to all universities, polytechnics and colleges a letter for transmission to their students' unions. This stated the view that it was improper to employ union funds to support or oppose political parties or promote campaigns on issues that did not affect students as students – for example, to press for illegal drugs to be made lawful. Nor should students call upon union funds to back one side or the other in industrial disputes, by hiring coaches to carry them to demonstrations or picket lines, or by any other means. Expenditure was legitimate only for 'the purpose of representing and furthering the interests of students, for example by providing channels for the representation of student views within the college or by improving the conditions of life of the students and in particular providing facilities for their social and physical well-being'. There was a difference between the interests of students and the causes that some students were interested in. As parent bodies allocating funds for 'charitable educational purposes', college authorities must ensure that these moneys were being properly applied. On being informed of 'major items of improper expenditure', they should 'cease to fund the union until the position has been rectified'.

Jo White, the General Secretary, denounced the Attorney-General's letter as 'an attempt by the Government to muzzle the students' unions as one of the most articulate and coherent sources of opposition to its policies'. Another student took issue with her and called it unreasonable to expect the country to foot the bill for 'non-educational political activities'. After all, the law was not just aimed at left-wing causes, and also restrained the unions from funding such organisations as the National Front, the Conservative Party and the Paedophile Information Exchange.

Not content with expressions of indignation, the Union Executive set out to establish a separate private limited company, Materialise Ltd., to handle the Union's profits from games machines and the hiring-out of sun beds (the idea came from the Union manager). The Union as a body would be shareholders in this enterprise, and the Executive would be the directors, while the company's articles of association would entrust it with the task of providing the Union with transport and other financial support for 'non-educational political campaigns'. It would also be possible to run benefit discos for the purpose of funding CND demonstrations and other such activities. Some students, interested in defiance rather than fancy footwork, saw Materialise Ltd. as a capitulation to the Government and a 'tool of the capitalist machine'. But it seemed a promising device, an alternative to expensive and probably futile campaigns for the defence of Union autonomy. The University Council agreed that the Union's auditors should be commissioned 'at the expense of the University if necessary, to report and certify that no payments had been made from charitable funds *ultra vires*'.

Dislike of Thatcherism was widespread, though not universal, among students. When the Left Alliance made great gains in the Executive elections of 1983, an Economics postgraduate described it as 'an unholy alliance of Libs, SDP, carved-out Labour people and general well-meaning middle/upper-class charitable-minded students who I feel don't like Thatcher, don't like the Labour Left, don't understand the Union or the political system . . . '. Strong student sentiment opposed the Government for its policies, not only on education, but also on defence and policing. Many students sympathised with workers who resisted the Government, first with the health workers and then, even more strongly, with the miners. They were anxious to help them with deeds as well as words, and some students were involved both with industrial picketing and with CND demonstrations. A few suffered or witnessed arrests and complained of aggressive police tactics, random snatches, confused evidence in magistrates' courts, and biased media reporting designed to praise police heroism in the face of 'mob violence'.

If students were brought before the courts, would the Union be entitled to pay their fines and legal costs? Between 1983 and 1985 students were arrested, one or two of them several times, on the picket lines of the National Graphical Association at *The Stockport Messenger*'s plant in Warrington; during a CND demonstration at Burtonwood, where a military air base was believed to be 'one of the United States's major storage depots for its nuclear arsenal in Britain'; and on a picket line at Kirkless Colliery, near Wigan. When magistrates fined one student £40 with £25 costs, the Union agreed to pay the costs, whilst the money for the fine came from a CND benefit disco and a benefit performance of Steven Berkoff's fringe play *Decadence* at Owens Park.

Greater uncertainty surrounded the Union's support for the miners during the prolonged and bitter strike against pit closures which began on 7 March 1984. In the spring term of that year the Union adopted a policy on human rights which included a clause pledging it in general terms to support the 'struggle' of all workers. On 1 May this was put to a specific test, when a branch of the National Union of Miners (NUM) at Bold Colliery asked the Union Executive to arrange accommodation for secondary pickets, who were miners from Yorkshire and Northumberland. One account suggested that the original request referred to 500 miners and the Union decided that they could cope with 100. Should they put them up in the Union building? Julian Sampson, the Education Officer, a Conservative member of the Union Executive, opposed the idea, arguing that hitherto 'support' had meant nothing more than sending sympathetic telegrams or allowing some use of office facilities to those supported. To offer accommodation to 'flying pickets engaged in a highly politicised industrial dispute' would fly in the face of the Attorney-General's letter; the Union's trading company, Materialise Ltd., could not lawfully pay, because its object was to enable students to attend demonstrations, not to give direct assistance to members of the public who were not students. 'Even if there were no expenditure involved, money in kind would have been provided in a building set up by public funds.' By virtue of the Trust agreement of 1963, the University had the power to prevent the use of the building for any purpose 'which in the opinion of the University Council shall be deemed of such a character as to injure or cause discredit to the University'.

Unbidden, Julian Sampson consulted the Registrar, who apparently told him that, having taken soundings, he thought that Council might intervene and fine the Union for misusing the building. The Executive decided to compromise by agreeing to put up the miners, not on Union premises, but in the houses of student volunteers. Jo White, the General Secretary, doubted the wisdom of challenging the University authorities in the summer term, the worst possible time to galvanise members, because most undergraduates would be obsessed with revision and preoccupied with exams. Although the miners had received practical help, some political posturing followed and the Executive stood accused of timidity in missing an opportunity to take on the University, the Attorney-General and other members of the Establishment, and in backing down at the instigation of a Conservative officer. They could reasonably claim, however, to have had no authority from any General Meeting to accommodate trade unionists on Union premises, and no time to summon a General Meeting to settle the matter.

On 10 October 1984 a General Meeting pledged more specific support to the striking miners. The Union undertook to support all miners' initiatives; to make its own publishing facilities and a minibus available to local NUM branches and Miners' Support Groups; to form a Miners' Solidarity Society to give support within the University; and to purchase at cost price 7,000 copies of *The Miner* (the NUM bulletin), distributing them with *Mancunion* so long as the dispute continued. It was the last of these measures that appeared to overstep the mark, and probably accounted for an item of about £700 in the Union accounts which the University auditors chose to query. It seemed possible that the University might withhold the sum – equivalent to about 0.13 per cent of the Union's grant – from the Union's allowance for 1985–86; but nothing more was heard of the matter, and no furore broke out. When the Union Council proposed to donate £1,300 to the NUM from a 'now defunct rent strike fund', a student objected on the different grounds that there were other causes, such as famine relief in Ethiopia, whose claims were equally strong. Much of the money for the Union's Miners' Support group, which 'adopted' Parkside Colliery at St Helens, came from daily collections taken at the University and weekly collections taken at Piccadilly Station.

Sharper conflict between the Union and the University eventually arose from the policy of 'No Platform for Racists and Fascists' which had originated with the NUS in the 1970s and exercised a strong influence over the Union. Many students had criticised its loose terminology and the practice of applying it only to movements of the Right, whereas in their view Marxist ideologies were equally inclined to totalitarianism, and the 'Fascism of the Left' was as much to be feared. In debate, some students argued that tyranny was a perversion of Marxism, but essential to Fascism, and so the discriminate treatment of the conflicting ideologies could be justified. As John O'Farrell wrote in his account of eighteen miserable years as a Labour supporter, the great Voltairean principle of free speech was giving way to another – 'I don't agree with what you say, and you can't say it because you're a Fascist'. In 1981 Geoff Glover, a member of the Union Executive, felt moved to explain a fundamental difference between Conservatism and Fascism: Conservatism had nothing to do with making the State 'the be-all and end-all of human existence' but wanted to shrink it and emphasise the principle of individual liberty. He warned of the violent, intimidating language used by the Left – 'the Tories must be smashed', 'Big Business must be destroyed', 'the Fascists must be kicked off the streets' (possibly with the aid of the

Doctor Marten boots favoured, at least in cartoons, by members of the Socialist Workers Students Party). In future, however, many students would associate the Government with heavy-handed policing, 'racist' immigration policies and the suppression of dissent; they would find it hard to perceive the Conservatives as a party of liberty. The supportive State might be withering away, but the oppressive State was gathering strength.

There was a risk that the Union would close its ears to speakers who challenged its agreed policies and lose the opportunity of refuting in public debate any arguments which it disliked. The dilemma was whether to wait for speakers to make inflammatory remarks, rule these out of order and prosecute the offenders under the Race Relations and Public Order Acts, or whether to disqualify the speakers in advance on the grounds of the opinions they were believed to hold or their membership of proscribed organisations. If the Union Executive gave a platform to an unpopular speaker, were members of the audience entitled to seize the initiative and disrupt the meeting? The Executive occasionally employed other forms of censorship by denying certain organisations the right to distribute literature or make presentations on Union premises; it accorded such treatment not only to the Reunification Church, otherwise known as the Moonies, but also to the Central Council for British Naturism, not because nudism was tyrannical, but rather on the grounds that the organisation's literature was sexist and homophobic. Disapproval of such tactics was not confined to politicians of the Right. When David Owen, the leader of the Social Democratic Party (SDP), visited the Union in October 1985, he called the 'No Platform' policy an erosion of democracy. Should twenty people wish to start a National Front Society in the Union they should be allowed to do so, for it was better to see these faces 'out in the open' and allow debate to take place.

Between November 1983 and November 1985 the visits of three Ministers of the Crown to the Students' Union gave rise to scenes of public disorder which were widely reported in the media, much to the University's discomfort. At the heart of the disturbances were Michael Heseltine, the Defence Secretary; Leon Brittan, the Home Secretary; and David Waddington, the Minister of State at the Home Office. Some commentators believed that the visitors (or their hosts, the Conservative societies) were bent on provocation: that their aim was to force the issue of free speech in university unions, and to manoeuvre supporters of the Far Left into committing acts of ritual hooliganism before the cameras in such a way as to discredit all students in the public eye. Heseltine and Brittan, or their advisers, insisted on facing demonstrators at the front of the Union building rather than entering discreetly by a side door. Heseltine's visit coincided with the installation of American Cruise missiles at Greenham Common in Berkshire and at Molesworth in Cambridgeshire; Brittan's with the final collapse of the miners' strike. Waddington was held responsible for 'racist' immigration controls and heartless deportations of visitors to the country.

There were both similarities and contrasts between the three visits and the actions which ensued, and the events doubtless influenced each other. One theory held that the failure of the police to protect Heseltine put them on their mettle and accounted for their brutal efforts to ensure Brittan a safe passage into the Union building. After Heseltine's visit the University blamed outsiders, rather than its own students, for the worst disturbances on the Union steps and in the Debating Hall. In the wake of Brittan, numerous public order offences allegedly committed outside the Union came before the magistrates' courts, and many questions arose about the conduct of the police and the University's duty to protect its students from persecution at the hands of maverick officers. In the Waddington case, disorder arose only within the Union building and the police were little involved, the magistrates not at all, whilst only Manchester students were blamed. For the first time, too, the University censured the Union Executive and, considering their discipline too feeble, set up its own tribunal – a move construed as an attack on the Union even by students who did not sympathise with the tactics of the accused.

Michael Heseltine's hosts, the Federation of Conservative Students, gave short notice of his impending visit and only divulged the news the day before his arrival. In the time available the Union officers hastened to appoint stewards for the meeting and to hire a security firm to control the entrances to the Main Debating Hall; if they had little time to prepare, it was also true that the opposition to the Minister had little time to organise. According to the account which the Vice-Chancellor later gave to the University Council, Mr Heseltine and his escort, approaching the Union building at midday on 15 November 1983, passed through a crowd of between fifty and eighty persons, some hostile and others encouraging. Then 'a man in the second rank of the crowd squeezed a plastic bottle full of thinned paint and directed the jet towards the Minister. The red paint hit him on the forehead and, as he turned away, on the back of his head.' The assailant disappeared into the crowd and his victim was hastily taken to the barber's shop in the Union to be cleaned up and enabled to face his audience with dignity. A group of twenty or thirty persons, hell-bent on disruption, forced their way into the Main Debating Hall. Despite their efforts the Minister succeeded in holding forth for about twelve minutes. *Mancunion* reported that he spoke of the 'most precious asset of university life – the freedom to speak and say what you want', and rebuked hecklers with, 'If the only intellectual contribution you can make to this debate is to shout, at the top of your voice, inarticulate and irrational abuse, then the British democracy will judge you for what you are.'

Two student journalists provided, under the headline 'HASSLETIME REVISITED', a dispassionate analysis of media treatment of the event. It was hardly surprising that neither *The Sun* (which screamed of an 'AMAZING GAUNTLET OF HATE') nor *The Daily Telegraph* should have a good word for the crowds, while television crews, focusing on a small group of troublemakers, presented students as hooligans. Even the more liberal papers underplayed the student CND's opposition to violence. For this the CND subsequently apologised to the Minister, although they denied having caused the disturbances themselves.

Advocates of discipline and punishment pointed out that the University of Warwick had recently fined its Students' Union £30,000 (equivalent to about 10 per cent of the Union's grant) for its part in recent demonstrations against Sir Keith Joseph, who had taken lunch on the campus. But the situations in Warwick and Manchester could hardly be compared, for at Warwick a Union General Meeting had itself organised a would-be peaceful demonstration and the Union had failed to control it or prevent damage to University premises. At Manchester the Vice-Chancellor and Council found no evidence to convict their own students of affray; anyone could walk on to the Union steps from Oxford Road, the paint-sprayer had escaped, and the foul-mouthed invaders of the Debating Hall had not been carrying student identity cards. Leaders of the student CND blamed Socialist Workers and Revolutionary Communists for the upheavals; student Socialist Workers were not displeased by the accusation, but made no moves to own up. The University was not moved to rebuke the Union officers, but could only acknowledge the harm which such incidents could inflict on the reputation, not only of Manchester, but of all universities. Council therefore set up a 'liaison group to oversee security arrangements for future visits to the University by persons in the public eye'; these measures had become too important to be left to the Union alone.

Some correspondents blamed the Union paper for publishing bowdlerised reports of the Heseltine affair which said nothing about police brutality towards demonstrators. This soon became a crucial issue, for events surrounding the visit of the Home Secretary sixteen months later earned the name 'Battle of Brittan', in memory of a violent encounter between police officers and a crowd trapped on the Union steps. On this occasion the student officers were well warned of the Home Secretary's impending visit and had ample time to discuss arrangements with the police. However, according to the left-wing journalist Martin Walker, they made a tactical error by agreeing that the steps of the Union building should be regarded, just for the night of Brittan's visit, as a public highway. 'In terms of public order law and police authority, they had just ceded their right to lawfully demonstrate on their own private property.'

A later report described how a good-humoured body of demonstrators and spectators assembled on the Union steps and surrounding pavements on the early evening of 1 March 1985, and the police made no attempt to stop them from so doing. 'The matters of concern for the protesters ranged from VAT on tampons, to immigration controls, and the policing of the miners' strike.' A banner exhorting 'SUPPORT THE MINERS ONE YEAR ON' topped the entrance to the building. Suddenly, a column of between twenty and forty police officers, marching in pairs, emerged from Dover Street and, without uttering any warning or calling upon the demonstrators to disperse, proceeded with the aid of reinforcements to clear the steps by driving a wedge into the crowd. Compressed into a narrow space, partly because Union security staff had closed the doors of the building, the crowd could only shove back. Pressure against the side railings was so hard that one of these snapped and several demonstrators fell on to bicycles parked six feet below.

One view of the incident was that the police involved, who were drawn from a paramilitary force known as the Tactical Aid Group, applied their training in riot control although they had no riot to contend with, and set out to occupy the Union building and its surroundings in the manner of a besieging army. Sinister significance was attached to a plan of the area chalked on a blackboard at Longsight police station, which a freelance photographer spotted and snapped through an open window. This diagram suggested to suspicious minds that the police had planned their assault in advance, regardless of the size or mood of any demonstration they might encounter. Rejecting the insinuation, the police report on the affair, published more than three years later, was to blame incompetence rather than confess to conspiracy: the police had planned a 'low-key' operation despite evidence that a large demonstration was likely, and arrived with no loud-hailer. Whatever the truth of the matter, the violence which occurred both before the Home Secretary's arrival and after his departure injured about forty people and resulted in forty arrests. Thirty-three persons were subsequently charged with public order offences, though only three were accused of assault, and only two of them were convicted: an outcome which suggested that it was not the crowd that resorted to rough tactics.

The Home Secretary arrived and police officers escorted him into the building with an elaborate show of force. Six members of the Executive had met and decided by majority vote, despite concern for the safety of Union members and staff, to let the meeting proceed. It proved to be hot-tempered and disorderly, inflamed by the events outside, but the officers of the Union could claim to have upheld Mr Brittan's right to free speech as far as they were able. Many of the audience had intended to demonstrate silently by turning their backs on the speaker, but now changed their tactics and voiced angry protests against the behaviour of the police. In the words of *Mancunion*, the Home Secretary's speech on law and order degenerated into an 'improvised rant'. He was disconcerted only by a question 'from one Jew to another' demanding why the police had to use excessive force. Otherwise he replied in kind to the protesters, saying, 'You're not worthy of your educational privileges', and (according to *The Manchester Evening News*) calling them 'rent-a-crowd, cowardly bullies, yobboes, a bunch of lunatics and fascist cheer-leaders guilty of the worst kind of intellectual hypocrisy'. A medical student wrote: 'How I would have loved to see this unpleasant man embarrassed, not by constant abusive heckling, but by constructive questioning on his racist policies, on his policing tactics, etc.'

As with the Heseltine affair, some public and media reactions were hostile. Even the *THES* spoke of 'infantile Scargillism among some students' and warned of its consequences: 'Not only do such outbreaks, which of course make perfect primetime television, give higher education a bad name with the public, but they are widely interpreted as proof of the inability of universities, polytechnics and colleges to manage their own affairs with reasonable discipline.' But a mother wrote to *The Guardian* in support of her daughter, a pacifist, aged nineteen, whom she had seen on the nine o'clock news emerging backwards at the bottom of the Union steps 'from under the feet of dozens of charging policemen'. She added that 'contrary to what the media would have us believe, the police now bring serious trouble whenever they descend *en masse*'. Attention began to shift from student disorder to police misconduct, and in the series of inquests which followed the BBC played a prominent part.

Within a few days a general meeting of students packed the Whitworth Hall and censured four Union officers for having the doors of the building closed when the police wheeled into the crowd and for allowing Brittan to speak in the wake of police violence. At the request of James Anderton, the Chief Constable of Greater Manchester, the Somerset and Avon Constabulary embarked on a prolonged investigation which proceeded under the umbrella of the newly-established Police Complaints Authority; a full summary of its long-delayed report was to appear only in 1988, some three-and-a-half years after the events of 1 March 1985. This document would admit to peccadilloes, but not to iniquities or conspiracies, on the part of the police. Sceptics distrusted any inquiry which involved the police investigating the police and objected to the University's decision to allow the investigators a room in St Peter's House, as well as to the chummy relations which apparently existed between the two forces, the judges and the judged. But the Home Secretary rejected pleas for an independent tribunal. In an effort to create one, the City Council's Police Monitoring Committee, whose aim was to insist that the police be accountable to the people, set up an unofficial inquiry of their own under the chairmanship of John Platts-Mills, a left-wing Queen's Counsel and peace campaigner who had proved too radical for the Labour Party.

Both the police and the Platts-Mills inquiries disposed of incomplete evidence, in that no police officer would talk to the City's investigators, and the Students' Union refused to co-operate with the police inquiry. Individual students spoke to the police and at least one came to regret it, but many others distrusted them, not only in principle but also from a fear that evidence given to the police might be disclosed to prosecutors in the magistrates' courts. At trials held in April and May 1985, nineteen defendants were convicted (some convictions were later quashed on appeal) and fourteen were found not guilty, partly as a result of confused and inaccurate police evidence.

Having received 102 eye-witness statements, representing one-fifth to one-quarter of the crowd which had awaited Brittan, the Platts-Mills panel reported in November 1985 that virtually all of them had testified to aggressive and violent policing, while forty-eight witnesses claimed to have been assaulted by police officers. 'In our view, the failure to give the demonstrators an opportunity peacefully to move from the steps was unreasonable, unjustifiable, and, in the circumstances, highly irresponsible.' The BBC screened a programme, 'A Fair Degree of Force', in a series called *Brass Tacks*, to coincide with the publication of the report. The makers focused on violent police action at essentially peaceful gatherings, not only in Manchester but also at Orgreave coking plant and at Stonehenge.

Platts-Mills and his colleagues took seriously some alarming reports of the persecution of two Manchester students who were believed to be in possession of evidence against police officers and well placed to complain of them. One was Sarah Hollis, a third-year medical student; the other, Steven Shaw, who was in his final year, reading Politics and Philosophy, and writing a thesis on police technology under the supervision of Roger Williams, the Professor of Science and Technology Policy. Both told appalling stories, not only of being trailed and threatened with unlawful arrest by men who appeared to be plain-clothes policemen, but also of having their homes burgled, as though to relieve them of incriminating documents. Steven Shaw claimed to have had his thesis stolen, to have been strip-searched for drugs in Bootle Street police station, and to have been assaulted and burned with cigarettes on the cheekbone during a return visit to Manchester in January 1986 some months after graduating. The police inquiry appeared to have no interest in investigating these allegations and to prefer to turn on the people who had made them, for it found no corroboration of Sarah Hollis's statements, questioned her integrity, and went so far as to recommend that Steven Shaw be prosecuted for attempting to pervert the course of justice.

Academics, particularly elected members of Senate, were horrified by the reports and strove, together with the Union officers, to bring the matter at intervals before the Senate and the Assembly and to press the police to publish their report without further delay. They were anxious that the University should take action to protect its students, and grew impatient with the non-committal attitude adopted, at least in public, by the University administration. More than a year after the Battle of Brittan, the plight of the two students influenced the election of the new Chancellor, in which victory went to the distinguished lawyer John Griffith, in the summer of 1986. An article in *The Guardian* reported that 'Many students and staff were already disappointed by the ostrich-like position of the authorities over Hollis and Shaw' and described Griffith as 'a man with a sterling record on civil liberties, who might be expected to take an interest in the unlucky two'.

Sarah Hollis's case was all the more poignant because her natural instinct was to refute indiscriminate attacks on the police; a clergyman's daughter, she had, she once said, grown up in a quiet part of Suffolk where citizens trusted them. She had criticised in a letter to *Mancunion* the provocative behaviour of student activists who had got themselves arrested in a demonstration in Manchester on 23 November 1984 against the erosion of the student grant – 'I do not say I condone any police violence which occurred on Friday, but I do say that the whole incident could and should have been avoided.' Injured after the Home Secretary's departure on 1 March 1985, she became the subject of a famous news photograph which showed her lying unconscious at the foot of the Union steps with senior police officers kneeling at her side. The *Daily Mail* published the picture with the caption 'Police Aid Demo Girl' as evidence of police chivalry and compassion (this was misleading, at least in the sense that she was not a demonstrator, but was present as a member of the Union Council and had been helping to issue tickets for the meeting). Sarah Hollis objected to the tone of a book on the Brittan affair by Martin Walker, who had already written, or collaborated in, two books about the miners' strike. Though favourable to her personally, Walker advanced arguments which she could not accept, for he depicted the 'paramilitary police' as supporters of the State against the people and as hostile, by virtue of their 'right wing lumpen ideology', to students in general and socialist students in particular. 'Students', he wrote, 'are a good anvil for the hammer of this new order; by their very nature they do not appear to produce and the liberal structure of the institution of learning allows them to develop life-styles which are different. And if it is the case that they do not much feel like causing trouble, then trouble can be thrust on them.' Disliking such insinuations, Sarah Hollis thought the title of the book, *With Extreme Prejudice,* all too revealing of its own assumptions. 'I am saddened that he should use my story to perpetuate and accentuate the chasm of mistrust and misunderstanding which exists between the police and many of the public.'

But she had her own, more specific, complaints. She had lost all faith in the police inquiry and reported that Deputy Chief Constable Reddington of the Somerset and Avon Constabulary had asked her 'why they should believe me when I was publicly ambitious in the Students' Union (I was a member of Amnesty International and CND, and Grant and Welfare Secretary of the Union)'. She complained that an interim report produced by the inquiry had identified eight cases of assault by policemen, but held no senior officers responsible for the operation which had gone disastrously wrong. Eventually, in 1991, when a qualified doctor, she lost a civil action against Greater Manchester Police in the High Court: several police officers maintained that she had accidentally tumbled down the Union steps, and the judge did not accept her claim that a policeman had caused her fall.

Steven Shaw, however, was happy to endorse Martin Walker's book. Friends and supporters launched a 'Justice for Steven Shaw' campaign in May 1986. He left the country the following autumn to escape prosecution and the danger of further harassment. He became a hero and a martyr for students fearful of an incipient police state devoted to crushing dissent and determined to retaliate against anyone who complained. Some were anxious to create monuments to him and to the Battle of Brittan, for student folk-memory was notoriously short, and the next cohort would probably forget both the man and the event. In the words of a ballad published in *Mancunion* in March 1987:

> 'It's a few bad apples', the Liberals cry,
> 'The British Police's standards are high.'
> Go over to Ireland, ask dead children's mums,
> Ask Cherry Groce about police use of guns,
> Ask them in Brixton, in Handsworth, Moss Side,
> Ask Wapping pickets if Steven Shaw lied.
> When the statutes come in and the laws are
>   re-written,
> Who's left to fight for justice in Britain?
> When the history books shut and the gravestones
>   are written,
> Will you have fought for justice in Britain?'

Trevor Suthers, then a postgraduate student, wrote a play about Steven Shaw's experiences, which the student Umbrella Theatre Company rejected on artistic grounds in 1987. Revised, adapted and thinly disguised, with the Shaw character named Peter Avon and the poll tax revolt as background, it was performed at the Green Room five years later under the title *Conspiracy to Pervert* (the author was now a scriptwriter for *Coronation Street*). On 7 October 1987 the Union agreed that the new Union building, then in the offing but not yet in being, should be named the Steven Shaw Building. In 1990, when the building was in use as a nightclub, the Union Council agreed that it should indeed be called the Steven Shaw Building by way of a sub-title, but should for commercial purposes continue to be known as the Academy.

However, comparisons of Steven Shaw with 'the Birmingham Six, the Guildford Four and the Broadwater Farm Three' savoured of hyperbole. They provoked a mocking letter from 'The Birchfields Five', who were bored with left-wingers' tales of injustice. Their question, 'Steven who?', perhaps reflected a shift to the Right, or towards a lower degree of political awareness and a more hedonistic outlook, on the part of students in general. 'Students that go to the Academy', they argued, 'do not do so to hold earnest debate on the subject of whether the Steven Shaw case should merit a feature on *Panorama*. They are there to drink, dance and enjoy a band.'

In November 1985 the Deputy Chief Constable, John Stalker, wrote to the BBC rejecting the findings of the Platts-Mills inquiry and citing recent events as proof that the University contained violent students. He referred to the treatment of the Home Office Minister David Waddington, who had been expected to speak at the Union on the theme 'That no western country can get along without immigration control'. Waddington entered and left the Union building without hindrance. Police officers observed the proceedings but did not intervene. However, hecklers in the meeting hall almost drowned the Minister's remarks and the behaviour of about thirty students, which was uncouth rather than violent – they threw paper missiles, spat at the speaker and tried to grab the microphone – plunged the University back into public disapproval. As convention demanded, Mr Waddington denounced his tormentors with gusto as 'left-wing fascists'; predicted that 'however loud you shout you will not be able to stop freedom of speech in Britain'; and commented afterwards that 'those students were not fit to be educated at the country's expense. They acted like pigs.'

Fearing for the University's reputation, unable to blame the disturbance on outsiders, the Vice-Chancellor and the University Council for the first time taxed the Union Executive with taking inadequate precautions and failing to apologise to the Minister (the Union took the view that any apology should be made by the Federation of Conservative Students, who had invited him). The Council called for reports on the affair and dismissed the first, like a tutor rejecting a feeble student essay, as inadequate; the second, though an improvement, they found unsatisfactory. They refused to accept the student officers' claim that 'attempts at disruption were dealt with speedily and effectively'. The student officers contended that the Union's own disciplinary procedures ought to suffice, for these included 'fines, reprimand, suspension of membership and expulsion', and the purported offences had taken place on Union territory.

Council requested the Union officers to make the outcome of their proceedings public, which they might not otherwise have done. But in any case, as the Vice-Chancellor made clear, the University intended to invoke its own Statute XXI. This legislation empowered the Senate to establish a committee 'for the purpose of investigating and hearing cases of misconduct or breach of discipline', and the University's action marked the most determined move in almost twenty years to intervene in the Union's affairs. In the background was Ordinance XIV, which required every student to 'maintain at all times and in all places a standard of conduct and behaviour proper to academic life'. The Senate disciplinary committee was chaired by a Pro-Vice-Chancellor, A.A. Grant, the Professor of Restorative Dentistry, and consisted of another five academics and a student, who was to be nominated by the General Secretary of the Students' Union. Donald Redford, the Chairman of the University Council, proclaimed to the Court of Governors in January 1986 that 'Denial of free speech anywhere on our campus is a threat to us all: gross incivility and mindless braying must be banished forever.'

The establishment of the committee antagonised many students. Conflict arose, not for the first time, between radicals who wanted an immediate resort to direct action, and moderates (including Chris Grant, the General Secretary of the Union) who saw the occupation of the University offices as an ace to be played only when all other tactics had failed, and a move to be undertaken only with the support of other campus unions whose members would be affected. A General Meeting voted, by the narrow margin of 128 votes to 124, to occupy parts of the Main Building and the Beyer Building, and certain students did so for five days, between 23 and 28 January 1986. The University obtained a repossession order. The occupiers withdrew at the behest of an Emergency General Meeting attended by 1,200 students, at which the General Secretary argued that the Union should occupy only in the unlikely event of the University expelling the accused students. Chris Grant's dilemma was so painful that he contemplated resignation, saying in an open letter that he had 'become depressed by the undercurrent of values, attitudes and motives that determine the mainstream political discourse of the Union'.

The Senate tribunal passed sentence on four students, including the Conservative chairman of the meeting, who had compounded the disorder by kicking out at protesters in an attempt to protect the speaker. They preferred suspensions to expulsions. This decision was not, perhaps, a cunning move to confuse the situation, but an attempt to follow precedent. The University had last established a disciplinary committee in 1968, when students disrupted a meeting (not arranged by the Union) addressed by a Minister, Patrick Gordon Walker, and the guilty parties had been suspended for the rest of the academical year. In 1986, however, when general support for the culprits was stronger and the issues more complex, it was soon being argued that suspensions were tantamount to expulsions, for the students concerned would probably be unable to obtain grants to resume their academic work. As though prepared at last to recognise the University's disciplinary system, the students lodged an appeal and some of them retained the services of the Longsight solicitor Rhys Vaughan, who had defended students involved in CND demonstrations and in the Brittan affair. Another occupation followed on 11–14 February and ended in an eviction. Academics began, meanwhile, to divide into hardliners who wanted exemplary punishments imposed and softliners who believed that the University was over-reacting and making too many concessions to political expediency. One group accused the University of failing to observe natural justice and improperly disciplining some students for 'extra-curricular activities' whilst failing to defend others (Sarah Hollis and Steven Shaw) against police harassment.

The chairmanship of the appeal tribunal was entrusted to Sir George Kenyon, the former Chairman of the University Council, who had considerable experience as chairman of a bench of magistrates. He recognised the qualities of the defence advocate, 'an experienced campaigner in fighting for the rights of the weak, the oppressed and the left-wingers who were so monstrously ill-used by society and by those like me who always seemed to be appointed and not elected. My main struggle was to demonstrate to him that it was a fair hearing without, of course, making concessions.' The appeal tribunal inclined to leniency. Two suspensions were suspended in return for promises of good behaviour and the students concerned were allowed to continue their courses; one student who, the defence argued, had incurred guilt by association, saw his conviction quashed; the young Conservative chairman of the meeting was fined and reprimanded. Sir George conceded that Waddington had been 'very provocative'.

Left-wingers hailed the decisions as a triumph for their own tactics. Chris Grant pointed out, however, that the accused had neglected to defend themselves properly in the first round of the proceedings and that only when they consented to do so had a just result been achieved. Some University critics murmured of appeasement, and a member of the Estates and Services Department adapted Kipling to the occasion:

'It seems wrong to be so prudent when confronted
    by the students,
In the hope that they'll succumb and go away . . . '

Sir George sensed his own unpopularity, but noted with satisfaction in
his memoirs that no further trouble ensued and peace was restored.

The student officers were mollified when the Committee on Relations between the University and the Union, chaired by Fred Tye, an
infinitely patient and reasonable trainer of headteachers, agreed that
Union discipline would suffice to deal with some offences. In turn the
Union agreed that, while it had no duty to provide platforms for those
who would advocate 'political, religious or racial discrimination', it
would welcome speakers 'across the conventional spectrum of British
politics'. The appeal board sought clarification of the ordinance governing student conduct, and a Senate Committee duly proposed a
more precise but still elastic form of words. This new formula specified
that students would be liable to disciplinary action for behaviour which
was 'discreditable to the University or detrimental to the discharge
of the University's obligations under the Charter'; which disrupted
the University's work or damaged its property; which obstructed
or endangered 'the safety of officers, employees or students of the
University or visitors to the University'; or which involved cheating
in examinations.

Rephrasing only slightly the crucial sentence in the existing Ordinance XIV, the new draft ordinance generally required students to
'maintain at all times and in all places an acceptable standard of conduct'. Seeing in this all-embracing demand a gladiator's net in which
students could easily become entangled, George Wilmers, a mathematical logician and an elected member of Senate, resisted it in Senate.
Afterwards he fought a rearguard action in the Court, and almost succeeded in carrying a proposal to refer the new clauses back to Senate
and Council for further consideration. His motion was defeated, but
only by a narrow margin (47 votes to 42), and he hastened to upbraid
the student representatives for their sleepiness at Senate and their failure to attend the Court and support him. In his view the students were
failing to notice the threats to their own liberties and becoming slow
to resist them. There were some signs that from this point onwards the
real critics of the establishment were not to be students but academics
determined to resist the extension of central executive power in the
University, and that their chosen arena for constitutional and other
skirmishes would be the Court.

Parliament was soon to compel universities to take steps to protect free speech. Manchester was not unique; there had been several other incidents elsewhere, and Fred Silvester, the Conservative MP for Manchester Withington, was prepared to recite a long litany of these for the benefit of the House of Commons. Early in 1986, as though strongly moved by events occurring on or near his patch, he introduced a Private Member's Bill. His proposals eventually found a place in the Government's Education (No. 2) Act 1986, which imposed on the governing bodies of institutions of higher education a duty to work out a Code of Practice on Freedom of Speech. Manchester's version of this was in being by May 1987. But it seemed important to show that the Union could make satisfactory arrangements of its own volition before the new procedures came into effect.

In October 1986 the visit of Edwina Currie, the Junior Health Minister, passed off well and offered proof that a Tory Minister could enjoy a hearing in Manchester in the face of profound disagreement and a large body of demonstrators gathered outside the Union. Although duty-bound to disapprove of the lady, *Mancunion* conscientiously reported repartee which suggested that the Minister had given as good as she got. Rebuking students for smoking, she reminded them that the duty on tobacco would go to finance Trident missiles. To a heckler she replied: 'I understand you are a member of the Socialist Workers' Party. You are not a socialist but a Marxist and if you're a worker I'm very surprised.' In the matter of free speech, she advised students to listen to all known racists and then prosecute them for any breaches of the law they might have committed. She called it 'A very good, very lovely meeting which I thoroughly enjoyed.' Less engaging members of the Government and the majority party found themselves addressing thinly attended meetings, as did, between November 1986 and June 1988, Kenneth Clarke, the Employment Minister; Neil Hamilton, the Member for Tatton; Peter Walker, the Secretary of State for Energy; Lord Joseph, now retired from office; Sir Patrick Mayhew, the Attorney-General; and Tim Janman, the Member for Thurrock, who objected to students' unions compelling their members *en bloc* to be members of the NUS. Neil Hamilton, according to *Mancunion,* attracted an audience of thirty-three and Lord Joseph an audience of forty-one. Newsworthy unpleasantness recurred only at a meeting addressed in June 1990 by John Selwyn Gummer, the Minister for Food and Agriculture, who was regaled with ritual obscenities by members of the Socialist Workers' Student Society.

Manchester's code of practice on free speech outlawed the NUS policy of 'No Platform for Racists and Fascists'. It denied students and

others the right to refuse the premises of the University and the Union
to any individual or body of persons properly invited, on grounds connected with 'the belief or view of that individual or body' or 'the policy or objectives of that body'. In some circumstances the Registrar
might pronounce it impracticable to hold a 'controversial' meeting,
presumably on the grounds that it would be impossible to guarantee
order without overspending on security, or that the bounds of lawful
speech would inevitably be transgressed. The decision to grant or
refuse a platform would no longer rest with students, but the organisers of the event and the chairman of the meeting would be held
responsible for ensuring that the proceedings stayed within the law.
Should the University feel that its good name had suffered, the principal organiser (for Union events this would be the Education and University Affairs Officer) would have to report fully to the University and
provide details of any disciplinary action the Union might be taking.

The new code came up for testing in October 1987 on a potentially
disastrous occasion – the visit, to take part in a debate, of Ray Honeyford, a former Bradford headmaster who held controversial views on
multicultural education. The subject of the discussion was 'The
Advantages and Disadvantages of Segregation on Ethnic Lines'. No
serious incidents occurred, partly because Honeyford was diluted by
less provocative speakers, and partly because of his own self-restraint.

The Brittan affair dragged on long after the Waddington upheavals
had subsided and the good faith of the police inquiry continued to be
disputed. Fragmentary pronouncements were issued in February
1987, at which point the Police Complaints Authority sent a letter
exonerating the Union Executive and the Manager 'from blame for
the unfortunate events on the steps'. Since the inquiry was recommending a number of prosecutions, the Director of Public Prosecutions delayed publication of a full summary of the report on the
grounds that it might conceivably prejudice fair trials. Three constables were prosecuted, one for assault and two for perjury, but some
students believed them to be scapegoats picked on to divert attention
from the failings of senior officers, and they attracted a measure of
sympathy. The case against all these defendants proved to be flimsy
(had they, perhaps, been chosen for that very reason?) and they were
acquitted. Another defendant was charged with attempting to pervert
the course of justice, but he too was found 'Not Guilty'. This was a
local man named Frank Logan, who had signed a sworn statement to
his solicitor to the effect that two detectives had encouraged him to
burgle Sarah Hollis's flat in John Nash Crescent, Hulme. 'One of

them said that if I was going to do anything I should do Sarah Hollis's place.' The only case which did not end in acquittal was the one which was never tried, that of Steven Shaw. After the failure of the Logan prosecution in May 1988, Senate resolved to ask the Director of Public Prosecutions to reconsider the charges against Steven Shaw, but he refused to drop the case.

The report of the Independent Police Complaints Authority, at last summarised publicly and fully in the autumn of 1988, admitted to some errors but trapped no big fish, and rejected the allegations made by Sarah Hollis and Steven Shaw. It concluded by dividing the blame between a minority or 'hard core' of the demonstrators, who had supposedly set out to stop Mr Brittan entering the building, and a minority of the police. In the words of the report, 'errors of judgement on the part of two senior officers, and the excessive use of force by relatively few policemen, enabled the hard core to turn what was intended by the majority to be a normal political demonstration into a violent and unnecessary confrontation with the police'. John Platts-Mills later commented, in his autobiography *Muck, Silk and Socialism*, that 'They might as well not have bothered.'

With time, in the later 1980s, it proved possible to build up a more amiable image of the police, which did not present them as the fist of the State. The friendly officer on the beat had faded into distant memory along with *The Blue Lamp*, *PC 49* and *Dixon of Dock Green*, but in University and student eyes there was a role for the police as advisers on security, on the avoidance of rape, burglary and mugging in a dangerous city. Jack Richards, a superintendent at Longsight police station, gave a friendly interview to *Mancunion* in which he denied that his officers were generally hostile to students; their commonest complaint was that students lacked caution and were careless of property. WPC Hazel Fenwick, a part-time Psychology student, took up office as police-student liaison officer in 1988. It was her task to advise students on ways of securing their houses, and with help from students she ran a 'Women and Safety' road show and organised publicity for the new Rape Crisis Centre at St Mary's Hospital.

Like the trade unions, the Students' Union in Manchester lost some of its liberty during the 1980s. Reformed financial arrangements, however, caused less friction than predicted. Wrangling over a capitation fee of £25 had roused more passion than discussion of a block grant of £500,000. Much credit was due to the patience and courtesy of Fred Tye and much to the willingness of student officers to compromise and avoid incurring costly legal proceedings. A new entrepreneurial spirit made the Union less dependent on public funding and able to finance its own new building. Although a separate entity, the Union could not hope to be treated in all circumstances as a self-governing polity: actions committed on the premises of the Union, a building owned by the University, undoubtedly reflected on the University's reputation. 'Extra-curricular' they might be, but the University could hardly ignore them.

Politically conscious students were themselves divided on the everlasting issue of whether or not to allow free speech to those who would be the first to destroy it if given the chance. Universities presented themselves as theatres in which all issues could be debated and unpopular opinions advanced in the belief that reason would eventually prevail. Should that image be tarnished, they and their students would sink even lower in public esteem, and academic freedom, as interpreted by academics, would be in danger. Debaters had been more numerous but disrupters had tended to get their way. According to some shades of student opinion, to listen to and argue with opponents was to clothe them in respectability; disapproval of their attitudes would not be made plain enough. To silence them, however, was perhaps to take greater risks: it was to invite the media to condemn students, to identify the whole with a vociferous minority, to portray them as simpletons and parasites incapable of argument or tolerance, who could not exercise the skill which the University should have taught them and the country paid them to learn. The cumulative effect of three unhappy incidents in Manchester eventually goaded the University into actions which forfeited the sympathy of moderate students. Rough police tactics placed students on the same plane as industrial pickets and political subversives; talk of 'liberal degeneracy' and bureaucratic timidity blamed the University for not defending oppressed students with greater vigour. At last, however, a certain inbred moderation, a desire on both sides to respect legal procedures and avoid excessive harshness, an impatience with the escapades of the hard Left, helped to restore a working relationship between the University and the Students' Union.

10

Efficiency and academic freedom

Always inclined to describe grim situations in dispassionate tones, the Vice-Chancellor delivered on Founder's Day 1985 a speech packed with foreboding, as he analysed a four- or five-year plan hatched by the Government and the University Grants Committee. From October 1986 the UGC would begin to shift resources from universities deemed weak to universities deemed strong in research. Some might either go bankrupt or, being deprived of research funding altogether, fall to the rank of Liberal Arts Colleges, as in the United States. Universities (as he might well have reminded his audience) had complained in the 1970s of being treated by the Government as superior grammar schools whose sole function was teaching the young; unwelcome attention was now to be paid to the quality of their research, and the results of inquiries and surveys would be used to establish both the status of an institution and its entitlement to finance. Within a few days, or so rumour had it, the UGC would pass the black spot to some ill-favoured universities. 'It seems to be a central dogma for this Government that all large organisations need to be shaken up, and from such shake-ups advantages flow. The shake-up of the university system is at hand. If it develops in the way that seems to be foreshadowed it will produce much turbulence and not a little acrimony and pain. It might lead to greater efficiency by some measures, but will the quality of the output be improved at the end? I find it hard to convince myself that it is likely . . . '

Events would suggest that the Government, like some eighteenth-century barber surgeon, believed in the therapeutic value of letting blood. Year by year it reduced university funding by a series of 2 per cent cuts, not merely to relieve the taxpayers of their burdens, but to compel the universities to become more efficient. Towards the end of the 1980s the Government ceased to argue that the system had to shrink because the number of youthful customers was declining. It began to sing a new song, which called for an expansion of student numbers, a widening of access to universities, and a reduction in the unit of resource, which the UGC had once tried to protect. Allegedly, there was waste and mismanagement in universities. If they administered their resources with greater skill, adopted a corporate ethos and a system of line management, and used more economical methods of teaching (for example, by holding forth to large lecture audiences and classes), they would increase their productivity, churn out more graduates and publications, and be able to do everything that Government and society required of them. Intense competition both for fee-paying students and for research funds would best serve the customers of universities and get them the best deals at the lowest prices. All should live in what Dorothy Parker, discussing a different kind of poverty, called 'a state of stimulating insecurity'.

In material terms, the entire university system would be deprived of some funding, but some universities would fall faster than others. For Manchester and other reputable universities, the main consolations would lie in the occasional year in which (as in 1988–89) the University's block grant appeared for a time to have slightly outstripped inflation, and in the knowledge that some institutions were faring worse than they did, on La Rochefoucauld's principle that 'In the misfortunes of our friends, we always find something which is not displeasing to us.' Relatively modest cuts were sometimes termed 'votes of confidence'. In most league tables, particularly those relevant to the distribution of grant money, Manchester appeared among the top ten or twelve of the forty-odd universities in the country. Only in 1990 did its reluctance to pull in great numbers of additional students cause it to drop down the published lists and remind it forcefully of the fragility of all reputations.

Manchester University's liberal tradition, brilliantly expounded in the past by such writers as Gerald Aylmer, the History lecturer, and Eugène Vinaver, the famous Professor of French, was still in being. It rejected analogies between a university, an institution devoted to free inquiry, and a business corporation dedicated to the pursuit of material profit. Administrative hierarchies, and systems of rewards and promotions which made younger academics dependent on the favours of superiors, were in reality profoundly inefficient. They had always been sanctioned by the customs of Victorian civic universities, but they ought to be modified and not accentuated, because they interfered with the central purpose of the institution. They also weakened its resistance in the face of threats, on account of the mutual suspicion that existed between senior administrators and the rest of the University, who were being transformed from colleagues into employees. The growing obsession with competition, the intrusion of the market into academic life, threatened to destroy collaboration and the sharing of secrets between universities.

A major problem, however, was that the Government's tolerance for free inquiry was limited and that what it wanted was immediately useful inquiry, precise accounts of how its money was being employed, and assurances that resources were being well managed. Academics, none the less, found a spokesman for the liberal tradition in the Chancellor who was elected in 1986. Some of them set out to curb the growth of executive power by awakening from its 'ancient, dreamless, uninvaded sleep' the largest and hitherto most passive body in the University's constitutional machinery – the Court – and persuading it, like Tennyson's Kraken, to rise to the surface and roar.

In 1984 the Vice-Chancellor joined a committee established by the Committee of Vice-Chancellors and Principals (CVCP) to conduct a series of 'efficiency studies' of universities and make recommendations. This body consisted of six academics (five heads of universities and colleges and one registrar); of four businessmen, who were chairmen and directors of large international companies, including Plessey plc and the Ford Motor Company; of a civil servant, the Prime Minister's Adviser on Efficiency, with the Head of the Efficiency Unit as alternate; and of Sir Peter Swinnerton-Dyer, the Chairman of the UGC. Two of the businessmen involved were also the constitutional monarchs of universities. Sir Alex Jarratt, the ex-civil servant who presided, was the Chairman of Reed International and the Chancellor of Birmingham University; Sir Adrian Cadbury, the Chairman of Cadbury Schweppes, was Chancellor of Aston University, one of the three which had suffered most gravely in 1981. Jarratt's name was more ephemeral than that of Robbins, and his report far slimmer, but he and his committee likewise promised to leave an indelible mark on British universities; ministers turned to his pages before specifying the reforms they expected universities to introduce in exchange for their grants. Mark Richmond was said to have modified the more forthright opinions of the industrialists and civil servants round the table, but his connection with the report was to cause some difficulty with colleagues.

Jarratt criticised both the Government, for springing on the universities so many exercises in crisis management, and the universities themselves, for their habit of avoiding unpleasantness by imposing a mixture of equal and random misery when faced with cuts. At the core of the document was a call for long-term strategic planning and for the identification of strengths and weaknesses by the systematic use of so-called 'performance indicators'. On these should informed judgements depend, and on these should the management rely when deciding (presumably with outside help, for example from the UGC) which departments it should cherish and which it should permit to wither away or even dissolve. At present there were 'pressures to pre-serve cohesion and morale which lead to a reluctance to set priorities and even to discuss openly academic strengths and weaknesses'. Uni-versities should abandon the comforting fiction that one academic department was as good as another. Appendix G propounded long lists of telltale signs: 'internal' indicators, such as graduation rates, the classes of degrees awarded, teaching quality, and the capacity to attract research grants; 'external' indicators, such as publications, patents, inventions, consultancies, conference papers, medals and prizes; 'operating' indicators, such as staff–student ratios, class sizes, the range of optional courses offered to students, and the supply of books and computers. 'Input' and 'output' should now be measured as though the university were some vast processing plant. Inviting uni-versities to discharge superfluous committees, which consumed valu-able academic time, Jarratt and his colleagues implicitly called for more hours to be spent on compiling quantitative records and assess-ing colleagues' ability. Let talking shops fall silent and filing cabinets bulge with judgmental paper.

The Jarratt report called for the establishment in all universities of a central committee to control resources. It sought to reinforce exec-utive power and the capacity to take hard-headed decisions by empha-sising the Vice-Chancellor's role as Chief Executive and strengthening the hand of Council, responsible for financial management, against that of the supreme academic body, the Senate. For 'financial and aca-demic priorities' were 'potentially in conflict' and some friction might increase the health of the body politic. No longer should the Vice-Chancellor be the scholar who did the will of Senate, which was a nat-urally conservative body (this description, which perhaps applied to the Manchester Senate, would scarcely have fitted Stopford, Mans-field Cooper or Armitage). Seats on Council, urged Jarratt, should go to young and vigorous business executives, at the expense, if need be, of the representatives of local authorities. Deans and heads of depart-ments should acquire managerial skills and not be mere scholars reluc-tantly doing a little administration on the side. Deans should be expected to pursue the policies of their universities rather than the sectional interests of their constituents, and heads of departments should henceforth be appointed by councils on the recommendation of Vice-Chancellors after due consultation. Academics' performances should be 'appraised' every year 'with a view to their personal development' and the advancement of their careers.

Furthermore, the Jarratt Committee disapproved of the concept of 'academic-related' staff, of librarians, administrators, accountants, engineers, assistant bursars or managers who enjoyed tenure and were paid on the same scales as academics. Let their conditions of service be determined instead 'by the nature of their duties and in relation to similar employment outside the university'. It was better that university administrations should be unified under a single head, a registrar or secretary – not divided, as in Manchester, into two or even three domains of equal standing, under a Registrar, a Director of Finance and a Director of Estates and Services, lest the Vice-Chancellor have to spend his valuable time co-ordinating their efforts.

In general, stated the Jarratt Committee, 'in our view universities are first and foremost corporate enterprises to which subsidiary units and individual academics are responsible and accountable'. The notion of a university, or its board of directors, being accountable to its members seemed to have disappeared entirely. All these measures were represented as crucial to the survival of the organisations under review.

The University received the Jarratt report with due caution. Some of its recommendations reflected existing Manchester practice; the University Council eventually told the UGC that Manchester's JCUD was 'almost exactly in line with the central planning and resources committee described by Jarratt', and that planning and resources sub-committees already existed for the five principal academic areas. Other recommendations, concerning appraisal schemes and the appointment of heads of department, were under discussion. The Council were saddened by the resigned tone of parts of the report, which seemed willing to accept that no-one would pay for the huge backlog of maintenance and repair work on university estates. Donald Redford, the Chairman of Council, did not seem enamoured of the 'creative tension' which Jarratt advocated. 'All laymen', he said, 'are doubly sensitive about creating academic problems. We have no wish to depart from the strong tradition of not bringing Council and Senate into confrontation.'

Swinnerton-Dyer had written that it had not been Jarratt's intention to 'offer an inappropriate industrial solution' to the management problems of universities, but not everyone believed him. Those who referred to the Vice-Chancellor as the Chief Executive usually did so

with satirical intent. Some found it strange that, given the poor performance of British industry, its managerial techniques should be held
up as models. Some came to believe, in the years which followed, that
the talk of five-year plans savoured more of a kind of anaemic Stalin-
ism than of any policies appropriate to a liberal institution where
inspiration ought to spring from within the individual, could not be
imposed from above, and did not gain from being constantly watched
and controlled. Would the rise of 'senior management teams', the
stress on 'leadership' rather than self-government, create a world to
which academics had become incidental?

Lessons, said many, not without malicious satisfaction, should be
learned from the failure of one appointment in particular. In 1984 a
middle-aged accountant who had served ICI for twenty-three years
was appointed to the post of Director of Finance. He was expected,
as *This Week* told its readers, to 'bring wide industrial experience to
the task of running the University at a time of financial strain'. For
whatever reason, however, the University's problems appeared to
overwhelm the man of promise. When he resigned his post after
barely a year rumours spread that the University, which had not
insisted on a probationary period, had been forced to make a substantial *ex gratia* payment. Pointed questions were asked in Senate and
Court, and a 'torrent of information-free verbosity' from one Pro-
Vice-Chancellor did little to allay discontent. In December 1986 two
academic members proposed to Court that in future no-one should
be granted tenure immediately unless they had previously been
employed in a university (Manchester or another) for at least three
years. Their motion was referred to Council, which, while talking of
'flexibility' and declining to accept the proposal formally, agreed to
take some notice of the misgivings which lay behind it. Wisely, the
University now appointed to the Director's post one of its Deputy
Bursars, Garth Roberts, who had spent twenty years becoming inured
to its ways and had introduced a number of innovations. Industrial
experience, it seemed, would not always equip a person for academic,
or even para-academic, life.

In the summer of 1986 the election of a new Chancellor gave liberal
academics a chance to reaffirm the old values threatened by Government interference and the spread of 'managerialism'. The Duke of
Devonshire had resigned and been highly praised as 'a model Chancellor, always accessible but never interfering'. Even his many admirers
would not have claimed that he had an intimate knowledge of the
working of universities; nor, perhaps, would he have thought it proper

to acquire one. Five of the University's seven Chancellors (three of whom had been Dukes of Devonshire) had inherited titles long ago established; two of them, Morley of Blackburn (1908–23) and Woolton (1944–64), had been newly created peers. In 1986 the Chairman, Clerk and Committee of Convocation made some attempt to follow tradition by nominating Shirley Vaughan Paget, the Marchioness of Anglesey, although she was also the first woman candidate for the job. Neither a nonentity nor a philistine, she had a respectable record of public service, to the environment, to the arts, and to Women's Institutes; she had earned her own title as a Dame of the British Empire. She was the daughter of two novelists, one of them Hilda Vaughan, and the other the late Charles Morgan, the author of *The Fountain, The Voyage, Sparkenbroke, The Judge's Story* and other works alternately admired and derided by the intelligentsia from the 1930s to the 1950s. But, although she had received an honorary Doctorate of Laws from the University of Wales, she appeared to have no other experience of universities, and it could well be argued that in the 1980s the role of a Chancellor needed to be more than emblematic and ceremonial. The Marchioness lived in Llanfairpwll, Gwynedd, and had no obvious connection with the Manchester region.

Although there had never previously been a contested election, and many people would therefore have supposed that it was for the officers of Convocation to find a willing candidate and for the rest of Convocation to back their choice, members of the University became restive and uneasy. A postgraduate student, John Spencer, put up against the Marchioness like a stalking-horse testing the support for an established Conservative leader, in the belief that in the interests of academic democracy there ought to be a contest. His move turned out to be more than just an expensive stunt.

The election of the Chancellor lay in the hands of the Convocation, which had 80,000 members. Under Statute XVI, of 1973, the Convocation had come to include, not only the whole body of Manchester graduates, but also all members of the Assembly, many of whom did not hold Manchester degrees. Broadly speaking, the Assembly comprised all persons who held academic appointments and were actively involved with the University. They could be expected to influence strongly the result of any election, especially because the tight timetable imposed by the ordinance on the subject tended to disenfranchise overseas voters. Perhaps a contested election had seemed unlikely; let one unexpectedly occur, and the defects of the arrangements became apparent. The Chairman and Clerk of Convocation were now involved both in conducting a ballot and in sponsoring a candidate, a confusion of roles which put their impartiality in doubt. They had allowed little time for anyone to put up a rival contender for the title. Certainly no-one would be able to secure a list of backers comparable with the battalions of supporters who had lined up behind the Marchioness, as a result of the officers' pre-emptive strike. Despite this handicap, a group (sometimes described as 'rebel lecturers') succeeded in organising support for a serious challenger, at which point the postgraduate student withdrew from the contest.

The new candidate was John Griffith, Emeritus Professor of Public Law at the London School of Economics. He had written (among much else) a famous book on *The Politics of the Judiciary;* he had been a friend and collaborator of one of Manchester's greatest lawyers, Harry Street, who had died suddenly when walking in the Lake District in 1984; and he had delivered in Manchester the first Harry Street Memorial Lecture. As a founder member of the Council for Academic Freedom and Democracy (CAFD), Professor Griffith had led in 1970 the unofficial investigation into the decision of a Manchester committee not to appoint a young lecturer critical of the establishment, Anthony Arblaster, to a permanent post in Philosophy. A CAFD pamphlet had invited the University to clear its name by authorising its own judicial inquiry into events that cast a shadow upon its integrity. Rhys Vaughan, the solicitor defending student members of the CND charged with offences at Burtonwood in 1984, had used arguments which John Griffith was said by *Mancunion* to support – to the effect that it was lawful to use reasonable force to prevent the greater crime of preparing to inflict indiscriminate murder and destruction upon fellow creatures. Some supporters of Griffith saw in him the champion of the oppressed who would be capable of overcoming the University's reluctance to protest openly at the ill-treatment of Sarah Hollis and Steven Shaw. This issue apart, he was an outspoken critic of all measures that threatened the independence of universities in the face of government, and the freedom of individuals within them by the strengthening of hierarchies.

When agreeing to stand, John Griffith doubted his chances of winning the contest, but thought it important to challenge 'establishment procedures'. Unlike the Marchioness of Anglesey, he issued a statement to members of the Assembly (to send it to all members of Convocation would have been prohibitively expensive). ' . . . it is clear', he wrote, 'that the next five years or so will be the most critical since 1946. Progressively, universities are being drawn more and more under the control of central government authorities. This is a tendency I have continuously opposed . . . My principal concern today is with the crucial necessity that universities, their students and their academic staffs, should remain free to pursue their primary purpose of enlarging the understanding of their disciplines . . . When the universities are required to divert their efforts to the short-term ends of politicians, they begin to lose their freedom and to die.'

Ballot papers went out in preparation for an election to be held on 4 July 1986. They listed the number of persons who had nominated each candidate, thereby creating the impression that the Marchioness of Anglesey (1,100 names were arranged in twenty-four full columns) enjoyed overwhelming support. Between seventy and eighty supporters had nominated John Griffith and succeeded in occupying a mere three half-columns. For all this, Griffith, believed to have been strongly supported by the Assembly, won the election by an ample margin, mustering 2,881 votes against his opponent's 2,018; about 6 per cent of the electorate had taken part in the election. Lady Anglesey was gracious in defeat, saying that at least the electors had wanted somebody Welsh, and that supporters of Professor Griffith had run a very professional campaign. Some of the new Chancellor's supporters declared in their triumph that the result humiliated, not the losing candidate, but 'the cabal of academics and businessmen who feel free to run the University as if it were their family estate'.

By custom the formal duties assigned to the Chancellor consisted of presiding at meetings of the Court and of conferring honorary degrees. Little else was laid down. The Chancellor was expected to use on the University's behalf such influence as he possessed in high places, and his rights might perhaps have been explained by invoking Walter Bagehot on the Victorian monarchy – they surely included 'the right to be consulted, the right to encourage, the right to warn'. Professor Griffith would clearly be no King Log; might he, perhaps, prove to be King Stork and gobble up some of the University's juicier frogs? The students greeted him with good reason as a sympathetic presence, a 'voice on our side': he became the first Chancellor to address an Introductory General Meeting of the Students' Union and made diplomatic but firm statements in an article, 'Breaking the Mould', which appeared in *Mancunion* for 9 October 1986. 'My role is a limited one. The Vice-Chancellor is the person responsible for running the University and I have no doubt that there are many areas in which I shall have no right to interfere or, indeed, would think of doing so. I want to be helpful to the University as a whole. However, I am very conscious, from my experience, that there is not just one unified view, but many views in a university. I certainly shan't be able to please everybody.'

Griffith's suggestion that the students needed some kind of ombudsman, separated from the University hierarchy, created alarm. It was inevitable that members of the central establishment should see him as the leader of a faction, as one who encouraged the dissidents with whom they had little patience ('the students, the unorthodox left-wing members of the Association of University Teachers, and the non-professorial members of Senate'). Perhaps, however, his role was really to restore balance and to act as a mediator, ensuring that proper attention was paid to the opinions of groups which higher authority was inclined to treat dismissively or to patronise with a show of courtesy.

Most controversial was the Chancellor's decision to break with precedent by attending meetings of the University Council, of which he was a member by virtue of the University statutes. Lay members, or some of the more senior among them, were as shocked as if the monarch herself had materialised in the midst of Margaret Thatcher's cabinet or joined an Old Bailey judge on the bench. University liberals, however, thought Council needed watching lest, in the name of the Jarratt report and despite its Chairman's assurances, it begin to encroach on the academic territory of Senate. The Chancellor's analysis of Council meetings was less than complimentary: one or two of the laymen might be well informed about the issues discussed, but the rest would simply back the Vice-Chancellor. Since he and the Chairman had usually thrashed out all contentious matters before the meeting began, there was little chance of getting decisions reversed and the Chairman was unlikely to oppose the Vice-Chancellor openly. When an officer of the Students' Union complained of being patronised at Council in 1987, the Chancellor sympathised and said so; he asked only that her successor should inform him in advance of matters which the students intended to raise ('it is difficult to intervene off the cuff and without background information'). As he later said, he was 'on tap, not on top'.

While attending Council the Chancellor called for greater openness on the part of Council's specialised committees. Surely the Estates and Services Committee ought to consult about proposals affecting the environment, and the Finance Committee ought to provide more information to justify heavy investment in a company which was losing money, the University's own Vuman. His views diverged from those of the Vice-Chancellor at a Council meeting in February 1989 which discussed the possibility of docking academics' pay if, by way of protesting against an inadequate salary settlement, they refused to examine their students.

It was plain that the Chancellor had no time for the theory that the University ought to resemble a company or adopt a corporate identity. In his view, a university was essentially a framework within which individuals performed the functions of teaching and research as effectively as they could. His remarks on this subject, for example at Founder's Day lunches, were greeted with visible embarrassment at parts of the high table, but brought tears of relief to the eyes of some of the academics present, who had begun to fear that the liberal traditions of the University would be buried in an unmarked grave.

Many of the Chancellor's critics conceded that he presided expertly and with impeccable dignity and fairness over the Court; a genuinely independent Chairman, he had no need to seek rulings from the Vice-Chancellor or the Registrar. In theory at least the Court had always been the sovereign body within the University and the long stop of the constitution, since all statutes and ordinances depended on Court's endorsement. Some universities were accustomed to send statutes directly from their own councils to the Privy Council for final approval, but this was not the practice in Manchester. The Court did not figure in Jarratt's calculations, but technically Court, and not Council, reigned supreme in the University. However, since it normally met only twice a year, it could hardly become involved in the day-to-day business of running the institution, and there was some temptation to treat it as a cipher and take its approval for granted.

Before the mid-1980s, the Court had for many years done little more than acclaim decisions already made by Council and Senate, approve the University's annual report and accounts after little or no discussion, and listen politely to statements made by the Chairman of Council, the Treasurer and the Vice-Chancellor. George Wilmers, the mathematician, described it in 1988 as 'a rather motley collection of some 200 souls', composed in such a way as to 'give an impression of democratic accountability while ensuring absolute control by a small camarilla which dominates Council', and thus provide legitimacy to a 'self-perpetuating oligarchy'. Now, however, it became a forum in which contentious matters already discussed by Senate and Council, such as the ordinance on student discipline, were reopened before a different audience. Here, University dissidents could sometimes join forces with City councillors serving on Court and oppose members of the University Council. It was doubtful whether Court could enact legislation which had never been before Senate or Council, but it was possible to initiate at Court discussion of certain matters, such as equal opportunities policy, which were then referred to Senate and Council for further action. Buried grievances were disinterred at Court in the presence of journalists, to the potential embarrassment of higher authority. Wilmers and his colleagues urged members of the University to use their right to vote for representatives of Convocation on Court (there were thirty of these and they accounted for about 15 per cent of Court's membership). It was surely desirable, or so they argued, to keep these places out of the hands of nominees of the central establishment.

Court first tested its new Chairman in December 1986. Addressing the Court the previous January the Treasurer had warned that the pay claims of university teachers, rushing like lemmings over the precipice, would lead to redundancies by forcing the University to shed staff it could no longer afford. When similar remarks appeared in the financial report and were coupled with predictions that a change of government would make no difference, they caused considerable offence. Ambiguous standing orders failed to make it clear whether an unsatisfactory Treasurer's report had to be rejected *in toto* or whether it could be amended. The Chancellor persuaded Court to vote on the matter and it chose to refer the report back to Council by a majority of 50 votes to 26.

The Chancellor's opinion carried great weight when an important constitutional issue arose as an indirect consequence of the Jarratt report. Following Jarratt, the University had determined that heads of departments should henceforth be appointed by Council on the recommendation of the Vice-Chancellor – the effect being to cast them in the role of middle management, responsible, not to their colleagues, but to the University's board of directors. In the session of 1989–90 Senate and Council followed up this move by proposing that heads of departments should now form an order or category of persons fit to be represented on Court. Indeed, they should have thirty places on it, as many as Convocation, for Senate recognised that 'Court had a key role to play at the apex of the University's governing structure'. Since the nine deans of the faculties were also to sit on Court, the 'managerial' component of the academic element on Court would – according to George Wilmers's calculations – increase from 54 to 75 per cent. This reform, in the view of critics, smelt perhaps of gerrymandering and certainly of a growing desire to manage Court lest it block vital legislation. But the Chancellor discouraged the move by pronouncing that the reform could properly be effected only through a change of statute and not a mere ordinance, as had been proposed. For it would bring about a major constitutional change by reducing the proportion of lay persons on Court. No statute could pass without securing a two-thirds majority in Court, and there was little prospect of obtaining this (a change of ordinance would need only a bare majority, of 51 per cent). Although the deans got their days in Court the heads of department did not, and the proposal which concerned them was shelved if not dropped.

Chancellor and Vice-Chancellor made an odd couple, and it was hard to resist the impression that each was there to mind the other. Relations between them were correct though not cordial, and they occasionally joined forces – for example, to write to the quality papers about the police inquiry into the Brittan affair. They were seen, if not as determined opponents, at least as representatives of contrasting points of view. Indeed, the Chancellor, addressing the Students' Union in 1988, advised: 'Don't get us mixed up. He wouldn't like it, and I certainly wouldn't like it!' Interviewed years later, Richmond remembered Griffith's remark about him: 'I don't think I've ever met anyone I like quite so much, with whom I've disagreed so profoundly!' For his part Richmond saw conflict in the contrasting roles of the Chancellor as the impartial Chairman of Court, which was the presiding body, and as an active member of Council, which was one of the recommending bodies. ' . . . if you actually quoted the legalities to him, being a lawyer he always backed off . . . he was almost like a monkey, wanting to get round the hurdles, but if you actually stated the hurdle, he'd always come back behind it . . . ' Richmond recalled his distrust of the Chancellor's willingness to issue aggressive or negative statements about the police – he referred, perhaps, to a sharp exchange in print with Sir Cecil Clothier, the Chairman of the Police Complaints Authority, after the publication of Griffith's article, 'A watch-dog with no bite', in *The Guardian* in 1987.

However, both Richmond and Griffith, in their contrasting styles, were outspoken critics of the Government and spirited defenders of academic freedom. In a pamphlet, *The Attack on Higher Education,* published by CAFD in 1987, and in an article in the THES, the Chancellor sought to expose the sinister intentions of the Government and their determination to conscript the universities into meeting the immediate needs of the economy. These proposals appeared in Government White Papers, soon to be translated into legislation through the Education Reform Bill passing through Parliament in the session of 1987–88: 'The whole amounts to a potentially complete take-over of policy-making in higher education . . . It is an almost total usurpation, a dissolution of the university system comparable to the dissolution of the monasteries.' Attempting to strike a conciliatory note, the new Undersecretary for Higher Education, Robert Jackson, jibbed at Griffith's description of the Government's approach to universities as 'totalitarian' in design. Writing in *The Observer,* the Chancellor doubted the Government's capacity to 'decide how many Japanese linguists . . . heart surgeons . . . and perhaps even a few historians, archaeologists, philosophers and sociologists we shall need in 1995'. He added that 'The dangerous folly of this government lies in its mistaken assumption that politicians and their appointees know better than the consumers (students) and professionals (industry and academia)'.

It fell to Richmond, as Chairman of the CVCP from 1987 to 1989, to lead much of the University lobbying against the more radical provisions of the Education Bill. The greatest dangers were that the Secretary of State for Education would acquire almost limitless powers to intervene in the affairs of universities; that financial relations between Government and universities would henceforth be ruled by a so-called system of contracts, which would specify in detail what each part of a university was expected to do in order to earn its money; and that the UGC would give way to a new body, the Universities Funding Council (UFC), which would have no power to advise Ministers on its own initiative, but have to wait for them to seek its opinion. As Griffith wrote, the proposed contracts would not be true contracts but rather devices to extend central control, in that universities could not freely choose whether or not to be bound by them. Nor were arrangements to be made for independent adjudication if one of the parties supposedly failed to keep its side of the bargain. The Department of Education and Science would assess a university's performance and renew or withhold funds in accordance with its own judgement. That express references to contracting disappeared from the Bill (it was said to cause problems for parliamentary draftsmen); that the Secretary of State agreed to limit his own powers; and that the Universities Funding Council gained the right to volunteer advice: these things were due at least in part to the efforts of the CVCP. An official eulogy of Richmond, on his departure from the University in 1990, declared that there was no stouter defender of academic freedom.

It was now certain that the Government would seek to abolish the strong form of tenure which prevailed in most universities and seemed to them like a hindrance to efficiency. Commissioners would descend on university statutes and overhaul them in such a way as to

allow staff appointed to the retiring age to be declared redundant
before they reached it. Certain safeguards were introduced in order to
prevent universities from solving their financial problems by dismissing costly senior staff and replacing them with juniors engaged to do
the same jobs for smaller salaries. It would be permissible to declare
redundancies only if a university intended to abandon an activity altogether, in which case it would be entitled to dismiss persons appointed
to engage in this pursuit. Could academic freedom survive if dismissal
for financial reasons became legitimate? There was a struggle to
include in the Bill a clause defining and protecting academic freedom
which the commissioners would be bound to respect, and it was eventually stipulated that any revised statute would have to 'ensure that
academic staff have freedom within the law to question and test
received wisdom, and to put forward new ideas and controversial or
unpopular opinions, without placing themselves in jeopardy of losing
their jobs or privileges'.

Richmond's pronouncements on the subject were forthright and
clear. At the annual residential meeting of the Vice-Chancellors and
Principals, in Manchester in October 1987, he said that 'Members of
the Committee have themselves experienced the sort of pressure that
can be brought to bear on academics by the likes of Joseph McCarthy
if they do not feel secure in speaking their minds. This is not a problem now, but times can change.' At a national seminar in London,
organised by the scientific journal *Nature* in January 1988, he argued
for three fundamental freedoms – not only to question received
wisdom, but also to research on subjects of as yet unrecognised importance, and to be protected from direct and narrow political interference by the Government of the day. For Manchester University there
was at least one poignant reminder of the damage that could be
inflicted by governments which decided that an academic subject was
superfluous or undesirable. Teodor Shanin, the Lithuanian-born
Professor of Sociology, arranged in 1989 for young Soviet sociologists
to attend summer schools in Manchester and to rectify, on behalf of
Gorbachev's regime, the shortage of sociologists in the USSR which
had occurred 'in the generation of Brezhnev'. Sociology had then
been proscribed as a bourgeois discipline, thus creating an extraordinary generation gap, for leading Soviet sociologists were either in
their sixties or in their twenties, with nobody in between.

Despite its desire to see an end of tenure, the Government did not
attempt retrospective legislation. Persons granted tenure before 20
November 1987 were entitled to keep it, unless they entered upon a

new contract of employment – for example, by accepting promotion. Rise from lecturer to senior lecturer, or accept a chair, and the price would be forfeiture of an important contractual right, so that the most able academics might well become the most vulnerable. In summer 1988 the Secretary of State, Kenneth Baker, named the five commissioners; they included two academics, Lord Butterworth, who had been one of the principal targets of E.P. Thompson's *Warwick University Ltd.*, and Professor David Williams, the Principal of Wolfson College, Oxford. Negotiations with the University of Manchester, such as they were, turned on the meaning of a Model Statute which was intended to apply to all universities but could be adjusted to local situations. Stipulations of the Education Act of 1988 were not open to discussion. A draft of the Model Statute reached Manchester early in 1990 and gave rise to much consultation and to-ing and fro-ing. An alarming clause which included as grounds for dismissal 'conduct liable to bring the institution into disrepute' was not in the end included. Incorporated as the revised Statute XVII, the new arrangements passed the Privy Council in November 1992. Members of Council were perturbed by the commissioners' failure expressly to limit the grounds for dismissal to good cause or redundancy. In principle, therefore, dismissals could be sought on other grounds, 'for example on the wholly imprecise common law ground of "fidelity"', 'thereby casting doubt on the concept of academic freedom as the Statute's guiding principle'.

Compulsory redundancy was still beyond the pale in the late 1980s. But the University could balance its books only by shedding a number of academic staff and by again encouraging early retirements, this time of younger staff, and on less generous terms than before. Turnover in some areas of the University, especially in Arts and Economic and Social Studies, remained very low; in Law, in summer 1987, it suddenly seemed alarmingly high, as a result of deaths, retirements, appointments to senior posts elsewhere, and secondments to the Law Commission. Underfunded Arts folk, their morale wilting, complained that expensive Science was getting all the bonuses while they were deemed to be in deficit. Against this it could be argued that faculties such as Science and Medicine, more favoured by the Government, were compelled to support supine and querulous Arts, which had not made its savings, and whose members were unfit for employment outside the university world. In September 1985 the University was able to fill three out of every five posts that fell vacant, but by May 1986 the proportion had dropped to one out of three and the Vice-Chancellor was saying that in principle there should be no replacements in Arts. Possible solutions, as yet mild ones, began to occur to the administration – that academics in the areas which had not made savings should seek secondments and take leave without pay, or that such departments should justify their existence by taking on extra students and increasing the University's income from fees.

Late in 1986 the University expected to have to seek about seventy early retirements by the end of the decade, for which the UGC would provide some but by no means all of the finance. Many regretted the move; Professor Ranger, about to depart for a chair at Oxford, lamented the disappearance of the 'grandfather factor', of older and wiser academics, from the University scene. In August 1987 the Vice-Chancellor wrote to all members of the academic staff over the age of fifty, encouraging them, if so minded, to apply to take early retirement in the years 1988, 1989 or 1990. When a chair committee resolved to appoint a candidate already in his late forties, a bold spirit asked the Vice-Chancellor which communication he proposed to send him first – a letter of appointment or an invitation to take early retirement. 'Shut up!' was the rejoinder. Over a hundred applications arrived, but the management interest in keeping staff was invoked more rigorously than before, and only ninety passed muster (seventy-four academics and sixteen members of the academic-related staff). On this occasion there would be nothing to prevent the University from replacing staff lost by early retirement.

Among Jarratt's recommendations were schemes for appraisal and development which would keep most academics under annual scrutiny throughout their careers and encourage self-betterment rather than torpor. A Senate committee had accepted the need for some such arrangement in order to convince Government and society that academics deserved their pay and relative security of employment, and to ensure that they could be removed from office only by 'due process'. Although it offered many refresher courses to fee-paying students engaged in other occupations, the University appeared to be doing little to help its own members towards professional advancement. Appraisal schemes were on the cards from 1985 onwards; pay settlements began to depend on their introduction; and the University made serious attempts to organise them from 1988.

A working party of five, headed by Professor J.D. Turner of Education, considered the question of appraisal and made recommendations. Hitherto most lecturers had encountered a searchlight at only three points in their career and at long intervals – first, when they were considered for tenure; secondly, when they approached the 'bar-line', a hurdle which had to be surmounted after eight or nine years' service before proceeding to higher points on the salary scale; and thirdly, when, if ever, they sought promotion to the rank of senior lecturer. These occasions apart, they would probably receive little systematic attention, and some would have been resentful if they had. Sixty-five departments answered the working party's questions. It appeared that only half conducted a regular review of their teaching staff, that only twenty-one conducted interviews at which their problems and progress were explored, and that only twenty put out questionnaires seeking student opinion on teaching. Professor Turner's party now urged Senate to call upon all departments to design schemes which would involve annual interviews by trained appraisers and reports of these encounters which would be placed on record and might be used in promotion exercises. Appraisal was generally to flow from the top downwards, but some of the more democratic departments salved their pride by providing for 'reverse appraisal', which would allow the appraisee to give the appraiser some opinion of the appraiser's performance. Professors were to undergo a biennial review by Pro-Vice-Chancellors, some of whom softened the process by visiting them in their rooms. Even the Vice-Chancellor was to be appraised by the lay officers of the University, who, for this purpose, would become the gods of Olympus or Valhalla, subject to scrutiny by no higher power.

In the summer of 1988 the University engaged a consultant, Roger Pryor, who had once been Chief Psychologist to the Australian Government Public Service Board, was now the managing director of Interactive Skills Ltd., and was helping a number of British universities to put appraisal schemes into effect. There was to be a 'pyramid system', in which the newly acquired expertise would flow downwards from the apex, a small elite being trained to train others in the new art, and the Vice-Chancellor and senior administrators attending the first day school. Progress was delayed by the AUT's refusal to co-operate with appraisal schemes until an acrimonious pay dispute was settled, but with this resolved the programme gathered momentum. Numerous senior academics attended day-long sessions at Holly Royde in West Didsbury, at which they engaged in role-playing, analysed each other's body language and assumed the guise of well-known departmental types, which ranged from the old soldier through the professional cynic to the victim of writer's block. They were advised not to be inquisitorial, warned not to set their colleagues unattainable goals, urged to encourage them to do what they did best, and treated to a John Cleese video on how not to perform the task. For many it was the only formal training they had ever received at the University's hands. They then went forth to put their newly acquired skills into practice.

Most appraisees, at least until the novelty wore off, enjoyed the experience of discussing themselves and grumbling about the University ('whoever appraises me is going to get an earful'). Self-criticism was often more in evidence than judgements from on high. One or two pompous characters lectured their appraisers with magnificent hauteur, whilst a few insecure souls regarded any hint of criticism as evidence of a plot to get them sacked. In general, however, the scheme worked smoothly enough and encouraged communication more often than it provoked resentment.

To counter the charge of failing to train its own people systematically, the University set up a Staff Training and Development Unit for the benefit of academics, para-academics and support staff. It was designed to bring together the activities of the Staff Teaching Workshop (used mainly by the Faculties of Medicine and Science) and those of the Training Section of the Establishment Office. A Lecturer in Adult Education was appointed to direct the new organisation and saw his work as 'harnessing human resources to the tasks that have to be faced in the more efficient and cost-conscious world of today'. The implied analogy between University staff and cart horses was doubtless accidental.

In Manchester the term 'head of department' had traditionally been regarded as faintly improper. Departments were ruled collectively by all their professors, and only in the absence of professors was a member of a department officially appointed to be its head. In 1986, however, as though in obedience to Jarratt, the Senate altered the role of professors by detaching their office from automatic managerial responsibility and associating it with 'academic leadership', a term perhaps intended to denote the intellectual influence which many saw themselves exercising. This reform did address the problem of the good scholar who had no capacity for administration but none the less refused to delegate authority. Another aim was to identify more precisely where responsibility lay, particularly for the control of resources, which increased in importance as resources shrank.

Departmental arrangements had varied. Sometimes the professors had recognised one of their number as so pre-eminent, or so enamoured of administration, that he or she could be regarded as the permanent head of department; other professors had rotated the job of speaking for the department, appointing a temporary chieftain to serve for perhaps three years; others still had managed to act as a headless body, dividing their duties 'along functional lines between two or more of them', and evading the question of which one, if any, was supposed to be the queen bee. If control over resources was to be devolved from the centre to a lower level – as it might be – it would become more important to identify a controller, and to be sure that this was one person and not a committee.

The reform could naturally be interpreted as part of a threatening managerial strategy, an attempt to put Vice-Chancellor's narks in charge of every vital point in the University. In practice, however, the appointment of heads of department depended on consultations conducted by the dean of the faculty concerned and not on the personal favour of the Vice-Chancellor. Multi-professorial departments generally wanted one of the professors to take charge of them, for they still clung to the notion that professors were paid to assume administrative responsibility. Should a department refuse to back a professor's candidature, as occasionally happened, he or she might be deeply offended and apply for a job elsewhere. In justice to Jarratt, it should be said that his committee had insisted that heads of departments should be obliged to consult and inform their colleagues; the University's charter and statutes had never done more than that.

By 1990 a system of devolved budgets was on the way, established in the interests of greater accountability for public money. Revenues were not supposed to disappear without trace into the maw of the University, and it must now be made clear how and where they were spent. Hence every department was to be assigned to one of thirty-seven 'academic cost centres', which corresponded to categories used by the UGC and its successor, the UFC. Cost centres were foci for the spending of money, and they ranged from a cluster of clinical medical departments at Centre 01 to the entire Faculty of Education at Centre 37. Some large and distinctive departments, such as Chemistry, Pharmacy or Computer Science, formed centres entire of themselves, while smaller entities, such as social science or language departments, were grouped together into many-celled units. This reform set out to bring more closely together income and expenditure (or, as official language had it, 'the allocation of resource and its actual use'). It would then become possible to show how a share of the block grant, plus fees, plus research overheads, plus equipment grant, plus other items, flowed into an academic pool, and how these things flowed out again in the form of salaries and wages and other expenditure. Cost centres would to some extent be able to cross-subsidise each other. Heads of departments would no longer be founts of academic wisdom and petitioners of higher authority, like feudal lords seeking royal favours for their vassals. Instead, they would become resource managers, entitled to manage their budgets as they would 'within agreed constraints'.

Efficiency in universities, their ability to attract, retain and inspire their staff, depended to some extent on the range of incentives and rewards at their disposal. Only idealists would continue to praise universities for teaching people to despise the money they prevented them from earning. In the early 1980s most lecturers had before them only the limited prospect of progressing by means of annual increments to the top of their salary scales. Once a lecturer had passed the bar-line, these increases were automatically granted and were not related to performance; opportunities for promotion to a higher rank and a higher scale had become very limited; and there was every sign that university salaries would keep pace neither with inflation nor with those commanded by other professions.

When settling money on universities each year, the Government would allow only a few per cent for salary and wage increases. Should the university employers, the Vice-Chancellors and Principals, agree with the AUT through their national negotiating machinery to pay anything above this allowance, the Government would almost certainly refuse to compensate them, and the universities' financial difficulties would become even more grave. On the other hand, if the heads of institutions stood their ground and closed their fists, they would fail to attract staff of the right calibre, especially in engineering, technology and academic support services, and they would probably provoke damaging strikes. *This Week* greeted the appointment of Tony Birley, the Professor of Ancient History, to a chair at Düsseldorf in 1990 as an example of a new brain drain which flowed in the direction, not of the United States, but of Europe, and was the result of poor salaries and working conditions in the United Kingdom. Sir Mark Richmond said in May 1990 that the 'most crucial' and 'most shattering' single event of his time in Manchester was the 24 per cent pay increase awarded in instalments over the years 1986 to 1988, when UGC funding allowed for a rise of only 14 per cent.

In 1988–89 the AUT's demand for a cost-of-living award, backdated to 1 April 1988, brought universities close to a general strike.

The national AUT voted in favour of refusing to examine students from 9 January 1989 onwards, thereby committing a breach of contract on a massive scale. Although for the time being few or no Manchester examinations had been derailed, crisis loomed in the summer. Students, whose careers were at stake, might sue the University if it denied them their degrees; the Registrar warned that the University had at its disposal legal remedies, including deductions of salary for failure to do the work; Council asked itself in February whether further admonitions would inflame the situation, and postponed sending them out until late March. The Senate recommended passing an 'enabling ordinance' which would empower the Vice-Chancellor, if need be, to appoint special Boards of Assessors (how they were to be recruited was not clear) to award degrees on the strength of such evidence as they could assemble, and to classify such students as they could. A majority of Senate refused to accept the argument that such degrees would have little academic worth, and the Senate cast 82 votes to 35 in favour of the proposal. Before the ordinance reached Court in May 1989, the AUT changed its tactics: papers would now be set and the examinations take place after all, but AUT members would withhold the marks until the dispute was settled. Fortunately a national postal ballot, the results of which were announced only at the beginning of June when the examination season was far advanced, declared in favour of accepting the deal offered – 11,549 votes for the settlement, 9,543 against. Only for 1990–91 did the AUT and the CVCP succeed in agreeing a pay increase of 9 per cent which exceeded the predicted rate of inflation.

In the middle to late 1980s pay settlements sought, not only to provide for general increases in salaries, but to clear the blockage in promotions and to provide other incentives to good performance. A portion of the money awarded was to be set aside for the purpose. They also strove to provide modest rewards, in the shape of additional increments or 'discretionary salary points', for academics who had done well or shouldered extra responsibilities. Such discretionary points proved attractive once it became clear that those who received them would not lose tenure, for discretionary points called for no new contract and were not supposed to be everlasting rewards (in theory they could be withdrawn after three years, but in practice seldom were). The process of agonising over the award of discretionary points added to the burdens of heads of departments, deans and former deans. New salary scales came into operation. Lecturers were placed on Grade A (the lower grade) or Grade B (the higher), and did not automatically advance from the first to the second grade, with its range of higher salary points. Unsatisfactory performers could be kept on Grade A until they improved, but proficient ones could move up to Grade B even before their probation had ended.

Few promotions to senior lectureships had been made in the early and mid-1980s, when the idea of rewarding everyone who reached a good but widely attainable standard had virtually disappeared, and fierce competition had supervened, allowing only candidates of exceptional achievements to succeed. In 1989, however, Senate approved twenty promotions, as in the years before the crisis of 1981–84. Two separate operations, whose results were announced in February and May 1990, cleared some of the backlog. Sixty-four promotions to senior lecturer, senior staff tutor or senior research fellow were then made, and twenty of these were reserved for good all-rounders and departmental stalwarts – persons at the top of the Grade B scale who were unlikely to gain promotion by the usual criteria, but had 'made a strong, positive and continuing contribution to the Department across a range of activity'.

For years lecturers had complained that promotions depended too heavily on research achievements and failed to reward good teaching. Judgements on teaching were haphazard, depending too much on anecdotal or impressionistic evidence. It was all too easy for a professor, urging the case of a good publisher, to exaggerate the candidate's excellence as a teacher and never be challenged. In 1990 a working party under Professor Cox of English attempted to tackle the problem. 'Teaching profiles', accounts of everyone's prowess as a teacher, were to consist of quantitative and qualitative evidence. To establish how many hours people had taught, and how many students, and how many courses, was a laborious but relatively straightforward task. Given the sensitivity of some academics, the job of measuring the quality of teaching was far more difficult; many tutors regarded the classroom as a sanctum that no observer should ever be allowed to invade.

Cox and his party did not discuss at length the problems of using student questionnaires, though many professors could have testified on the subject. Students, said some critics, would applaud charlatans, and enthuse about spectacular performers in colourful but conventional subjects; they would comment maliciously on rigorous teachers who tackled demanding issues, told no jokes, repeated no entertaining anecdotes, and refused to tell them what to think or to provide, in lectures and tutorials, substitutes for reading books. However, few lecturers who did well out of questionnaires were inclined to question their value. In defence of questionnaires it could be said that, though students were not experts on the content of their courses, they were experts on their own reactions to them, and could properly be consulted. They were likely to act responsibly, especially if they were advised that their judgements could affect lecturers' careers. If they could not hear properly, or found that too much knowledge was assumed, or were anaesthetised by a lecturer's monotonous tones and unenthusiastic demeanour, that critical information, if obviously given in good faith, was highly relevant and could profitably be used.

Cox and his colleagues, however, pronounced in favour of scrutiny by academic peers. Let a group of colleagues attend a lecture or seminar by each member of staff about once every three years or perhaps every five, and adopt some sort of scoring system in order to assess the performance. It seemed that they had nothing very rigorous in mind, and the mere fact of being observed was liable to change behaviour; but perhaps there were a few academics who could not give a decent lecture, even occasionally, and even when warned in advance.

Endless arguments arose as to whether the new and increasingly formal system of management adopted in the wake of Jarratt would actually make the University more effective. It provided machinery for procuring a general level of efficiency, keeping everyone up to the mark by constant scrutiny and seeking to motivate academics by material rewards and gains in status. In abeyance was the liberal notion that academics should be their own managers, doing their own work with some encouragement from colleagues and friends. Growing insecurity, affecting the young people without tenure rather than the middle-aged who continued to enjoy it, might act as a healthy stimulus. For many folk, it might be argued, jobs for life had not provided a chance to carry out great enterprises, to delay for twenty years before publishing some work of huge significance in its field. On the contrary, they had tempted academics to take life easily and surrender to an undemanding routine. One might well wonder, though, whether the practice of accentuating hierarchy in the new form of line management would make the University more original, creative or inspiring. Much time would now be diverted to the systematic compilation of records, documents, programmes and codes of practice, and to sitting in judgement on colleagues. So-called 'efficiency gains' were often no more than euphemisms or flimsy pretexts for cuts, exercises in doing things, not better, but with less expenditure of time and money. Preoccupation with measuring performance, talk of account-ability, in order to demonstrate that universities gave value for the money allotted to them, became increasingly insistent and oppressive. From the mid-1980s a growing concern, perhaps the gravest of all, was with the quality of the University's research as judged by outside bodies, and that will be the subject of the next chapter.

11

Research and rationalisation

In 1985 the UGC began to reveal the formula which it proposed to use in order to calculate the block grant for each university ('transparency' became one of the managerial watchwords of the late 1980s). About two-thirds of the grant would now depend on criteria related to teaching (student numbers, rather than proven pedagogic excellence), the rest on criteria related to research. It appeared that the Committee intended to divide universities into 'cost centres'; to arrive at a 'resource requirement' for each; to add all of them together; and to make extra allowances for certain unusual items which did not fit into the ordinary departmental framework, such as, in Manchester, the Museum, the Whitworth Art Gallery, and the John Rylands University Library. The grant thus arrived at would be composed of T for Teaching, R for Research and S for Special Factors.

On close inspection, R turned out to be the most elaborate compound, for it would consist of four elements, called SR, DR, CR and JR. SR would depend on the number of staff and of research students. DR would reflect the sum total of the grants obtained by members of a university from the Research Councils, charities which supported research, and other sources. By way of rewarding self-help, the UGC would make the university an allowance equivalent to 40 per cent of this sum. This arrangement echoed the time-honoured 'dual support system', whereby the university provided a well-equipped laboratory and researchers applied to the Research Councils or elsewhere to seek additional finance for specific, expensive projects. CR, the third element, depended on carrying out contract work for industry, business and Government departments: a total of £10m. would be distributed to universities in proportion to the sums they had raised by this means. They would be expected to charge their clients overheads at a realistic rate, and not to subsidise them out of public money.

Fourth came JR, which was to cause the greatest trouble and anxiety, for it would depend, not on counting bodies or money, but on judgement: on the UGC's opinion of a university's recent achievements and future promise in research, as described in its returns and plans. Before long a university's excellence in research would become the clearest indication of its standing and have a strong bearing upon its finances. The quality of each department, as the UGC saw it, would be proclaimed to the world when the results of the UGC's Research Selectivity Exercise were announced. Among the consequences would be elation and humiliation, depression and indignation, guilt and perplexity, at least in the early stages of the operation before the procedures settled down and the results became reasonably predictable. In the 1980s people could be seen wearing badges which announced 'I Hate J.R.', though doubtless they referred to J.R. Ewing, the villain of the soap opera *Dallas*, portrayed by Larry Hagman, rather than to the UGC's latest device. Like student questionnaires on teaching, this was loved by those who did well out of it and reviled as a devilish invention by those who did not.

As time passed JR became increasingly important in the algebra of public finance. When the UFC replaced the UGC and declared its hand in 1989, it seemed that the judgemental element in research funding could be expected to grow and that by the mid-1990s it would weigh twice as heavily as SR, which rested on mere numbers. DR – the slice of the grant related to income from the Research Councils – would now disappear from the block grant and be transferred to the Research Councils themselves. They would cover all the costs of expensive undertakings in scientific research, except for the salaries of those involved and the cost of the premises on which the work was done. Costly research in the sciences or social sciences would therefore depend heavily on obtaining the approval of Research Councils for specific projects, and the old system of dual support would be under threat.

Like new arrivals at a posh public school, awaiting initiation into its peculiar vocabulary or its esoteric version of football, fives or lacrosse, academics at Manchester approached with apprehension the task of compiling research plans for the UGC. Clearly there were hidden rules in the game, buzz-words to be learned, fashionable topics to be stressed, ways of impressing panels of judges that could only be picked up by experience. Would the UGC and its collaborators get at the substance of a department's achievement, or would everything depend on the skill with which the department was presented by the compilers of its return, on the wrapping paper rather than the gift? Members of Senate objected to the amateurish methods the UGC proposed to use, presumably to save itself time – especially their chairman's request for 'the titles of five books which represent the best and most representative scholarship of each subject group in each university'. It was hard to see how, in an individualistic department, a book could represent anything other than its own author. Addressing Senate in November 1985, the Vice-Chancellor urged those responsible 'to portray a forward-looking and dynamic university, not one dwelling on past successes', and warned that 'there were well-informed people outside the University . . . who were quite capable of matching the University's internal analysis with an external view of its strengths and weaknesses'.

The judgements of the UGC panels were first published in May 1986 and complacently described by Sir Keith Joseph as 'a landmark in university funding' (a Labour spokesman, the Member for Denton and Reddish, preferred to call them 'a landmine under higher education'). To the CVCP Swinnerton-Dyer said that his own Committee had done nothing more than expose their judgements for all to see. 'We do not ask that universities should accept our judgements', he explained; 'they can make and implement their own. But there is hardly a single institution which can say with plausibility: "All our departments are equally strong".' It seemed that the UGC was not presuming to dictate exactly how the block grant should be used, or suggesting in detail how rewards and punishments should be dispensed; a university was entitled to invest in bringing a weak department up to scratch, as well as in encouraging a strong one. John Griffith, Manchester's Chancellor, wrote in his pamphlet *The Attack on Higher Education* of 'a half-baked exercise purporting to assess research performances in university departments, the arbitrary results of which met with both hilarity and anger, but were deployed by university planners, selectively, to suit their prejudices for the management of cuts'.

Half-baked or not, the exercise pronounced sixteen Manchester cost centres above average and awarded rosettes to eleven departments or subject areas which it regarded as outstanding (these were Clinical Dentistry, Psychology, Physics, Applied Mathematics, Computer Science, Geography, Social Anthropology, Accountancy, Spanish, History of Art, and Drama). Some, such as Physics and Computer Science, had succeeded very well in attracting additional posts in the New Blood and Information Technology initiatives which had followed the 1981 cuts. Accountancy was attracting strong support from the profession. Iconoclasm seemed to be at large, proclaiming to be merely average, as though to dispel smugness, certain departments which had once enjoyed a glowing reputation – as had Government under Mackenzie and Finer; History under Tout, Powicke and Namier; and Electrical Engineering under Freddie Williams. Certain areas fared poorly and were declared below average, as were Pharmacology, the Biological sciences, Architecture, Town and Country Planning, and Education. The Arts Faculty did badly, in that only one sizeable department with more than fifteen members, Geography, which was part science and part social science but located in Arts, scored highly in the exercise, whereas the large departments of History and English did not.

Guides for the perplexed were not forthcoming. Judgements were not officially explained, and inquiries produced only polite commiseration from civil servants and bland assurances that the evidence had been 'weighed again and again'. Disappointed departments asked themselves how to improve, whilst cynics urged them to accept that they were merely average and always would be. Had there been enough collective activity, should the department have launched a learned journal, should a major conference be organised, did the professors know enough influential people?

Fortunately, no doubt, a rather more systematic exercise took place in 1989. Departments named the recent publications of each individual member of staff, submitted quantitative evidence of various kinds, and were graded on scales of 1–5. There was some movement both up and down, and History, for example, a department which had lost several of its ablest members to chairs elsewhere, succeeded in improving its reputation and rising to Grade 4, which placed it on a par with a large number of good History departments in the country but did not make it outstanding.

Taken as a whole, the results of both operations were pleasing to Manchester. Using a crude measure – the number of departments regarded as outstanding – it was possible, at least from within, to identify Manchester as the fifth of the large institutions in 1986. No match for Oxford, Cambridge and University College London, it ran closer to Bristol and neck and neck with Edinburgh. In October 1989 *This Week* published an analysis which suggested that Manchester had maintained this position and was still fifth in the race, so long as one counted only large, wide-ranging institutions (defined as those with thirty-five or more departments or at least twenty-one cost centres – Manchester had twenty-six cost centres). Add more compact institutions such as LSE, and Manchester dropped to eleventh place. The average score, on the new 1–5 marking scale, of all Manchester units was 3.56 (an Arts undergraduate with an average score of just over 70 per cent in his or her final examinations would almost certainly get a first-class degree, though not a first with distinction). Geology, regarded as merely average in 1986, had now joined Physics and Computer Science at the pinnacle; Social Anthropology had again earned the highest possible rating; and Nursing and Dentistry, rated at 4, had notched up the highest scores awarded by the parsimonious panels which assessed those disciplines.

Weak departments in vital scientific subjects were likely to attract remedial action and have money thrown at them. In some areas of the University it was possible to improve both performance and image by casting down old-fashioned departmental barriers and abandoning worn-out subject divisions. A traditional way of overcoming such hindrances to progress had been and still was the creation of interdisciplinary centres, which left departments intact but brought together scholars with shared interests to consider common problems. Lawyers, philosophers, theologians and doctors could all profitably discuss medical ethics together. However, where the departmental structure was so obsolete as to block intellectual progress, stronger measures were called for, not only on scholarly but also on economic grounds. For the creation of larger departments, or the absorption of departments into schools with a common administration, would lead to economies of scale – one accounts office, one store, one electronic microscopy unit, one safety officer, where previously there had been several – and to savings of administrative time. Some changes arose from within the University and were prompted by groups of like-minded professors. Others were imposed or encouraged by the UGC, by the subject reviews which it commissioned, and by the transfers of academic staff to Manchester which it brought about.

Far from unexpected was the UGC's lack of enthusiasm for the research performance of Manchester's biological sciences. This was an area of special interest to the Vice-Chancellor. He had already urged remedial action by appointing through the JCUD in November 1983 a working party of seasoned professors, both medical and scientific, who were not themselves biologists, 'to investigate the biological sciences associated with Science and Medicine'. Headed by a Pro-Vice-Chancellor, the physicist John Willmott, the working party held sixteen meetings and eventually reported in June 1985. Pressure to reform came as much from the younger professors within the biological sciences as from without: especially from Maynard Case of Physiology, Michael Grant of Biochemistry, Mark Ferguson of Basic

Dental Science, and Tony Trinci of Cryptogamic Botany. Ten older professors had retired or left the University in the previous three years, and the way to change seemed clear. A discussion paper, wholeheartedly supported by eleven professors and with reservations by five others, proposed to the Willmott working party the establishment of a new Bioscience Faculty, which would assemble staff at present scattered through thirteen academic departments and two other units (those concerned with Marine Technology and Pollution Research). Some of the departments concerned lay in the Faculty of Science, others in the Faculty of Medicine, and they were physically and intellectually separated in a manner which hindered collaboration.

As Willmott and his colleagues later recognised, some of the existing departments had arisen almost a century before and 'reflected the division of material seen at that time', whereas recent developments in research had cut across those lines. It was no longer fruitful to think of anatomy, bacteriology and virology, biochemistry, botany, immunology, pharmacology, physiology and zoology as if they were separate organisms or distinctive species which could not cross-fertilise each other. Efforts to bring them together in the past had not, however, proved outstandingly successful, as witness a history of the Botany Department, published in the 1990s, which described the all-too-tentative attempts of the Departments of Botany and Zoology to come together in the 1960s and 1970s.

Advocates of the new Faculty contended that it would give rise to larger and more effective research groups which could more easily be identified by Research Councils and by 'clinical academic staff and others seeking assistance or collaboration'. Expensive equipment, to be shared by many different users, could be purchased and serviced in a more rational and efficient manner; it would be possible to design a curriculum encompassing all the biological sciences; and the Faculty would be able to organise preliminary training courses on subjects of interest to all postgraduate students – including 'computational methods, statistical analysis, instrumentation, care of animals, information retrieval, report writing', and other matters. One reason for reorganising and concentrating the biological departments was to enable them to 'underpin' clinical medicine, by ensuring that budding doctors acquired a thorough grounding in basic science before they embarked on patient care. 'Clinical medicine', reported Willmott and his colleagues, 'is poised to make major improvements in diagnosis and treatment, based on advances in molecular and cell biology.' This approach appealed to the Vice-Chancellor (at his school, Epsom College, the first-year Biology Sixth had been the portal to the more advanced Medical Sixth). However, the idea proved less popular with others, who did not wish to see classical botany and zoology eclipsed by research which was more intimately related to medicine.

Despite these reservations, the Willmott working party rejected the concept of an independent Faculty of Biosciences. To establish one might be to sever these disciplines from clinical medicine and encourage separatists in other parts of the University to demand faculties of their own; received wisdom favoured coalescence into larger units, not fission into smaller ones. Willmott and his colleagues therefore recommended that Biological Sciences should become a section or wing of the Medical Faculty, ranking equally with Clinical Medicine and Dentistry, and endowed, as they were, with a Dean.

By October 1986 staff from ten departments had regrouped into four larger ones, entitled Biochemistry and Molecular Biology, Cell and Structural Biology, Environmental Biology, and Physiological Sciences. Within these departments, research groups and interests were clearly labelled and identified in the University Calendar, such as 'Contractile and Excitable Tissues' (within Cell and Structural Biology) and 'Smooth Muscle' (within Physiological Sciences). Members of old departments were not transferred *en bloc* into these new units, but redistributed: fourteen botanists, for example, went to Cell and Structural Biology, four to Environmental Biology. Appointments were to be made during the coming session to chairs in Molecular Biology (the most neglected rising subject in the field) and Immunology. The four new departments conferred membership of both the Medicine and Science Faculties.

A semi-official statement in the University's house journal explained the significance of the reforms and extolled the power of the biological sciences to change the world through genetic engineering – 'genes can be purified, sequenced, changed at will, reintroduced into individual cells of all kinds and expressed therein as protein. These advances, together with the development of techniques for culturing cells and the availability of many new and powerful laboratory instruments, give a range of experimental approaches which can be applied to a wide variety of biological problems – from fighting disease to improving the quality of crops . . . '.

The original professors' proposal for a Biosciences Faculty had urged the need for 'high-quality saturation publicity in all quarters'. Much was now done to present the new organisation, Manchester's beautified if not yet beatified Cinderella, as one of the University's greatest success stories. The interests and achievements of Mark Ferguson provided good copy. While still in his late twenties he had been appointed to take charge of the newly created Department of Basic Dental Science, which, since it was rapidly absorbed into the new school of biology, became the most short-lived unit in the University's history. His own research, on palate development in the embryo, had some popular appeal, especially on account of its connection with alligators. These were 'swamp sophisticates' which had adapted excellently to their environment and combined primitive with advanced features: 'Study of their biology has led to unique insights into the mechanism of sex determination in a wide variety of animals and the developmental causes of cleft palate in man'. Honours rained upon him, conferred by the International Association for Dental Research and by the Royal College of Surgeons. *This Week* did not fail to comment on his, and the biological sciences', growing ability to attract research money. In 1988 the new school, eager to keep itself before the public eye, launched the *Biological Sciences Review*, a journal designed to present the latest developments in the subject to A-level and first-year students of biology.

Since the early 1980s there had been talk of reducing the range of activities undertaken by individual universities, and even of depriving the weaker institutions of all funding for research. Whole universities did not in the end suffer such drastic penalties, but the UGC's planners did wish to concentrate certain costly subjects in institutions of their choosing, and to transfer to them staff from other establishments. In pursuit of this aim, the UGC commissioned Sir Ronald Oxburgh, the President of Queens' College Cambridge and future Rector of Imperial College London, to carry out a survey of Earth Sciences departments (those specialising in geology, petrology, mineralogy, and so forth) throughout the country. He at first recommended that departments be placed on three tiers, the first of which would be amply funded for research and the second moderately funded, while the lowest, destined merely to provide support for other scientific subjects, would not receive research money from the UGC.

Oxburgh's stark distinctions were later blurred and the contrasts toned down, but Manchester's Geology Department, skilfully steered by Jack Zussman, emerged with credit and stood to gain large numbers of staff and students. It was placed in Category M1, within a group of six top departments deemed capable of laying on substantial single honours courses and engaging in both teaching and research. 'M' indicated that it was 'mainstream', '1' that it deserved to be generously provided with resources. Subsequently renamed Earth Sciences, the

Department attracted six new staff by transfer from other universities and three by new appointments; the number of students planned for rose from 141 to 215, consisting of 156 undergraduates and postgraduates taking taught courses, and 59 postgraduate researchers. Manchester, which had two collections of geological specimens, one in the Department and the other in the Manchester Museum, was designated in 1989 one of the five Collection Centres in the country, together with Birmingham, Cambridge, Glasgow and Oxford. It could now expect to receive items from within an area which included the Universities of Durham, Lancashire, Leeds, Liverpool and Newcastle. As Jack Zussman's eulogist told Senate when he retired in 1989, he had at enormous expense of time and effort contrived a 'bid' which resulted in Manchester receiving more additional resources in his field than did any other university. The effect of the review was to recognise the quality of Manchester's Department as equivalent to level 5 in the ranking system used in the Research Selectivity Exercise.

During its sunset years the UGC conducted, apart from its general surveys, a number of smaller subject reviews whose results proved generally favourable to Manchester departments. From the Dental School through Occupational Health to Sociology and to Social Policy and Administration, most received praise and encouragement, and only Celtic Studies (no longer an independent department) was recommended for closure. Unusually, the University chose to ignore this last piece of advice, for it regarded Celtic Studies as a harmless and inexpensive activity, and thought it good that about seven students a year should continue to be taught Welsh by part-time lecturers.

As it announced in a letter of August 1985, the UGC was inclined to question the efficiency of small departments. These were most likely to be found struggling on in, or on the fringes of, the arts and social sciences, and to occur in such fields as drama, history of art, music, social anthropology, and the history and philosophy of science. Their minimum effective size, in the UGC's opinion, might well range from four to nine full-time members. Below that level they would probably provide little intellectual stimulus and, since they could spare no-one for any length of time, prove incapable of arranging study leave. Transfers to other universities might benefit individuals and create much stronger units elsewhere; Manchester profited from these arrangements in several fields other than Geology. Both its metropolitan status and its proximity to other universities acted in its favour, and it became an importer rather than an exporter of talent in certain fields. Indeed, when Richmond resigned in 1990 it was said that in his time thirty academics had chosen to come to Manchester as a result of UGC rationalisation schemes, and only one had wanted to leave.

When a review in 1987 identified the Department of Science and Technology Policy as one of four centres of excellence in the country, some extra staff were close to hand in UMIST, which still had a tiny Department of the History of Science, despite the plans of the former Principal to close it down. Both Middle Eastern and Russian Studies gained from rationalisation exercises and from reports which recognised their practical value, not only for the understanding and interpretation of the contemporary world, but also for the assistance of the business and diplomatic communities. There was some talk of reorganising the existing thirty-six architecture schools in the country into sixteen super-schools, a move which might entail merging Manchester's school with that of the neighbouring Polytechnic, but for the time being nothing came of the idea. On its own initiative, the University performed various other acts of reorganisation, which usually involved mergers between departments or the absorption of small faculties into large ones, minnows swimming into the mouths of whales. Music in 1987 and Theology in 1992 abandoned their status as separate faculties and joined the Faculty of Arts as departments. The days of the one-person department, a piece which would fit into no existing jigsaw, appeared to be numbered. So were those of the department which existed only as a symbol, and consisted only of one or more honorary lecturers whose main concerns lay elsewhere.

Research in many subjects depended heavily on the approval of the research councils and charities which alone could finance them. Revenue from these sources was important not only for its own sake but for its influence on the University's block grant; making the necessary claims on the grant-giving bodies was an important activity within the Finance Department. The Vice-Chancellor spoke in May 1988 of larger earnings from outside research funding, which had risen in the past four years from £8.5m. to £15m. a year. Science and Medicine were generally the big earners, to be especially cherished and encouraged, but the largest grant of all, a sum of £2.8m., was credited in 1989 to the Faculty of Education. This went to a consortium known as STAIR, headed by Tom Christie, a Senior Lecturer in Education. STAIR, whose name stood for 'Standard Tests and Implementation Research', had made a successful proposal to develop tests for pupils at the end of the first stage of the National Curriculum, on behalf of the School Examinations and Assessment Council.

Understandably, the University's house magazine gave prominence to large grants for projects which promised to confer generous social benefits. All research appeared to be priced, and there was a danger that research which cost little might seem to be of less value; readers did well to remind themselves now and then that what counted was not so much the extent of the grant as the use to which it was put. Compilers of the magazine seemed surprised at the news that £60,000 was on its way from the Leverhulme Trust to the Department of Music, to finance over the next five years research towards a monumental edition of the works of Berlioz. The arts were not yet known for great collective enterprises, conducted by teams and involving the employment of research assistants. On average, it was said in 1987, each member of the new school of Biological Sciences had earned grant money of £15,000 in the first six months of the school's existence.

Much of the research conducted in the University was useful in a direct and obvious sense. Some of it was concerned with the diagnosis and prevention of disease, with the relief of pain and suffering, with the repair of injuries, with the extension of care into the community. Sociologists and members of the Department of Social Administration and Social Policy investigated important social problems, ranging from the social and environmental consequences of open-cast mining in the North West and North East to the amateurish and inconsistent behaviour of magistrates and their fondness for custodial sentences. Educationalists worked on projects designed to promote awareness of economic issues and counter economic illiteracy among schoolchildren aged between about fourteen and sixteen. The new Centre for Ethnic Studies in Education won a grant of £65,000 to explore the pressing subject of inter-ethnic relationships in secondary schools. The centre for Policy Research in Engineering, Science and Technology (PREST), developed a line in research on research – in determining the value of the costly programmes or institutions operated by other people. For five years the centre was engaged in evaluating an ambitious project based at the Department of Industry and known as the Alvey initiative, from which (see Chapter 7, above) the Department of Computer Science had benefited. This operation cost about £300m. and was designed to involve academia and industry in exploring several aspects of the development of information technology, defined as 'software engineering', 'intelligent knowledge-based systems', 'very large-scale integrated circuits' and 'man–machine interface'. PREST also assessed the work of the Natural History Museum in South Kensington, by asking who used, and for what purpose, its attempts to classify the vast numbers of animals and plants within its walls. Members of the centre helped, by devising, distributing, collecting and analysing over 16,000 questionnaires, to carry out a comprehensive survey of equipment held by universities and polytechnics, with a view to discovering how up-to-date and well maintained it was.

Research in medicine and the life sciences had several particular strengths. The University was said to boast 'the largest concentration of connective tissue work in Europe', which meant research on cartilage, bone, blood vessels and skin, much of it under the direction of Michael Grant, the Professor of Biochemistry, and much of it relevant to the relief of osteoarthritis, heart disease, and some aspects of cancer. The Kay Kendall Leukaemia Fund awarded over £900,000 to Michael Dexter, of the Department of Medical Oncology, and his research group at the Paterson Institute for Cancer Research at the Christie Hospital in South Manchester. The grant would enable them to construct a new laboratory to explore the formation of blood cells and investigate new methods of treating leukaemia. *Mancunion*, which seldom took much interest in the scientific work of the University, none the less reported on work being done on the AIDS virus and on a new female contraceptive in the Department of Biochemistry. Members of the Department of Pathology, with the support of the Medical Research Council, brought an electron microscope to bear on the formation of senile plaques in the brain in the early phases of Alzheimer's disease. The North Western Regional Health Authority offered £300,000 to provide Magnetic Resonance Imaging, an advanced alternative to X-rays, for patients suffering from neurological disorders. Professor Iain Hutchinson, of the Immunology Research Group in Biological Sciences, concerned himself and his colleagues with methods of preventing the rejection of transplanted kidneys. Hope Hospital had the only Accident and Emergency department in the country to be provided with clinical staff who were also senior academics. Hence the new North West Injury Research Centre was well placed in the hospital, and the Centre's director, Rodney Little, a specialist in trauma research, spoke of the wide range of injury victims from other casualty and burns units in the area to whom the Centre would have access. Miles Irving, the Professor of Surgery, mentioned the benefits, including the service to industry, of getting patients back to work as rapidly as possible.

Much of the University's work was concerned with the education of doctors, pharmacists, nurses and even patients themselves, in order to supplement the efforts of the National Health Service and to assist in putting Government policy into effect. Its importance was as much social as scientific. Geriatric medicine had long been a speciality of Manchester, and it was concerned with such matters as brittle bones and muscular deterioration, as well as with the even broader subject of decline in the performance of elderly people and their diminishing ability to cope with the problems of everyday existence. Specialists in geriatric medicine helped to educate general practitioners, community nurses and others about the problems of incontinence in old people. Professor Stephen Tomlinson and certain colleagues raised money by appeal to cover much of the cost of opening a new Diabetes Centre in two converted houses in Hathersage Road, an enterprise which involved not only doctors and nurses but also dieticians and chiropodists. It was designed to relieve patients of the grim and tedious experience of queuing for up to three hours in the Manchester Royal Infirmary with, at the end of the long wait for attention, nothing more than a brief consultation, an encounter which would concentrate on finding problems rather than preventing them or educating patients about their condition.

The release of mentally ill, or mentally handicapped, people into the community, created problems for local authorities, and members of University departments undertook to investigate them and make recommendations. University pharmacists helped to address the task of training some 2,700 pharmacists in the region as 'community pharmacists' who would be better equipped to diagnose minor ailments and give proper advice to customers. Karen Luker, a Lecturer in Nursing, won a substantial grant from the Department of Health and Social Security to collaborate with a consultant nephrologist at Withington Hospital and develop methods of training which would enable patients to manage their own portable kidney dialysis machines.

The social as well as the medical aspects of the AIDS epidemic claimed the attention of University researchers. Sue Scott, a Lecturer in Sociology, collaborated with colleagues in the University of London in an inquiry called WRAP (the Women, Risk and AIDS project). This set out to investigate the sexual knowledge and behaviour of British women aged between sixteen and twenty-one and the extent to which they had been affected by the spread of HIV infection. The inquiry would not pay excessive attention to the traditional social and economic classifications of the women involved, but rather to 'the amount of autonomy the women have in their life'.

As the journalist George Monbiot would write some years later, in *Captive State: the Corporate Takeover of Britain,* until the 1970s and

1980s British universities had generally fought shy of close engagement with industry – unless, as he might have added, the university
could clearly retain the initiative, as in the partnership with Ferranti in
the late 1940s, when the engineering firm which constructed the early
computers was working to the instructions of a university professor at
the behest of the Ministry of Supply. The danger, as Monbiot put it,
was that contacts with industry might persuade the universities to 'concentrate on immediate technological needs rather than on the more
profound scientific questions'. Some members of the University were
aware of this danger. Brian Dawson, the Secretary to the Faculty of
Science in Manchester, spoke to *Mancunion* in November 1987 of the
fear that too much funding might be directed towards applied
research, and suggested that Salford's dependence for more than half
its income on research contracts and consultancies was leading to
research only in very constricted areas. Manchester's reputation, he
said, was, and should remain, in 'research for curiosity's value'. Industry, remarked a student journalist, Naomi Koppel, did not always know
what it wanted and was liable to change its mind. But dependence on
industry would grow if and when public funding of the Research
Councils became inadequate. Already, she had heard, projects rated
Alpha by SERC were failing to attract funding.

   Should universities move closer to business and industry, would
research be subordinated to the pursuit of commercial profits, and
would scientists encounter restrictions on publishing some of their
results? The Vice-Chancellor rightly warned against involvement in
enterprises whose sole purpose was to make money, but some forms of
collaboration seemed less dubious. Arguably, there was nothing wrong
with making businesses aware of discoveries made in universities, so
that they might arrange to develop them if they chose, and certainly no
harm in encouraging discussions and exchanges of information between
businessmen and academics. These appeared to be the aims of CURID
and the Science Park, and there was much talk of working on academic
areas which happened to be of 'industrial relevance', but in which
'good, sound, basic science' could still be practised. The Universities of
Manchester and Liverpool formulated between them a successful collaborative bid which enabled them to establish in Liverpool an Interdisciplinary Research Centre in Surface Science ('the business of how
atoms and molecules intersect with surfaces of metals, semiconductors
and oxides'). This appeared to be crucial to developments in the chemical industry, which was one of the country's biggest earners abroad. An
endearing photograph appeared of the Vice-Chancellor and Baroness

Blackstone, the Master of Birkbeck College London, who seemed to be at the controls of a train pulling into St Pancras. Sir Mark wore a hat bearing the slogan 'Universities Work', designed to advertise a new publication of the CVCP describing various industries and services, British Rail among them, which had benefited from university research.

In practice, relations between the University, business and the professions were complex and varied, taking at least eight different forms, apart from exchanges of information and expertise.

First, the University was a customer of industrial concerns, from which it purchased, with financial help from the Research Councils or charities such as the Wellcome Trust, certain highly sophisticated instruments. Among these was the 'mini-supercomputer' supplied by Floating Point System (UK) Ltd. of Warrington in 1988; this was designed to make the calculations necessary for molecular modelling and intended to contribute to such matters as 'rational drug design, catalysis and material science'.

Secondly, having acquired expensive equipment, the University could give scientists in industrial employment access to its treasures and charge them for the privilege of using them – as representatives of ICI, Colgate-Palmolive and the United Kingdom Atomic Energy Authority (UKAEA) resorted to the centralised Electron Microscope Unit at the heart of the Medical School. Since it commanded the most powerful university computer centre in the UK, the University could look forward to exploiting its 'excess supercomputer power' and entering into 'lucrative contracts' with industrial concerns.

Thirdly, it occasionally happened that large concerns made generous gifts to the University, including the wind tunnel which British Aerospace presented in 1990. This was set up at Barton Aerodrome and for a time provided, under contract, testing facilities to the TWR Jaguar Racing Team.

A fourth kind of link began to develop through the professor or senior academic who had considerable experience in business or industry and continued to maintain connections with it after appointment to a University post. New academic types began to appear on the scene and to be greeted with applause. David Warren, who became Professor of Computer Logic in 1985, had founded two years earlier, in the United States, a company called Quintus Computer Systems Ltd., of which he was now a Vice-President. Brian Warboys, who had spent his working life with ICL (International Computers Ltd.) combined an ICL Fellowship with a chair of Software Engineering in the Department of Computer Science.

Fifthly, there were some fields in which firms sponsored students or took a direct interest in the education of bright young things who might be attracted into their employment. Certain firms were willing to give students in Electrical Engineering problems to solve and projects to carry out; these usually entailed developing under supervision a complicated piece of equipment up to the point at which the students could construct a prototype for production. Designs worked out in the Department under this stimulus included a complex portable computer for analysing digital control systems on board ships. And if engineering firms could help educate students, the University could provide academic direction for engineers working on industrial premises. The Department of Anaesthesia at Withington Hospital undertook to supervise graduate engineers working at Ohmeda, a firm which formed part of the BOC Health Care Group, on the development of new anaesthetic breathing systems which would be widely used in operating theatres and intensive therapy units.

Sixthly, it was possible for intellectual reasons for University groups or units to address themselves to the problems of industrial machinery and industrial buildings. Since 1980 the Wolfson Maintenance Unit had worked closely with the Department of Engineering, and had carried out consultancy work. This involved, among other things, using sophisticated instruments to keep watch over the condition of machinery and to anticipate trouble, by predicting failures before they occurred. Among the Unit's clients was Ford of Europe, which commissioned it in 1986 to conduct a pilot study ranging across seventeen of their plants. In the Department of Architecture, the Architecture for Industry Research Unit, headed by Dr James Harris, investigated the formidable problems faced by British industry in that it had to struggle, to a greater extent than did its leading foreign competitors, with obsolete buildings and overcrowded sites.

A seventh area of collaboration lay in the endowment of chairs and other senior posts by businesses and by successful firms of accountants, consultants and solicitors. Their generosity appeared to provide welcome relief from the bleak and threatening climate of the early 1980s, in which many posts had fallen to the financial axe. There was a price to pay, in the form of suspicion (even in the absence of evidence) that a benefactor would acquire some kind of hold over the University. It was, after all, an axiom of the Thatcher period that no free lunches were ever to be had. Left-wing critics might well suggest that Manchester was in thrall to capitalism, whose philanthropy could never be disinterested. They might seek, or imagine, evidence of pressure to produce a certain type of useful graduate, or of expectations that research would be steered in directions useful to business.

However, some departments concerned with vocational training existed almost by definition to serve the needs of the professions and made no secret of the fact. Peat Marwick (later Peat Marwick McLintock, described in 1989 as 'the UK's largest accountancy and management consultancy practice'), endowed two chairs in the Department of Accountancy and Business Finance and also supported a Readership and Senior Lectureship. Herbert Smith, the London firm of solicitors, topped up a lectureship and endowed a chair of Corporate and Commercial Law, their senior partner noting the risk that the legal profession (sometimes said to be approaching saturation in the past) would soon be insufficiently supplied with graduates. David Milman, the senior lecturer appointed to the chair, was co-author of an *Annotated Guide to Insolvency Legislation*, a work read avidly by accountants; he also became the director of a new Centre for Law and Business. Halliwell-Landau, a Manchester firm specialising in commercial law, funded a new lectureship, sponsored a reading room in the Law Faculty Library, and pledged almost £250,000 to the Faculty over a period of ten years.

It became known in 1989 that ICI Pharmaceuticals and Glaxo were about to support two new chairs in the Department of Physiological Sciences. ICI's object was, by founding a chair in Molecular Pharmacology, to strengthen the University's work on the design, development and analysis of drugs; Glaxo's, through a chair in Neuroscience, to encourage investigations of the brain and nervous system. In the same year Boots the Chemist Ltd. established a new chair of Pharmacy Practice in the Department of Pharmacy. A British Gas Chair of Urban Renewal arose in the midst of the Department of Architecture. The UGC commended the University for seeking industrial funding for a chair in Occupational Health and raising enough money to support it for seven years.

Some business folk endowed posts which had nothing specifically to do with their own economic interests. John Hinnells, the Professor of Comparative Religion, launched in 1986 an appeal for funds to support a post in modern Jewish studies, thus enabling Manchester to extend its concerns beyond the field of early classical Judaism. From his campaign came a chair which was eventually financed to a large extent by the Alliance Family Trust, David Alliance being the Group Chief Executive of Coates Viyella, which had long had business interests in the region. Here the intention was not to serve the practical needs of a particular business, industry or profession, but to enlighten and inform those who would soon become influential professional people. As Professor Hinnells promised, 'we will produce graduates with an informed and sensitive view of Judaism. As they go on to careers in such opinion-forming professions as teaching, the media, the Civil Service and social work, which so many of our students will do, they will be well equipped to counter anti-semitism.'

It was also true that professional or industrial firms were not the only sponsors of chairs in vocational subjects. To mark its own centenary in 1987, the Queen's Nursing Institute endowed the first chair of Community Nursing in the country. This went to Tony Butterworth, originally trained as a psychiatric nurse, who had been a Nursing Officer at Withington Hospital and a Lecturer in Applied Community Studies at Manchester Polytechnic. He had worked with AIDS patients and had helped to develop courses for nurses working with drug addicts and alcoholics.

The last and perhaps most intimate bond with industry grew out of collaboration in the development of new products, the exploitation of inventions. These things could be done either through the University's own company, Vuman, and its subsidiaries, or by entering into partnership with an independent company. Roger Hambleton of Pharmacy, and Edward Duff, the University Research Consultancy Officer, took a prize in an 'academic enterprise' competition set up by the British Technology Group – a reward for their initiative in developing, together with Lantor [UK] Ltd. of Bolton, the device known as the Lantor Cube Engineer's Autoclave Test Pack. This was used to test the hospital machinery which sterilised surgical instruments. By 1989 'industrial collaboration' was far advanced in the physiological sciences, in which area twenty-three joint projects with fourteen different pharmaceutical companies were under way.

It was also possible for the University to work on its own, although its efforts to do so were not always crowned with immediate success. In 1985 the University Council had set up a Committee on Research Exploitation, and this body was to ensure that Vuman, acting as the University's agent, would be the first to assess the commercial potential of University research, to make an initial patent application, and to discuss the matter with possible licensees. Should Vuman not wish to proceed, the Council Committee would decide whether or not to offer the work elsewhere. There was some uncertainty as to whether Vuman ought itself to become involved in manufacturing or in basic development work, designed to bring products to the point at which they could be commercially exploited. Any expectations that the company would immediately and consistently record large profits were soon disappointed. Vuman sustained a loss of over £70,000 in the financial year 1986–87 and made a pre-tax profit of about £60,000 in 1987–88. But it required heavy initial investment in order to build up its working capital for the purposes of development. The call to put in a further £500,000 in 1988 prompted questions in Council and requests for more candid financial statements. Seeking to reassure the doubters, the University Treasurer and others urged that Vuman 'represented the public image of the use of the University's expertise' and justified its activity, particularly in the field of lasers, as potentially 'of great value to society in general'.

In 1988–89 Vuman again showed a modest profit, but, like the University itself in the eyes of the UGC, it appeared to have both strong and weak performers. At least for the time being the strength appeared to lie in Medeval and Predictive Control, but the Laser Division, the Delta Division and Vuman Computer Systems Ltd. had failed to meet the high expectations entertained of them. It could then be said that, although the company 'operated within a highly competitive commercial environment where risks were higher and outcomes less certain', a profit had been made and the University had received some royalties. Unfortunately, in the following year Vuman incurred a heavy operating loss of some £230,000, when even Medeval's profits were falling, and the company was compelled to cut its costs. The loss was partly due to delays in making available commercially a new version of Vuwriter (the word-processing programme for scientists) and to development costs carried by the Laser Division. At this point the Deputy Vice-Chancellor, Sam Moore, who was holding the fort after Mark Richmond's departure, expressed the view that 'Vuman should not be involved in development funding or actual manufacturing, but should rather be a company responsible solely for the exploitation potential of the University's research products, through the activities of licensing and trading'.

The University's reputation for effective research depended to some degree on its ability to supervise postgraduates, and particularly to persuade doctoral students to bring their theses to completion. Only completed works, the visible and tangible products of their labour, solid additions to knowledge and understanding, marshalled on library shelves and properly catalogued for readers to consult, would convince the dispensers of funds that public money was being well spent. Few would be impressed by suggestions that defaulting research students had learned a great deal on the way to the non-production of their dissertations or by pleas to the effect that the investment in their future had not been entirely lost.

Doctoral students were initially registered and most of them financed for three years of concentrated work on their dissertations, and few of them succeeded in writing up their results within that time. University regulations allowed them to dally for another five years, sometimes more, before presenting their results. Ill-defined expectations and the absence of word limits, particularly in arts subjects, encouraged students to embark on ever more ambitious topics which they could not hope to exhaust. Grants normally ran out after the first three years, students took part-time if not full-time work and the dissertation was driven to the wall. Some blamed chronic poverty, anxiety for immediate employment in order to lead a normal life, mounting disillusionment with the academic world and the evaporation of prospects within it, misguided perfectionism and lack of confidence. All these things tended to deter the less determined students. One thinks of poor Zipser, in Tom Sharpe's *Porterhouse Blue*, of his unequal struggle with 'The Pumpernickel as a Factor in the Politics of Sixteenth-Century Westphalia', and of all the distractions that overtook him before his untimely death. Real-life Zipsers needed a sense of urgency and rather firmer direction from above.

Postgraduate students and their representatives complained of casual supervision and of the lack of official procedures for complaining about it to anyone other than the errant supervisors themselves. Academics were inclined to blame indiscipline and the absence of organised basic training in the techniques of research. Students supported by the Economic and Social Research Council (ESRC) gave particular cause for concern. By way of a partial remedy the ESRC backed a doctoral training programme organised by Professor Brian Robson of the Geography Department. This scheme, launched in 1985 and drawing on the skills of seventeen departments, endeavoured to provide doctoral students with a sense of structure and purpose during the first year of the three, when they might all too easily drift into uncertainty and isolation.

It was hardly possible to sue defaulting students for breach of contract; they had received grants, not publishers' advances. But, since the ESRC allotted a certain quota of studentships to each department considered worthy to receive them, the Council could apply sanctions against institutions whose students performed poorly and could cast them into limbo until, suitably chastened, they promised to mend their ways. The ESRC expected a certain proportion of its students to complete their work within four years and stepped up its demands as time passed. It increased the requirement from a mere 10 per cent in 1985 to 25 per cent in 1986, 35 per cent in 1988 and 40 per cent in 1990, when a hurdle of 50 per cent was in prospect. Early in 1988 the University began to suffer from these measures, in that the ESRC refused to go on supporting certain courses and departments, whilst in 1990 it judged the institution as a whole and found that its overall submission rate was no better than 27 per cent. By way of penalty the ESRC then withdrew all studentships from Manchester for the time being, and it was feared that the consequent fall in student numbers might reduce the University's block grant. This measure bore hard on the Faculty of Economic and Social Studies, which had achieved rates of over 50 per cent but been dragged down by the poor achievements of others. The Faculty could only comfort themselves with the reflection that the Research Council would in future invite universities to nominate departments for recognition and base its calculations only on their performance. It was unlikely that the University would back the weak and inefficient.

By way of concentrating the postgraduate mind, the University began to make its doctoral regulations a shade less indulgent. It reduced from five years to two the period after full-time registration in which Doctor of Philosophy (Ph.D.) students were automatically allowed to submit their dissertations after completing them. After that time they would have to explain themselves at intervals and apply for extensions, although they would be able, if their excuses proved convincing, to continue as doctoral students for another four years.

There was a growing danger that the Faculty of Arts in particular would develop into the University's poor relation. It might come to resemble one of those peripheral provinces, like Catalonia in the old Spanish monarchy, whose inhabitants complained endlessly of their exclusion from the honours and privileges enjoyed by those closer to the centre of royal power and patronage. The arts contributed little to the much-vaunted 'links with industry'; even writing business histories presented certain problems, in that scholars describing recent events might be prevented from publishing their results lest they disclose professional secrets. Engineers and other scientists contributed their consultancy fees to the University's coffers; a member of JCUD once argued passionately that arts authors ought likewise to hand over the royalties (should there be any) of books they had written in the course of duty. Had the University subsidised arts research adequately, the argument might have cut some ice. As it was, most scholarship ran at a loss. A complaint of arts academics was that they had to support their research from their own pockets as if it were some form of private self-indulgence, the University entertaining the delusion that they could do it for little or nothing in their ample vacations.

In the aftermath of the second Research Selectivity Exercise in 1989 grievances began to be voiced in the correspondence columns of *This Week*. Lecturers in Italian, in French and in Turkish complained of having to finance from their own salaries the work they were contracted to do and of having to subsidise their own departments lest these suffer from poor research ratings. They spoke of poor or non-existent allowances for photocopying, of the high cost of materials ordered from abroad by Inter-Library Loans, of the cost of travel to conferences, of the price of stationery, of the need to purchase one's own word processor, of the Inland Revenue's reluctance to allow items of expenditure to be set off against tax. Colin Imber, an expert on the history of the Ottoman Empire, told of the near-impossibility in his situation of obtaining sabbatical leave, and described how, when he had decided to sacrifice 'several thousand smackers' to obtain release to do research in the form of leave without pay, he had been told how lucky he was to be granted such a privilege. A difficulty for the arts was that, unless their topics were of clear economic or social significance, they had no Research Council from which to seek large grants. The British Academy, which administered postgraduate studentships in arts, could offer small grants for travel and other research purposes, and was able to award a few coveted Research Readerships to academics in mid-career. But it was not yet well placed to subsidise research leave on a large scale.

Since 1984 the University had striven to remedy the shortage of research awards in all subjects by providing its own Research Support Fund (there was no particular intention to favour the arts). Sir Francis Graham Smith, the chairman of the committee which administered the fund, felt moved by Dr Imber's lament to give an account of its activity. Since its establishment the committee had received 443 applications and had been able to afford only 53 grants; hence the success rate appeared to be no more than 12 per cent.

Close to hand lay a superb resource for historians, literary scholars in many languages, Hebraists and others. But the John Rylands Library in Deansgate was (or so some critics maintained) in danger of declining into a mausoleum, a depository for a vast but inaccessible treasury of manuscripts and archives which it was unable to sort and list. The Vice-Chancellor told the University Council that on a good day the richly appointed but sepulchral building of Basil Champneys might receive five visitors, on a bad day none. Arguably a library which stored items but did not make them available to readers was failing in its duty to the citizens of Manchester, to the University and to the wider scholarly community. This pessimistic view of the Library was not universally shared, but it carried weight among influential people. The subject specialists on the Library staff could not easily be spared to work on the collections, and even if they could their results were unlikely to reach the standard established by the professional archivists whom other institutions employed.

There arose the idea, in itself admirable, of establishing a John Rylands Research Institute which would provide bursaries and fellowships for scholars prepared to work on the Library's collections, with a view both to arranging them and to interpreting their contents. David Miller, the second Deputy Librarian, drew up plans in a paper of 17 November 1986, and the process gathered momentum under his leadership at a time when the University Librarian, Michael Pegg, had fallen gravely ill and was slowly recuperating from treatment. In 1987 the Library Committee and Senate endorsed the project. They were told of proposals to raise funds by publishing facsimiles and microfilms of the Rylands treasures; by appealing to local businesses (which might be moved to give luncheons in these dignified surroundings and make suitable donations in return for the privilege); and by selling so-called 'duplicate copies' of books. Approaches might be made to educational trusts; to the Jewish and Chinese communities; to the French Government, since the Library held on deposit a fine collection of pamphlets relating to the French Revolution; and to the Hellenic Foundation.

Most of these proposals, though optimistic, were unexceptionable. But bitter controversy, damaging to the University's reputation, began to arise over the proposed book sale, for it became clear that what the small circle of librarians working with Dr Miller had in mind was not an auction of recent publications or ordinary nineteenth- and twentieth-century works. Rather, they were proposing a sale of books published before 1500, of other early printed books, and of some hugely valuable illustrated works on natural history. These items might be expected to raise between them £1m. or more, and endow the new Institute with an annual income of some £70,000. There might be talk of 'duplicates', but could that term be applied to early printed books, and could an edition printed on paper be called a duplicate of a similar edition printed on vellum and prepared for a famous connoisseur? Meeting in October 1987, the Library Committee were warned of the difficulty. In this connection, 'duplicate' could never mean 'an exact replica'. Before 1801, they were told, 'type was set by hand, text was often proofread and corrected after printing had begun and a variety of different media was used . . . the Library had considered [for possible sale] copies which duplicated the text but were not necessarily duplicated in all other respects'. As a writer in the *Times Literary Supplement* (*TLS*) subsequently observed, 'The very notion of duplicate books is one which meets with hollow laughter from scholars, bibliographers and collectors. No two copies of early printed books are ever exactly alike: they vary in small but significant ways.' Peter McNiven, a historian and librarian, was to write some years later that the Library laid itself open to charges either of failing to appreciate this fact, or else of trying 'to give the impression that "true" duplicates were involved in order to allay legitimate concerns'.

As its defenders maintained, the Library proceeded circumspectly, consulted with interested parties within the University, informed some other libraries of its intentions, and got a mixed reaction from them. On the advice of the librarians immediately involved, the Library Committee determined to put ninety-eight items on sale at Sotheby's on 14 April 1988. Most of these came from two major collections: that of the second Earl Spencer (1758–1834), previously housed at Althorp and purchased by Mrs Rylands in 1892 from his descendant, the fifth Earl, who was then the Chancellor of the University; and that of a versatile Manchester professor, Richard Copley Christie (1834–1901), who had bequeathed his books to the University. Indignant denials greeted the suggestion that the sellers had chosen the best copies and put them up for auction with a view to making the most money. When in doubt, they replied, they had chosen the Spencer volumes, more of which had been cleaned up, freed of marginalia, and rebound. The present Lord Spencer and the present Lord Crawford (the owner of one of the most valuable collections deposited in the Library) were members of the Library Committee and as such party to its recommendations; the involvement of the father of the Princess of Wales increased public interest in the transaction about to take place.

Within two or three weeks of the impending sale it became clear that certain influential figures in the world of libraries and book-collecting had not been persuaded of the arguments for disposing of the books. Among them were Fred Ratcliffe, now the University Librarian of Cambridge, who had helped to bring the University and John Rylands Libraries together in 1972; Lord Crawford, whose family had sold a substantial collection to Mrs Rylands in 1901, and had deposited other holdings in the Library; and Nicolas Barker of the British Library, editor of *The Book Collector* and a member of the mainly aristocratic Roxburghe Club. Letters published in *The Times* and the *TLS* accused the University of breaking faith with its benefactors and the people of Manchester, and urged it to cancel the sale. One came from Fred Ratcliffe and several distinguished librarians, together with the Master of Emmanuel College Cambridge and a former Chairman of the Friends of National Libraries. Six members of the Roxburghe Club, of which the second Earl Spencer had been a founder in 1811, swelled the chorus of condemnation and asked: 'Who can imagine the distress which this sale would cause Mrs Rylands?'

Subsequent controversy produced no meeting of minds and no agreement as to Mrs Rylands's likely attitude; everything said about this was speculative. The dispute was represented all too neatly in the University as a contest between bibliophiles and scholars, between hoarders of books and readers of books, as if these were mutually exclusive categories. Was it not possible for scholars to be interested in the history of books, printing and taste? It was probably true, however, that there were many whose interest lay in the essential content of a text, and some who regarded each book as a unique object, which should be considered as a whole, together with its provenance and with the history of the collection to which it had belonged and from which it ought never to be parted. There were also scholars who took an interest in the textual variations of copies of what was essentially the same work. Arguments about duplicates continued and were never settled. There was much dispute about the coherence of Lord Spencer's collection and some impatience with the tendency to regard it as sacrosanct. Had the Spencers themselves ever hesitated to sell books when they found it convenient and what respect had they shown for damaged medieval bindings? Was it true, or was it not, that Lord Spencer had declined a higher offer than that of Mrs Rylands in order to prevent his books from going to America, and was there or was there not a tacit understanding that the collection should always be kept together (it was not kept in one place in the Library)? Surely, said some participants in the debate, Mrs Rylands had believed in a 'dynamic' Library which would be of use to the citizens of Manchester, and she would not now be shocked at proposals to sell a few items in order to make the rest more accessible.

The Library did not fail to cite clauses from legal agreements and bequests, including the agreement drawn up when the University and John Rylands Libraries merged, which authorised the sale of items at the librarians' discretion. Dr Ratcliffe did not dispute the Library's legal right to act in such a way, but he questioned its moral right to do so, and argued that the legal provisos (almost obligatory in trust documents) had never been intended to permit the sales of the 'great books' in the Library's collections. These had not been expressly protected because it had occurred to nobody that they could ever be at risk: 'We put our faith in scholarship, not the law'.

Whatever might be said of Lord Spencer (and Nicolas Barker claimed that his collection had a 'historic unity'), Professor Christie had expressed his wishes clearly in the introduction to his catalogue of his books. 'The Collection as a whole will be found to have a uniform aim and a principle of unity pervading it. It has been formed with a view of illustrating the classical Renaissance of Italy and France. I believe that no other Library in England or the Continent contains a more complete collection . . . ' A fine stained-glass window beside the staircase in the Christie Building depicted the professor, in full academic dress, reading at a desk and flanked by the figures of Erasmus and of Aldus Manutius, the Venetian printer, several of whose books figured in the sale. The Christie Building, which had once housed the Science library, was now an empty shell. Was Christie's collection to be violated and his wishes ignored?

Interviewed years later, in 1999, Dr Ratcliffe said: ' . . . it was totally out of character with Manchester . . . I couldn't believe it at first . . . I was very upset by it because I was the person who'd really persuaded the Rylands and the trustees that this could never happen . . . '. The Rylands could, towards 1970, have solved all its financial problems by selling just one book – its copy of the Gutenberg Bible, one of the finest in the world – but had chosen instead to put all its holdings in trust at the University. At the time of the controversy in 1988 Dr Ratcliffe argued that the University ought to have used the investments of the Rylands Library to finance the Rylands Research Institute.

Undaunted and resentful of opposition, the University proceeded with the sale, from which it reaped the unexpectedly large sum of £1,620,000. Peter Stockham, the bookseller, distributed a mock-Victorian penny-dreadful handout to those attending the event, which called it 'A Cruel and Inhuman Murder Committed upon the Body of the University of Manchester'. *This Week*, which had never echoed the official point of view with greater fidelity, gloated over the proceeds of the sale and dismissed its distinguished critics as ill-informed, without referring to their status and qualifications or answering their arguments. Two members of the Departments of Greek and Latin, Harry Jocelyn and David Bain, rebuked it for insensitivity. Professor

Jocelyn wrote: 'The vulgar triumphalism of language like "sale of the century" must embarrass even some of those who think the sale justified'. David O'Connor, an art historian, compared the Library unfavourably with the Whitworth Art Gallery, which, being short of space in which to display its fine collections of prints, textiles and wallpapers, had sold no treasures but launched an appeal for funds. Nicolas Barker published in the pages of *The Book Collector* an outspoken attack on the actions of the librarians responsible, calling the saga of the Rylands 'a story in which stupidity and duplicity go hand in hand'. He professed to see in the affair a reflection of the classic conflict between the landed aristocracy and the rising bourgeoisie, evinced in 'a mean-minded dislike of owning such frankly aristocratic objects'. The wittiest counterblast blew from the *PN News*, formerly *Poetry Nation*, in which the poet Michael Schmidt, founder of the Carcanet Press and a Special Lecturer in the English Department, defended the University's position and reflected on the outlook of the fifth Lord Spencer, who, finding himself financially embarrassed, had sold the books to Mrs Rylands rather than dispose of his china.

Much debated was the role of Lord Crawford in the affair. Was he a generous benefactor or an avenging fury, and why, being a member of the Library Committee, had he apparently waited until the last minute to object? Through him had arisen, once more, the possibility of selling a single, immensely valuable book to solve the Library's financial problems. At issue now was not the Gutenberg Bible but *Birds of America*, the work of the 'American woodsman', naturalist and illustrator, John James Audubon (1785–1851). Lord Crawford had offered the Library his copy of this work on condition that it sold its Audubon instead of the ninety-odd books proposed for Sotheby's; the Audubon would probably have fetched at least as large a sum. But the Library refused the offer, presumably on the grounds that Lord Crawford was only proposing to lend or deposit the book and could have withdrawn it when he chose. After the sale it was he who demonstrated the sanctions in store for libraries held to have broken faith with benefactors. By way of penalty he chose to remove from 'indefinite deposit' in the Rylands his fine collection of materials relating to the French Revolution. It was not among the neglected holdings, for considerable time and money had been spent upon it. The Library had no redress, except to resolve to accept no collections in future without either a guarantee of tenure in perpetuity or a guarantee that on their removal compensation would be paid for the service of having kept them safe and in good order.

How seriously had the University's reputation suffered? John Zochonis, the Chairman of Council, felt obliged to refute the suggestion that a fit of philistinism had overtaken a great liberal institution. It seemed that the Rylands book sale was being coupled with another pragmatic decision, which concerned Tabley House near Knutsford. The owner of the estate, Lieutenant-Colonel John Leicester-Warren, had bequeathed the house to the National Trust, which was unable to accept it, and it had passed, about 1976, to the University as residuary legatee. The University had decided to lease a large part of the house for 125 years to Cygnet Health Care, a company which proposed to open a home for elderly people. But the University had also agreed to open a museum on the premises, and by way of a curtain-raiser organised an exhibition of paintings from Tabley House, including Turner's 'Windy Day', at a London gallery in Jermyn Street.

In view of the furore it was doubly important to extol the work of the new Institute. There was no question of using the proceeds of the sale for any purpose other than the Institute's support. By the autumn of 1989 the Institute had a staff of six research workers, funded by investment of the proceeds of the sale, and they were working on collections which ranged from the papers of landed families in the North West to the Library's remarkable Hebrew–Jewish collection. Peter Slade, a pioneer of children's theatre, gave his personal archives to the Rylands at Deansgate. A newly formed editorial board had already redesigned the *Bulletin of the John Rylands Library,* the Library's staid learned journal, in such a way as to bring out every year one issue devoted to the Rylands collections, as well as a thematic issue and a learned miscellany. From time to time new discoveries were reported. A rare book, the *Oratio* of Alexander Cortesius, printed at Rome in 1483, had come to light by chance among 12,000 uncatalogued items in the Robert Shackleton Collection. Who knew what systematic investigations might reveal?

If the price of liberty had always been constant vigilance, it seemed that the price of survival in the late 1980s was constant surveillance and the price of efficiency constant competition and the publication of results. In return for their employment, still reasonably secure despite the erosion of tenure, academics must now submit to scrutiny, designed in part to establish whether or not they were giving value for money, and in part to identify strengths and weaknesses. Concern with the Research Selectivity Exercises threatened, as time passed, to become obsessive. The fairer these operations aspired to be, the more time they consumed and the more mountains of paper they threw up, senior academics spending precious long vacations, not on creativity, but on judging their colleagues. 'Publish or your department perishes' became a nagging admonition, impossible to ignore. However, the improvement of research performance was a legitimate goal. The reorganisation of biological sciences demonstrated the University's ability to reform itself; it provided a model and a precedent for the refashioning of groups of departments into schools in other parts of the University.

One of the University's main intellectual concerns was to preserve a balance between pure science and scholarship, and things of more immediate application, which were both more lucrative and more likely to impress the public and the Government. Developing 'links with industry' was not intended to suggest that the University should be dominated by business ethics and industrial capitalism, although there was a suspicion that it might take on this meaning unless care was exercised. As Sir Mark Richmond explained when reminiscing about the 1980s, 'one of the inexorable things about universities at the moment is that the money-spinners are medicine and science, and that's where the dynamo is'. Hence the need to concentrate on the 'big hitters', whose research ratings and capacity for attracting funding would most affect the University's budget. The consequence of this was, on the part of arts departments, a sense of relief at being left alone, but also one of resentment at being neglected and poorly funded. It seemed hard that one of the more vigorous efforts at self-help, the foundation of the John Rylands Research Institute, should have been made in such a way as to bring the University into disrepute and even, in some circles, to impugn its reputation for intellectual honesty and good faith.

12

Student culture in the 1980s

At intervals journalists, commentators and left-wing politicians would accuse students of losing their idealism, of becoming materialistic and beady-eyed, obsessed with good results and good jobs, addicted to hedonism and pop culture rather than intellectual pursuits. An article demanding 'Where have all the rebels gone?' appeared on the twentieth anniversary of the events in Paris in 1968. After the Waddington affair in 1985–86 students seldom resorted to direct action within the University, although they still picketed and petitioned by way of protest. Demonstrators still clashed with the police, and a few Manchester students were arrested for public order offences, but in London, not in Manchester. In 1989–90 the Union Executive temporarily lost faith in the effectiveness of demonstrations. Symptomatic of a new mood was the failure of the Socialist Workers' Students Society, in February 1990, to win support for their proposals to occupy the University offices in protest against the introduction of student loans the following autumn. To authorise such action, an Emergency General Meeting needed to attract 500 students. This one mustered only 108. 'Occupations achieve nothing', declared the Academic Affairs Officer.

Students did not lack contentious issues or grievances, but now tended to focus on matters directly related to student welfare and to relations between students. These naturally included grants, benefits and loans, which were of almost universal concern. Increasingly prominent throughout the 1980s were protests against sexism, sexual harassment and crude misogyny. Campaigners strove to invade masculine preserves, to ensure respect and consideration for women, to protect them against indecent and violent acts, and to procure more genuine equality of opportunity – a concern which extended not only to women, but also to ethnic groups and disabled people. Interest in southern Africa and in nuclear disarmament became less intense in the late 1980s. No longer did students seek allies in fellow victims of Government policy, friends in health service workers or striking miners.

Levels of student radicalism were related, among other things, to the job prospects of university graduates. Both good and hard times tended, for different reasons, to stimulate student protest and win it sympathy from apolitical students – good times because they bred self-confidence and a sense that students deserved a hearing; hard times because they alienated students from an economic system which offered even graduates little hope. There were in-between times, such as the later 1980s, when prospects were far from dim but the superiority of and demand for graduates could no longer be taken for granted. These competitive periods were more likely to produce a swing to the Right or result in a lower level of political consciousness.

In the late 1970s Conservatives had briefly dominated the Union Executive. Ten years later change depended on the 'Cosmo-ites', supporters of a shrewd politician, Richard 'Cosmo' Hawkes, denounced by his enemies as a closet Tory, whose professed aim was to restore the Union to the average student. Although vowed to a deeply unpopular loan scheme, the Government seemed less obnoxious to students than in Keith Joseph's day. It was now encouraging universities to expand and widen access to higher education, although it intended to pay as little as possible for the increased numbers, and students could only anticipate a decline in the quality of their education.

Throughout the decade students struggled with financial problems as the value of the standard maintenance grant wasted away. Year after year the Government announced grant increases which fell short of the general rate of inflation and took no account of rising prices in areas of special interest to students, such as books, bus fares, and the movement of rent. In November 1984 the Vice-Chancellor quoted figures supplied by the CVCP which suggested that the purchasing power of the full grant in the previous year had fallen by 22.1 per cent since 1968. In May 1986 he argued, in a letter to MPs about student financial problems, that the grant's real value had declined by about 15 per cent since 1979. Rises in University rents did not outstrip grant increases as dramatically as they had done in 1980–81, the year of the great rent strike, but they were almost always steeper, especially in the catered halls which had to pay large wage bills.

The NUS, as the national negotiating body, ceased for a time to argue for increases which would have restored the grant to its old level. Such ill-timed demands would have seemed absurdly unrealistic, dwarfing the wage claims made by public sector workers, and would have stigmatised students as greedy and naïve. Few tangible results flowed from ritual protests, such as burning Sir Keith Joseph in effigy or conducting all-night work-ins in the John Rylands Library with a conjuror-comedian for light relief. In 1984 a *Mancunion* campaign special urged the case for a New Deal (students no longer had good job prospects to console them for their penury while they studied). Three years later the national campaign was aptly christened GBH, which stood both for the grants, benefits and housing allowances which had been reduced or withdrawn, and for the grievous bodily harm which Conservative policies were inflicting on higher education.

Government policies under Joseph seemed designed to discourage young people from attending universities. Inadequate maintenance grants were not the only problem. The minimum grant, once payable even to the children of affluent parents and affording them a modicum of independence, was first halved and then abolished. No longer could students make special claims for travel expenses, since a flat-rate travel allowance was included in the grant and supposed to satisfy everyone. This bore hard on students living in outlying halls of residence such as Needham in Didsbury, and on certain other groups, such as senior medical students, who had to travel from one hospital to another. Travel costs were among the forces which drove students towards the Hulme estate, hard by the University, and drew them away from more secure and salubrious areas several miles away.

However, in 1984 the Secretary of State introduced two measures which might be described as redistributing wealth, since they were harder on affluent parents and easier on those with modest incomes. He raised the point on the income scale at which parents were first called upon to contribute towards their children's maintenance at university. To the outrage of many, he also proposed to charge tuition fees of about £500 to parents whose residual income exceeded £22,000. As the Vice-Chancellor told Council in November, this was 'a radical departure and returned to a situation not seen in the United Kingdom for more than twenty years'. It had long been accepted that university places themselves should be free, in that tuition fees were always paid from the public purse, even where a student's maintenance at university was not. Any departure from this principle suggested a move to privatise higher education, for if places ceased to be free universities might begin to resemble public schools and well-to-do parents be better placed to buy opportunities for their children. The Vice-Chancellor also objected to another Government tactic, the device called 'coupling', which consisted of reducing student support in order to provide resources for other purposes – perhaps to buy research equipment. Some had said that the move was good for universities, but bad for students and parents. 'In the Vice-Chancellor's opinion', reported the Council minute, 'it was a most regrettable way of thinking that contrasted students with their University in this way.'

Joseph's move to exact tuition fees proved unpopular enough to provoke a Conservative back bench revolt. He withdrew the fees proposal, but clung to his other reforms. Suggestions of using extra tuition fees to top up the income of impoverished universities were to recur for many years to come, together with proposals that students' parents or sponsors or even the students themselves (by means of loans) should be made to pay them.

By May 1986 students were clearly about to suffer from changes in the social security system. They would forfeit their entitlement to supplementary and unemployment benefits during the short Christmas and Easter vacations, and students living in halls of residence would no longer be able to claim housing benefit. Most students spent up to two years in privately rented flats and houses, which they had to take for the whole academical year, even though few occupied the premises during the long vacation from June to the end of September. Henceforth they would receive only limited benefit for the summer. Cuts in housing allowances, argued a Campaign Special issue of *Mancunion* in 1987, were especially serious for students because they spent as much as 39 per cent of their income on accommodation, and this was believed to be more than any other group in the population, with the sole exception of single pensioners.

Indebtedness became a feature of student existence. By the autumn of 1984 banks had realised that students were almost certain to overdraw on their accounts and were allowing many of them to overstep their initial credit limits of £100 or £200. They asked only that students should arrange these facilities in advance, and reproved those who helped themselves. However, banks seemed to favour the disciplines most likely to lead to lucrative jobs with high starting salaries, and budding accountants, lawyers and engineers might well fare considerably better than future librarians, schoolteachers or social workers. Hence the Vice-Chancellor complained of the furtive introduction of a 'loan-scheme by omission with certain courses being assessed as more credit-worthy than others'.

By the autumn of 1986 the Vice-Chancellors and Principals appeared to have convinced themselves that an impartial public loan scheme, designed to raise grants to subsistence level, would be better than one operated by the banks according to their own criteria. Student politicians, however, would not ditch the idea of restoring the grant. Hence any suggestion that loans might be formalised by a Government scheme was sure to be deemed a shameful surrender. Richmond, once hailed as the students' champion, fell from grace with his Vice-Cancellarial colleagues as precipitately as Prince Lucifer and the rebel angels. Only in the autumn of 1990, however, did the Government introduce a mixed system of loans and maintenance grants.

Generalisations about student wealth and poverty depend excessively on anecdotal evidence. James Vernon, a student in the 1980s, remembers having enough money for survival but being chronically overdrawn, while certain contemporaries found themselves 'in a meltdown situation'. Some enjoyed good relations with generous parents; others did not. One barometer of student poverty was the popularity of the decaying Hulme estate. *Mancunion* estimated in 1984 that at the 1981 census 21 per cent of Hulme residents had been students (students constituted about 4.4 per cent of the city's population). In 1988 it suggested that they accounted for about one-third of Hulme's population of 19,000. Crime rates were high and insurance unobtainable, but the consolations were many. 'Beasts and Bullies aside', said a guide to places to live, 'Hulme is the place to be if you're living on a student grant. At £24 a week for a three- or four-bedroomed, centrally heated, double-glazed flat it is possible to add a spot of luxury to the average student's life-style. But you don't get this for nothing! Cockroaches and mice are not unknown, while asbestos panels and ultra-thin dividing walls pose problems to an individual's health and sanity'.

Some students accused their contemporaries of exaggerating their misfortunes, of having little idea of the nature of true poverty. Some of their penury may, indeed, have resembled what Victorian sociologists had once called 'secondary poverty', due to mismanagement of a tight budget or expenditure on diversions rather than essentials. But entertainment, not all of it cheap, was needed to make life tolerable, to colour what H.G. Wells, in *Love and Mr Lewisham,* dubbed 'the greyness of the life of all studious souls'. Drunkenness remained a problem even at times when, in theory, students had no spare cash; some of it was fuelled by the bar promotions of brewers and distillers. Heads of University residences noted in 1988 that 'the level of alcohol consumption among the student population continued to be a cause for concern and was leading to unruly behaviour, vandalism, criminal damage and an increased incidence of medical problems'. Television, soft drugs and music clubs figured prominently in the leisure hours of James Vernon and his friends. He had come north, like the Mass Observers who studied Bolton in the 1930s, in the hope of discovering the world of the working class; but he also wanted to be close to Factory Records, which managed the Hacienda Club and enabled fans to rub shoulders with the music-makers. Smoking cannabis proved cheaper than getting drunk, although it involved frightening encounters with sinister parts of the city, in Hulme and Moss Side – 'you were shitting yourself, you got your drugs and you legged it back home!'.

Students were increasingly inclined to take paid work during term and, unlike their American counterparts, to look for jobs outside the campus. Since the University was a major employer of local people, opportunities for waiting at University tables were rare, although Union bars offered some paid work. Many laboured long hours two or three nights a week in restaurants and pubs. Some students became care assistants or nursing auxiliaries, a job which required 'no medical training, just common sense, a strong stomach and a caring outlook'. The Manpower Skill Centre helped companies to cover staff holidays and sick leave, and welcomed students for temporary work during holidays. Drug-testing for Medeval, though 'inconvenient', was not strenuous and could bring in much-needed cash.

Rumours spread towards the close of the 1980s that Manchester was pulling in more prosperous students and attracting them by the fame of the Manchester music scene. Most took care to dress down and make themselves inconspicuous. An article, 'A-Car-Demia', of 1988, esti- mated that one student in eight owned a car, with all the social cachet it conferred and all the attendant problems of parking and security. Much student dismay had greeted a recent decision of the University to increase its parking charges, to which a car-less population would have been indifferent. For this article at least the question was, not how poor, but how rich students had become: 'Although designer clothes and filofaxes proliferate in the Union coffee bar, that bastion of hip and trendiness, are we all that wealthy?'

Students endured the picturesque squalor of dank and dilapidated Victorian houses and were afflicted by a chronic lack of ready cash. But they owned hardware and software that made them the envy of local residents, the victims of burglaries, and the despair of the police. The neighbours, wrote a student journalist, knew students when they saw them. 'You are the ones that never sleep, but never seem to get up . . . They know you haven't got a proper job. But they also know each of you has a stereo, and if you come from the south, a telly as well. Thus, they fiddle with your Yale locks, smash your windows, and crawl through gaps in your walls to steal your precious belongings. At last your redistributive socialist ideals are realised, as some poor deprived Mancunian buys your whole "Earth, Wind and Fire" collection for 50p. at a well-known second-hand store.' Personal computers and word-processors were still comparatively rare, but by the autumn of 1988 the NUS and the Midland Bank had contrived a scheme which would enable students to buy them, with loans of up to £1,000 to be repaid within two years of graduation. More and more students, reported *Mancunion*'s 'Housing Special' issue in February 1989, were choosing to buy houses rather than rent accommodation. Since prices were still rising at the rate of 10–15 per cent per annum, there was some prospect of making a tidy profit at the end of one's university career. About some students there was a touch of the rising bourgeoisie, of the Young Urban Professional in the making, of the owner (not always for long) of expensive electrical or electronic toys and perhaps a modest car.

At the start of the 1980s there were alarming reports of graduate unemployment, which seemed, in the short run, to justify the decision to reduce the number of graduates by paring down the universities and cutting student numbers, especially in the arts, humanities and social sciences. Gratification was not only deferred but remote; student privation was unlikely to be instantly relieved by well-paid jobs rewarding a good degree. From 1980 to 1984 prospects were bleak; indeed, the Careers Advisory Service described them as the worst since the Second World War. Reduced public spending on education, which had always absorbed many of the educated, led to higher unemployment, with fewer graduates embarking on research degrees or training as teachers. When recession overtook manufacturing industry, the prospects for arts and science graduates seemed equally poor. Whilst unemployment ran high in 1983 for those with degrees in Philosophy or Archaeology, Zoology and Botany graduates fared only a little better. Graduates were taking jobs appropriate to school-leavers (for example, as clerical assistants in the Civil Service), and one report referred ominously to 'unemployment in relation to developed talents'. Expert advice suggested the need to adapt, to go where jobs could be found, to cultivate basic numeracy (at least by acquiring a Mathematics O-level), and to build up a varied curriculum vitae. For a time the best chances seemed to lie in occupations which idealists regarded with deep suspicion – the army, the police, or the Government centre at Cheltenham for the gathering of intelligence. A lecturer in Metallurgy had supposedly advised the class of 1982: 'There's no point in applying to anything but South African companies or those involved in nuclear weaponry or power.'

From 1985 onwards economic revival inspired greater optimism, although, as one expert warned, the 'concept of the graduate as Crown Prince has gone'. The willingness of large firms to endow chairs in accountancy and law suggested a demand on their part for good graduates. It was probably true that the market for lawyers, accountants, trained managers, engineers of all kinds and computer scientists remained most consistently buoyant, but there was now some comfort for arts and science students so long as they were not 'trapped' by the confines of narrow degree subjects. The formal logic learnt by readers of philosophy was said to speed careers in computing, and employers, it was now reported, wanted graduates with general abilities and 'all-round balance', both academic and social.

By 1989 the increasing confidence of graduates was causing them to look upon visiting employers with a cool, appraising eye. The Careers Service complained of students who attended company presentations only with a view to descending on the buffet and bearing off the bottles. An unrepentant writer in a Union careers leaflet replied that since the talks given on those occasions were uniformly uninspiring, 'the best way to distinguish between firms is the quality of their refreshments . . . Megacorp Telecoms had done us proud. There were two tables of alcohol. There were vol-au-vents stuffed with prawns. There was cheese and pineapple stuffed with enough cocktail sticks to keep a low-tech acupuncturist busy for weeks . . . Remember that you are in a seller's market. In general these firms want graduates more than you want them. This food is there as an incentive to promote their image. A full buffet and a free bar at the Britannia suggests to me job satisfaction and maybe a company car . . .'. The first Alternative Careers Fair, for those who were not by nature the future servants of large companies, was held in the Refectory on 27 February 1990 and attracted about 1,100 students, opening their minds to such diverse possibilities as 'acupuncture, co-operatives, modelling, journalism, and starting your own business'.

In this climate, benign but changeable, it was not surprising that the pattern of student politics should begin to alter and one of the periodic reactions against student radicalism set in. For many years the same criticisms of the Students' Union had circulated among its more moderate and conservative members. The Union purported to represent all students, but in fact spoke only for a vocal, left-wing minority addicted to slogans; its constitution permitted, indeed encouraged, the manipulation of General Meetings by small bodies of politicos and endowed such meetings with undue importance; campaigns for left-wing causes took precedence over services to the whole student body; intolerance and intimidation lay in wait for the holders of views which conflicted with Union policy on such matters as women's rights to choose abortion.

Mancunion, the Union's paper, was accused of biased reporting, particularly in 1982–83, when it could not advertise the Bogle Stroll without calling the event 'politically redundant' and urging 'Save your boots for a Grants Demo instead'. A postgraduate complained of the disingenuous use of 'sarcastic titles and smug little editorial notes' to discredit letters expressing opinions which conflicted with those of the *'Mancunion* hierarchy'. Indeed, the editor was formally criticised, though not censured, by the Union Council for breaking his pledge to avoid 'cheap propaganda and sensationalism'. His General Election headline, 'THROW OUT THE TORIES', gave considerable offence; a correspondent argued that the paper had been 'both outré and gauche at the same time', and that its overt bias had disenfranchised some 60 per cent of Manchester students. In September 1984 the Conservative Association claimed that 42 per cent of students had voted Conservative in the Election of 1983 (a disaster for Labour), and declared that 'Conservatives strive to ensure that the Union serves all students and their needs and not just the minority of politically active ones.'

Satires on left-wing middle-class poseurs multiplied in subsequent years, demanding a ban on 'pseudo-proletarian uniforms' such as NUM jackets and North West Gas coats. A self-styled 'average Chinese dentist' observed the vogue for 'long, dark overcoats, post-apocalypse make-up, torn jeans and training shoes' which prevailed among the more raucous left-wing students. The impending departure of a leading student Marxist prompted rhetorical questions:

> Whither Ranting Rob now his time is nearly done?
> Follower of Trotsky and Hampstead's famous son?
> . . . .
> But whither now that intellect, to join the NLR
>   elect,
> Or hit his local Labour branch with analysis
>   correct?
> Some say to sunny Mexico and others say Peru,
> To rant and rave and find himself in Marxist
>   pastures new.

Elsewhere on the spectrum lay the Hon. Gaston de Wimpson, a kind of Alf Garnett in reverse who specialised in saying the unsayable, a fictitious upper-class twit who entertained readers of *Mancunion* with a regular column. 'If there is any consolation to be drawn from my vastly unhappy three years at Manchester, there has been a certain anthropological fascination in observing the student sub-species in its natural milieu.'

Bored with earnestness, self-righteousness, ideology and pomposity, some students had always found relief in joke candidates; elections, after all, tended to coincide with the carnival season. A stuffed duck named Colin had narrowly won the presidency of OPSA in 1982 on the manifesto 'Quack! Quack! Quack!', but had been dethroned on the grounds that he was not a registered student and not entitled to a room in the student village. A joke candidate with a difference was Richard 'Cosmo' Hawkes, originally a BA (Economics) student from Wolverhampton Grammar School. He was able to storm the Union itself and hold sabbatical posts for three successive years (1986–89) because the University had amended its ordinance on student discipline after the Waddington affair in such a way as to bring sabbatical officers within its ambit. The Union then argued that if officers were deemed to be students for the purposes of discipline they must also be so for electoral purposes. Cosmo sported an elephant hat, which his enemies were quick to dub a phallic symbol, and put out rhymed manifestos remarkable for the absence of any political message:

Big nose
No chin
Cool and handsome
Vote for him

and

If I was an apple
I'd be a total bore
But underneath my skin
I'd have a pip-filled core.

In the elections of March 1986 Cosmo attracted attention by standing for all the Executive posts save those of Women's Officer, Overseas Officer and Postgraduate Officer. He won three contests, became the sabbatical Events Officer, and held concurrently two non-sabbatical posts. His serious message for the next three years, 'It's your Union – claim it', was addressed to students interested in services rather than in politics.

In 1988, after some false starts, Cosmo succeeded in carrying, through a cross-campus ballot involving about 1,800 students, his proposals for constitutional change, the pip-filled core of the Cosmic apple. He invited the Union to make the whole Executive, rather than a single officer, responsible for campaigns. To that end, the post of NUS/Externals Officer, hitherto responsible for campaigning, was to be abolished, and a Communications Officer appointed instead. The Executive would also include a non-sabbatical Halls Liaison Officer, in the hope of bringing the Union and the halls of residence closer together. Cosmo further argued that the notoriously low quorum for General Meetings should be raised from 200 to 300, whilst the number of these gatherings should be reduced to three a term and a priorities ballot should prepare the way. This vote would determine the order of considering the motions submitted, thus allowing time to debate subjects, rather than debate which subjects to discuss. 'The overall objective of these changes is to encourage more students to have greater involvement and more control over the Union and its activities.' More trenchantly, an ally from the Labour Club called on rank-and-file students to reclaim Union democracy 'from the ideologues, the zealots and the bigots'.

Despite enthusiastic attendance at the meetings which considered Cosmo's constitutional changes, few General Meetings proved attractive even after the reforms. One Pro-Life campaigner found them still marred by aggressive behaviour, by a tendency to discuss complicated issues such as abortion in a simplistic manner, and by 'personal bitching, lies, accusations and personal insults' – all of which discouraged attendance. One consequence in the Cosmo and post-Cosmo era was a shift of authority towards the Union Council, which did not always justify its actions to General Meetings – not even when it disciplined an Education Officer in 1989 and a Communications Officer in 1990 for neglect of duty and unseemly conduct.

In the Executive elections of 1987 five candidates from the 'Cosmo slate' were victorious, and an editorial bridled at the fact that half the Executive had been elected on the strength of one person's popularity. A large headline, 'RIGHT TURN', proclaimed the news. But the Cosmo-ites did not launch the usual Conservative attack on Union membership of the NUS, and Cosmo became an active NUS politician, rising to the position of national Secretary after his departure from Manchester, and seeking to influence rather than boycott the national organisation.

An uncharitable column, 'Sylvester's Trash Can', quoted with glee some cheerful remarks of Sarah Dodd, the Cosmo-ite General Secretary of the Union, during a previous spell as Socials Secretary of Ashburne Hall – 'We are the only traditional hall mentioned in *The Sloane*

Ranger's Directory'. 'Exchange Dinners. These are an absolute hoot. It has been known for some Ashburnians to get the man of their dreams here . . . ' She was a firm opponent of direct action, though reluctant to deny the value of demonstrations as 'a symbol of feeling, the symbol of a democratic state', and argued that 'The Union can be a hard campaigning force, without being perceived as "Hard Left" or "Right". Students have got to feel that the Union represents them.' A new column, known first as 'Hall Stories' and then as 'H-Block', relayed news of events in traditional halls to readers of *Mancunion*, and these accounts were sometimes lively, though articles on 'average' students and their habits proved too boring to catch on. Karl Cheese, the first Executive Officer responsible for Halls and Societies, was at the time of his election, already serving as Senior Student of Needham Hall and President of the Senior Students' Council. In the following year he became General Secretary. The traditional separation, not to say antagonism, between the Union and the halls appeared to have been modified, if not brought to an end.

Cosmoism, if it was an ideology or a distinctive attitude, stood for reconciliation between two student cultures. At one pole lay the hearty, beery mentality, faintly reminiscent of *Doctor in the House* and the *Carry On* films, associated with male traditional halls, rugby clubs, medical students' revues, Rag Day, Rag Magazine, and other capers designed to raise money for charities. At the other were the 'right-on', Liberal/Left, politically correct attitudes and conduct fostered by the official policies of the Students' Union and the NUS and the activities of Community Action. Sexism, aggressive heterosexuality and homophobia were all fiercely attacked during the 1980s. The conflict between the two cultures became acute in the 1980s over the issue, not so much of women's rights, as of respect and consideration for women. Old-fashioned chivalry and gentlemanly behaviour had expired of their own accord or been dismissed as a veneer which concealed a deep-seated sense of male superiority. But some substitute for these was badly needed, some antidote for the sinister side of masculine behaviour, for the undertones of violence and contempt for women latent in boys' locker room talk and in the ambivalent 'all-lads-together-in-the-shower' mentality. Manchester was a dangerous city and students faced a certain threat of violence on the streets. But did not some of the danger spring from within, in the form of harassment and coarseness on the part of students and even of some academic staff, who were in positions not only of trust but also of power over their pupils? In the middle and late 1980s some of the old castles fell and their garrisons surrendered, as the traditional halls, both male and female, began to mix. Some changed willingly; in others junior common rooms resisted reform imposed from above and ran vigorous campaigns in defence of the traditional way of life.

Women did not yet account for half the University, but they could hardly be dismissed as just a tolerated minority. Despite prophecies in the early 1980s that Government predilections for science and engineering would prove hard on women students, the proportion of women undergraduates and postgraduates at Owens increased throughout the 1980s. Among full-time students it rose from 38.83 per cent in 1981 to 40.88 per cent in 1985 and 42.22 per cent in 1989. By 1989, doubtless as a consequence of the introduction of part-time undergraduate degrees, part-time women students had come to outnumber men: in that year 891 women (53.80 per cent of part-time students) and 765 men (46.20 per cent) registered at the University. There had been no dramatic changes in the distribution of women between the faculties, though some innovations, such as pre-university courses designed to encourage women to read physics, had had a local effect. Ten years earlier, in 1979, fifteen women freshers and eighty-five men had embarked on courses in physics; in 1989, 31 women and 109 men started the single-honours course, although the proportion of women reading joint degrees which included physics was far smaller (only seven women to thirty-eight men). In engineering, again, the number and proportion of women (now 28 women to 226 men in the first year, compared with 13 to 222 in 1979) had increased, but they were still in a small minority. This did, however, include some outstanding students, for in summer 1984 the University's house magazine listed five women students who had topped their years in various engineering courses (including the 'elite' four-year course in Engineering Manufacture and Management) and carried off scholarships and prizes. As always, women favoured the biological sciences, whose status was now rising, and in 1989 the full-time student population of the school was divided almost evenly between women and men.

Women complained of the absence of women lecturers in physics and the very small number holding posts in the History and Government Departments. In 1987 the University agreed to declare itself an Equal Opportunities Employer, formally adopted the codes of practice of the Commission for Racial Equality and the Equal Opportunities Commission, and issued statements condemning discrimination in the recruitment and treatment of students and staff. In some areas it had a long way to travel in order to correct the imbalances of the past, and opportunities were few, because fewer appointments were made. Women, however, were increasingly strong in the Students' Union, which in 1985 first appointed a sabbatical Women's Officer, elected by female suffrage only and perhaps recalling the separate Women's Union of earlier years. The new post of Black Women's Secretary was added to the Union Council. In 1986, for the first time, women officers, helped by the fact that Cosmo held three posts, came to form a majority of the Executive. Women had long distinguished themselves in student journalism – indeed, two of them, Liz Fawcett in 1980 and Sue Ash, the editor of *Mancunion* in 1985–86, had won the national NUS/*Guardian* competitions as the best student journalists of the year.

Some women's groups urged that closer attention be given to women in their own academic disciplines. The question 'Why have women hidden from history?' began to be asked in the 1980s, and a women's history group opened in the spring term of 1985 by holding a session on witches. The Women in the Arts Group wanted more women writers included in the canon of English Literature, as defined by the English Department. Jane Austen, it was said, had too long reigned in solitude as the token woman author, and needed more companions (had George Eliot, Elizabeth Gaskell and the Brontës really been neglected?). Members of the group pressed the claims of women writers of the twentieth century, and Katherine Mansfield, Doris Lessing and Iris Murdoch began to figure in the syllabus. Classic films of the 1930s, Hollywood versions of *Wuthering Heights*, *Pride and Prejudice,* and *Jane Eyre,* were shown in the Main Debating Hall of the Union.

The Women's Festival, held in November 1981, included talks by the English Collective of Prostitutes and by a speaker from Chorlton's Women's Refuge. There were lectures and discussions concerning images of women in the media, women in politics, women and peace, women at work, women in Ireland, and women in education (stimulated by a showing of the film *Blue Murder at St Trinian's*). Gay Sweatshop presented in the Solem Bar a play which promised to examine 'the problems experienced by lesbian and feminist mothers', and a short film, *Comedy in Six Unnatural Acts,* led into a discussion on women and sexuality.

Women were more forcefully asserting their need for recognition, equality, respect and security. Their struggle advanced on a number of different levels and entailed both conflict and diplomacy. Feminists tended to divide into at least two camps. Some wanted to counter the cliqueish nature of masculine society by establishing exclusive organisations, women discussing the problems of women unobserved by men. Other campaigners questioned the wisdom of distancing women from men, who needed to be educated and disarmed, for their ineptitude often sprang from nervousness or fear of women rather than deep-seated arrogance or malice. Separatism and diatribes against men were likely to make the problem worse. Taxed with practising sexism themselves, the fiercer campaigners rejoined that this vice could only be practised by oppressors, and therefore by men alone. In December 1983 they won from a Union General Meeting recognition of their right to hold meetings confined to women.

Some women confessed to embarrassment at the aggressive slogans used on women's marches, such as a protest in October 1988 against masculine violence in which some placards urged retaliation: 'Castrate, Mutilate, Don't Hesitate'. But a writer in *Mancunion* warned women not to soften up, and not to be beguiled by the insidious forms of patriarchy practised by liberal young men. 'In the enlightened '80s many University boys will expect, and, yes, encourage their girlfriends to be aware of "women's issues" – a little feminism is sexy – every "right-on" couple should have some. Even more important, however, is that a woman should be able to perform mental gymnastics and produce a feminist critique which never, but *never,* implicates her man. Women don't always have to be beaten into submission, they can be socially blackmailed into it by the withdrawal of approval by peers. Let's not rock the boat, girls, or the rats might bail out . . . '

Campaigners' targets ranged from the 'gender-specific' language used in lectures and official communications, through the dissemination of pornography and sexist jokes, to at least one case involving allegations of brutal sexual harassment. The practice of referring to students only as 'he' was fairly widespread, and the familiar defence that 'the masculine includes the feminine' failed to impress critics, especially those who believed that language created reality as well as reflecting it. Old-fashioned stereotyping of the Janet and John variety seemed to underlie the suggestion that 'On Wednesdays, when the boys are playing football, the girls can use the books; on Fridays, when the girls are washing their hair, the boys can have the books'. Emma Gladstone, of the History Department, entertained readers in 1983 with a piece on 'The Male Art of Bad Language'. Why did women gossip when men talked, women giggle while men laughed, and women get hysterical whereas men got angry?

Rag Magazine and its lewd contents were ancient subjects for complaint, which had been bombarded by the religious societies in the 1950s long before the women's groups attacked them. When, in

1984, the Union banned the sale of Rag Magazine on its own premises, it probably enhanced the publication's appeal. *Inmate,* the house
bulletin of Whitworth Park, incurred censure for similar reasons, and
the Women's Group objected to the shameless activities of a 'porn
mag swap club' at Whitworth Park. The Twenty-Eighth Medics'
Revue, presented in 1983 with the aim of raising £1,000 for charity,
crawled with references to 'tarts', 'whores', 'queers' and 'fairies', and
the producers and scriptwriters did not seem to have heard of women
doctors – all female members of the cast were 'relegated to suspender-
flashing, nymphomaniac nurses, who merely fed the males in the audience with the myth that women enjoy being sexually harassed'.
Indecent Rugby Club antics incurred justifiable complaint which was
rebutted on the interesting if illogical grounds that 'the individuals in
our club do more good in the charity field (and for the image of Manchester University) than our so-called caring Union'. Less easily assail-
able were the Cricket Club. When reproved for allegedly holding a
Compulsive Hookers' Party, they replied that the event was to be a
Compulsive Hooking Party, and that the name had been picked
because '"compulsive hooking" was a cliché used on cricket commen-
taries during the recent Ashes series, referring to the Australian open-
ers' habit of playing the HOOK shot instinctively and, quite often,
stupidly'. Seldom did wit or humour enliven the exchanges of feminist
campaigners and their opponents. But one writer relieved the solem-
nity with an engaging account of a visit to the Lancashire Cricket Club
at Old Trafford:

> Yes, it seems they have a rule, both sexist
>   and silly,
> You can only sit in the pavilion if you
>   possess a willy . . .
> I was suddenly enlightened by this wondrous
>   disclosure –
> So THAT's why they call it the Members'
>   Enclosure!

Most complaints were of a generalised, institutionalised sexism
which portrayed women students as 'silly little girls' and otherwise
devalued or even degraded them by exposure to unwanted sexual
advances. A few more serious and specific charges of sexual harassment
were made. At least two were against prominent student members of
the Labour Club, which took action on the complaints. Another, which
gave rise to a long campaign designed to carry the war into the

normally deferential Medical School, involved a lecturer in physiology, who was alleged to be choosing his victims ('shy, timid, anxious to do well') with great cunning and to be abusing his position of authority and trust. The Senate took the issue sufficiently seriously to consider appointing advisers on sexual harassment. Some members took alarm – did this mean that no male tutor should ever be alone with a woman student? Certain men, indeed, fearful of false accusations, did refuse to see women alone behind closed doors. Other persons complained that Standing Committee had discussed the issue in the presence of only one woman, and persuaded it by way of remedy to invite a group of women to attend on the next occasion that the subject arose. By March 1987 the Registrar had compiled a list of twelve selected volunteers who would be prepared 'to act as a point of help and advice for any woman student feeling threatened as a result of sexual harassment'. They were to communicate with the Registrar in cases where it might prove necessary to discipline a member of staff, and with the professional counselling and advisory services where the student might need further help. Campaigns on the streets against the lecturer, whom the Women's Officer had named, began to subside.

Violence and even murder seemed to threaten women students in the early 1980s. A serial killer, the 'Yorkshire Ripper', had struck twice in Manchester, leaving one victim at the rear of the Manchester Infirmary, and two women students, Barbara Leach at Bradford and Jacqueline Hill at Leeds University, had died at his hands. Police arrested the murderer, Peter Sutcliffe, in Sheffield in January 1981, but the fear of attacks on women, not only on the streets but in University areas, in or near Whitworth Park, Owens Park and the female halls of residence, still remained. There were calls for improved lighting, locks on ground floor windows, more security patrols, more use of rape alarms, more self-defence classes, more 'assertiveness training' lest women convey, by their bearing, a dangerous air of vulnerability. At the end of the decade two local men were charged and received long prison sentences for a series of rapes and indecent assaults on students.

Feminists were infuriated by any suggestion that the nocturnal crimes of men should inflict a curfew on women. They would surely have echoed the 'Poem for Jacqueline Hill' written by a woman in Leeds, where the November night was fifteen hours long:

And we, the women who as yet survive, we say:
'We have waited a long time for anger,
But we are angry now
For each and every betrayal of trust

For each and every degradation, the greater
 and the less,
For each and every evil done to women . . . '

Some women complained that the Union's injunction, 'Don't Walk Home Alone', was little better than the police's advice to women not to go out at night at all. In the winter of 1983 the Union, treating the symptoms since it had no power to cure the disease, began to organise a minibus which would leave the building hourly in the darkness, up to midnight, and deliver women members to their homes. 'Reclaim the Night' marchers walked the city in 1985 and 1986. Hazel Fenwick, the Police Liaison Officer, agreed that women must not be forced to retire into fortresses after dark.

Some feminists argued that rape and violence were only projections or extensions of attitudes which were deeply rooted in masculine preserves, in rituals and customs which portrayed women as objects – especially in sporting clubs and traditional male halls of residence. Men students in halls were not always tolerant of departures from the norms which they imposed, and some gay students suffered from homophobia. Re-education was urgently needed.

Woolton Hall, once called a 'secretive little bastion of misogyny', again became the target for attacks. These were reinforced by former denizens of Woolton who had found deeply repugnant both the rowdy atmosphere and the resort to punitive practical jokes and cold baths for those who offended against the hall ethos or broke the rules by arriving late for dinner and getting 'spoonbanged'. Ian Willmott, a prominent member of the Union and the Labour Club, infiltrated the introductory meeting of the Junior Common Room in October 1981 and reported the practice of alluding to women as 'dogs' and greeting each reference to a female with 'a manic chorus of "Woof Woof" and cries of "shag 'er"'. Another account of the hall's traditions had described the competition for the MUCUS award, a vulgar artefact presented to the Wooltonian judged 'to have the most ugly girlfriend'. A woman student, Rhetta Moran, maintained that Wooltonians were contravening Union policy by holding such meetings. To ban them was thought to be beyond the Union's powers, but she strove to get them publicly condemned. Woolton residents defended their behaviour as typical of 'any lively, all-male environment'; this, said their critics, was (if true) a sad reflection on contemporary society. Woolton escaped such concentrated public attacks for several years afterwards, though several women were anxious to keep the issue alive, and to assert at intervals that there had been no improvement in the language, behaviour and mentality of those who set the tone of the hall.

Traditional halls began to lose their popularity during the 1980s. They were expensive to run and fewer students wished to afford them; charges for waitress service and damages for vandalism pushed up the fees at Woolton and Allen. Many new arrivals at the University were unenthusiastic about single-sex communities, and fewer applicants were placing them at the head of their lists. Some first-year students, therefore, found themselves assigned to halls which they had not chosen, that the places might be filled. Many adjusted to the manners and customs of their new homes, but a significant number found the atmosphere puerile and oppressive. Some wardens and senior members believed that mixed halls would prove more popular and that a strong female presence would civilise the men. Should women be introduced into a male hall, it would eventually prove necessary to introduce men into a women's hall, to maintain the supply of catered places for men, who were believed to have fewer culinary skills and to want their meals provided. Hence, if one single-sex hall sold the pass, another would have to move in parallel, and the skittles would begin to fall.

In 1984 the University Council established a working party to consider the admission of women to Hulme Hall, one of the University's oldest and largest traditional residences. Council then approved a proposal that from the autumn of 1985 seventy women (forty freshers and thirty more senior students) should be admitted to the hall and that the experiment should run for three years. Freshmen already in Hulme, not yet steeped in hall tradition, favoured the change more than their seniors did, and, being more numerous than anyone else, carried the day when authority consulted the student body. Despite initial misgivings, the experiment worked smoothly. As a first-year woman student testified, 'When we heard it was mixed corridors, my mother bought me some "sensible" nightshirts and a long dressing-gown . . . We felt slightly embarrassed about being here at first, but the boys made us feel really welcome.' The Senior Student (no longer called the Senior Man) enthused about the friendlier atmosphere and the absence of food fights. The University Council firmly declared Hulme a mixed hall in June 1988 and fixed the quota of female residents at 135, or 36 per cent of the community's total population. During the following session, Needham Hall decided to make forty places available to women. It had long suffered from its remoteness from the University – Didsbury was a safe and desirable suburb, but bus fares discouraged many students from living so far away. Needham's

social arrangements with Greystoke, a nearby women's hall run by
the Polytechnic, had fallen apart when Greystoke determined to mix.
Karl Cheese, the Senior Student, reported that over 90 per cent of
Needham's residents had voted in favour of following suit.

Fierce resistance, however, greeted proposals in 1989 to mix
(though not with each other) both Woolton and Langdale, which was
a women's hall in Victoria Park. Reform was urged by the Hall Committees which managed them and consisted of a number of academics,
who were advised by administrators. The Junior Common Rooms
(JCRs) of both establishments were determined to defend the traditional ethos. Resentment ran higher in Woolton because the reform
appeared to be punitive, a remedy for bad behaviour, the JCR protesting that they were suffering unjustly from their past reputation, that
(like Rag and the Rugby Club) they had an excellent record of raising
funds for charity, and that other residences were equally guilty of dis-
seminating smut. Had not Oak House, their despised neighbours, contributed a 'Tarts and Vicars' float to the latest Rag procession?
Eighty-five per cent of the Langdale JCR voted against mixing; almost
150 of the 180 residents of Woolton did so in a ballot supervised by
the Students' Union, in which only sixteen votes were cast in favour of
the change. The new Warden of Woolton had, it seemed, put an end
to formal hall meals and cracked down on 'gross and offensive conduct' at the traditional Bar Nights. In describing the affair, which provided lurid copy, *Mancunion* veered between praising the attempt to
civilise the community and deploring the determination to do so
against the wishes of the residents.

More horror stories came from nonconformists, including 'An
Ashamed Ex-Wooltonian', who recalled that 'the place was full of
muscle-bound pissheads whose idea of fun was urinating under your
door or getting the pass-key from the porter on some transparent
excuse and intruding in your room in the middle of the night (especially if they thought your partner might be with you) . . . This bully-
ing atmosphere led to many all-day absentees on sporting days.' The
writer argued that Woolton had everything to gain by mixing and
applauded the University's action. More soberly, the Warden and the
Chairman of the Hall Committee reported that 'incidents of wilful
damage and abuse of staff by students had continued to occur'.

Both JCRs told the Working Party that single-sex halls were more
secure than mixed halls, and Langdale depicted male residents as
rowdy intruders; both swore that it would be harder to field sporting
teams when they had smaller numbers of each sex to draw upon; both

urged the University to describe their halls more seductively in its accommodation prospectus, thus attracting more willing applicants, and eliminating the need for conscripts. Langdale feared for its social arrangements with St Anselm Hall. It would be hard for Langdale, which had a small bar and could not hold discos, to sustain its own social life, and the hall (with 122 residents, dwarfed by Hulme's 400) was not large enough to become properly mixed. Some women, for religious or cultural reasons, could only contemplate living in segregated women's halls, and opportunities for them to do so must be preserved at all costs.

Eloquent though they were, the arguments of the JCRs failed to persuade the University Council, which decided in April 1990 to mix both Woolton and Langdale, again for an experimental period of three years. Meanwhile, Woolton's defence had not stopped at polite remonstrations with University authorities. Once contemptuous of the political campaigns of the Union, the hall's JCR launched a paper war as vigorous as any declared by radical activists. They prepared a substantial pamphlet for circulation to the Students' Union, to the newspapers, and to a selection of influential people, including Lord Woolton's widow; they conducted a secret ballot which resulted in a massive vote of no confidence in the Warden; and they put out a leaflet, 'The Warden and You', which purported to expose the Warden's failings and complain of his arbitrary acts. With restraint, the Warden remarked that this product contained 'misinformation in every paragraph'. When the University had pronounced sentence, the newly elected JCR Committee were anointed, as tradition demanded, with tomato ketchup and HP sauce, and their President prophesied that with nothing left to lose an excellent summer term lay ahead.

At the end of the 1980s, two fundamental changes promised to disturb still further the traditional patterns of student existence: a sustained increase in numbers, which was to be described in the 1990s as 'massification'; and the introduction of a new system of maintaining students at university, by the use of both grants and loans. No doubt the two moves were related, for the Government could not or would not contemplate financing mass university education by restoring the standard grant to its former glory.

Student loans had been lurking in the wings for almost thirty years, hesitating to make an entrance. They had figured in the Robbins Report of 1963, but had been postponed for fear that the prospect of heavy debts would discourage many potential students. In the 1980s proposals to lend rather than give harmonised with Thatcherism.

Loans, it was argued, would make students more self-reliant, and dispel the mistaken belief that the State should be the great provider from its inexhaustible cornucopia. Well qualified graduates were potentially big earners, and had a moral obligation to repay the public from their ample salaries. Loans could be made to students without means-testing parental income, thus meeting students' desire for greater independence. The present system of grants worked badly (partly because the Government had shown little desire to repair it), and in any case most students already depended on overdrafts for financial survival. Loan schemes supposedly worked well in other countries, from Europe to the United States, and there was no reason for the British public to be uniquely generous, providing economic advantages and never demanding repayment.

Opponents of the scheme argued that other countries' schemes did not work well and that in any case they functioned in a different social context, students working while they studied, taking longer to obtain their degrees, and more frequently giving up. Efficient, well-respected and attractive to overseas students, the British system, characterised by the intensive three-year first-degree course, would be jeopardised by the introduction of loans. Since working-class folk had a horror of debt, loan schemes would frustrate the Government's vaunted aim of broadening access to universities. Were they, perhaps, a none-too-subtle attempt to entice students into taking vocational courses, which would enable them to enjoy high starting salaries and clear their debts quickly? Even if they were the schemes would be flawed, because they would be especially hard on medical students and others following long courses in professional schools, whose burdens of debt would be the heaviest of all. Students' Union policy in Manchester consistently opposed loans throughout the 1980s, arguing (among much else) that they would be very costly to set up and administer, whilst expensive concessions would have to be made to unemployed graduates who could not afford to repay them.

For these and other reasons the Government repeatedly deferred the introduction of loans. But from the autumn of 1988 the prospect of these bulked larger, when the Government began to outline proposals to top up grants by the addition of loans from the session 1990–91 onwards. Loans would be provided, at the rate of £420 for each full academic year, and £310 for the final year of a degree course; on the other hand, the parental contribution and the grant would remain at the same cash level after 1990–91, and would not be adjusted for inflation. As soon as graduates obtained jobs which paid them more than £9,600 a year, they must begin to pay off their loans. 'It will give students a greater economic awareness', trumpeted the Education Secretary, Kenneth Baker; 'it's time they realised nothing in life is free.'

Intense politicking followed. The Students' Union's faith in demonstrations appeared to decline, at least in the autumn of 1989, and they recommended other tactics, such as writing to back bench Tory MPs and putting pressure on banks (these were in any case less than enthusiastic about the Government's scheme, and the ten banks which had originally agreed to co-operate pulled out in December 1989). The Union considered removing its account from the Royal Bank of Scotland unless the bank withdrew from the scheme, and stressed the economic power of student customers, both as individuals and as collectives. Some MPs were sympathetic to the student cause, others much less so. Nothing, however, prevented the Student Loans Bill from completing its passage through Parliament in May 1990.

Student numbers remained stable throughout most of the 1980s, the total number of full-time undergraduates and postgraduates varying between about 11,000 and 11,500. There was less incentive to build new residences, although, when the Corporation planned to demolish flats in Hulme, the University added another extension, Holly Court, to Oak House in Fallowfield in 1988. Measures were taken to help overseas students: the same year saw the opening of Arthur Livingstone House in Whitworth Park, a new block for students taking the course for overseas administrators which Arthur Livingstone had founded, and accommodation for overseas married students was planned in Grafton Street.

By 1987, however, it was clear that the Government had changed its views on student numbers and was bent on increasing, from 14.2 per cent in that year to 18.5 per cent by the end of the century, the proportion of eighteen- and nineteen-year-olds in the population who would embark upon higher education. It also seemed that the income of universities would be more and more closely linked to their success in recruiting students, with a heavy stress on the fees so earned, and with rewards for institutions prepared to take on students at the lowest practicable cost – including those which agreed to accept a certain number in exchange for fees only, receiving no subsidy over and above those fees.

In the autumn of 1989 a sudden, unplanned increase in student numbers propelled the University some way towards the Government's goals and gave rise to a dearth of accommodation. The number of full-time students registered at Owens jumped from 11,554 to 12,237, for more candidates had succeeded in jumping the A-level fences set before them by admissions tutors, and more applicants, finding Manchester attractive, had chosen to take up its offers. Students appeared to be gravitating in larger numbers towards the north, where the cost of living was lower than in London and the Home Counties; the prospect of loans and heavy debts heightened the desire for a cheap deal in a lively if dangerous city. The University was unable to honour its guarantee to find places for all its first-year students, but showed ingenuity in providing unorthodox solutions. These ranged from fitting up the Senior Common Room in the refectory as a temporary doss-house, offering beds to fifty homeless students at £2 a night, to leasing from the Atomic Energy Plant a property near Warrington equipped with 170 study bedrooms and conveying the residents into Manchester daily by bus.

It was now clear that the University's ability to maintain its range of activities would depend on its willingness to increase student numbers by a further 15 per cent between 1990 and 1994. In April 1990 the University Council recognised the need for more accommodation, and for residences of a higher standard to meet the rising expectations of postgraduate and other students (this meant, in effect, providing *en suite* washrooms and showers, suitable for mixed accommodation and appealing to the conference trade). Visiting and exchange students, married students with families, the new fashion for mixed residences: all would swell the demand for rooms in University flats. Resume building on a large scale, and it might eventually prove possible to offer more years in residence to undergraduates, rather than abandon them to the struggle to find affordable flats or houses in the city, some of which would be situated in dangerous areas, subject to burglary, mugging and worse.

In the late 1980s students had come to distrust the gesture politics and rituals of left-wing protest, partly, perhaps, because they offered no solution to the practical and material problems of student life. Student officers in 1989–90 came close to agreeing with the views adopted by the Vice-Chancellor in 1981 – to the effect that the best way to impress the Government was not to demonstrate on the streets but to lobby behind the scenes. Much of the fiercest campaigning, by Woolton Hall, was in the name of a traditional order, rather than in favour of change. Sexism rivalled, perhaps even replaced, racism and fascism as the principal target of progressive thinkers in the 1980s; it too was recognised as an evil which flourished within the University as well as outside it. Women students were now numerous, influential and self-confident enough to demand the respect which was due to peers.

In the early 1980s, perhaps for the first time since the Second World War, politicians on the Government benches had challenged the doctrine that universities ought to expand and graduates multiply in the interests of national prosperity. By the last years of the decade the arguments for expansion were again prevailing. They were now coupled with the convenient belief that, should universities manage their money more efficiently and spur their staff to greater achievement, they would be capable of handling increased student numbers without commensurate increases in public funding. Before long, Government decrees would create new, competing universities as the status of polytechnics changed and the old binary line of the 1960s became obscured. As the demand for graduates revived and steps were taken to increase the supply, student outlook seemed to become both more pragmatic and more hedonistic – increasingly inclined to regard higher education as a form of financial investment, especially with the advent of the student loan and the steady decline of the maintenance grant.

13

Epilogue

In October 1989 Senate and Council heard that Sir Mark Richmond had resigned his office with effect from 30 September 1990. He was destined, it later transpired, for a spell of five years as Chairman of the Science and Engineering Research Council, in which capacity he was soon to face the familiar task of announcing a shortfall in the budget and warning of 'a sharp cutback on our activities next year'. He had presided with stoicism and courage over the most critical years in the University's history, when the position of Vice-Chancellor brought the least pleasure and the most pain. Like many Vice-Chancellors in the same unhappy situation, he had been suspected of deferring unduly to the Government or approving of the cuts it imposed; opponents and critics had seized on any hint, however slight, that he regarded the enforced economies as less than catastrophic. As a judicious appreciation explained to Senate shortly after his departure, Sir Mark 'has a strong element of pragmatism in his outlook. He believes that when a government has a large and powerful majority and is determined to carry through its programme there is little point in marching down Whitehall with banners. Better to demonstrate that universities are indeed well managed and that the public are receiving excellent value for money. To behave defensively would, he strongly believed, increase the severity of the attack and ultimately undermine the principles he held dear.' His criticisms of Government, particularly of its failure to adjust the student grant and its carelessness of academic freedom, had been outspoken and acute. It was inevitable that critics should at times have wished for a little less unglamorous realism and for even louder rage against the dying of the light:

When statesmen gravely say – 'We must be
  realistic –'
The chances are they're weak and therefore
  pacifistic:

But when they talk of Principles – look out –
   perhaps
Their generals are already poring over maps.

In retrospect Sir Mark was widely praised for urging the reform of
the life sciences and bringing them closer to the Faculty of Medicine.
His own vision, and that of the younger professors in the field, had
happily coincided. He had seemed stern and abrasive, but a few years
later administrators and managers were to criticise his regime for not
being ruthless enough. Manchester, they said, should either have cut
its staff more drastically or agreed, more promptly and readily than it
did, to take on more students and expand its way out of trouble.
Other universities, including Leeds, explains Eddie Newcomb, who
became head of the University administration in 1995, rapidly
expanded from the late 1980s onwards by about 50 per cent and
(through not increasing their expenditure at an equal rate) 'got a bit
of a cushion'. In Sir Mark's view (as he put it nine years after leaving
Manchester), with 11,000 students at Owens the University was
already too large, and further growth would make it not merely difficult but impossible to control. In his thirteen years at Bristol, from
1968 to 1981, the student population had grown only from about
5,600 to some 6,300, and had remained very manageable as a result.
   Conscious of encountering a highly politicised University, Richmond had met with the kind of resistance that Sir Edward Parkes
might have called 'mulish', though the description would not have
been entirely just. Many hoped to defend values which were by no
means obsolete and inappropriate to universities. There was a justified fear of upsetting the balanced relationship between teaching,
research and administration on which the character of the University
depended, and of inflicting grave intellectual damage in the process.
Misgivings were to grow in the 1990s. In the 1950s, although most
students remained deferential, they had complained of the University's indifference to their welfare, of the pontifical style of teaching
which prevailed in many courses, of the substitution of frequent
examinations for genuine pastoral care. In the two decades which
followed, during and after the great expansion of the university system, many of the younger academics had struggled to win proper
respect for teaching and recognition of the virtues of dialogue
between tutors and students. In the late 1980s and the 1990s, however, the advent of Research Selectivity Exercises threatened, once
more, to reduce the University's esteem for teaching, since the estimated quality of its research was beginning to influence its finances

far more strongly than did the excellence or otherwise of its lectures and classes.

In some parts of the University tutors began to meet their students fortnightly rather than weekly in order to devote more time to research and improve their department's rating. From mathematics to social sciences some excellent teachers were urged to switch their energies from things they did superbly to things they did only moderately well, as the pressure to publish grew more intense. The demand for publications and the increase in student numbers threatened to combine and destroy the personal relationships between tutor and student that had once been the pride of certain departments; a few, such as Social Administration and Social Policy, succeeded against the odds in maintaining them throughout the 1990s, metaphorically using string and sellotape to keep the show on the road. There was some danger that the most successful researchers, the self-perpetuating stars of the University, would become detached from their departments like absentee bishops and cardinals in the medieval Church: their teaching would be done by substitutes, by tutors paid by the hour or by young temporary lecturers engaged, sometimes for spells of nine months or even less, to take on their undergraduate courses. Temporary lecturers and tutors were often competent, enthusiastic and approachable, but the old relationship between the undergraduate and the distinguished scholar, now so often absent on research leave, threatened to melt away. Only postgraduates and doctoral students would now be likely to know the more senior academics well, as the staff–student ratio fell from the time-honoured 1:8 of the 1960s to something closer to 1:20 or even, in some parts of the University, 1:30.

There was a further danger that students, streetwise and increasingly inclined to regard education as an asset which they had borrowed heavily to obtain, would become obsessed with the all-important Upper Second Class degree. For those bent on entering the professions this tended to mark the boundary between possible success and certain failure; an indifferent degree would mean the end of an ambition. It was unlikely that reputable accountants and solicitors would accept as trainees anyone who had fallen below the line which divided the Second Class. Concern with qualifications did not always, however, make for independent learning. When students worked to earn money during term and suffered from a chronic shortage of books and of the means to buy them, they were tempted to rely on forms of predigested knowledge which they were content to regurgitate – not only lectures, but also hand-outs and printed aids to study. Was this an effective way of preparing students for professions which called for independent research? In the words of an experienced Law lecturer, Maureen Mulholland, 'A senior partner is not going to say, "I want to know about this problem, so could you please go and read about it, these are the pages you need to look at." He'll say "Find out about it", and I think we should be teaching them research skills.' In some areas, however, a new approach to teaching did begin to promote a new kind of self-reliance. Under Leslie Turnberg's Deanship of the Faculty of Medicine, from 1986 to 1989, medical education had changed its spots. Confronted with an avalanche of specialised and rapidly changing information, it had abandoned the practice of saturating students (who had resembled New York street kids trying to drink from a fire hydrant in summer), and invited them to teach themselves and to learn what they thought appropriate.

Relentless pressure to publish, partly at least for financial rather than intellectual reasons, created its own pitfalls. Reluctance to publish inferior work had sometimes been the lazy academic's excuse for doing nothing, idlers posing as perfectionists with impossibly high standards, and it was perhaps right that some should be exposed. But rushing into print did not always produce happy results. Older scholars complained of superfluous journals crammed with 'Lilliputian pfaff', of the recycling and repetition of indifferent material, of the impossibility of contemplating a *magnum opus* which would burst on the world with the force of Darwin's *Origin of Species* or Namier's *Structure of Politics,* even of a growing reluctance to produce either substantial books or elegant ephemera. It sometimes seemed that the place where one published – the prestige of the journal in which an article appeared – had begun to matter more than the content of the article itself; it was as if a kind of gamesmanship was intruding on every aspect of academic life. Research management, the demand for a steady flow of published work, might be replacing individual self-government; it would certainly produce a larger volume of papers, but would it give rise to a larger quantity of inspired and original work?

Demands for accountability, for efficient record-keeping, and for the effective management of shrinking resources threatened to feed bureaucracy and divert energy into paperwork. Not unnaturally, the shrinking of resources created a reasonable suspicion that the University would do a less good job, and therefore it must be more closely watched lest its standards deteriorate. As Mike Buckley has described the philosophy behind the increasing obsession with quality controls: 'All right, we've taken a large slice of your money away, but now we want to make sure you're still doing as good a job as you were when you had lots of money, and what's more you can't have any money unless you convince us that you're good at what you're doing.' Inspections, visitations and reviews called for the compilation of increasingly elaborate documents, designed, not to present unsalted truth, but to enter into the psychology of the inspectors and create the best possible impression. Faced with complaints about the burden of administration, however, higher authority had its own answer, in the establishment of schools rather than departments, and in the savings of administrative time which such measures would supposedly create. First, however, it would be necessary to persuade conservative academics of the value of economies of scale and of the merits of casting down the departmental walls behind which they had long ago taken shelter.

During the 1980s and again in the 1990s University teachers suffered from a loss of public esteem and sometimes of self-confidence as well. This decline in morale, especially on the part of the older generation, sprang from at least two roots – from the failure of academic salaries to keep pace with those in other comparable professions, and from a sense that academics had lost their independence: that they were no longer to be trusted to drive themselves forward and to produce work of distinction in their own time. Perhaps they had been spoilt and had become arrogant and self-satisfied; perhaps the attack on universities was part of a more general assault on complacent, self-regulating professions, an attempt to instil into them the healthy sense of insecurity that ruled the business world. Academics had escaped inspection by anyone more formidable than the external examiners who oversaw the conduct of degree examinations and incidentally commented, when strongly moved, on the quality of the teaching that had prepared the students for those ordeals. The loss of this immunity, long taken for granted, made the verdicts of outsiders seem all the more intrusive. It removed one of the consolations for living on a modest income and having little power; academics would be less inclined to say:

Let other folk make money faster
In the air of dark-roomed towns;
I don't dread a peevish master
Though no man may heed my frowns . . .

Academic bosses were still inclined to mildness rather than fits of peevishness, and despite the loss of cast-iron tenure dismissals were almost unknown, even if short-term contracts had become all too familiar, and heavy hints at the desirability of early retirement could easily be dropped upon the burned-out scholar. But academics had more reason to look over their shoulders, to ask themselves constantly if they were doing things correctly in the ways demanded by some higher agency or responding adequately to the pressure exerted by their peers. In one or two areas, such as law and engineering, they felt themselves a little despised by ambitious, materialistic students who would soon be earning higher salaries than theirs.

This pessimistic view of the University was not, however, universal, and it was not generally shared by the younger generation of academics appointed during the 1990s. They were more content to ride the surf, to play the system as they found it, with enthusiasm rather than resignation. They were less inclined to sit down and weep by the waters of Babylon when they remembered Zion. They developed methods and skills which enabled them to teach classes of thirty, and minded less when they could not remember names or tempt students into anything more than the occasional intervention. They wrote impressive research proposals and were successful in obtaining grants. If anything, they were inclined to despise their elders for complaining so loudly and refusing, like species destined for extinction, to adapt to a changing world.

The University's history in the second half of the century might perhaps be seen as a three-act play, best described, in neutral language, as a drama rather than a tragedy or comedy. In the 1950s and for some of the 1960s the old professorial hierarchy had ruled. At its best it had combined paternalistic authority with a laissez-faire philosophy, a belief in encouraging scholars to develop at their own pace and pursue their own lines of inquiry, publishing when they were ready. In the second act of the play, during and after the long debate on the revised charter and statutes, departmental democracy had risen to challenge the old authority. Some said it strengthened the sense of academic community and protected academic freedom. Others thought it self-defeating, believing that it would foster a cult of mediocrity, that it would give the power of veto to obstructionists and wreckers, that it would indulge the negative, critical streak in so many academics – that stubborn, conservative tendency which made them, in Dennis Austin's words, 'marvellously arranged to oppose but ill-equipped to govern'.

From 1985 onwards, as resources shrank and choices had to be made, the University began to enter a third, less democratic phase. On the surface it was less formal and secretive, marked by an instant recourse to first names, an almost North American cordiality, and a lapse in standards of dress; long gone were the days when a young demonstrator in Pharmacy had been rebuked for turning up (on a sports day) in a sports coat and flannels rather than a suit. But it was also a third age in which academics had grown weary of long meetings and lost faith in their power to influence events; effective financial management reigned supreme, together with the power to bring in research money and other forms of funding that would enable the University to survive. No longer automatically sharing in the headship of departments or schools, professors *qua* professors were losing their authority to the programme directors and heads of resource centres who formed, for their years in office, a new elite; the system was democratic, or at least republican, in the sense that its key figures were not permanently entrenched, but would return to the sergeants' mess when their spell as officers was over. Few administrators, in this world of proliferating deans and directors, of 'senior management teams', 'profiles' and 'leadership', were likely to ask themselves the traditional Manchester question, once recommended by Vincent Knowles (who had probably got it from John Stopford): 'I know I'm an evil, but am I a necessary evil?'

In 1989 the Senate and Council established, as tradition demanded, a joint committee to seek a successor to Sir Mark Richmond. Their quest proved to be long and arduous. Sam Moore, a popular and approachable Deputy Vice-Chancellor with a talent for diplomacy and an understanding of figures, had the task of holding the University together throughout a two-year interregnum. A sense that Manchester's constitutional and administrative structures were antiquated, a fear that they would never 'deliver', probably made the job of Vice-Chancellor an uninviting prospect in the eyes of all but the toughest and most determined of the persons approached. One year after Richmond's departure, Martin Harris, then Vice-Chancellor of the University of Essex, agreed to succeed him in another year's time, eventually arriving in August 1992. Professor Harris's intellectual interests were in linguistics, and he was the author of a book on *The Evolution of French Syntax* and co-author of another on *The Romance Languages*. An old Manchester hand and, as were Armitage and Haszeldine before him, a member of Queens' College Cambridge, he had been a Pro-Vice-Chancellor of Salford University and a resident of Didsbury before departing for Essex in 1987. He had been a member of the UGC at the time when it instituted the Research Selectivity exercises. The Registrar at Essex, Eddie Newcomb, was to follow him to Manchester in 1995 after a spell at Leeds. Together, they were to put into effect one of the

remaining recommendations of the Jarratt Committee – the establishment of a unitary administration under one head, with the title of
Registrar and Secretary.

Martin Harris had the formidable task of adjusting to the system of
devolved management in the University of Manchester, whose staff
was six or seven times larger than that of the University of Essex,
where personal government had been much more practicable. It
would be his task to solve – or at least to contain – the University's
financial problems, and perhaps enable it to do something better than
break even, by expanding its way out of trouble; to maintain morale
across the generations and persuade the more conservative sectors of
the University of the advantages of change; to keep the centre of the
University in harmony with its periphery; and to cultivate good
relations with the City. Professor Harris set out – as he would say later
– to persuade the University to acknowledge the need for 'academic
goals, purposes and priorities and sufficient management to manage,
but not so much as to destroy the individuality of individuals'. An
optimist in the Armitage tradition, with great faith in the University's
capacity for self-improvement, he aspired above all to raise it to its
rightful place in the league table. Oxford, Cambridge, University
College London, Imperial College and perhaps Edinburgh would be
hard to overtake, but Manchester should at least be Number Six in the
national race for acknowledged excellence in teaching and research.

Sources and bibliography

Primary sources

This book draws on the following written records and other sources for information and opinions. For oral sources see the list of people interviewed by Michele Abendstern in the next section.

Official records

Minutes of the University Court
Minutes of the University Council
Reports of Council to the Court of Governors
Annual Reports
Minutes of the University Senate
Calendars of the University
Presentations for Honorary Degrees

Reports and surveys

Capital Provision for University Libraries. Report of a Working Party of the UGC [Professor Richard Atkinson and colleagues] (London, 1976)
Committee of Vice-Chancellors and Principals. Report of the Steering Committee for Efficiency Studies in Universities (March 1985) [Sir Alex Jarratt and colleagues]
Report of the Committee established by JCUD on 21 November 1983 'To investigate the biological sciences associated with Science and Medicine'. Reported 6 June 1985 [Professor J.C. Willmott and colleagues]
Leon Brittan's Visit to Manchester University Students' Union, 1 March 1985. Report of the Independent Inquiry Panel. Commissioned and published by Manchester City Council, November 1985 [Mr John Platts-Mills, QC, and colleagues]
Report to Senate of the Disciplinary Committee established on 12 December 1985 'in view of prima facie evidence of misconduct' during the visit of David Waddington, Home Office Minister, to Manchester University Students' Union, 8 November 1985 [Professor A.A. Grant and colleagues]
Report of a Student Accommodation Committee Working Party on Mixing of Accommodation [Mr Geoffrey North and colleagues], 9 March 1990.

University newspapers and journals

Communication
Manchester Independent
Mancunion
Staff Comment
This Week

Parliamentary papers

Higher Education. Report of the Committee appointed by the Prime Minister under the Chairmanship of Lord Robbins, 1961–63 (London. HMSO Cmd. 2154]. Presented to Parliament, October 1963.

Fifth Report from the Expenditure Committee, Session 1973–74. Wages and Conditions of African Workers Employed by British Firms in South Africa (ordered by the House of Commons to be printed, 22 January 1974).

Copyright and Designs Law. Report of the Committee to Consider the Law on Copyright and Designs. Chairman the Honourable Mr Justice Whitford (London. HMSO Cmd.6732). Presented to Parliament, March 1977.

House of Commons Papers. H.C. 552–I (1979–80). First Report from the Education, Science and Arts Committee, Session 1979–80. The Funding and Organisation of Courses in Higher Education (ordered by the House of Commons to be printed, 16 April 1980)

House of Commons Papers. H.C. 787–II (1979–80). Fifth Report from the Education, Science and Arts Committee. The Funding and Organisation of Courses in Higher Education. Vol. II, *Minutes of Evidence* (ordered by the House of Commons to be printed, 12 September 1980)

House of Commons Debates, 6th series, vol. 8, coll. 458–501; vol. 9, coll. 553–78, 635–46 (debates on Higher Education, 8 and 23 July 1981)

Papers and documents on University affairs

Papers of Professor John Griffith; Sir George Kenyon; Professor A.P.J. Trinci; Dr George Wilmers; Professor Joan Walsh

Bibliography

For items relating to earlier periods of the University's history, see Brian Pullan with Michele Abendstern, *A History of the University of Manchester 1951–73* (Manchester, 2000), pp. 255–7.

The following abbreviations are used:
BMFRS *Biographical Memoirs of Fellows of the Royal Society*
PBA *Proceedings of the British Academy*

THES *Times Higher Educational Supplement*
TLS *Times Literary Supplement*

Allen, Geoffrey. 'Geoffrey Gee, C.B.E., 6 June 1910–13 December 1996', *BMFRS*, 45 (1999), pp. 185–94

Austin, Dennis. 'Salva sit universitas nostra: a memoir', *Government and Opposition*, 17 (1982), 469–89

Barker, Nicolas. 'The rape of the Rylands', *The Book Collector*, 37 (1988), 169–84

Berrington, Hugh. 'Samuel Edward Finer, 1915–1993', *PBA*, 90: *1995 Lectures and Memoirs*, pp. 347–66

Bland, Lucy. 'The case of the Yorkshire Ripper: mad, bad, beast or male?', in Phil Scraton and Paul Gordon (eds), *Causes for Concern. British Criminal Justice on Trial?* (Harmondsworth, 1984), pp. 184–209

Booker, Christopher. *The Seventies* (Harmondsworth, 1980)

Bosworth, Stuart (ed). *Beyond the Limelight. Essays on the Occasion of the Silver Jubilee of the Conference of University Administrators* (Reading, 1986)

Boyson, Rhodes. *Speaking My Mind. The Autobiography of Rhodes Boyson* (London and Chester Springs, Pennsylvania, 1995)

Bradbury, Malcolm. *Cuts* (London, 1987, 1988)

Broadbent, T.E. *Electrical Engineering at Manchester. 125 Years of Achievement* (Manchester, 1998)

Carswell, John. *Government and the Universities in Britain. Programme and Performance, 1960–1980* (Cambridge, 1985)

Charlton, H.B. *Portrait of a University, 1851–1951. To Commemorate the Centenary of Manchester University* (second edition, Manchester, 1952)

Charlton, W.A., and Cutter, E.G. *135 Years of Botany at Manchester* (Manchester, no date)

Cox, Brian. *The Great Betrayal. Memoirs of a Life in Education* (London, 1992)

Crequer, Ngaio. 'Creating the right mix of town and gown', *THES*, 27 October 1978, 8–9.

Curtis, Simon. *On the Abthorpe Road, and Other Poems* (London, 1975)

Firth, Raymond. 'Max Gluckman, 1911–1975', *PBA*, 61 (1975), pp. 479–96

Fortes, Meyer. 'Max Gluckman', *Dictionary of National Biography 1971–1980* (Oxford and New York, 1986), pp. 341–2

Frend, W.H.C. 'Richard Patrick Crossland Hanson, 1916–1988', *PBA*, 76: *1990 Lectures and Memoirs*, pp. 411–22

Griffith, John. *The Attack on Higher Education* (CAFD, 1987)

Hain, Peter. *Political Trials in Britain* (Harmondsworth, 1985)

Hartwell, Clare. *Manchester (Pevsner Architectural Guides)* (London, 2001)

Hattersley, Roy. *Fifty Years On. A Prejudiced History of Britain Since the War* (London, 1997)

Hennessy, Peter. *The Prime Minister. The Office and its Holders Since 1945* (London, 2000)

Kelly, Alison. *The Missing Half: Girls and Science Education* (Manchester, 1981)

Kennedy, Michael. *Portrait of Manchester* (London, 1970)

Kilburn, Tom, and Piggott, L.S. 'Frederic Calland Williams', *BMFRS*, 24 (1978), pp. 583–604

Knapp, John, Swanton, Michael, and Jevons, F.R. *University Perspectives* (Manchester, 1970)

Lodge, David. *Nice Work* (Harmondsworth, 1989)

McNiven, Peter. 'The John Rylands Library, 1972–2000', *Bulletin of the John Rylands Library*, 82, no. 2–3 (2000), 3–79

Marsh, Nora. *Developing Nursing Studies in a University Setting* (University of Manchester M.Sc. thesis, Department of Nursing, 1976)

Marshall, I.H. 'Frederick Fyvie Bruce, 1910–1990', *PBA*, 80: *1991 Lectures and Memoirs*, pp. 245–60

Monbiot, George. *Captive State. The Corporate Takeover of Britain* (London, Basingstoke and Oxford, 2001)

O'Farrell, John. *Things Can Only Get Better. Eighteen Miserable Years in the Life of a Labour Supporter* (London, 1998, 1999)

Pailin, David (ed). *Seventy-Fifth Anniversary Papers of the University of Manchester Faculty of Theology, 1979* (Manchester, 1980)

Parkinson-Bailey, J.J. *Manchester. An Architectural History* (Manchester and New York, 2000)

Phillips, C.B. 'Thomas Stuart Willan, 1910–1994', *PBA*, 101: *1998 Lectures and Memoirs*, pp. 557–63

Pimlott, Ben. *The Queen. Elizabeth II and the Monarchy* (London, 2002)

Platts-Mills, John. *Muck, Silk and Socialism. Recollections of a Left-Wing Queen's Counsel* (Wedmore, 2002)

Pullan, Brian, with Abendstern, Michele. *A History of the University of Manchester, 1951–73* (Manchester, 2000)

Robertson, Alex. *A Century of Change. The Study of Education in the University of Manchester* (Manchester, 1990)

Rose, M.E. *Everything Went On at the Round House. A Hundred Years of the Manchester University Settlement* (Manchester, 1995)

Rowley, E.E., with Lees, Colin. *The University of Manchester at War, 1939–1946* (Manchester, 2001)

Schmidt, Michael. 'The Rylands Affair', *PN Review*, 15/5 (1989), 8–12

Sharpe, Tom. *Porterhouse Blue* (London, 1974, 1976)

Smith, J.C. 'Harry Street, 1919–1984', *PBA*, 72 (1986), pp. 473–90

Stewart, W.A.C. *Higher Education in Postwar Britain* (Basingstoke, 1989)

Thompson, E.P. (ed). *Warwick University Ltd. Industry, Management and the Universities* (Harmondsworth, 1970)

Ullendorff, Edward. 'Stefan Strelcyn, 1918–1981', *PBA*, 67 (1981), pp. 479–90

University of Manchester Athletic Union 1885–1985 (Manchester, 1985)

Walker, David. 'Old familiars stay at the top', *THES*, 19 December 1975, 6

Walker, Martin. *With Extreme Prejudice: an Investigation into Police Vigilantism in Manchester* (London, 1986)

Wood, Christopher, and Jay, Stephen (eds). *Reflections on 50 Years of the Manchester School of Planning and Landscape* (Manchester, 2000)

Woolfson, M.M. 'Henry Solomon Lipson, 11 March 1910 – 26 April 1991', *BMFRS*, 39 (1994), pp. 229–42

Woudhuysen, H.R. 'Squandered inheritance', *TLS*, 1–7 April 1988, 358; also 23–28 April 1988, 458

Zarnecki, George. 'Charles Reginald Dodwell, 1922–1994', *PBA*, 105: *1999 Lectures and Memoirs,* pp. 389–96

People interviewed

This is a list of those people interviewed by Michele Abendstern whose testimony relates wholly or in part to the years 1973–90. The brief biographical notes given here are not intended to be complete. They are designed to focus mainly on people's connections with the University during that time, and sometimes on their activities immediately after leaving the University or in the interval between two periods at the University.

Aaronovitch, David. Journalist and broadcaster; columnist of *The Independent* and lately of *The Guardian*. Undergraduate, Department of History, 1974–78; participant in *University Challenge,* 1975. NUS Vice-President (Services), 1976–77; NUS President, 1980–82.

Ahmed, Sarah. Undergraduate, Faculty of Law, 1984–87.

Beswick, Frederic Bakewell (Bill). Doctor and administrator. Associate Dean, then Executive Dean, Faculty of Medicine, 1969–79; Bursar, 1979–84; Hon. Ll.D. (Manc.), 1986. Chairman of Salford Health Authority, 1984–94.

Boucher, Joyce. Schoolteacher and life-long resident of Fallowfield, active in the Civic Society. Graduate in English, 1949.

Brazier, Margot (born Margot Jacobs). Authority on torts and medical law; Chairman of the NHS Retained Organs Commission. Taught in Faculty of Law from 1971; Professor of Law from 1989.

Bromley, Peter. Authority on family law. Professor of Law and three times Dean of the Faculty, 1965–86. Pro-Vice-Chancellor, 1977–81. Member of the UGC, 1978–85.

Buckley, Michael. Administrator. Member of Registrar's Department from 1966; responsibilities included the Business School and the Academic Staffing Office; Deputy Registrar, with responsibility for Court and Council, 1986–94. Honorary Lecturer in Overseas Studies.

Burchell, Robert. Historian of the United States, also famous for generous hospitality. Taught in Department of American Studies, 1965–96; Head of Department, 1989–94; Professor of American Studies, 1991–96. Sometime elected member of Senate. Chairman, British Association for American Studies, 1989–92; Director of the Eccles Centre for American Studies in Britain, at the British Library, 1991–2001. FRSA, 2001.

Cameron, Harry. Electrician and engineer. Joined Electrical Services Department, 1951; apprentice, subsequently electrician, planned maintenance engineer, Assistant Electrical Engineer (1978), Electrical Engineer (1981) and Assistant Chief Engineer (1985–88).

Cameron, Ian. Administrator. Personnel Officer, later Personnel Manager, 1977–2000.

Carling, Ellen B. Secretary, from 1964 Personal Assistant, to the Professors of Astronomy (Professors Kopal, Kahn and Dyson), 1954–95

Cox, [Charles] Brian. Poet, critic and writer on education. Professor of English Literature, subsequently John Edward Taylor Professor, 1966–93; Dean of the Faculty of Arts, 1984–86; Pro-Vice-Chancellor, 1987–91. Co-editor of *Critical Quarterly* from 1959; of *Black Papers on Education*, 1969–77; Chairman, National Curriculum English Working Group, 1988–89. CBE, 1990; FRSL, 1993.

Cummings, Patricia. Librarian, particularly concerned with the Manchester Medical Collection. Joined the staff of the Medical Library as Library Assistant, 1950; later Assistant Librarian; ALA, 1971; member of the Department of Information Resources, John Rylands University Library. Hon. MA (Manc.), 1997.

Davies, Rodney. Radio astronomer. Worked with the Radio Astronomy Group at the Jodrell Bank outstation from 1953; Professor of Radio Astronomy, 1976–97; Director of the Nuffield Radio Astronomy Laboratories, 1988–97. President of the Royal Astronomical Society, 1987–89. FRS, 1992; CBE, 1995.

Denton, Jeffrey. Historian of the medieval Church. Taught in Department of History, 1965–97; Professor of Medieval History, 1988–97; Research Professor, 1997–2000.

French, Elizabeth (Lisa). Archaeologist and academic administrator. Warden of Ashburne Hall, 1976–89; afterwards Director of the British School at Athens.

Griffith, John. Academic lawyer. Emeritus Professor of Public Law in the University of London (LSE). Chancellor of the University of Manchester, 1986–93. Hon. Ll.D. (Manc.) 1987. Founder member of the Council for Academic Freedom and Democracy. FBA 1977.

Haddy, Pamela. Clerical supervisor. Joined staff of Registrar's office as Clerical Assistant, 1949; Supervisor of the Awards Office, 1963–93.

Hallett, Christine. Lecturer in Nursing and historian. Undergraduate, Department of Nursing, 1981–85; district nurse and health visitor, Oldham Health Authority and Bolton Health Authority, 1985–89; part-time student, Department of History, 1985–93; research assistant in Department of Nursing, 1989–93; part-time Lecturer, later Lecturer, in Nursing from 1993. Ph.D. in Nursing, 1995; Ph.D. in History, 2002.

Harris, Martin (afterwards Sir Martin). Vice-Chancellor and Professor of Romance Linguistics, 1992– . Member of the UGC, 1983–87; Chairman of the CVCP, 1997–99. CBE, 1992; knighted, 2000.

Hunt, Christopher. Librarian. Sub-Librarian, Social Sciences, Manchester University Library (later John Rylands University Library of Manchester), 1968–74; University Librarian, James Cook University of North Queensland, 1974–81, and of La Trobe University, Melbourne, 1981–85; Librarian,

London School of Economics and Political Science, 1985–91; University Librarian and Director of the John Rylands University Library of Manchester, 1991–2002.

Imber, Kee Kok (born Kee Kok Lee, writes as Kee Kok Lee). Philosopher, with particular interests in environmental philosophy. Taught in Department of Philosophy, 1966–99; retired as Reader.

Jones, Peter. Taught in Department of Electrical Engineering, later School of Engineering, 1963–97; retired as Senior Lecturer. Elected member of Senate. Chairman of the Electronics Computer- Aided Design Initiative, 1984.

Kemp, Sarah (born Sarah Bentley). Managing Director, Explore International (a subsidiary of National Geographic and a distributor of documentary films); formerly Managing Director, Hulton Getty Picture Collection and President, Archive Films and Photos (New York). Undergraduate, Department of History, 1975–78. FCMA, 1994; FRSA, 2000.

Kent, Harry. Administrator. Joined Bursar's Department, 1947; Establishment and Superannuation Officer, retitled Deputy Bursar in Charge of Personnel, 1971–82.

Kenyon, George (afterwards Sir George). Engineer, industrialist and banker. Member of Council, 1960–88; Treasurer, 1970–72, 1980–82; Chairman, 1972–80; Chairman of Vuman Ltd., 1982–88. Hon. Ll.D (Manc.), 1980. Knighted, 1976.

Kitchen, Kenneth. Administrator. Joined Registrar's Department, 1965; Deputy Registrar, 1971–79; Registrar, 1979–94. Honorary Lecturer in Government. Co-organiser of the Northern Universities Administrative Training Programme (first run 1971); Administrative Training Officer to the CVCP, 1975–77; Business Secretary to the Conference of Registrars and Secretaries (later the Association of Heads of University Administrations).

Knowles, Vincent. Administrator. Registrar, 1951–79; subsequently Schools Liaison Officer. Special Lecturer in Greek and Latin. Hon. Ll.D. (Manc.), 1979. OBE, 1977.

Leitch, Diana. Librarian. Joined staff of John Rylands University Library of Manchester, 1973; subsequently Sub-Librarian, Science; Head of Acquisitions; and Head of Information Services. Deputy Librarian and Assistant Director since 1995.

Lowe, Peter. Historian of diplomacy in the Far East. Taught in Department of History from 1965; retired from full-time work as Reader, 2001. Elected member of Senate and of Standing Committee of Senate. Officeholder (on many occasions) in Manchester branch of AUT.

McCulloch, Walter. Chief Technician, University Library, Photographic Section. Member of the University staff, 1935–81; sometime Chairman of William Kay House.

McFarlane, Jean (afterwards Baroness McFarlane of Llandaff). Pioneer in nursing education. Senior Lecturer and Head of Nursing, Department of Social and Preventive Medicine, 1971–73; Senior Lecturer and Head of

Department of Nursing, 1973–74; Professor of Nursing, 1974–88. Member of Royal Commission on the National Health Service, 1976 –79. Life peer, 1979. Hon. M.Sc. (Manc.), 1979; Hon. D.Sc. (Manc.), 1998.

McKenna, Gerard. Administrator. Joined Registrar's Department, 1967; Secretary to the Faculty of Medicine, 1970–80; Assistant Registrar in charge of the Accommodation Office, 1982–97. Tutor and later Vice-Warden of Allen Hall, 1967–78.

Mays, Wolfe. Philosopher. Taught in Department of Philosophy, 1946–79; retired as Reader. Officeholder (on many occasions) in Manchester branch of AUT.

Moore, Stuart Alfred (Sam). Econometrician. Lecturer, later Senior Lecturer, in Economic Statistics, 1964–92; Robert Ottley Professor of Quantitive Studies, 1992–97. Dean of the Faculty of Economic and Social Studies, 1980–83; Pro-Vice-Chancellor, 1985–90; Acting Vice-Chancellor, 1990–92; Deputy Vice-Chancellor, 1990–96.

Mulholland, Maureen (born Maureen O'Brien). Legal historian, also concerned with law and medicine. Taught in the Faculty (later School) of Law from 1964; now Honorary Lecturer.

Newcomb, Edgar (Eddie). Administrator. Registrar and Secretary, 1995– . Chairman of the Association of Heads of University Administration, 1998– . OBE, 2002.

North, Geoffrey. Geographer. Taught in Department of Geography, 1954–93; retired as Senior Lecturer. Adviser in the Central Academic Advisory Services from 1972. Chairman and member of numerous University committees (at one time between thirty and forty). Hon. MA (Manc.), 1996.

Ogden, Rev. Eric. Administrator, clergyman, and transport historian. Assistant Accountant, Bursar's Department, 1968–89, responsible for academic salaries and halls of residence accounts, and later for research grants; Treasurer to the Chaplaincy, 1970–79. Took North-West Ordination Course, 1973–76.

Pailin, David. Philosopher and theologian; Methodist minister. Taught in Faculty of Theology from 1966; Dean, 1979–80. Professor of the Philosophy of Religion, 1994–2001.

Parry, Geraint. Political theorist and writer on politics. Taught in Department of Government, 1971–74; Edward Caird Professor of Politics, University of Glasgow, 1974–76; Professor of Government, later W.J.M. Mackenzie Professor of Government, 1977–99.

Perera, Katharine. Member of the Department of Linguistics and of the University's Senior Management Team. Postgraduate student, Department of Linguistics, 1972–74; rejoined Department as Lecturer, 1977; Professor of Educational Linguistics (first in United Kingdom), 1991– ; Pro-Vice-Chancellor, 1994–2000; Senior Pro-Vice-Chancellor, 2000.

Prothero, Iorwerth (Iori). Historian, especially of radical movements in the early nineteenth century; taught in Department of History from 1964.

Retired from full-time work as Senior Lecturer, 2001. Elected member of
Senate and of Standing Committee of Senate. Officeholder (on many occasions) in Manchester branch of AUT.

Purdy, David. Economist, especially interested in the labour market and the
social security interface. Taught in Department of Economics, 1968–94
(subsequently transferred to Department of Social Policy and Social
Work). Now Senior Lecturer.

Radcliffe, Philip. Communications Officer (retitled Director of Communications, 1978), 1970–95. Honorary Lecturer in Adult Education, 1974–95.

Ratcliffe, Frederick. Librarian. Librarian, University of Manchester, 1965–80
(Director of the John Rylands University Library of Manchester, 1972–80);
Librarian, University of Cambridge, and Fellow of Corpus Christi College,
1980–94 (subsequently Life Fellow); Parker Librarian, 1995–2000. CBE,
1994.

Rhodes, Gay. Secretary in the Dean's office, School of Medicine, 1968–79;
Personal Assistant to the Dean, 1979–99.

Richardson, David. Administrator. Joined Registrar's Department, 1967;
Assistant to the Vice-Chancellor (Arthur Armitage), 1970–74; Secretary to
the Faculty of Arts, 1974–79; Deputy Registrar, 1979–94; Academic
Secretary, 1994–97; subsequently concerned with the establishment of a
University Foundation, to pursue the possibility of fundraising in North
America.

Richardson, James. Pseudonym of a student in the 1970s.

Richmond, Mark (afterwards Sir Mark). Bacteriologist and academic states-
man. Vice-Chancellor and Professor of Molecular Microbiology, 1981–90.
Chairman of CVCP, 1987–89; Chairman, Committee on Microbiological
Food Safety, 1989–91; Chairman of SERC, 1990–94; Group Head of
Research, Glaxo Holdings, 1993–95; Member of the School of Public Policy, University College London, 1996– . Hon. Ll.D (Manc.), 1990. FRS,
1980; knighted, 1986.

Rose, Michael. Social historian of the nineteenth and twentieth centuries.
Taught in Department of History from 1962; Head of Economic History,
1982–89; Professor of Modern Social History, 1989–99.

Smith, Ian. Civil engineer. Taught in Department of Engineering (later
School of Engineering) from 1967; Professor of Geotechnical Engineering, 1984– .

Tallentire, Alan. Pharmacist and sports enthusiast. Taught in Department of
Pharmacy, 1953–96; Professor of Pharmacy, 1979–96.

Trinci, Tony. Mycologist. Barker Professor of Cryptogamic Botany, 1981–
2001; first Chairman of the School of Biological Sciences, 1986–90.

Turnberg, Leslie (afterwards Lord Turnberg of Cheadle). Physician and
specialist in gastroenterology. Taught in Medical School from 1968; Professor of Medicine, 1973–97, particularly concerned with developing the
academic community at Hope Hospital, Salford; Dean of the Faculty of
Medicine, 1986–90.

Tye, Frederick. Headmaster and trainer of headteachers (Director of the North West Educational Management Centre, 1972–81). Member of Court, 1962–98, and of Council, 1967–92, particularly concerned with University–Union relations, disabled access, and car parking. Hon. M.Ed. (Manc.), 1993. CBE, 1980.

Vernon, James. Historian, specialising in British history of the nineteenth and twentieth centuries. Undergraduate, School of Politics and Modern History, 1984–87; postgraduate, Department of History, 1987–91.

Walsh, Joan. Mathematician, with special interests in computing. Taught in Department of Mathematics, 1963–97; Professor of Numerical Analysis, later of Applied Mathematics, 1974–97; Pro-Vice-Chancellor, 1988–94. Member of National Computer Board, 1981–86.

Welland, Dennis. Literary scholar and academic administrator. Taught in Department of American Studies, 1962–83; Professor of American Literature, 1965–83; Dean of the Faculty of Arts, 1976–78; Pro-Vice-Chancellor, 1979–83; Acting Vice-Chancellor, 1980–81. Hon.Ll.D. (Manc.), 1992. Chairman, British Association of American Studies, 1980–83. Died 2002.

Williams, Olwen. Administrator. Welfare Officer in the Establishment Unit, Bursar's (later Registrar's) Department, 1971–89. Founder of Retired Staff Association.

Willmott, John. Physicist. Professor of Nuclear Structure, later of Physics, 1964–89; Director of the Physical Laboratories, 1967–89; Pro-Vice-Chancellor, 1982–85; Adviser to Vice-Chancellor on Research Exploitation, 1988–93. CBE, 1983.

Wilmers, George. Lecturer in Department of Mathematics from 1970. Elected member of Senate and of Court.

Young, Margaret L.M. French scholar; specialist in Renaissance literature. Taught in Department of French Studies, 1948–84; retired as Senior Lecturer. Adviser in the Central Advisory Service, 1972–78; Dean of the Faculty of Arts, 1978–80.

Zussman, Jack. Geologist. Professor of Geology, 1967–89; Dean of the Faculty of Science, 1980–81. President of the Mineralogical Society of Great Britain and Ireland, 1980–81.

Statistical appendix

by Michele Abendstern and Steve Chick

The following graphs are based on statistics derived from the University Council's Annual Reports to the University Court for the years 1974 to 1990, and also on the figures for student numbers reported to the Senate in October or November of each year. Some of the supplementary figures on accommodation were gathered directly from the Accommodation Office. It is hoped that the graphs will speak for themselves and complement the story told in the main text of the book. A brief commentary on the figures follows.

Information is more complete for these years than for 1951–73 and it has been possible to demonstrate more fully the growth and changing pattern of some sectors of University life. In particular we have been able to gather statistics on student accommodation, an area of student life that changed dramatically during these years. The number of student places in University residences increased substantially between 1974 and 1990 from about 4,700 to over 6,600. In 1976 the University also initiated a direct leasing scheme, whereby it took over the tenancy of houses owned by private landlords and then sublet them to students. According to the University Calendar for 1989–90, 'Some 750 to 800 places are available and new accommodation is constantly sought.' The biggest expansion was in self-catered accommodation, provided for about 1,300 students in 1974, for about 3,300 in 1979, and for some 3,700 in 1989, chiefly through the growth of Oak House in Fallowfield and Whitworth Park on the Oxford Road site, mainly in the 1970s (there was comparatively little new building in the 1980s, although the direct leasing scheme was extended). The proportion of students in University-provided accommodation increased over the period from 32 per cent to 43 per cent of the whole student population.

The figures on income show a steady growth in cash terms throughout the period. However, as the text explains, the real value of University income, its power to purchase essential goods and services, was constantly being eroded by inflation. Parliamentary grants remain the largest single source of income throughout the period, though in 1990 they drop below 'other' combined sources of income for the first time. As a proportion of total income the parliamentary grant falls substantially from just below 80 per cent in 1974 to approximately 48 per cent in 1990.

Total full-time student numbers rise between 1974 and 1990 from 14,684 to 17,842 if UMIST is included, an increase of 18 per cent. Most faculties contract in response to the cuts imposed by the Conservative Government in 1981–84, but thereafter begin to recover. The Faculty of Music was 'discharged' and assigned as a department to the Faculty of Arts in 1987–88.

The gap between male and female student numbers closes during the period by about 7 per cent. If the Faculty of Technology/UMIST is included, women accounted for 30 per cent of total student numbers in 1974 and for 37 per cent in 1990. For Owens alone the figures for women are greater, rising from 36 per cent to 42 per cent.

Student numbers have been broken down faculty by faculty, showing which areas remained predominantly male preserves throughout the period. Women students never make up more than 28 per cent of the total in the Faculty of Science, whilst in the Faculty of Technology/UMIST, although their numbers double in the period in question, they remain a minority at 26 per cent in 1990. On the other hand, women outnumber men in the Arts Faculty throughout the period, having first overtaken them in the early 1970s. The numerical dominance of male students in the Faculty of Medicine that can be seen in 1974 no longer exists in 1990.

Graph 20 shows the increase in the proportion of part-time students during these years. This rises from roughly 5 per cent in 1974 to 10 per cent in 1990, partly as a result of the introduction of part-time undergraduate degrees in 1985.

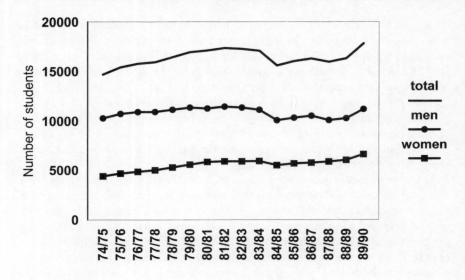

1. Total Full-Time Students
(including Faculty of Technology/UMIST)

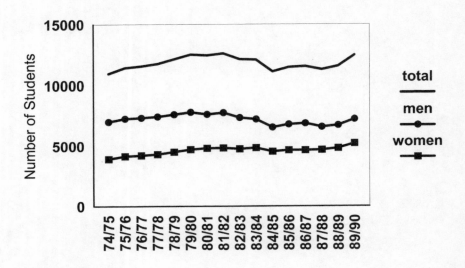

2. Total Full-Time Students
(excluding Faculty of Technology/UMIST)

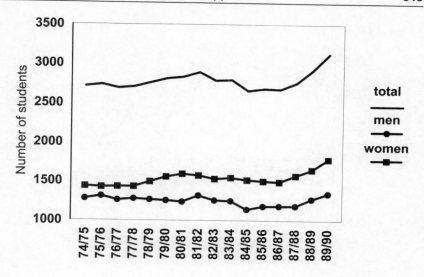

3. Faculty of Arts

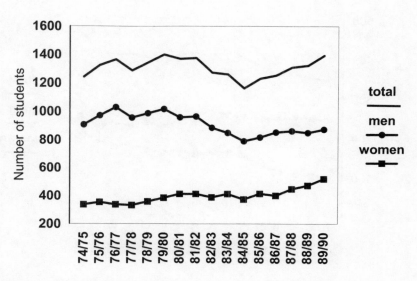

4. Faculty of Economic and Social Studies

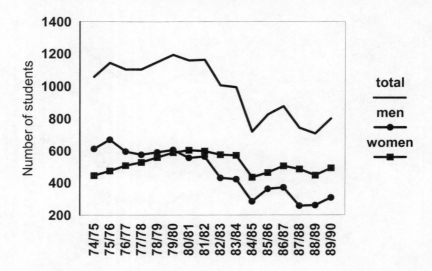

5. Faculty of Education

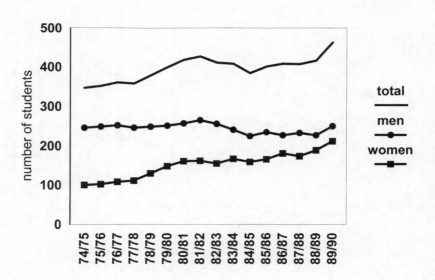

6. Faculty of Law

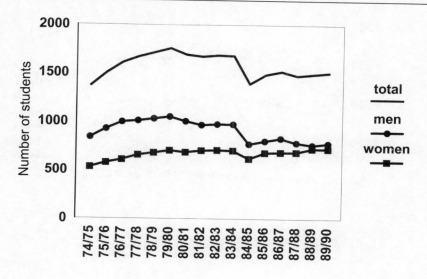

7. Faculty of Medicine

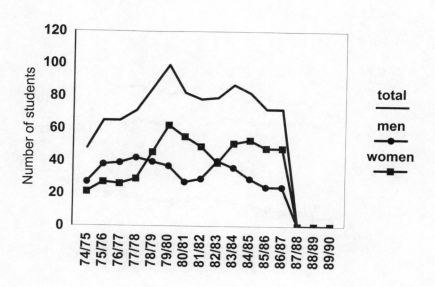

8. Faculty of Music

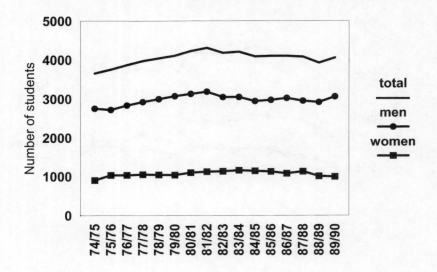

9. Faculty of Science

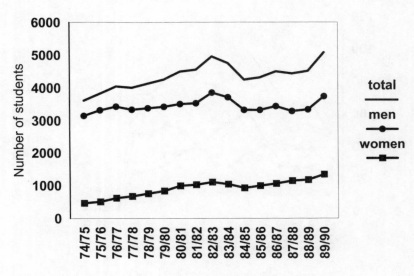

10. Faculty of Technology/UMIST

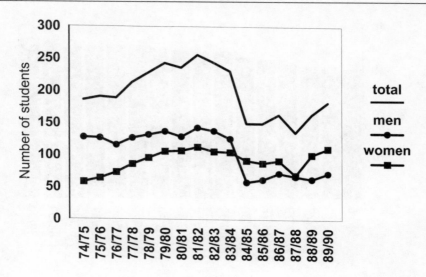

11. Faculty of Theology

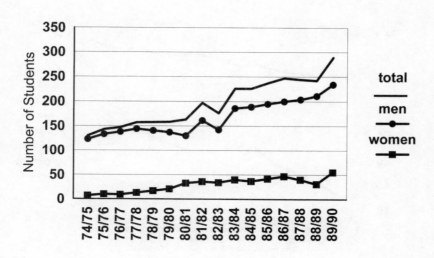

12. Faculty of Business Administration
/The Business School

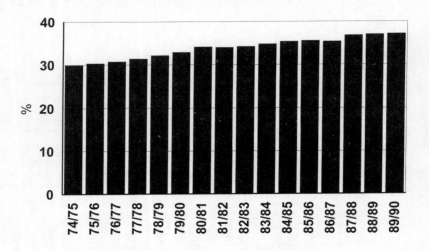

13. Women as % of Total Students
(including Faculty of Technology/UMIST)

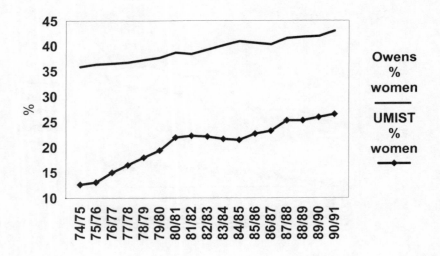

14. Comparison of Owens and Faculty of
Technology/UMIST intake of Women

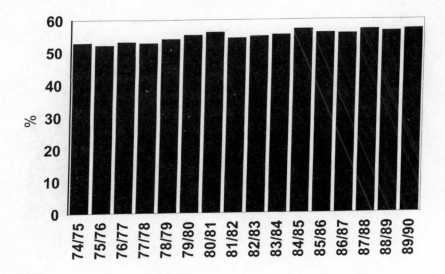

15. Percentage of Women Students (Arts)

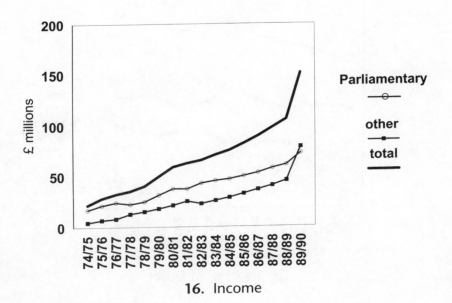

16. Income

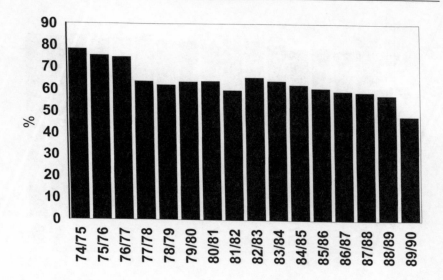

17. Parliamentary Grants as a % of total income

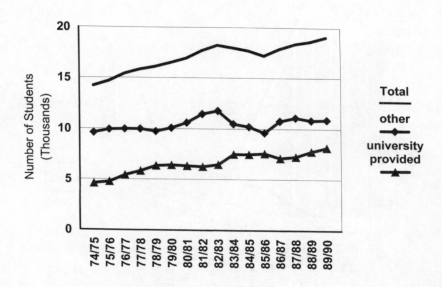

18. Accommodation

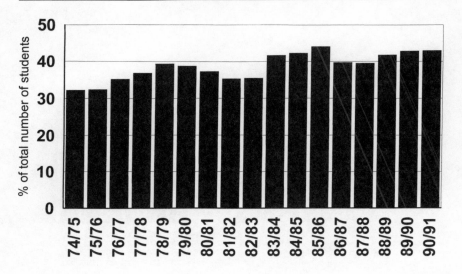

19. % of Students in Accommodation
Provided by the University

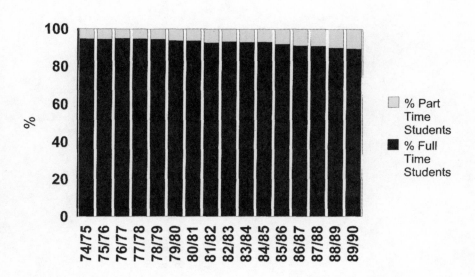

20. Growth in Proportion of Part-Time Students
(including Faculty of Technology/UMIST)

Index